Keeneland's Ted Bassett

"Ted Bassett has been our ambassador for Thoroughbred racing around the world, and he has placed his stamp on every aspect of the sport, accomplishing this with the grip of a Marine and the air of a gentleman."
—William S. Farish, former U.S. ambassador to Great Britain and master of Lane's End Farm

"Ted Bassett is a man of all seasons. Wherever he has been involved, he has brought a level of ethical behavior, professionalism and sincerity of purpose."
—Peter J. Timoney, former director of the University of Kentucky Maxwell H. Gluck Equine Research Center

"Throughout his distinguished career as a Marine and as a private citizen, Mr. Bassett has continued to epitomize 'Once a Marine, always a Marine.' Mr. Bassett's selfless patriotism and dedication reflect great credit upon him and are in keeping with the highest traditions of the Marine Corps and the U. S. Naval Service."
—General James T. Conway, commandant of the U.S. Marine Corps

"Ted Bassett is a legend in the Kentucky State Police today for those officers who served through the 1960s and 1970s."
—Colonel A. D. Fortner, Kentucky State Police commissioner, 1980–1981

"Ted Bassett has been a pervasive force for the good of international racing. No one has been as focused or as energetic, or has his persuasive wit and charm. I hold him in awe."
—The Honorable Andrew S. Peacock, former Liberal Party leader and Australian ambassador to the United States

"Perhaps only in Kentucky can one move effortlessly from serving as director of the State Police to managing one of the world's unique racetracks and dining with the Queen of England."
—Terry L. Birdwhistell, associate dean of special collections and digital programs, University of Kentucky

Keeneland's
Ted Bassett
—— *My Life* ——

James E. "Ted" Bassett III
and Bill Mooney

THE UNIVERSITY PRESS OF KENTUCKY

Published by the University Press of Kentucky
Scholarly publisher for the Commonwealth,
serving Bellarmine University, Berea College, Centre
College of Kentucky, Eastern Kentucky University,
The Filson Historical Society, Georgetown College,
Kentucky Historical Society, Kentucky State University,
Morehead State University, Murray State University,
Northern Kentucky University, Transylvania University,
University of Kentucky, University of Louisville,
and Western Kentucky University.
All rights reserved.

Editorial and Sales Offices: The University Press of Kentucky
663 South Limestone Street, Lexington, Kentucky 40508-4008
www.kentuckypress.com

13 12 11 10 09   2 3 4 5

Library of Congress Cataloging-in-Publication Data
Bassett, James E., 1921–
Keeneland's Ted Bassett : my life / James E. "Ted" Bassett III and
Bill Mooney.
      p.   cm.
Includes bibliographical references and index.
ISBN 978-0-8131-2548-0 (hardcover : alk. paper)
1. Bassett, James E., 1921– 2. Keeneland (Lexington, Ky.)—
Employees—Biography. 3. Horseracing—Kentucky—
Lexington—Biography. 4. Keeneland (Lexington, Ky.)—History.
5. Horse racing—Kentucky—Lexington—History.
I. Mooney, Bill. II. Title.

SF336.B36A3 2009
798.4006'876947—dc22   2008052396

This book is printed on acid-free recycled paper meeting
the requirements of the American National Standard
for Permanence in Paper for Printed Library Materials.

Manufactured in the United States of America.

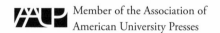

Member of the Association of
American University Presses

To my dear wife Lucy,
who has always been a voice of reason and
my safe harbor of reassurance.

Contents

Foreword

IT WAS AN honor to be invited to write this foreword as it is about a man who, for as long as I have known him, has been something of a hero.

I first met Ted Bassett at an early Breeders' Cup meeting, and we have been friends ever since. I was fortunate, a few years ago, to experience my first Kentucky Derby in the company of Lucy and Ted Bassett and a few of their oldest friends. It was on that occasion that I became aware of Ted's breadth of acquaintanceship, for wherever we went at Churchill Downs, he was greeted with huge enthusiasm by a myriad of people from every corner of the racing industry. They were all, everyone, just as delighted to see him as he was to see them.

Considering that one of Ted's most endearing characteristics is his innate modesty, the very existence of this book is something of a miracle. We, the readers, are the beneficiaries of this great, good fortune, as this is a book that will give enormous pleasure to many, many people, as well as insights into a wide range of national and international events over the past seventy-five years. There is much of Ted's life that I was unaware of, and I am fascinated by every chapter of the Ted Bassett story.

And Ted has had a fascinating and unusual life—he has been successful in just about every area to which he has turned his hand and his considerable charm. In this book, we share his journeys from his early days at Kent School, thence to his beloved Yale, and on to his enlistment in the U.S. Marine Corps and his combat experience in World War II. The Marine Corps experience has played a seminal role in Ted's life, and in his later years, he has been the recipient of the Corps' coveted Semper Fidelis Award and the USMC Superior Public Service Award.

Following the war, Ted was a newsprint salesman based on the East Coast. He returned to Kentucky in the mid-1950s and was later appointed director of the Kentucky State Police, serving with distinction during a critical period in the state's history that was disrupted by labor strife and divisive racial tensions.

It was then on to Keeneland in 1968, a move that became a springboard for him, as Ted went on to serve the Thoroughbred industry for nearly forty years. For it was Ted's Keeneland experience that provided him the opportunity to take on a broad range of responsibilities, such as president of the Thoroughbred Racing Associations, the Breeders' Cup, Equibase, and the World Series Racing Championship. Ted's efforts have earned him the Eclipse Award of Merit, the Thoroughbred Club of America Honor Guest Award, The Jockey Club Gold Medal, the John H. Galbreath Award, and a host of other prestigious recognitions, including three honorary doctoral degrees.

Moreover, Ted has traveled to the four corners of the globe advancing the merits of Thoroughbred racing and breeding and earning the sobriquet "International Ambassador of Racing."

Throughout this book, Ted Bassett's uncanny ability to charm and persuade is frequently masked by his reticence and leads the reader to underestimate the pivotal and key roles he has played within the Thoroughbred industry. But do not be fooled. His is truly a remarkable story.

Stoker Devonshire
The Duke of Devonshire CBE

Preface

EVEN AS THIS project progressed from a vague, somewhat whimsical notion that I have a few stories that people might be interested in hearing me tell, through the humbling task of actually putting words on paper, I have never been completely comfortable that it is a sensible idea. Who am I to do a book? What possible interest might anyone have in reading it? This is not any sort of attempt at false modesty. It is a genuine and sincere concern.

No decision I have made in my life has ever altered the course of history. I have been more than fortunate through the years, through fate and circumstance, to have been at the right place at the right time. In many respects, my life has been a series of oblique turns and fortuitous journeys down unexpected roadways.

During my teenage years at Kent School and my early days at Yale, it never occurred to me that I would become a member of the U.S. Marine Corps. And when I was in the Marines, fighting on Okinawa and subsequently participating in the post–World War II occupation of Japan, I never realized that I was destined to become a newsprint salesman for the Great Northern Paper Company, for which I spent a great deal of time on Piedmont Airways and Trailway buses, traveling to conduct business with newspaper publishers in the Middle Atlantic region and the South.

There was never any grand plan in my mind to become a tobacco farmer—yet that is something I did for three years, and I will tell you candidly that it was a backbreaking way to make a living. I subsequently spent eleven years with the Kentucky State Police, including three as its organizational head, yet this is also something that happened largely through happenstance and not because of any career intent on my part.

After my tenure with the State Police ended in 1967, I was offered a pair of opportunities: (1) to become president of Kentucky Fried Chicken, and (2) to become Louis Lee Haggin II's assistant for the Keeneland Association. After discussing the situation with my dear wife, Lucy, I decided to accept the latter offer. In the ensuing decades, I have often suspected that the franchise founded by Colonel Sanders was the party that really lucked out in this matter.

My years affiliated with Keeneland—as Louis's assistant, as president, as chairman of the board, as trustee, and as trustee emeritus—now number more than forty. I can sincerely say that for four decades I have been blessed with one of the most serene commutes to work in the world, winding through the backwoods of the Bluegrass in the early-morning hours, scarcely passing another car. And there has never been a morning when I have entered those rear gates at Keeneland that my mind was not filled with the curiosity and anticipation of what the day may bring.

Reasons for this are ample. Working at Keeneland has been an exercise in the pure joy of being involved with people, from the backside to the frontside, from the barns to the grandstand and clubhouse to the general offices, who love what they do for a living and are constantly energized by it.

The most fascinating aspect of the Keeneland experience is there's never a lull, there is never a day that can be described as average, and there is no long, laborious, repetitive routine that dulls the enthusiasm. Keeneland is a continuing, year-round exercise in January sales, wintertime construction, spring race meets, summertime construction, promotional travel, September sales, fall race meets, and November sales. It is an exhilarating exercise in keeping the intellectual engine active.

Keeneland came into existence in 1935 and continues to be blessed by the vision of its founders, particularly Hal Price Headley and Major Louie Arnold Beard. Of equal importance are the foresight and dedication of Keeneland's long list of directors, who, for seven decades, have served the not-for-profit association pro bono, their reward being the pride they have realized from their efforts.

But the lion's share of the credit for Keeneland's success truly belongs to the men and women who daily work within its confines and whose responsibilities are to meet the public's high expectations. It is these people, more than any other group, who have maintained the deep sense of loyalty and responsibility that has molded and maintained the association's heritage. While the horses may get the credit, it is the Keeneland employees who most deserve it.

A recognition of the need to change with the times, though, has also been a Keeneland strength. When I first went to work there, Keeneland had three general managers and two completely separate staffs. The Keeneland Association conducted the race meets. And the Breeders' Sales Company conducted the horse sales. Thus, there were two different organizations operating under the same roof, each possessing its own board of directors, philosophies, viewpoints, and employee components.

One of my first responsibilities was to help Louis Haggin effect a merger. And we accomplished this without a vote by either board of directors. We did it subtly and slowly through our advertising, by changing the name "Breeders' Sales" to "Keeneland Sales" and eliminating all references to "Breeders' Sales" from our stationery and press releases.

The boards were subsequently combined into a single entity, and I recall about a year or so later the breeder Warner L. Jones Jr. making the cryptic, combative statement, "The minnow has swallowed the whale." He felt resentful, as did others, that suddenly, without any input from them, the name Breeders' Sales Company had vanished.

But Warner remained on our board, as did most of his colleagues, many of whom were appointed to Keeneland's executive committee. They eventually understood that our intention was not to conduct a political coup d'etat. Keeneland was expanding; it was beginning to establish a global identity. International buyers were becoming active at our sales, and it was important for the association to have a uniform marketing brand and promotional message that could be distributed worldwide.

In 1968, my first year at Keeneland, we generated gross receipts totaling slightly over $22 million at our horse sales. In 2007, the figure exceeded $815.4 million. In 1968, the gross handle generated at Keeneland's race meets was slightly over $16 million, every dollar of which was wagered on-site on a live product. In 2007, the combined live and simulcast wagering during Keeneland's race meets exceeded $298.1 million. And Keeneland now conducts simulcast wagering all twelve months of the year on Thoroughbred races run at other tracks, both national and international.

It has been my privilege to have witnessed this growth. Among other things, it has allowed Keeneland to expand its landholdings to 1,024 acres; to expand the seating and dining capacity of its frontside to 8,535; to increase its stabling facilities to 57 barns with accommodations for 1,951 horses; to install a European-style turf course; to build a sales pavilion that is the most modern, expansive, and comfortable in the horse industry; and to construct a research library that is open to all members of the public. Further, Keeneland annually serves as a benefactor for charities throughout the central Kentucky region.

Keeneland's success has opened up so many doors for me, personally. It has allowed me to travel beyond North America's shores to five other continents, to meet the rulers, prime ministers, and other government and racing officials from many other countries. It has allowed me to serve as host for the first visit by Queen Elizabeth II to a U.S. racetrack and to be, in turn, invited as her guest to Windsor Castle and the Royal Meeting at Ascot.

Further, my association with Keeneland has led me into roles with such organizations as the Breeders' Cup, Equibase, and the World Series Racing Championship. As dear to my heart as anything, it has allowed me to develop firm and lasting friendships with Keeneland's employees, horse owners, trainers, jockeys, grooms, journalists, politicians, statesmen, and so many others from all points on life's compass. This book is intended as a tribute to all of them.

And it is also a tribute to the cul-de-sac that constitutes central Kentucky, where I was born, raised, and have spent most of my adult life. There is something so wonderful about this region of the country and especially about the Lexington community. If you live here long enough, you cannot help but develop a deep appreciation of the culture, the environment, the land, the genuineness of the people, the heritage and traditions—it all melds into a special, special thing.

Maybe the greatest source of strength emanates from the region's women. If you marry a central Kentucky girl (and I was fortunate enough to do so) and move away, the magnetism and gravitational pull of the Bluegrass region are always there, no matter how successful you might be somewhere else. There is always that subtle lure to return home. Many, if not most, men who grew up here share the same feeling, but it seems stronger on the female side. I am not sure I can explain it any better than I have, but to central Kentuckians, I do not have to. They seem to understand.

I guess if there is a central theme to this book it is that life can be interesting, and even intriguing, if one is willing to accept the risk of challenges. Granted, in adhering to this philosophy there are bound to be some dramatic changes in course. But if one has some degree of self-confidence and courage, the intricate parts of the puzzle may come together. I think, largely because of fortuitous chance, they did for me, although I will leave it to the individual readers to make the final judgments.

James E. "Ted" Bassett III
Keeneland Cottage

Chapter 1

Early Years at Keeneland

I WAS FORTY-SIX years old and out of a job. I was unemployed! One of those crossroads we sometimes reach in life loomed directly in front of me, and what it presented seemed nothing short of a harsh, hazardous dilemma.

A few weeks earlier, I had resigned as director of the Kentucky State Police. I did this anticipating that the first Republican governor in twenty years would demand a broad-based change in the Democratic appointees. It was an uneasy and uncomfortable time for me, and I welcomed any inquiry regarding my future. And so, on the afternoon of the third Sunday in December 1967, I was thankful for Louis Lee Haggin II's invitation to visit him at his Sycamore Farm home near Lexington.

Although more than forty years have since elapsed, that day remains vivid in my mind. The outside temperature was cold, the sky was dreary, and snow flurries danced in the air. I met with Louis in his library. He had on a blue button-down shirt and a yellow cashmere sweater. He had lit some logs in the fireplace, and blazing away they provided a warm, reassuring atmosphere, which was something I needed.

For more than a decade I had been an employee of the state of Kentucky. I had started out as deputy commissioner of public safety and for the past three years had held the Kentucky State Police directorship. But suddenly I was no longer in either of those positions. I did not have a position anywhere, involving anything. My mind was bulging with unanswered questions. What did my future hold? What employment was available? Should I jump at the first job offer made to me?

My conversation with Louis turned out to be one of the most fortuitous conversations I have ever had with anybody. He was president of the Keeneland Association Inc., and we talked seriously, specifically, about what I might bring to Keeneland if I was hired to work there in an executive capacity.

1

I had known Louis for more than twenty years. He was a good friend of my father, James E. Bassett Jr. They knew each other through their Thoroughbred breeding and racing activities and by way of the Lexington social scene. And I had other Keeneland contacts. William Arnold Hanger, a distinguished breeder and owner of both Thoroughbreds and Standardbreds, was a trustee of the association. Hanger was also a longtime member of The Jockey Club and served as a director of Churchill Downs in Louisville and Hialeah Park near Miami, Florida. Arnold was a very successful corporate business leader, too. The construction management firm Mason & Hanger-Silas Mason Company Inc., for which he served as chairman of the board, had overseen the building of the passenger terminal at Blue Grass Field in Lexington, as well as the downtown Civic Center. Arnold was a good friend of my in-laws, Gus and Elizabeth Simms Gay, and I counted him as one of my mentors.

At the time, all the offices at Keeneland, including the presidency and two vice presidencies (which were held by Leslie Combs II and Dr. Charles E. Hagyard), were honorary positions. But during the decades immediately following World War II, the association had undergone substantial growth in both its race meetings and its horse sales. In 1946, the first full year of operation for Keeneland after the war, pari-mutuel wagering for its race meetings had averaged $278,640 per day. The association's daily purse distribution averaged $20,717. And the gross receipts for its sales totaled $6.52 million.

But in 1959, the commissioner of the Internal Revenue Service had issued a ruling that the Keeneland Association's activities had expanded to the point that it no longer qualified as a tax-exempt corporation. In 1967, Keeneland's race meets had averaged $521,958 per day in pari-mutuel wagering. Purses distributed averaged $36,000 daily. Gross receipts from sales had totaled $18.1 million. Indeed, over a twenty-one-year period, daily wagering and daily purses had nearly doubled and sales receipts had nearly tripled.

Louis was a man of wealth, and his primary interests were his Thoroughbred racing and farm operations. The tedious, day-after-day devotion to the corporate agenda his Keeneland position increasingly required was not his forte. Both he and Arnold had concluded it was time to have a full-time, paid executive attending to the responsibilities of operating Keeneland—a CEO, so to speak, who would oversee both the race meets and the sales operations. And that's how it came to pass that I was sitting in Louis's library on a mid-December Sunday. He might have been inter-viewing other people for the job, but if so, Louis never revealed their names to me.

John Y. Brown Jr., who would later serve as Kentucky's governor, was then the head and principal stockholder of Kentucky Fried Chicken. He had made me a very lucrative offer—an annual salary of $100,000 along with 5,000 shares of stock—to join the company as its president. Taking the job would require me to relocate to Nashville, Tennessee, which was then the locale of KFC's executive offices. Brown and I had been discuss-ing this possibility for about ten days. I was scheduled to meet with him and his father, John Y. Brown Sr., for breakfast at the Campbell House in Lexington the morning after I talked with Louis, to give them my final decision. A good friend of mine, Lou Karibo, had attended the University of Kentucky with John and had played football there under Paul "Bear" Bryant. Karibo had worked for me as a public relations officer for the State Police, after which he had become a KFC franchise holder. Karibo had been urging me to accept John's offer.

But despite the financial incentives, I did have reservations about ac-cepting the KFC offer. John had purchased the company for $2 million from its founder, Colonel Harland Sanders, in 1964, with the intention of expanding it into the global enterprise which it indeed became. John needed an infusion of money to do this, so he sold a major interest in KFC to Jack Massey, who had made a fortune in the health care business. John had told me, "I'd like for you to meet him and for him to meet you, and see if there's a comfort level." So I went down to Nashville for an interview with Massey, who wore a Texas-style, leather-thong bow tie and sat with his feet up on his desk throughout our meeting. Actually, Massey and I had a pleasant talk. But I still got the impression he regarded me as John's man, and I don't know how comfortable Massey was with that. Further, John was not a disciplinarian, and I think what he wanted was someone who could bring strong administrative control to the company. Many of the KFC franchises had been awarded to John's college associates, young men who became overnight millionaires. And, truth be known, while I had a strong administrative background because of my State Police work, I didn't know how to fry as much as a few chicken wings or a drumstick. The initial attitude of KFC franchise holders toward me would have been, "Who the hell are you? What do you know?" I would have had my hands full.

3

Louis needed to know about the situation with Kentucky Fried Chicken, so I told him, in detail. He responded, "If you are interested in coming to Keeneland as my assistant, I would like to know by this coming Tuesday, when our board of directors meets. I would like to make my recommendation to hire you, and have them vote either 'yea' or 'nay.'"

I returned home, which was and remains Lanark Farm on Old Frankfort Pike in Woodford County, and discussed the matter with my wife, Lucy. She said, "If your preference is to go to Keeneland, I think you ought to call Louis Haggin tonight and tell him how much you appreciate his consideration and that you accept his offer. You don't want to give him the impression you're entering into a negotiating position between Kentucky Fried Chicken and the Keeneland Association."

About 8:30 that evening, I phoned Louis and told him I would accept. And he said, "Wonderful!" He would take it up with the Keeneland board and let me know the results on Tuesday. The board granted Louis his wish, and in the final issue that year of the weekly trade publication the *Blood-Horse,* on the 101st page at the bottom of the middle column, there was a seven-and-a-half-line item (encompassing all of one inch of print) informing the readership I had been named assistant to the president of the Keeneland Association. The item was sandwiched between a note that a newspaper tout named Clem Florio had recently given a presentation titled "How to Handicap" at Laurel Park in Maryland and a note that Mr. and Mrs. Ephraim Jessup of Hill-N-Dale Farm in Maryland were planning "a stay of several weeks in California while their horses are racing at Santa Anita."

Keeneland's hiring of me, it seems, was not earthshaking news.

§

I started working at Keeneland on January 1, 1968. My salary was $30,000 a year. There were no shares of stock or stock options in the package, because Keeneland was and remains a not-for-profit corporation. I did not have a contract or any sort of written agreement. Indeed, I have never had a contract anywhere I worked, and I have never wanted one. There is a very simple reason for this—I have never sought to be any place where I was not wanted. The understanding with Keeneland was that I would be Louis Haggin's assistant for a year or so, and if things worked out well, I would eventually succeed him as president.

My arrival was not met with wild enthusiasm by the entrenched

Keeneland staff. Subdued resentment would be a much more accurate description. The staff included four senior executives: William T. Bishop, William S. Evans, J. B. Faulconer, and Frank O. Werner Jr. Bishop, Evans, and Faulconer all bore the title of general manager. Bishop presided over the racing operation and was also assistant secretary and treasurer. Werner, whose title was assistant general manager, worked directly under Bishop. Evans was the general manager of the Breeders' Sales Company, which was formally listed as "a division of the Keeneland Association Inc." but in reality, it was a separate entity. And Faulconer was the general manager of public relations.

Racing at Keeneland dates back to October 15, 1936, when the track's very first race was won by a horse named Royal Rainment, who, interestingly, was owned by John Hay "Jock" Whitney, a gentleman who was a factor in the development of my father's career and mine as well. The Breeders' Sales Company was formally incorporated on November 13, 1943, as a cooperative for the purpose of marketing Thoroughbreds. The idea was for the Breeders' Sales Company to lease the use and grounds of the Keeneland Race Course from the Keeneland Association. In other words, Keeneland Race Course and the Breeders' Sales Company were created as two separate entities, each with its own officers and board of directors.

The Breeders' Sales Company was formally absorbed into Keeneland in 1962. But the association's management and staff remained largely composed of old loyalists who were divided into those loyal to the racing operation or to the Thoroughbred sales operation. Further, within those divisions there were individual fiefdoms, small centers of power that were carefully guarded. Keeneland also had two different work schedules. Racing employees worked five and a half days per week, with their hours ranging from 8:30 A.M. to 4:30 P.M. Sales Company employees worked five days a week, from 9 A.M. to 4 P.M. The two entities had different salary scales, along with different pension plans, vacation schedules, and benefits.

From these factors alone, you can realize the administrative problem that confronted anyone who came in for the purpose of developing a comprehensive, coordinated, and effective management team. But old ways of doing things are not easily altered. With the exception of his years in the military during World War II, Bishop, a highly competent, dedicated, and committed employee, had been with Keeneland since its beginning. Hal Price Headley, who led the group that had founded Keeneland

(and was Louis Haggin's father-in-law), had selected Bishop to be foreman of the construction crew that built the original facilities. Werner had been with Keeneland for fifteen years, Evans for twenty-one, and Faulconer for fourteen.

Frequently during my first year at Keeneland, I would look in the mirror and say to myself, "What the hell am I doing here?" During my tenure with the State Police, which was a quasi-military organization, a stern look and a raised eyebrow from me would result in a click of the heels. But at Keeneland, even if my gaze was stern and I raised both eyebrows, these actions would barely evoke a yawn. I realized that gaining the staff's confidence was going to be a long, tedious process.

And I couldn't really fault the staff for that. Here I was, coming in from the outside with no experience to speak of in the Thoroughbred racing and breeding industries. I was immediately put into an executive position with supervisory authority over capable people, many of whom had served Keeneland and the Breeders' Sales Company for many years, even decades.

Still, Keeneland's management structure was unwieldy, and racing executives throughout the United States knew it. Santa Anita, which is a racetrack in Southern California, was one of the true jewels of the racing industry. It drew enormous crowds—they averaged over 27,000 per day and generated an average daily mutuel handle in excess of $2.5 million. In 1968, I had a meeting with Fred H. Ryan, who was the track's vice president and general manager. Ryan had a national reputation for his organizational skills and efficiency. He was very courteous, and we started out by extending the usual platitudes and small conversation that such occasions require. I then said to Ryan, "I'm here to ask for advice about the possible restructuring of the Keeneland administrative staff. And I'm wondering if you could make some suggestions?"

Ryan replied, "Keeneland is the enigma of the racing business. Its corporate setup is a mystery to the rest of us in the racing world."

I said, "What do you mean by that, sir?" I was somewhat stunned by what Ryan had said.

He then told me, "Yours is the only racetrack, not only in the United States, but as far as I know anywhere in existence on the globe, that has three general managers. How do you function? Whose word carries the most weight? Who makes the final decisions?"

With Ryan's questions anchored in my mind, I went back home, mulled things over for a few days, and then went to Louis Haggin and asked him, "How did we ever arrive at this corporate setup of three general managers?"

Louis said, "That's why we brought you in here, to do something about it."

I said, "Well, I think the first thing I have to do is get us down to one general manager."

Haggin said, "I think maybe that should be you."

I said, "Well, I'll have to work this out in a diplomatic way."

We did not fire anybody. But as the months went on, we changed people's titles. Bishop became Keeneland's director of finance, Werner became director of operations, Evans became director of sales, and Faulconer became director of public relations. And I became Keeneland's sole general manager.

In the fall of 1971, Bishop resigned from Keeneland to become vice president and general manager of Oaklawn Park in Hot Springs, Arkansas. At almost exactly the same time, Werner left our employ to take an executive position with a Lexington construction firm, White and Congleton. And on December 1, Faulconer resigned to become a bloodstock agent and commercial Thoroughbred breeder. Bill Evans, however, remained with us as sales director until he retired in 1980.

After Bishop, Werner, and Faulconer left, we were able to attract four very bright and committed young men to fill four critical positions. One was William C. Greely, who in December 1971, at the age of thirty-three, was hired to be my assistant general manager. Bill was from a family of horsemen. Both his grandfather and his father had trained horses throughout the Midwest and the South, including at the old Kentucky Association track, which was Keeneland's predecessor in Lexington. Bill himself had been an administrator at some of the nation's leading racetracks—Churchill Downs, Arlington Park, and Hialeah among them.

Another was Stanley H. Jones, who was thirty-six years old, a fellow Marine Corps veteran, and a brilliant certified public accountant. Stan had been a partner in the Lexington firm of Potter, Hisle, Sugg and Nolan, of which Keeneland was a client, and was hired to fill our newly created position of controller. It became his job to make sure that every dollar of the final bids on horses at our sales was collected. (This wasn't always easy—there was one case where a gentleman from Mexico who did not speak English was bidding in what he thought was pesos and received a tremendous shock when he received the bill from us in U.S. dollars.) Stan totally revised our auditing and accounting systems and paved the way for Keeneland's entry into the computer age.

R. James Williams was hired to fill the newly created position of director of publicity. Jim was twenty-five years old when he came aboard in 1971. He had a bachelor's degree in journalism from the University of Kentucky, had already served as an assistant publicist during race meets at Keeneland and Monmouth Park in New Jersey, and was a sports reporter for the *Lexington Herald*. Jim possessed a combination of youthful energy and experience as a journalist who had covered racing, along with an extraordinary sense of logic and fairness.

The fourth person hired was Howard L. Battle, who joined Keeneland in January 1973 as our racing secretary and handicapper. Howard was forty-two years old and had a master of fine arts degree from the University of Notre Dame. His great passion was painting horses—he was a splendid artist—and in his younger days he had ambitions of teaching art in college. But he came from a racing family. His father, Howard H. Battle, had trained Sweet Patootie, who won the inaugural running of the Alcibiades Stakes at Keeneland in 1952. The younger Howard had worked as a placing judge and assistant racing secretary at tracks in Florida, New Jersey, Pennsylvania, Illinois, Michigan, and Ohio. He was a superb fit for Keeneland.

§

It didn't take me long during my first year at Keeneland to realize that my expertise, whatever it was worth, did not include the pedigrees and conformation of Thoroughbreds. It would be in the association's best interest, and in my best interest, to leave those areas to our sales professionals and experts, which I steadfastly did thereon.

The four auctions the Breeders' Sales Company at Keeneland annually staged in those days were formally known as the Midwinter Horses of All Ages Sale, the Summer Sale of Yearlings, the Fall Yearling Sale, and the Fall Breeding Stock Sale. As time went on, the names of the auctions were changed to include the months in which they were held (January, July, September, and November). Keeneland added an April Two-Year-Olds in Training Sale in 1993. The July Selected Yearling Sale was put on hiatus in 2003, and I do not know if we will ever see it return.

Throughout most of my tenure with Keeneland, though, the July sale was the one that created the most interest, the most electricity. The days leading up to it were almost like the days leading into the World Series. During my early period at Keeneland, there weren't many hotel and motel rooms in Lexington and the surrounding area, and the demand to reserve them by July sale participants was frantic. And the demand to reserve seats in Keeneland's sales pavilion was huge, too. Consigners and buyers wanted seats for clients and family members, and the general public wanted to be in attendance as well. The media covered the July sale as a major event.

In July 1968, Keeneland was auctioning yearlings from the first crop of Sea-Bird, who three years earlier had won the Prix de l'Arc de Triomphe, which for nearly a century has been France's premier horse race and remains one of the most prominent races anywhere on the globe. Mrs. Julian G. Rogers had consigned to the sale a Sea-Bird filly out of a wonderful mare named Libra, who had already produced a colt named Ribocco, the winner of the 1967 St. Leger Stakes and Irish Derby.

At the time, Mrs. Rogers was in the midst of a run where she was one of the leading consigners at the July sale for several years. But on the first day of the sale in 1968, a small, bespectacled fellow wearing a suit and bow tie walked into the pavilion and sat in Mrs. Rogers's seat. He was Wendell P. Rosso from Norfolk, Virginia. When Mrs. Rogers arrived, an unpleasant confrontation promptly ensued—she could be impatient, on occasion—and we put Rosso, who we didn't know, in another seat next to Max Self, who was our man in charge of seating.

I subsequently found out that Rosso owned a chain of open-air food markets in Virginia's Tidewater region. "Twelve big ones and 37 little ones," he told Kent Hollingsworth, editor of the *Blood-Horse* magazine. Rosso had been a racing fan for nearly four decades, and a year earlier he had started a small racing stable, entrusting his handful of claiming horses to a New Jersey–based trainer named Bob Durso.

Rosso, however, wanted to make a bigger investment in the sport. Following the death of his wife, Rosso had taken a trip to Europe—to Italy, to see the old country, and to France, to see the Arc. That was the year Sea-Bird won. His margin of victory was six lengths. "After I saw him run, I knew he was the greatest horse there ever was," Rosso told Hollingsworth. "And when I saw these Sea-Bird yearlings here in the sale, I thought I might as well buy them."

Mrs. Rogers's filly was Hip Number 226, scheduled to be sold on the sale's second day. Seated in the pavilion's third row was a group that included Charles W. Engelhard, a man of enormous wealth and one of the most prominent yearling buyers in the world; Mackenzie Miller, the trainer for Engelhard's Cragwood Stable; and Robert Sangster, who, among his other accomplishments, would be honored five times as England's leading Thoroughbred owner.

The bidding on the filly started and soon escalated into a duel between Engelhard and company versus Rosso. The price reached $395,000, which was then the highest bid ever made for a yearling at a public auction. There was a pause, and Keeneland's head auctioneer, George Swinebroad, in his inimitable fashion, looked at Engelhard and said, "Hey, Charlie, can't you afford another $5,000?"

Engelhard confided with Miller and Sangster, gave a nod, and the bid reached $400,000, with George thinking he was going to hammer that down as the new world record. But in the back of the pavilion seating area, Rosso raised his hand one more time. His bid was $405,000, and the filly went to him.

The next morning we were in Bill Evans's little office in the pavilion. I was feeling my oats, even though I was not really informed on any matter regarding the conduct of sales. Bill and I were wondering out loud who Rosso was and by what means he was going to settle up with us—forty-one years ago, $405,000 was a lot of money for Keeneland. And during the sale, Rosso had also been the high bidder on three other Sea-Bird yearlings. He actually owed a total of $602,000 for his purchases.

Suddenly, unexpectedly, Rosso walked into the office. And as he did I quickly decided I would try to do something helpful and productive. I said, "Good morning, Mr. Rosso. I want to thank you for your support of the Keeneland sales. In reviewing our credit records, I see that you haven't purchased horses from us in the past. Could you advise us on how you plan to pay for these yearlings?"

Rosso looked at me in a stern manner, as if I had challenged his integrity. He reached into his shirt pocket and pulled out half a dozen certified checks worth $100,000 each, threw them at me, and indignantly said, "Is this sufficient?"

And I got down on my hands and knees and picked up those checks off the floor and said, "Yes, sir. Thank you very much."

(The postscript to this story is less than wonderful, although assuredly it could have been worse. Rosso named his $405,000 filly Reine Enchanteur and sent her to a training center in Virginia. There, somehow accidentally or otherwise, a stable hand stabbed her in the left knee with a pitchfork. The exact details were never made public, but Rosso's trainer, Robert J. Durso, later said that "four or five grooms" were fired because of the incident. Reine Enchanteur raced seven times, with all her efforts coming at age three. She won her first race at Aqueduct in New York in November 1970, never finished worse than third, and earned a career total of $9,305 in purse monies. Reine Enchanteur was never a stakes horse. As a broodmare she produced half a dozen sons and daughters, none of which were noteworthy.)

§

During the early portion of my Keeneland tenure, the association was involved in a highly contentious legal situation. A prominent, locally based veterinarian, Dr. Arnold Pessin, and his business partner, Rex Ellsworth, had an antitrust suit in federal court against the Keeneland Association, the University of Kentucky Research Foundation, the Bank of New York, and some twenty other defendants, alleging an illegal conspiracy to create a monopoly and restrain trade. Pessin and Ellsworth were seeking $30 million in damages.

Pessin, an alumnus of the Texas A&M University School of Veterinary Medicine, had been operating his practice in central Kentucky since the mid-1950s. Ellsworth, a highly religious man who lived at the time in Chino, California, was a former cowboy who had purchased eight broodmares for a sum of $600 in 1933 and subsequently became one of the most prominent horsemen in North America. Ellsworth had bred and campaigned the 1955 Kentucky Derby winner, Swaps, and had led North America's breeder and owner standings (with regard to purse monies achieved) in both 1962 and 1963.

By the time the lawsuit came to trial on January 27, 1969, the controversy surrounding it had been raging for eighteen months. At its center was an attempt by Pessin and Ellsworth to purchase Maine Chance Farm, a 721-acre property adjacent to two tracts of land owned by the University of Kentucky near Lexington. In late July 1967, Pessin and Ellsworth had submitted a bid of $1,942,500 to purchase Maine Chance. Their plan was to set up a breeding center, a training operation, a jockey school, and a Thoroughbred sales company on the property.

Well, at this point in time, the Breeders' Sales Company at Keeneland had been conducting Thoroughbred auctions in Kentucky since 1944, virtually with no competition. In 1968, the Breeders' Sales Company had sold 40 percent of the yearlings consigned nationally to public auction and had generated 48 percent of the gross receipts for yearling sales. Keeneland's gross receipts from its horse auctions in 1968 totaled $22,009,500, from which the association netted more than $1.1 million. Some of the sales company profits—about $350,000 that year—were utilized to supplement purses at Keeneland's race meets. A portion of the remaining $850,000 went to charity.

No one had ever before really challenged the way Keeneland operated. Neither Louis Haggin's predecessor, Hal Price Headley, nor Louis himself ever held press conferences. Louis Haggin had been elected Keeneland's president in 1940, five years after the association had been incorporated, and he always did what he believed he had to do and did not see a need for explaining his actions. Article III of Keeneland's Articles of Incorporation, filed on April 17, 1935, in Fayette County court, stated:

> The nature of the business and objects and purposes proposed to be transacted, promoted and carried on (at Keeneland) shall be the conducting of horse shows, fairs, race meetings, horse sales, and to conduct any other business, whether herein specifically enumerated or not, which in the opinion of the Board of Directors of the corporation will improve the breed of livestock of any kind.

Undeniably, that is a nice, simple statement that gets directly to the point. But a number of people, including several members of Keeneland's board of directors, believed the association had become insular and insensitive to the growing needs of the overall Thoroughbred industry. And I cannot, in good conscience, suggest that their belief was completely unwarranted. What is often referred to as the "old boys' network" was very much in place at Keeneland at the time. Important business decisions were sometimes made not after a careful analysis of a situation and an assessment of what would bring the greatest good for the greatest number. Rather, they were made by a couple of "old boys" exchanging friendly nods and handshakes.

The Maine Chance property had been owned by Mrs. Elizabeth Arden Graham. Following her death in October 1966, the Bank of New York became coexecutor (along with two other banks) of her estate and subsequently announced they considered $2.5 million a fair price for the Maine

Chance property. The following year, Pessin and Ellsworth made their offer to purchase Maine Chance and made public their reasons for doing so, further stating that they intended to put another $3 million of improvements into the property. The University of Kentucky, which already owned two parcels of land adjoining Maine Chance on the latter's south, west, and north sides, then made a $2 million offer for the property through the University of Kentucky Research Foundation.

George Swinebroad, who was Keeneland's director of auctions, was also serving as UK's real estate agent in the situation. The Keeneland Association, over the signatures of Louis Haggin and Arthur Boyd Hancock Jr., sent a letter to the Bank of New York endorsing the university's bid. Four days later, on July 31, 1967, the executors announced that Maine Chance would be sold to the University of Kentucky.

At that point, so to speak, all sorts of hell began to break loose. A Fayette County judge, Joseph E. Johnson III, protested that the sale of Maine Chance to the University of Kentucky would remove the property from Fayette County's tax rolls. University president John Oswald angrily defended the sale, and his position was ratified by the university's board of trustees. And Pessin and Ellsworth submitted another bid of $2,058,000 for Maine Chance and filed their $30 million lawsuit.

During the next year and a half, pretrial briefs, depositions, pleadings, memoranda, motions, and exhibits produced a file that was several feet thick. The Kentucky state legislature got into the fray when thirteen of its members drew up a resolution petitioning the University of Kentucky to abandon its plans to purchase the farm so that the $2 million could be used for other purposes within the university's budget. And in midsummer 1968, U.S. District Court judge Mac Swinford denied defense motions to dismiss the case.

The trial began on January 27, 1969, in the federal courthouse in Lexington, Judge Swinford presiding. Kent Hollingsworth published a column in the *Blood-Horse* that listed all the organizations and individuals alleged by Pessin and Ellsworth to be involved in the conspiracy:

Keeneland Association: (Louis) Lee Haggin II, president of Keeneland and, at the time this controversy started 18 months ago, president of Thoroughbred Racing Associations; the TRA; George Swinebroad, Keeneland director of auctions and a realtor handling the sale of Maine Chance Farm; attorney Gayle Mohney, a director and secretary of Keeneland, counsel for the late Elizabeth N. Graham, and one of three trustees of the estate which owns two Lexington newspapers; Fred B. Wachs, editor and publisher of one Lexington newspaper, general manager and publisher of the other, and one of three trustees of the estate which owns both papers; the University of Kentucky Research Foundation; John Oswald, president of the university when the controversy started; Carl Cone of the university; Robert F. Kerley of the university; Robert M. Odear, law partner of Mohney and trial counsel for the firm representing Keeneland in this case; Edward T. Breathitt, governor of Kentucky when the controversy started; the Thoroughbred Racing Protective Bureau; Spencer Drayton, president of the TRPB and executive vice president of the TRA; the Bank of New York, James J. Clinch, Frederick Dohrman, Charles M. Bliss, Anthony M. Simonette, Thomas P. Tredway, J. Howard Carter, William J. Sweeney, Alexander R. M. Boyle and Edward M. Mayer, all of New York, "and others known to the defendants, but unknown to the plaintiffs."

During the ensuing three and a half weeks, the testimony filled 5,200 typewritten pages. Nine defense lawyers endeavored to dismantle the plaintiffs' case. The jury consisted of three men and nine women, and in giving them instructions before they began their deliberations, Judge Swinford narrowed the issue to one basic question: Did the defendants, as a group or individually, conspire to prevent Pessin and Ellsworth from purchasing Maine Chance Farm in order to protect Keeneland's virtual monopoly in regards to the sale of Thoroughbreds in central Kentucky?

After a day's deliberation, the jury came back with its verdict. A conspiracy did not take place on the part of any parties en masse, individually, or otherwise. And no damages of any kind would be awarded.

That was that. But looking back at the testimony from forty years ago, I believe one has to conclude that Keeneland, the University of Kentucky, the Bank of New York, et al. were extremely fortunate to have prevailed. In today's litigious environment, where there is so much pro-underdog and anti-establishment sentiment, the jury's verdict might be entirely different.

I did not participate in the trial. I was a bystander and was not called by lawyers on either side to testify. But I recall the bruised feelings the trial caused throughout the local Thoroughbred community, which included many responsible members who felt it was wrong for Keeneland not to have competition. Among other things, this was a gigantic wake-up call, informing us that our customer relations needed major improvements.

My official appointment as president of Keeneland was postponed until the trial was over—Louis Haggin asked me to consent to this, because he did not want the impression created that Pessin and Ellsworth had driven him out. In the months immediately following the trial, construction began on a new $700,000 sales pavilion at Keeneland. It was completed in time for that year's Summer Sale of Yearlings in July.

And in 1970, I became president of the Keeneland Association. Louis Haggin became Keeneland's chairman of the board, a position he continued to fill until his death from leukemia on April 18, 1980.

§

I made my first visit to Santa Anita in February 1969. Louis Haggin had sent me there to solicit nominations for the Blue Grass Stakes and the Ashland Stakes. The Blue Grass was and is for three-year-olds, and the Ashland is for three-year-old fillies. Both races had $25,000-added purses back then, which were small incentives for trainers to ship their horses from the West Coast to Kentucky.

But Keeneland did possess some powerful promotional tools for these races. During the 1960s, six horses that finished first or second in the Blue Grass went on to win the Kentucky Derby. And four fillies that finished first, second, or third in the Ashland had gone on to win the Kentucky Oaks, which is run at Churchill Downs the day prior to the Derby.

On this rainy morning at Santa Anita, though, I was very dejected and somewhat depressed. I had mud up to my ankles from walking around trying to decipher the geographical layout of the barns, which had an unusual numbering sequence. About 8:15 A.M., they closed the track for harrowing, and I went into the backside kitchen for a cup of tea and breakfast.

At the table next to me was a loud, joking group that included Oscar Orting Otis—he was known as "Triple O" because of his name. At the age of thirteen, he had sold special editions of the *San Diego Evening Tribune,* featuring racing results, on street corners and had advanced from there to become a *Daily Racing Form* columnist and dean of the West Coast turf writers. In 1959, Otis had secured an exclusive interview with FBI director J. Edgar Hoover, which gives you an idea how powerful a journalistic institution the *Racing Form* was in those days. Otis's column usually appeared on the *Racing Form*'s back page and was titled "Between Races."

Also at the table were Charlie Whittingham, who was the most prominent Thoroughbred trainer in that region of the country, and another well-known trainer, Noble Threewitt. Whittingham had already twice won the track's biggest race, the Santa Anita Handicap, and he would go on to win it another seven times. My back was turned to the group, but Otis said to me, sort of over my shoulder "Are you the new man from Keeneland?"

My response was, "Yes, sir. I am."

Otis said, "Well, what is your title back there?"

I told him, "I'm the assistant to the president, Louis Haggin."

Otis said, "You're his assistant? What do they need a fellow like you for?"

I said, "Well, you'll have to ask Mr. Haggin."

Otis was persistent. He said, "What is your claim to fame? Have you done anything?"

I did not want to get into my tenure as director of the Kentucky State Police and so on. I did not feel it was appropriate. So I said, "No, I haven't done anything in racing. I'm relatively green."

"Well, good Lord," Otis said, "I would like to write a story about you, but what have you done? Were you in the Army?"

That really got my ire up. I said to him very slowly and very pointedly, "Mr. Otis, I was in the United States Marine Corps." And then I just stared at him.

You would have thought a sorcerer with a magic wand had arrived. Oscar was an old Marine, having achieved the rank (not surprisingly) of sergeant. Whittingham was also an old Marine—he was in the Corps' Second Division, which fought on Guadalcanal. Our conversation in the track kitchen became warm and comradely as we exchanged stories. The fact that all four of us had served during World War II (Threewitt had been in the U.S. Army) opened a door I otherwise might not have been able to get through.

As the years went on, Otis and I developed a very firm friendship. He and his wife, "Ticky," had a farm in Manteca, a small town in the San Joaquin Valley, where they raised crops of almonds and had a vineyard. With a lady named Eunice Wallace, Otis coauthored a novel titled *The Race*, which was a fictional account of the 100th running of the Kentucky

Derby. Later, with the help of Hollywood director Mervyn LeRoy, Otis had tried to get a movie made out of the book. But his story contained references to the doping of horses and fixed races. John W. Galbreath, who was chairman of the board of Churchill Downs, didn't like the inclusion of unsavory episodes about racing. Galbreath was a man of powerful influence, and he put a stop to the film project.

§

Throughout the years, there had been a series of very preliminary conversations between Keeneland trustees and several members of the board of directors of Churchill Downs about the possibility of some type of merger or working alliance involving the two tracks. These conversations went back to the early days of Keeneland under Hal Price Headley and extended through the period when Warner L. Jones Jr. served on the Keeneland and Churchill boards. For the most part, the conversations never progressed very far. But Arnold Hanger and Warner Jones remained strong advocates of pursuing the merger possibility.

In early 1969, a company called National Industries Inc. attempted a hostile takeover of Churchill. National Industries operated a string of large discount department stores and a taxicab company in Louisville, had a Kentucky-based trucking firm, and operated 300 retail stores nationwide that dealt in goods ranging from dairy products to institutional furniture.

This was long before Churchill became the conglomerate it now is. The track's stock was sold over the counter in Louisville, and at the time it was held in various quantities by 2,327 stockholders, many of them horsemen. The value of the stock had recently ranged from $18 to $21 per share, but National was willing to pay $30 a share for it, in an attempt to acquire a controlling interest of greater than 50 percent.

National's president, Stanley Yarmouth, said his company viewed Churchill as "an investment opportunity for entry into the ever-expanding leisure-time field." And, at the time, this appeared to be a trend with more than a few racetracks. The year before, Gulf and Western Industries had purchased controlling interests in the two major tracks in the Chicago area, Arlington Park and Washington Park. And in January 1969, Realty Equities Corporation closed a deal to purchase Suffolk Downs in East Boston, Massachusetts, and the Ogden Corporation purchased Waterford Park and Wheeling Downs in West Virginia, Scarborough Downs in Maine, and Fairmount Park in Collinsville, Illinois.

The idea of something along these lines happening with Churchill was abhorrent to members of the track's board. They sent out a letter to stockholders imploring that the Kentucky Derby continue under the ownership of those primarily interested in racing. It was noted in the letter that National produced and sold "inexpensive plastic toys, carbonated beverages [, and] flavoring concentrates," which were items, the board felt, that could never blend well with horses.

National's plan ultimately failed, even though the company raised its purchase offer to $37.50 a share. For every time National upped the ante, a group that included Jones, his fellow Churchill directors A. B. Hancock Jr. and Cornelius Vanderbilt Whitney, Galbreath, Hanger, Leslie Combs II, and John Y. Brown was willing to match the offer. In late March 1969, National abandoned its bid. And as the *Blood-Horse* reported, the value of Churchill's shares promptly "dropped with a thud" to $22.

But just because one try at a hostile takeover was stonewalled, this didn't mean there was no possibility of another attempt in the future. Both Hanger and Jones were strong advocates of pursuing the possibility of a merger. In the early 1970s, because of the expansion of its yearling and bloodstock sales and the escalating influx of foreign buyers at those sales, Keeneland's financial position had become stronger than Churchill's. In 1972, Hanger and Jones initiated a preliminary study to evaluate the feasibility of Keeneland purchasing a majority of the shares held by the stockholders of Churchill as a protective measure from possible tender offers from outsiders.

J. J. B. Hilliard, W. L. Lyons Inc., a noted brokerage house in Louisville, was commissioned to draw up a proposal whereby Keeneland would purchase 137,000 shares of Churchill stock for $35 per share. This would provide Keeneland with 50.13 percent of the shares in Churchill, making the association the major holder of the 273,292 shares outstanding. Two-thirds of the $5,795,000 needed to purchase the stock would be financed by a ten-year bank loan with an annual interest rate of 12 percent.

The plan would provide benefits for parties on both sides of the transaction. Churchill Downs stockholders would be protected against further attempts at hostile takeovers of the company. For fiscal year 1975, their earnings would increase by a projected 30.6 percent, from $3.40 per share to $4.44 per share. The best possible racing schedules could be designed for both tracks. And there would be more efficient use of full-time managerial personnel.

To document and validate a bank's request for collateral, Keeneland contracted with R. W. Crabtree, a noted Lexington appraiser, to put a value on the 169 acres and physical facilities of Churchill. On August 1, 1972, Crabtree provided a detailed appraisal, complete with photographs and other documentation that assessed Churchill's value as $10,976,000— of which approximately $6.5 million was attributable to the raw land.

One of the purposes of recalling this exercise is that the nearly $6 million that Keeneland had to raise (to pay the $4 million principal of the loan and the interest on the loan) was a very high number for us back then. And we had to explore creative ways that we thought would be practical in generating the funds.

Well, we developed this Rube Goldberg plan involving the clubhouse and grandstand boxes for the Derby. Even thirty-seven years ago, they were prized items—when a box holder passed away, there frequently was, and still is, great concern among members of the family as to whether or not they could retain the box. (This has long remained true for box holders at Keeneland, as well.) George Evans, who was a member of the Kentucky Racing Commission, provided us with a list of all the holders of premium Derby boxes at Churchill. This involved 300 boxes. Evans himself had obtained the list from the Louisville & Nashville Railroad, which for many years transported thousands of people from throughout the Midwest to the Derby.

The conclusion we reached was that the quickest and surest way to raise money would be to raise the price of the premium boxes. Our plan was that to guarantee the annual right of renewal for a Derby box for a twenty-year period, the box holder would pay $20,000. Payments would be made in annual $5,000 installments over a four-year period. This is what would become known, three decades later, as "seat licensing." In recent years, it has been adapted by many major sporting establishments in the United States. But Keeneland almost became a pioneer of the concept.

Yes, I said almost. We sent Stan Jones, who was now our director of finance, to Florida to visit with Arnold Hanger, to advise him of the details of the idea, and to find out if he would give us his recommendations and his blessing. Stan (who is no relation to Warner) was and is a very good detail person. He made his presentation and pitch, and Arnold listened to him intently. And then, after some consideration, Arnold said, "I do not think it is appropriate to do this, nor do I think it would be acceptable to Churchill Downs."

And with that, the plan for a merger between Keeneland and Churchill Downs pretty much ended. Arnold believed that any proposal that required a box holder to pay a fee to guarantee retention of his or her seats would be impractical and unpopular in the minds of Churchill's shareholders. But that was thirty-four years ago. Today, Churchill has embraced the practice of seat licensing for the Derby. The fees to do so run well into five figures, and they have added some nice profits to Churchill's bottom line. Viewpoints change, and time marches on.

§

Harbor Springs, a very nice two-year-old colt, was a homebred that raced for Louis Haggin. Woody Stephens was his trainer. In 1975, Harbor Springs had registered his first career victory at Saratoga and then had won in allowance company at Belmont Park. Louis then brought him home to run on the opening day of Keeneland's fall meet in the Breeders' Futurity. It had a purse that year of $130,725, making it the first race Keeneland ever staged with a six-figure value.

The Breeders' Futurity was a seven-furlong event (a furlong is an eighth of a mile) in those days, and that year's edition lured a field of ten horses. Harbor Springs was the 8–5 second choice in the betting, and he was ridden by a jockey named Eddie Maple. It was a rough race. A colt named Vuelo forced another colt named Scrutiny to brush into Harbor Springs at the top of the stretch. Harbor Springs then bore inward on Scrutiny, who sort of got ping-ponged between Vuelo and Harbor Springs until nearing the eighth pole. At that point, Scrutiny dropped out of contention. At the wire, less than half a length separated the three top finishers —Harbor Springs, the late-charging Best Bee, and Vuelo. Harbor Springs appeared to be the winner by a very narrow margin. But the "photo finish" sign went up, and the stewards also posted the "inquiry" sign on the tote board. Further, Larry Snyder, the jockey aboard Scrutiny, who had finished fourth, lodged a claim of foul against Vuelo, alleging interference in the stretch and while going down the backstretch as well.

There was no public-address system at Keeneland, so there was no announcement as to exactly what was going on. To me, the tote board seemed to be one big mass of warning signs not to do anything but stay put. Photo! Inquiry! Objection! And once the unofficial order was posted, the numbers of Harbor Springs, Best Bee, Vuelo, and Scrutiny (1, 5, 4, and 6) kept blinking on and off, on and off—indicating that a change (or changes) in the order of finish might be nigh.

Louis had always said, "Don't take anyone across the track to the winner's circle until the race is declared official." This was something he had hammered into me time and time again. "Don't ever do it!" To accentuate his point, Louis had told me, many times, about a very embarrassing incident that had taken place at Hialeah back in 1958: Jewel's Reward, a homebred colt representing Maine Chance Farm, had finished first by a head in the Flamingo Stakes, which back then was a premier prep race for the Kentucky Derby. But a stewards' inquiry sign had gone up on the tote board. And Bill Hartack, who rode the second-place finisher Tim Tam, a colt bred and owned by Calumet Farm, claimed foul against Jewel's Reward and his jockey, Manuel Ycaza, alleging interference "all the way through the stretch." Nevertheless, Elizabeth Arden Graham, who owned Maine Chance and Jewel's Reward, walked arm in arm with her trainer, Ivan Parke, across the track to the winner's circle in the Hialeah infield. She was in there for ten minutes, accepting congratulations. And then the stewards disqualified Jewel's Reward. They took his number down and put him in second position. This made Tim Tam the winner. Mrs. Graham, who had left a sickbed to attend the race, walked away briskly. The sustained booing that followed—there were 31,303 people at Hialeah that day—was so loud that Mrs. Lucille Markey, the owner of Calumet and Tim Tam, refused to go into the winner's circle and instead was presented with the trophy in the Hialeah directors' room.

The Flamingo had been televised nationally, and the Hialeah press box was packed with major sports columnists—Red Smith, Arthur Daley, Jimmy Cannon, Shirley Povich, Stanley Woodward, Walter Haight. They had all witnessed a great race, along with a postrace fiasco. "We cannot allow something like that to happen at Keeneland," Louis had said. And during my first seven years working there, it didn't.

Now, though, on Breeders' Futurity day in 1975, there was Louis himself rushing up with his wife, Alma, and preparing to run across the track to the winner's circle. I said to him, "Uh, umm, uh [I might have thrown a 'duh' in there, too], don't you think we should wait until it's official?" So we waited. For three minutes. And Louis was glaring at me. We waited five minutes. And he looked up toward the grandstand roof and started glaring at the stewards' stand. We waited seven minutes. And Louis glared at me, glared at the stewards' stand, and then glared at me again. Ten minutes went by. "What the hell's taking them so long?" Louis said. By this time, he was stomping around in circles. He glared at me again, and I half expected him to start shaking his fist at the stewards.

Twelve minutes elapsed. Fourteen minutes. Louis began snorting loudly. He was furious. A volcano, the scope and size of Mount Vesuvius, seemed to be on the verge of eruption. And then, suddenly, there was an explosion of lights on the tote board. The stewards had sorted everything out. Vuelo was dropped down to fourth position. Scrutiny was elevated to third position. Best Bee was second. And Harbor Springs, by the margin of a head, was officially the Breeders' Futurity winner. Louis and Alma went across the track to receive the winner's trophy, while I heaved a gigantic sigh of relief.

§

In the winter of 1976, Keeneland was struggling to find a national television network that would be interested in broadcasting the Blue Grass Stakes. These were the days before ESPN and ESPN2 and Fox Sports and all the other channels available today via cable and satellite systems.

The trio of ruling powers were NBC, CBS, and ABC. Most of their sports coverage—beyond the baseball playoffs and the World Series, Monday-night football, and the college and professional basketball and National Hockey League finals—was focused on weekends. Back then, the Blue Grass was run on a Thursday afternoon, which to television network executives was not an enticing time slot for a live sporting event.

In 1975, CBS—for decades a force in televised horse racing—had lost the Kentucky Derby to ABC. The latter network had also telecast the Blue Grass via a two-day tape delay in 1975 but had decided not to do so in 1976.

At Keeneland, we sensed that CBS wanted to get back into the horse race telecasting business. I was in New York City for other matters, but on what wasn't much more than a whim, I decided to take a chance on meeting with Robert Wussler, who was the president of CBS Sports. Being a greenhorn, little did I know that the chances of getting an appointment and meeting with Wussler were slim to none. Nevertheless, I marched over to his office at 1:00 P.M. on a Friday, approached the receptionist, and asked "if I could meet with Mr. Wussler about televising Keeneland's Blue Grass Stakes." The receptionist told me that Mr. Wussler's appointment book was filled that afternoon but I could sit down and wait if I wished, and maybe there would be an opportunity if I was patient. I sat outside Wussler's office until 6:00 P.M., at which time the receptionist got up to leave for the day. She suggested I do the same.

The following day was Saturday, and I had nothing more important to do, so I decided to go back to Wussler's office to see if I could gain an appointment or perhaps see him that morning. I got to his office at 9:00 A.M., just as the receptionist was arriving, and she asked me, "Did you spend the night here?"

I told her, "No, but I'm going to stay here until I have the opportunity to see Mr. Wussler, even if it's only for five minutes." At 10:35 A.M., Wussler came out and said hello and invited me into his office. He was courteous and apologized for the long delay but at the same time told me that his schedule was very busy. Perseverance does sometimes pay off, and it did on this occasion. Wussler called in his assistant, Bud Lameroux, and the three of us discussed the Blue Grass and its role as a major prep race for the Derby. We agreed that CBS would pay Keeneland a fee of $25,000 to televise the Blue Grass via tape delay (to be shown on the following Saturday) for a period of two years. The race would be shown as part of the *CBS Sports Spectacular* program.

Letters of agreement subsequently followed. And I was absolutely elated. Ted Bassett, self-appointed, self-acclaimed super salesman! For I had obtained a $25,000 commitment for the Blue Grass Stakes to be shown in its entirety on national television two days after it was run! And CBS did a nice job. Jack Whitaker handled the anchoring chores. Heywood Hale Broun was the color man. And Charles "Chic" Anderson did the call of the race.

But little did I realize (I found this out later) that Wussler's primary interest was not in the Blue Grass Stakes. What he wanted to gain was the support of the Keeneland directors who also served on the Churchill Downs board—Leslie Combs II, Seth Hancock, Arnold Hanger, and Warner L. Jones Jr. You see, what CBS really wanted to do was to get the Derby back, and Wussler and Lameroux viewed our race as a vehicle that might lead to the achievement of that goal. Unfortunately for them, that is not the way it turned out. ABC had many successful years telecasting the Derby with Jim McKay as host. More recently, NBC has telecast the Derby. It has yet to return to CBS.

§

I do not recall the exact year of the story I am about to tell you. It had to have taken place prior to the fall race meeting of 1976, when we moved from the old wooden grandstand into a new concrete and steel structure.

It was back when the members of our maintenance crews were outfitted in white coveralls with green Keeneland logos stenciled on the upper left-hand areas of the chest. We were very concerned about cleanliness and about letting our patrons know about our concern, and the maintenance people were always roaming around on race days, picking up discarded tote tickets and programs and cups and whatever else might be discarded on the floors of the grandstand and the lawn in front of it.

One afternoon, Stan Jones and I were walking through the crowd, and we observed this one fellow dressed in Keeneland coveralls with a trash receptacle at his side. He wasn't moving around, though; he was just standing there, and people kept coming up to him. They would engage him in a brief conversation and hand something to him, and then he would reach into the receptacle, pull something out, and hand it to them. He was pretty discreet about it, but this happened again and again. Stan and I began to watch him more closely. We said to each other, "What in the world is he doing?" Suddenly, we figured it out. The fellow was selling half-pints of whiskey for what we later learned was $1.75 a bottle. It was not exactly bootlegged booze. Keeneland had a liquor license, and we sold whiskey at the concession stands for $1.75 a shot. But this fellow was selling the equivalent of eight shots for the same price. And he had a line of regular customers. So I went over to him. And I began telling him what a great job he was doing, helping to keep Keeneland clean and comfortable and so on and so forth. Then I took a hold of his trash receptacle and said, "You know, you seem to be so busy. I don't think this receptacle is big enough to handle all this paper you're picking up. Let me get a bigger one for you." First he began to stammer. Then he began to choke. Tears started coming out of his eyes. And when I actually picked up the receptacle and began to walk away with it, I thought he was going to have a heart attack. I was confiscating all his whiskey! But he did not say anything. Not that it mattered, for he soon joined the ranks of those who were formerly employed at Keeneland.

§

Now I am going to let you know about a fellow named Lazlo Urban, one of the most intriguing horse sale participants from my early years at Keeneland. He was a veterinarian, originally from Hungary. A story that accompanied him is that when the Russian army invaded his home country in 1956, Urban escaped by hanging on to the bars on the underneath of a railroad car and did not release his grip until the train steamed into neutral territory. Urban eventually made his way to France, where he set up a clinic and developed a reputation for working with mares that had fertility problems. In 1980, he came to Keeneland's January sale and purchased a broodmare named Valoris II, who during her racing days had been a champion three-year-old filly in Ireland.

Early on in the breeding shed, Valoris II had produced a trio of foals that placed in stakes races in England, Ireland, and France. She also produced a colt that had won the Geoffrey Freer Stakes, which is one of the more prominent races in Ireland. But at the time she was put in our January sale, Valoris II had failed to produce a live foal for three consecutive years. During two of those years, she hadn't even conceived. Urban nevertheless bought her for the substantial sum of $200,000. Suggestions were made in our sales office that Urban had no clue pertaining to what he was doing.

Urban promptly bred Valoris II to Secretariat, which in itself was pretty expensive. Somewhat surprisingly, the mating produced a filly named Salva. But she never raced. And although Salva subsequently went to the breeding shed, only one of her foals made it to the racetrack, and he earned only $6,250. Predictably, no windfalls came from Urban's Secretariat venture.

Then in 1981, Urban bred Valoris II to Northern Dancer, the most expensive stallion in the world, commanding stud fees as high as $750,000. The idea seemed crazy, and a trade publication, the *Thoroughbred Record,* did an article about it. The article included mention of Urban's practice of having Valoris II stand in a running stream, with the water providing support for her impregnated belly. This would facilitate growth, healing, and all sorts of benefits, according to Urban. But the article inferred that he might be a man who had lost his mind.

Well, the following year, Valoris II gave birth to a dark bay daughter of Northern Dancer, a nice-looking filly possessed of not only a pedigree but also fine conformation. As the months went on she proved sound and strong. And in 1983, she was cataloged in the Keeneland July Selected Yearling Sale as Hip Number 185. That was the first year the airplane manufacturing magnate Allen E. Paulson bought horses at Keeneland. His yearling purchases at our July vendue numbered ten, for a gross expenditure of $5,435,000. Among them was Urban's Northern Dancer/Valoris II filly, for whom Paulson had bid $2.5 million, which equaled the world-record price for a yearling of her gender sold at public auction.

Urban was at the sale, and he invited Stan Jones, Bill Greely, and several other Keeneland employees to dinner. At everybody's place at the table was a laminated copy of the *Thoroughbred Record* article. When dinner was over, Urban he handed out Monte Cristo cigars, which were very expensive and from Cuba and could not legally be purchased in the United States at the time. Urban had obtained the Monte Cristos in France and brought them over. And he walked around lighting them for us with big, long cedar reeds. All the time, Urban was wearing a big Cheshire Cat grin. But he said nothing. He did not have to say anything. Urban had proved a lot of people wrong, including us and the writer from the *Thoroughbred Record*. In July sale folklore, Urban's turned out to be one of the true Cinderella stories, one in which his coach most definitely did not turn into a pumpkin.

A few postscripts. The Northern Dancer/Valoris II filly turned out to be a pretty fair racehorse. Paulson named her Savannah Dancer and turned her over to my dear friend Ron McAnally to train. At age two, Savannah Dancer finished fourth in the inaugural running of the Breeders' Cup Juvenile Fillies at Hollywood Park. At age three, she won four stakes, one of which was the Del Mar Oaks. Savannah Dancer's career race record included sixteen starts, six wins, a second-place finish, and one third-place finish, and her purse earnings totaled $360,600. In the breeding shed, she produced a filly, Sha Tha, who was a stakes winner in both France and the United States, and a colt, Brier Creek, who was a multiple stakes winner in England and went on to do stud duty in France.

§

There was a buyer who used to come to the Keeneland September Yearling Sale from Panama named Luis Navas. One year, there were some sales tickets that were signed in his name. But somebody came into the sales office and told Stan Jones, "Navas is not signing those tickets. It's somebody else." Stan tried to find out who it was. A Keeneland employee spotted the man and informed Stan that, indeed, it wasn't Navas. The employee further said the man had just gotten into a rental car, or maybe it was a cab, and was headed for Blue Grass Field across the street. Stan decided he had better head for the airport, too, to find this fellow before he left town. Bill Greely was going with Stan, as was an employee named Paul Hollar, who did triple duty as a bid spotter, emergency medical technician, and roving sales office representative and knew what the man looked like.

Their plan was to confront him and learn if he had the authority to sign those tickets.

The immediate problem involved a means of transportation. If Stan and his posse delayed, the man's plane might take off before they got there. Well, the automobile most readily available was mine. It was parked in its usual spot at the top of the hill near the general offices, and they knew I always left the car keys on the floor mat on the driver's side (which for some strange reason I thought would serve as a deterrent to thieves). Bill Greely grabbed the keys, jumped in, started the car, and, with Stan and Paul, sped off to the airport's main terminal.

I did not know anything about this. The sale session ended; I came out to drive home, and my automobile was gone. My first and only thought was, "Someone has stolen it!" I went back into the general offices, phoned the State Police in Frankfort, identified myself, gave them a description of the car, provided the license plate number, and asked them to put out an ATL—an "attempt to locate." Listen, I was a former State Police director and knew how to do things by the book.

Meanwhile, over at Blue Grass Field, Stan, Bill, and Paul could not find the man they were seeking. (Not that it really mattered—everything subsequently turned out to be fine, and the yearlings were paid for.) They came back from the airport, returned my automobile to its proper spot, got into their own cars, and went home for the night.

At the same time, I was trying to get security or somebody else to give me a ride home but was not having any luck. After about a half hour, I walked outside and, to my shock, there was my automobile! No one was around to tell me what had happened. I looked at the car very carefully to see if it had been abused in any way. When I decided it had not, I got in and started to drive home, forgetting all about the report I had phoned in to the State Police.

A mile or so out of Versailles, I was pulled over by a State Police cruiser with siren sounding and blue light flashing. The trooper was H. C. Shipp, who was assigned to Woodford County and who also directed traffic at Keeneland's main entrance during race meets. Shipp had immediately recognized my automobile. And as he walked up to my car, he recognized its occupant. Because I had not rescinded my ATL request, had not informed the State Police that my auto had been returned or recovered, I had, in effect, been pulled over by Shipp for stealing my own vehicle.

This may amuse you. But it did not amuse Shipp, not even slightly.

Going strictly by the book (which is something Shipp never failed to do), he told me to show him my title to the car. Which, rather meekly, I did. "The next time, check with your office staff before you report it being stolen," Shipp said sternly. And I replied, "Yes, sir."

And, throughout my years at Keeneland, new chapters full of such tales as these seemed to keep emerging.

Chapter 2

Family Background and Kent School

BACK IN 1863, General William Temple "Temp" Withers was in command of the Confederate artillery forces during the siege of Vicksburg, Mississippi. Withers was thirty-eight years old at the time and a hardened veteran. Sixteen years earlier, while leading a charge at the Battle of Buena Vista during the Mexican War, he had been shot through both hips, a circumstance that effected a severe limp and equally severe headaches for the remainder of his life.

At Vicksburg, the opposing Union forces were led by General Ulysses Simpson Grant. Outnumbered, outgunned, and suffering from a lack of food and medical supplies, the Confederates surrendered to General Grant on July 4—which, interestingly, was just the day after Pickett's ill-fated charge at Gettysburg.

I have read that Withers shook Grant's hand, congratulated him for his victory, subsequently benefited from a prisoner exchange program, and completed his Civil War days serving with Confederate forces in Alabama. In civilian life, he was a lawyer and businessman, and after migrating during the postwar period to various locales in the Deep South, Withers moved his family to Lexington in his home state of Kentucky in 1871.

Withers was my great-grandfather—the grandfather of my mother, Jane Brooker. He became master of Fairlawn Stock Farm, a 153-acre enterprise that specialized in high-quality Thoroughbred and Standardbred breeding stock. Fairlawn's main house, stately and white, continues to stand today at 904 North Broadway in Lexington. General Grant and Hawaii's King Kalakaua were among the visitors my great-grandfather entertained at his residence.

I've seen photos of him. As a young man, he was thin-faced and clean-shaven. In the autumn of his years, Withers remained slim, but a thick white beard adorned his face, making him look a little bit like Confederate general Robert E. Lee. Withers was very religious, and when his health necessitated that he move farther south again in 1883, he resettled in Ocoee, Florida, and there began to build the Ocoee Christian Church.

Ocoee is about eight miles west of Orlando. My great-grandfather chose to live there because he had read a book by James Audubon that talked about the region's oak trees—some were so gigantic that it took six men with their arms extended to encircle the trunks. Withers reasoned that this was indicative that God, through the forces of Mother Nature, had blessed the area and that it was a wonderful place for crops. My great-grandfather got into the citrus business, oranges and grapefruit, and put most of his profits into the church.

The Ocoee Christian Church was constructed on land donated by another member of my mother's family, Captain Bluford Sims, who was a native of Tennessee and had also fought for the Confederacy. But the materials for the building, along with the costs of construction, were largely paid for by Withers. He died before the church was actually completed, and his widow imported three beautiful stained glass windows from Belgium to be placed behind the church altar in his honor. The windows were shipped across the Atlantic Ocean to Jacksonville, then by barge down the St. Johns River, and finally by oxcart to Ocoee. The Ocoee Christian Church opened in 1891. It is now the oldest Christian house of worship in continual use in Florida, and on March 28, 1997, it was put on the National Register of Historic Places.

During the later years of her life, my mother lived in Ocoee. Whenever I went to visit her, we attended services at the church—she always sat in the second row. After she grew terminally ill, I would frequent her bedside and she would tell me, "Don't forget the church." And in the ensuing years, I've tried to do what I can. Pay for a new roof on the church when it's needed. Help develop a plan for restoring the stained glass windows. The longtime pastor at the Ocoee Christian Church, Robert Clary, was a fanatic University of Kentucky basketball fan. I would bring him UK sweatshirts and T-shirts, and he would wear them around Ocoee. I think my mother would have liked this, too.

§

My grandfather on my father's side of the family was James Edward Bassett. There was no "Jr." or "III" attached to his name—he was the original. He was president of the Fayette National Bank, one of the oldest financial institutions in Lexington, and he was a very good businessman. He also had inherited S. Bassett & Sons Shoes, which was a famous old shoe store here that belonged to several generations of our family.

General John Hunt Morgan, the "Thunderbolt of the Confederacy," was anything but a hero in our household because, during one of his forays into Lexington during the Civil War, he and his raiders cleaned out the shoe store. My father's two sisters (my beloved, devoted aunts) would not, their entire lives, go into the Hunt-Morgan House on North Mill Street in Lexington, even though it is also on the National Register of Historic Places. That's how resentful they remained concerning what General Morgan had done.

During the Great Depression, the Fayette National Bank closed. My father had been working there and, needing a job, with a wife and two sons to support, he took employment at a horse farm named Mare's Nest. But my father was also a friend of Major Louie Beard, who was a graduate of West Point, a U.S. Army artillery officer, and a polo player of international stature. Further, Beard was a major figure in the founding of the Keeneland Association in 1935 (the track's 7-furlong, 184-foot Beard Course is named after him), and he managed Greentree Farm and Stud, which were owned by the Whitney family.

Beard hired my father to be the superintendent of Greentree—this occurred around the time Keeneland was founded, and he stayed with the Whitneys until 1948. This was during the period when Greentree had the champion homebred racehorses Jungle King and Devil Diver and the Kentucky Derby and Belmont Stakes winner Shut Out. My father had a significant role at Keeneland. He was elected a vice president and director of the racecourse in 1940 and continued serving in those capacities for the remaining seventeen years of his life.

You might conclude from this that, well, Bassett, you did indeed have a racing background when you came to Keeneland. But I assure you, I did not. During my father's tenure at Greentree and Keeneland, I spent almost all my time in college preparatory school, at Yale University, in the Marine Corps, or working on the East Coast for an outfit called the Great Northern Paper Company. I never worked with horses and have no recollection of ever going to Keeneland in my youth.

§

I was twelve years old when my parents sent me to Kent School in Kent,

Connecticut. My means of getting there was the Chesapeake & Ohio Railroad's George Washington train. I was on car 24, a Pullman, with green curtains and upper and lower berths. It was September of 1936, and at the time the farthest from home I had ever been was Michigan—I had never even been to New York City. Now, here I was, not a teenager yet, frightened and apprehensive. With one exception—a boy from Lexington named Logan Shearer who was three years my senior—everybody at Kent was a stranger to me. Following World War II, Shearer married a girl named Elizabeth, who was the sister of one of my closest friends, Alex Campbell. But when I first came to Kent, there was a time warp between the upperclassmen like Shearer and the new boys like me.

Kent School is administered by the Episcopal Church. It was established in 1906 by the Reverend Frederick Herbert Sill, who was an alumnus of Columbia University and a member of the monastic Order of the Holy Cross. Under Father Sill, the Kent student body never numbered more than 299 because he felt 300 students would be, in his words, "too many." Some thirty-five to forty states were represented in the student body, although the majority of the boys came from New England and the eastern seaboard. In 1960, Kent established a separate division for girls. Today, its student body numbers 560 students, and the school is fully coeducational—54 percent male and 46 percent female—and members of both genders share the same campus. But when I was there, Kent was strictly an all-boys school.

Father Sill remained the headmaster throughout my time at Kent. Physically, he was a small, slender man, but he possessed an enormous personality and physical presence. He had horn-rimmed eyeglasses, smoked Prince Albert tobacco in a curved pipe, wore a white monastic habit topped with a broad-shouldered cowl that billowed in the wind, and had a large black cross hanging from his neck. During his early decades at Kent, Father Sill taught English and religion; supervised admissions; presided over disciplinary matters; was the school's business manager, purchasing agent, chaplain, and dietician; and coached football, hockey, tennis, and crew. He believed in rigid adherence to discipline and saw to it that his students maintained something of a spartan existence. We wore stiff collars on Sundays and three-piece suits to dinner. We didn't have any free weekends, and until my final year there, we never had dances (and even then, we had only one).

The bell to rise rang at 6:00 A.M. Classes began at 8:00 A.M., and we had them six days a week. There were voluntary chapel services every morning and mandatory services every evening and twice on Sundays. We swept floors, washed windows, waited on tables, and were responsible for making our beds and cleaning our rooms. These things later became benchmarks for private boarding schools throughout the country, but they were rather unusual when I was a boy. The motto at Kent is *Temperantia, Fiducia, Constantia,* which roughly translated from the Latin means "Simplicity of Life, Directness of Purpose, Self-Reliance."

Kent's academic program encompassed five years, which were referred to as "forms," second through sixth. There was no first form—I do not know why, that's just the way it has always been. When you are in the eighth grade, it is your second-form year, ninth grade is third form, and so on through senior year, which is sixth form. The academic year extended from about September 10 through the first week of June.

Most of the faculty members were laymen, and the curriculum was very demanding. I took five years of Latin and four years of French at Kent. The core curriculum included four years of English and courses in history and biology. We were required to take math at least through the geometry level, which meant a minimum of three years. Our examinations were generally old College Board tests, and they were very tough.

Within the mystery of this new environment, I acquired a nickname, "Bluegrass," which I embraced without any particular degree of happiness. Otherwise, we were almost always called by our last names. If you had a brother at the school, you had a number attached. The brother in the higher form year was designated "One," and you thus became "Smith One" or "Jones One" or "Bassett One," and your younger brother became "Smith Two" or "Jones Two" or "Bassett Two," or whatever, depending upon what your surname was.

Every day at 6:00 P.M., just before dinner, there would be the Job Assembly, attended by the entire student body. Reports would be given on the day's activities, and announcements would be made, including ones pertaining to the quality of work that each student in the lower forms had been assigned. If my responsibility had been to sweep a hall or classroom, and what I had done was deemed insufficient, an upper former would "sting" me, which meant I had to go spend an hour washing windows or something like that. The announcement would be made at the assembly, "Bassett One, report to such-and-such hall," and I'd go and perform my penalty duty. But I don't want to give the impression that attending Kent was a never-ending exercise in all work and no play. I enjoyed my time there immensely.

One thing that would also occur at the Job Assembly is that, if a varsity game had been played that afternoon or the evening before and an athlete had played particularly well or scored a touchdown or the winning run or winning goal or basket, when he walked into the room the entire student body would start clapping. Nothing would be said. No shouting. Just applause. Subdued, steady applause. And this was always very meaningful to the athlete who was the recipient. And it would happen again if a second athlete had done well in the same game or contest.

The location of the school was, and is, beautiful. Kent is situated on what formerly was farmland in the northwestern part of Connecticut, between the Appalachian Trail and the Housatonic River. The Litchfield Hills, which are part of the Appalachian Mountain range, provide the backdrop for Kent's campus. The hills are a mass of sugar maple trees, whose colors are brilliant in the autumn.

Participation in athletics was required at Kent. The only way it could be avoided was for health reasons, and you had to have documentation from your doctor to prove it. Otherwise, everybody had to go out for football. Kent had varsity and junior varsity teams and intramural junior and midget leagues. One of the purposes was the health benefits of exercise. Another was to teach you how to compete. And another was to immerse you in the concept of school spirit. When the varsity football team played a home game, the entire student body would attend and ring the field. And I mean everybody—you wouldn't even think about not going.

Crew was huge at Kent. While at Columbia, Father Sill had been coxswain for the university's eight-oar shell team, and his love for the sport was transmitted throughout the school he founded. In the spring, we would stampede down to the Housatonic and line the river's shoreline as the Kent oarsmen raced against teams from Philadelphia and Washington, D.C., which were also centers of crew competition. Each form had a crew, and I was captain and seventh oar of the second form's eight-oar shell. It was not something I was really interested in, but my father urged me to do it. His boss, Jock Whitney, had rowed on the varsity crew at Yale. I did it for a year. But I developed severe blisters on my calves where they hit the sliding board on the shell. The blisters became so infected that by the end of spring term, I could not walk and had to be hospitalized. After that, I said to my father, "I really think I would prefer to play baseball."

And I was a lot better at that sport than I was at rowing. At Kent, I played center field. During the summer months, my father would take me to Crosley Field in Cincinnati, where we would see the Reds play teams such as the New York Giants. The Giants (who are now in San Francisco) had an outfielder in those days named Hank Lieber. He would stand there with his arms down, his hands parallel to the sides of his knees, until a fly ball got to within five or six feet of his head. Lieber would then put his hands together at waist level, with his palms turned upward, and he would catch the ball that way. He called it a "basket catch."

I was young and impressionable and thought it was really neat the way Lieber fielded fly balls. So I did it too, several times, while playing the outfield for Kent. The school's baseball coach, Bill Nadal, called me over and said, "That circus catch you're trying to make out there, Bassett—you better make darn sure you don't drop the ball, because if you do, you're going to the bench full time." Well, after that, I didn't try it anymore, at least not in games. But I still did it when practice flies were hit to me before games. (Lieber, by the way, eventually spent three seasons with the Chicago Cubs and then went back to the Giants. He played for ten seasons in the major leagues, and I don't ever recall him changing his ways. The basket catch, of course, was later popularized by another player for the Giants named Willie Mays.)

My best sport at Kent was basketball. I played center from my third-form year onward for the varsity team. Logan Shearer, whom I mentioned earlier, was the team's captain the first year I played, and I was the captain my final year. We played in the Tri-State League, which included seven other prep schools—Canterbury, Gunnery, Taft, Choate, Berkshire, Pawling, and Loomis—in the states of Connecticut, New York, and Massachusetts. These were the days of the two-handed set shot, where you tossed the ball toward the basket from a height midway up your chest. You did not see anybody shooting one-handed jumpers. For foul shots, we bent our knees almost halfway to the floor, sort of in a semisquat, and threw the ball toward the basket underhanded. You might recall that Wilt Chamberlain did his foul shooting that way during his early years in the pros, during the late 1950s and early to mid-1960s, and his fellow Hall of Famer Rick Barry did it that way throughout his entire professional career, which extended through fourteen seasons. In that regard, Chamberlain and Barry were throwbacks. But in my time, the underhanded method was the way every player shot fouls.

Pawling was the best team in the league the year I was basketball captain. They beat us twice, 27–21 and 28–20; finished the season undefeated; and were Tri-State champions. With a record that included eight wins and four losses, Kent finished second in the standings. I remember we lost a game to Taft 33–32 when one of their players hit a shot from half-court just before time expired. Our most lopsided victory, 86–27, was achieved over Gunnery—at the time, it was the most points ever scored by a Kent team. And in that game, I scored 25 points, which was the most in a game in school history by a single player (Shearer had set the previous standard of 23). At season's end, my overall point total was 143. This eclipsed the previous Kent standard as well.

Kent is where I first developed my Machiavellian sense of humor. We had several nicknames for Father Sill. One was the "Great White Tent." Another was "Fritz." Of course, no one dared call him either of these to his face—we would only do so behind his back. He was such a strict discipli-narian, the epitome of the all-powerful headmaster clad in flowing white vestments. Occasionally, I would find myself walking along through a building corridor with two or three of my classmates, and Father Sill would be walking perhaps thirty yards ahead of us. We would come to a doorway and I would cup my hands around my mouth and yell out, "Hey! Fritz!" Father Sill would stop and turn around, but before he did, I would duck into the doorway, leaving my classmates to stumble onward. Father Sill, enraged at the insult to his authority and dignity, would begin to reproach them. My classmates would also try to duck back through the doorway, but I would close the door on them. And Father Sill would proceed to give them a good dressing down.

But I received a pretty important lesson from my fellow students dur-ing the spring of my third-form year. My presence on the varsity basketball team was extraordinarily unusual for a lower former, and I had begun to develop a rather exaggerated notion of myself and my importance. Being center on the basketball varsity had suddenly thrust me into the athletic limelight, and my ego became overloaded. I campaigned to be elected to the Kent student council, which was the ruling body of the school. Self-confidence can often be a good thing, but in this case, it overwhelmed me. I was sure I would be elected. A majority vote was necessary, and the elec-tion went to three ballots. The entire student body voted, all 299 members. And I lost. It was a crushing blow of reality. I felt rejected, and my ego was deeply hurt. But it was also a turning point for my attitude, and it was needed, because from there on I knew there was much more to the process of gaining respect from my fellow students than being a basketball player.

I thought a lot about that over the summer, and it brought about a dramatic change in my thinking. I would never, ever be as cocky again.

There were other lessons to learn, too, and not all of them came at Kent. During the summer months, I worked at Greentree. I started out mowing grass. This was during the Great Depression, and many of the adult men on the farm were paid $2.50 a day. I started there when I was fourteen years old, and my pay was 25 cents a day. My first monthly paycheck was for less than $6, and I did not like this. I had figured, for no particular reason, that I was going to be paid the same as the full-fledged adults. And I had mentally made plans about how I was going to spend the money. So I went to my father and said, "I'm working just as hard, and I'm doing just as good a job as these other guys." And he told me, "That is true. But you haven't yet earned the right to be considered a full-time employee. And you don't have the responsibility of feeding a family. When you do, you will have the right to earn the same salary." Short. Brief. Right to the point. End of conversation.

In subsequent summers, I went from mowing grass aboard a little sit-down Toro to using heavy equipment to mow the fields. Greentree, of course, was privately owned and did not have public roadways, and I was driving trucks across the property before I had my driver's license. I was operating tractors. But my father kept me away from the horses. He did not want somebody as inexperienced as me with equine stock trying to handle them. And I think he was always also afraid that I might get hurt.

§

It was during the early spring of my final year at Kent when my brother, Spencer Brooker Bassett, was killed in an automobile accident. He was named after my maternal grandfather, who was an Englishman. I was nineteen at the time. Brooker (we always called my brother by his middle name) had been born on August 3, 1925, and was a little bit less than four years younger than me. Brooker was my only sibling. He also attended Kent and was president of his third-form class.

The accident occurred on March 22, 1941. We were home on spring vacation. A Saturday morning. Brooker and three of his friends had gone to Lawrenceburg, Kentucky, to pick up another friend, and they were on their way back to Lexington to attend a high school basketball tournament. They were traveling east on Route 62 in Anderson County and were on the approach to the Tyrone Bridge, which crosses the Kentucky River and leads into Woodford County, when their car struck a shoulder of loose rock on the right side of the road.

A boy named Johnsen Camden Stoll was driving. He was only fifteen, and he apparently slammed on the brakes and lost control of the car. I don't recall what the legal age was to drive in Kentucky back then, but nobody made an issue of it—what purpose would that have served? Police investigators concluded from the tire tracks that the car had swerved three times across the road before going over the embankment on the left side and plunging 200 feet down the steep, wooded hill, coming to a stop about 100 yards from the river.

Johnsen, his seventeen-year-old sister Susanna Stoll, and another boy, John Wheeler, who was sixteen, all were thrown from the car and killed instantly. My brother was also thrown from the car and suffered massive head and spinal injuries. (There were no seat belts in those days.) A fifth passenger, a sixteen-year-old boy named Cassell Stewart, somehow managed to stay inside the vehicle. Despite the fact that the car was totally wrecked, Cassell suffered only minor cuts and bruises. He climbed out of the wreckage, walked halfway up the hill, and was kneeling next to my brother, trying to talk to him, when the police arrived.

All five of the teenagers were from prominent families—the Stolls were the only children in theirs—and the devastating effects of the accident were felt by people throughout Lexington, which was a much smaller town back then. Brooker was taken to Good Samaritan Hospital. A specialist, Dr. Spurling, was brought in from Cincinnati to try to save his life. But Brooker was in a coma and completely paralyzed from the chest down, and the prospects of him recovering were very bleak. My parents told me to return to Kent, and I did as they wished.

At 3:15 P.M. on April 12, the day before Easter, Brooker died. The official cause of death was cardiac asthenia, which is a fatal weakening of the heart caused by the strain placed upon it by the body's attempt to deal with the injuries. My father phoned Father Sill and told him. I was in the Kent infirmary, for reasons which I do not recall, but I remember the Reverend William Scott Chalmers, who was Father Sill's assistant and the varsity basketball coach, coming up to me. He had a nurse with him. When I saw them, I had an apprehension of what he was about to say. Father Chalmers was as gentle and compassionate as you could ever expect a man to be—as he performed the immensely difficult task of letting me know my brother had died.

I immediately boarded a train for the journey home to attend my brother's funeral. It remains the most difficult trip I have ever taken in my life. Father Chalmers, who at the culmination of that school year would succeed Father Sill as Kent's headmaster, accompanied me. Services for Brooker were held in our house on Paris Pike on April 14, and he was buried that afternoon in Lexington Cemetery. Brooker had lived to the age of exactly fifteen years, eight months, and nine days.

§

Two months after Brooker's death, I graduated from Kent. On what was officially known as Prize Day, I was awarded the Yale scholarship, which did not have much monetary value, something less than $500, but it was an honor to receive it. I was also the recipient of the Columbia Cup, which Father Sill had named for his undergraduate alma mater and is annually given to "the boy who has shown in his life at Kent the most comprehensive grasp of life and work." The Columbia Cup was presented to me by Norman Thomas, who, beginning in 1928, was the Socialist Party's candidate in six consecutive presidential elections. He ran against Herbert Hoover, four times against Franklin Roosevelt, and against Harry Truman. Thomas's son, Evan, attended Kent, and the elder Thomas was the commencement speaker on Prize Day that year, and in the process of handing me the cup, he dropped it on my foot. He then said to me, "I hope your grasp is more comprehensive than mine."

Whatever levity that brought, however, did not last, for immediately following the Prize Day ceremonies, a window in memory of my brother was dedicated in the Kent sacristy, which bears the name St. Joseph's Chapel. My parents were there, of course, as was the entire third-form class. The dedication service was conducted by Father Sill and Father Chalmers. I remember Father Sill saying that this was "a very celebrated occasion" and that Brooker would remain a part of Kent School "for as long as it existed." He spoke these kind words from his wheelchair, for Father Sill, now sixty-seven years old, had suffered the first in a series of strokes that were slowly paralyzing him. The *Kent News,* our student newspaper, published a short article about the dedication service, which contained the following paragraph:

The window is of surpassing beauty. It is decorated with various colors of glass and is as beautiful a window as there is in the Chapel. The colored glass forms a picture of Our Lord giving Communion to two people kneeling at a table in front of Him. Under it is inscribed, "The Body and Blood of Our Lord Jesus Christ." This is a fitting tribute for a boy who was loved by the whole School. He was one who followed truly in the way of Our Lord and his classmates as well as his schoolmates have all felt his loss very keenly. It is a fine thing to have something in the Chapel to commemorate his name. May he rest in peace.

§

When Father Sill founded Kent, he believed very strongly in providing boys from families of modest means an opportunity to attend. (The phrase "from families of modest means" is in the governing charter of the school.) Unlike many New England boarding schools, which in Father Sill's estimation were content to cater to the sons and daughters of wealthy families, Kent from its inception went out of the way to make the experience available to any boy, regardless of his family's financial background.

An emphasis on scholarship assistance remains a Kent hallmark. During the first fifty-four years of its existence, until it went coeducational in 1960, there was no stated monetary figure for tuition or for room and board at Kent. A boy was admitted on his merits as a person. And if his family accepted the offer of admission, they would discuss with the headmaster the annual payment they would make—which could be far in excess of the cost of educating the boy, or equivalent to the cost, on down to no payment at all. This was called the "sliding scale" of tuition. If a family did pay in excess of the actual cost, the extra money would be put into a scholarship aid program.

The average cost when I attended Kent was about $1,200 a year. I do not remember exactly what my father and mother paid—I think it was about $900, which was a rather significant sacrifice for them. But what a given boy's family paid was never discussed or revealed by Father Sill, not even to the boy himself. That was one of Father Sill's cardinal rules. He made the decision as to what a boy's tuition would be, and it was no one else's concern.

Every year since my graduation, I have contributed money to Kent. Almost all the money realized from the school's annual fund-raising drive goes directly to scholarships. John S. Kerr, Kent's director of planned giving, has told me the participation by members of the class of 1941 in these fund-raising drives has almost invariably been 100 percent. We are a distinct group in that regard.

But because of the respect I have for Father Sill's mission, and in memory of my brother, I am also underwriting a scholarship in Brooker's name. It will be funded in perpetuity after my death by the proceeds from three life insurance policies and by a charitable remainder trust I established decades ago. The trust has other beneficiaries as well—the New Union Christian Church on Old Frankfort Pike in Woodford County, Kentucky, where Lucy and I attend services every Sunday; the Ocoee Christian Church in Florida; and Transylvania University, for which I have served as a trustee for nearly four decades.

My plan is that following my death, the Spencer Brooker Bassett Scholarship will be awarded annually to a young person, male or female, who is from the South. The people at Kent will decide who receives the scholarship. Tuition and room and board at Kent now cost $42,000 per year, and the scholarship will not cover the entirety of that sum. But it will defray some of the expenses.

§

During the year following Brooker's death, my mother and father were divorced. I was then twenty-one years old. What happened to my brother had devastated them, and their grief was omnipresent—it just would not leave. I have seen that happen as a result of a tragedy such as a child's death in other families, and it happened in mine. My mother went down to Ocoee, Florida, to stay at the property my great-grandfather had founded and stayed there probably a little bit longer than she should have, and by the time she returned to Lexington, my parents' marriage was over.

My father did not live to an old age—when he died on April 2, 1957, he was only fifty-nine years old. One of his habits each morning was to stop at a place called Jerry's Drive-in on East Main Street in Lexington. It was one of those car-hop eateries, and my father would sit in his automobile and have coffee. He liked to start the day that way. Well, at 7:45 A.M., they found him slumped over the wheel. A heart attack had taken him. We buried my father in our family plot in Lexington Cemetery.

But my mother—well, she lived past her eighty-eighth birthday. The later years of her life were spent in Ocoee, where she remarried and became Jane Brooker Bassett Wilson. My mother outlived her second husband as well.

Throughout her days, she was an energetic and dynamic lady who

41

always tried to advise her idiot older son about which steps to take and which ones should be avoided. Toward the end of her life, my mother was in a nursing home, and I would fly down to Florida about once a month to visit her. I can recall her sitting in a chair in that home, chatting with me, just passing the time of day. And then her gaze would extend beyond me to several other elderly ladies who were moving ever so slowly up and down the hallway with their walkers and wheelchairs. And my mother would say, "Look at those old crows, shuffling around here! They ought to be up and moving around! Just look at them!" The women she was describing invariably appeared to be at least ten years younger than she was.

My mother and I were both born under the sign of Scorpio, which led to occasional clashes of temper between us. But I loved her dearly. She died on January 11, 1985, and is buried in a cemetery in Ocoee.

§

While I do not view myself as an exceptionally religious man, attending church is something I rarely fail to do when I'm home. My father and mother mandated that I go to Sunday services, and the importance of doing this was fortified by my experiences at Kent School.

The pastor of New Union Christian Church is the Reverend Nancy Jo Kemper. Dr. Kemper, interestingly, is also executive director of the Kentucky Council of Churches and a key spokesman for Citizens Against Gaming Expansion (CAGE). Both groups oppose the legalization of slot machines at Kentucky's racetracks or at any facilities in the state. I will deal with the issue of slots in a later chapter. What I want to mention now is that I have composed a prayer that Dr. Kemper has me read before the New Union congregation about once a year. (I am not talking about a large congregation, for there are only about twenty or thirty of us there each Sunday.)

> One gets happiness from peace of mind. One gets peace from what one gives to others. This is where happiness resides: by being a giving person, a generous person, a kind person.
>
> It is important to have honor, for it is honor that helps you stand by people when they are in trouble or need; it is honor that will help make you a loyal person; it is honor that makes you help people when you are really too busy, when you are really too tired and too distracted, and when no one else will even know or credit you with helping.

Happiness comes not from your head, not from your intelligence, not from your ambitions; it comes from your heart.

To emphasize service above self; by embracing the spirit of caring for others, and following the true instincts of your heart will be the pathway to genuine happiness.

Well, maybe it is a not a prayer in the true definition of the word; perhaps it is more of a statement of beliefs. But I do truly believe these things, and the remembrances of my father and mother, Brooker, and my days at Kent School have had a major influence on the formation of these beliefs as the years and decades have gone by.

My time at Kent, with its spartan, restrictive environment and its emphasis on self-reliance and responsibility, coupled with a sense of purpose, were, I think, the most formative years of my life. They were a major factor in molding the person I became.

I went home from Kent that summer of 1941, immeasurably thankful for my experiences there but not certain what my next steps in life would involve. And then in midsummer, the letter arrived from Yale University informing me that my application to be a student there had been accepted.

Chapter 3

Yale and the U.S. Marine Corps

THE DAILY NEWSPAPER my Yale University roommates and I subscribed to was the *New York Herald Tribune*, and I remember opening our door at 50 Vanderbilt Hall early Monday morning, December 8, 1941, and immediately seeing that headline in huge type, one of the biggest headlines I have ever seen, "JAPS ATTACK PEARL HARBOR."

I was totally unaware of the broad implications of what had happened. I did not know where Pearl Harbor was. I really was not even sure what it was. The whole situation seemed something akin to that famous Orson Welles radio broadcast of *War of the Worlds* back in 1938, when many people on the East Coast thought Martians had actually landed and were rampaging the countryside. But this was real. Much of the U.S. fleet in the Pacific had been decimated if not outright destroyed. Many of our battleships had been sunk, were burning, or (in the case of the USS *Arizona*) had been blown apart. Thousands of American citizens—sailors, soldiers, and civilians—had been killed or injured. At the same time, conflicting information kept circulating via newspaper and radio reports and by word of mouth. We heard about hoards of Japanese planes poised to attack again, about an anticipated Japanese invasion of the West Coast. Commentators were saying the country had to be galvanized immediately to meet the threat.

New Haven Green is a gigantic place that encompasses three or four big blocks. It's owned by the city and is adjacent to the Yale campus. The night following the Pearl Harbor attack, New Haven Green was the site of what I can best describe as a student riot. There were 2,000 or 3,000 of us milling and marching around, drinking, carrying torches and American flags, and shouting, "To war! To war!" and "Join up!" In the midst of this, the Yale band was playing patriotic music.

There was no organization or any true direction on New Haven Green that night. It was just mass hysteria, with all of us caught up in the flame of patriotism. There were no brawls on the Green, in contrast to what you usually see when people are really worked up. But the sound and fury were enormous. We didn't really understand what was happening, except for the inalterable reality that our country had been attacked. We were drinking beer and whiskey and rum and yelling, "We'll do this! We'll do that!" It was one of the most incredible spectacles I've ever been part of.

Almost all the students were young, in their late teens or early twenties, and had not had any relationship with the First World War. And we certainly hadn't been around during the Spanish-American War, much less the Civil War. So war was something we didn't know much about. It wasn't like more contemporary times, when we have had Korea, Vietnam, Desert Storm, and our current conflicts in Afghanistan and Iraq, and there seems to be a war fought by every generation.

Prior to Pearl Harbor, there had been a strong leaning toward isolationism in many parts of the northeastern United States, and the isolationist philosophy was evident on the Yale campus. That vanished after the Japanese attacked. But we still didn't understand what was going on. Winter arrived, and the U.S. military buildup began. All men aged eighteen to forty-five were told to register for the draft. Since I was already in the Reserve Officers' Training Corps (ROTC), that directive did not apply to me.

There were continuous rumors that the Japanese were poised to attack the Hawaiian Islands again, that their ships were steaming toward the Washington, Oregon, and California coasts. The stories were circulating daily, nightly, in the corridors and rooms of Yale's residential colleges, classroom buildings, and libraries and in the taverns frequented by Yale students throughout New Haven.

January went by, as did February and March. One evening in April 1942, five of us were downing beers at Mory's, a famous old New Haven eating and drinking establishment. Its walls are covered with Yale memorabilia, and its tables are decorated with carvings made by Yale students, past and present. Mory's is also the only place in New Haven that serves Welsh rarebit. We were getting a little drunk and carried away, and somebody suddenly said, "We all ought to join the Marine Corps!"

"Join the Marine Corps! Yes, that's a great idea!" After a few more pitchers of beer, we all got into a Ford convertible owned by one of my classmates, Haskell Noyes. Two of us got into the rumble seat, and three others were in front. And we drove to New York City—to 346 Broadway Avenue to be precise—and enlisted in the Marine Corps. Had we not gotten so immersed in beer and patriotic fervor at Mory's, I wouldn't have done it.

Cell phones did not exist back then. And we did not have telephones in our dormitory rooms either. If I wanted to call home, I had to go to a pay phone and pump nickels, dimes, and quarters into it. But with regard to informing my parents that I had joined the Marines, I decided to forgo that option as well and instead wrote them a letter about it.

They were furious. My father sent a telegram ordering me to call him, and he was right to be so angry—at least to a degree. This was my freshman year, mind you, and I had no real understanding of what I had done. To make sure he had made his point, he came up to Yale to see me, which was a very unusual thing for him to do. And he told me, "Buckle down and concentrate on your academics, and let the war take care of itself."

But I was not the only college freshman to become hypnotized by the patriotic frenzy. This sort of thing was happening at campuses across the land. The federal government realized this and, in league with the colleges and universities, developed programs that allowed for the accelerated, year-round pursuit of degrees, at the culmination of which students would go directly into the armed services.

I came home that summer of 1942, but only for a brief stay. Yale had decided to go to a full twelve-month academic calendar, and I returned to New Haven within a few weeks to begin my sophomore year. The small group of Marines the university had among its student body was put into uniform, myself included, and a Corporal Moran was put in charge of us. He was all full of himself, and we called him "Corporal Moron" behind his back, but we didn't know rocks from dirt ourselves. Fortuitously, instead of being yanked away and sent to Parris Island, I was allowed to get my college degree first.

§

Yale had been the only university to which I had applied for admission. I had never visited Yale during my Kent School days. In fact, I had never been to see it, period. But as a boy I had read the stories about Frank Merriwell, the fictional Yale athlete who excelled in football, baseball, crew, and track and moonlighted during his university days by solving unsolvable mysteries and righting wrongs. Indeed, the chroniclers of Merriwell's exploits recognized virtually no limitations to his character. Beyond the university's athletic fields, Merriwell was also a playwright, campaigned a champion Thoroughbred racehorse, and traveled the world. He was something else, and I read those wonderful stories about him and fantasized I would grow up to be the same way.

Much more grounded in reality was a great football player from Kent School named James Riley. "Boogie" Riley, they called him, and he was from New Orleans. He was four years ahead of me, a nine-letter, all-around athlete who went to Yale and played on a freshman team that beat Harvard and Princeton. It all was written up in the *New York Times* and in our school newspaper, the *Kent News*. Riley was my school idol and hero and my inspiration to go to Yale.

The transition from Kent's spartan, restrictive life to the newfound freedom of Yale, where students could come and go as they wanted, was intoxicating. I can still recall my first football game in the Yale Bowl, with Yale defeating the University of Virginia 21–19. (It was the Yale Bulldogs' only football victory that year.) The following Monday morning in English 101, my voice was still hoarse from the excessive cheering and imbibing I had done on Saturday afternoon. My classmate Charles "Buck" Bradley had seen me at the football game and viewed my raucous behavior with disdain. Buck later became general counsel for the pharmaceutical giant Eli Lilly and Company, and a lifelong friend. But that morning in the classroom he said to me, "Bassett, you are the type of person my parents warned me about."

For good reason, I think. Here's an absolutely ridiculous story. My roommate Alexander "Zandy" Harvey and I went up to Cambridge, Massachusetts, for the football team's season finale against Harvard. As the game came to an end, with Harvard winning 27–14, the Harvard undergraduates ran to the Yale end of the field to tear down the goalpost. Zandy and I saw them and bolted toward the field. We, as enthusiastic, gung-ho freshmen, were going to defend our goalpost! Our "heroic mission" got us involved in a brawl in which we were substantially outnumbered. The goalpost came down, and as it did it broke into pieces, one of which conked me on the head and opened up a gash above my right eyebrow. Afterward, Zandy and I went to the Alpha Delta fraternity house where his brother Bartie, who played on Harvard's football team, was a member. We were refused entry, so we climbed up to a second-floor window, broke it, hoisted ourselves in, and confiscated the fraternity's Harvard University banner. We displayed that banner in our dormitory room for years.

And here's another story, also ridiculous. In the fall of 1942, because of wartime travel restrictions imposed by the federal government, it was agreed that the Yale-Princeton football game would be played at Columbia University's Baker Field in New York. Baker Field was about halfway between Yale and Princeton and was supposed to be a neutral site. But for some reason, Zandy and I decided that we were going to temporarily turn it into Yale's home field. The Friday night before the game, we purchased two gallons of blue paint and two paintbrushes. Our plan was to sneak into Baker Field and paint an enormous *Y* in the middle of the fifty-yard line so that people would come to the game and say, "Oh, you see, this is actually a Yale home game." We had a few drinks to fortify our courage, and it was about 10:00 P.M. when we climbed the fence, went onto the field, and began painting. Zandy and I had decided we would each be responsible for one of the arms of the *Y* and then meet in the middle. We were about 90 percent finished when we looked up and saw the beams of a couple of flashlights bobbing around. Apparently, someone had heard our voices and alerted security. We picked up the paint cans and brushes, ran back to the fence, climbed over it, discarded the cans and brushes, and ran as fast as we could down the road. Subsequently, we hailed a taxi to take us downtown to a popular New York nightclub called LaRue. We had dates waiting for us there: mine was a girl named Rosie Parsons, and Zandy's was a girl named Lucy Mitchell. When we got there, the maitre d' gave us the funniest look. We sat down and the girls asked, "What is the matter with you?" We were both covered with tiny speckles of blue paint.

The next day, Zandy and I went to the game, and we were a little bit nervous about what we had done. Had word gotten out about us? Our seats were well up in the stands, adjacent to the forty-yard line, and we climbed up to them and looked down. The *Y* we had thought was going to look so mammoth, impressive, and imposing appeared to be about a yard in length. And it was grossly deformed, all lopsided, with one arm longer than the other. Yale won the game, 13–6. We found out later that there was some discussion among the Yale, Princeton, and Columbia authorities about conducting an investigation into who was responsible. But I didn't go to them and say, "I cannot tell a lie. . . ." Neither did Zandy.

§

My first year at Yale, I tried out for freshman football. That venture lasted for about three weeks, and then I tried out for freshman basketball and made the team. One of the unwritten requirements at Yale is that to succeed there you have to stretch your abilities as far as you can. There is a subtle synergy, a sort of inner electricity that demands you do so. Yale recognizes and encourages involvement—academically, athletically, and within the university's organizations. A yearning to participate becomes ingrained in you, and it constantly pushes you to search for recognition. If you want to be a member of a public speaking team or a debating society, fine. If you want to be a member of an athletic team, that's fine, too. A member of the glee club—excellent. You are allowed to follow the routes of your fundamental interests, be they public affairs, dramatics, singing, baseball, basketball, or whatever. But don't just sit there and do nothing. You have to be active, stay active, and support the traditions of Yale. It is an embracing energy.

At Yale, students reside in residential colleges. These are magnificent places, with beautiful Gothic architecture, and you have to apply for acceptance to the one you want to live in. You are interviewed by the master of the college. Zandy and I wanted to reside in Davenport College, whose master was Emerson Tuttle. Davenport had a beautiful interior courtyard and a lovely dining room and chapel. A number of our classmates were also interested in Davenport, and many of the upperclassmen we had a great deal of respect for lived there.

At Yale, you were always aware of the upperclassmen who were the leaders on campus, and you tried to do things to earn their respect. And if you did something they did not respect, they had their ways of letting you know—they were masters at giving you the chilling experience of being ignored. There was an unwritten code of behavior, and in those days it was considered gauche and in poor taste to boast of your accomplishments or associations. It was a case of reverse egotism or subdued elitism.

There were twelve residential colleges at Yale while I was there, and if you were rejected by all of them, you had to get a room off campus. Generally, though, Yale made a supreme effort to assign everyone to a residential college, although it was not always your first, second, or even third choice.

Luckily, Zandy and I were accepted into Davenport. My sophomore year, I wanted very badly to become a member of Delta Kappa Epsilon fraternity (DKE). At Yale fraternities did not have residences as they did at so many other universities. You did not live in a fraternity house. But the fraternities did have dining rooms, bars, and meeting rooms. They were very important social clubs, particularly on big football weekends. They had dances, cocktail parties, and dinners.

Rush Week, the process by which fraternities recruit and accept or reject prospective members, actually involved several weeks at Yale. You were interviewed by members of various fraternities and subsequently given a time to report to learn the fraternity's decision when Rush Week concluded. A not entirely subtle message was contained in your time to report. If it was 8:00 to 8:10 P.M., you were on the preferred list for membership. If the fraternity was somewhat interested in you, but you weren't in the top eight or ten preferences, you were told to report at 8:15 P.M. And if your report time extended toward the half hour, this indicated the lessening degree of interest the fraternity had in you. If you were given a report time beyond 8:20 P.M., the inherent message was that the fraternity was suggesting you should look elsewhere. I was accepted into Delta Kappa Epsilon and before my Yale days concluded became the chapter's president.

My senior year I played basketball for the Yale varsity team. That experience was up and down—somewhat good, but mostly bad. Our coach was Red Rolfe, a former third baseman and shortstop for the New York Yankees. Red had been a teammate of Babe Ruth, Lou Gehrig, and Joe DiMaggio; had a career batting average of .289; and had been a member of five World Series–winning teams. He had also played basketball when he was a student at Dartmouth College. Red was hired to be Yale's baseball coach, and since he had nothing to do during the winter months, Yale appointed him basketball coach too.

Maybe Red had perused a couple of books about basketball. I don't know. He had a system that didn't make much sense to us players. He had what we called the "Yankee walk"—holding his shoulders up high, clapping his hands together—and I used to mimic him in the locker room. Inevitably, he caught me doing it one day, and that really burned him up. So Red sat me on the bench for a couple of games, just letting me stew. Then we played the University of Pennsylvania in Philadelphia at the Palestra, one of the hallowed cathedrals of college basketball. Red put me in during the second half of the game, and I got into a scuffle with one of the Pennsylvania players under the basket. Red took a shine to me after that. It was not my basketball ability that changed his mind; it was my willingness to get into a fight.

In the last game of that season, we played Harvard University at Cambridge. We beat them 44–43. I sank the winning shot—a two-handed set shot. I closed my eyes and threw it up, and it went through the net. This was February 1944. Shortly afterward, I graduated with a bachelor of arts degree in history. Then I boarded a train, along with twenty-two of my fellow graduates, and headed to Parris Island, the official Marine Corps Recruit Depot, located off the coast of South Carolina.

§

Parris Island is a 12.65-square-mile hole from hell that resides forever in the memory of anyone who ever went through basic training there. It is a furnace, a cauldron where young men (and, in the present day, women) are forged into Marines by way of the most intense challenges—both physical and mental—that most of them have ever encountered in their young lives. Basic training, which is uncompromising perdition, forms the bedrock of the Marine character, instilling confidence, building character, and creating pride not only in oneself but in the entire U.S. Marine Corps organization. It is a bonding experience that is woven into one's persona as a badge of honor, never forsaken, never forgotten.

For me and my classmates, Parris Island was also a spectacularly rude awakening. We arrived there at four o'clock in the morning, and from the moment we began to get off the train, the drill sergeants were yelling at us, berating us. "GET OFF! GET OFF! MOVE! MOVE! MOVE! STRAIGHTEN UP! PULL YOUR GUT IN!" We had our belongings in duffel bags and hadn't gotten any sleep during the thirty-six-hour trip from New Haven to New York to Parris Island. The hallowed halls of Yale, along with the residential colleges, fraternities, football weekends, and basketball heroics, quickly became vague memories. At Parris Island, we were privates, and, as we were immediately informed, that made us "lower than whale shit on the bottom of the ocean floor."

Further, it doesn't take a wide degree of imagination to realize that if your name is James Edward Bassett III, the drill sergeants are going to pounce on the portion of it that's a roman numeral. One of my fellow classmates and Marines was George Barrie IV, and that IV might as well have been emblazoned across his back with a branding iron.

The first place the sergeants marched us to was a barbershop that had twenty-five chairs. "Take off your hat! Take off your coat!" And your hair was gone in about ten seconds. It is shock treatment, and it has a purpose —when your hair is shaved off, part of your past is shaved off too, and your new regimented life has commenced. Whatever sense of pride or assurance we had disappeared with our hair. Then we were marched to the quarter-master. "WHAT SIZE PANTS DO YOU WEAR? WHAT SIZE SHOES DO YOU WEAR? TEN? HERE'S A PAIR OF TWELVES. GET INTO THEM!"

We were all dumbfounded. But what I can only describe as the Yale University camaraderie and sense of humor helped get us through. Had I gone to Parris Island by myself and not known anybody, I probably would have been devastated, destroyed. But together, we formed a bond nearly impossible to break. We were there for fourteen weeks, and both physically and psychologically the noncommissioned officers beat the hell out of us. We had a lot of laughs mimicking them, but only when they were out of earshot.

Our platoon sergeant was James Joseph, USMC. Believe me, you never forget, not for the rest of your life, your platoon sergeant's name. It is permanently committed to your memory. One day, we were in formation and he called out, "JAMES EDWARD BASSETT III! [with a huge emphasis on the roman numeral] OF YALE!"

I said, "Yes, sir!"

Sergeant Joseph said, "WHAT IS YOUR EXCUSE FOR BEING HERE? DID YOU FLUNK OUT?"

I said, "No, sir!"

"WELL, WHAT?"

"I volunteered, sir!"

"GOOD! I'VE BEEN LOOKING FOR A VOLUNTEER. JAMES E. BASSETT III! OF YALE! GET YOUR BUCKET! GET THE BROOM! CLEAN THE HEAD! AND HAVE IT DONE BEFORE CHOW!"

The "head" is the lavatory, where the urinals and toilets are. There weren't any toilet seats, just a bench about thirty yards long with holes in it, and a concrete floor. I'm an octagenerian, but in my mind I can still hear Sergeant Joseph, more than six decades ago, humiliating me: "JAMES E. BASSETT III! OF YALE!" (emphasis on the III). And after that, my fellow Marine Corps privates always kidded me about it. I was JAMES E. BASSETT III. With an emphasis on III.

There were three phases of boot camp. The first, called "forming," involved total immersion in the Marine Corps culture, and at times it was overwhelming. There was constant running, marching, drilling, lectures, and the pounding into our heads that we were totally worthless. Almost nothing we did was met with any approval from the drill instructors.

Every morning we would do calisthenics. It wouldn't solely be members of our platoon. It would be on the parade field amidst many platoons. There would be a sergeant in a tower, yelling out commands, and other sergeants with swagger sticks, hitting us on our butts. "Do more! Faster! Down! Down! Down!" We also spent a lot of time carrying our rifles in close-order drills, learning the cadence, learning to react to authority, learning to obey commands—massively, reflexively, as a group. "Left flank! Right flank! Parade rest! Rear march! Echelon left! Echelon right! Right shoulder arms! Left shoulder arms. Heels! Heels! Heels! I want to hear heels!" We weren't just walking on the soft parts of our feet. We were putting our heels down, hard, and when everybody was in cadence, it sounded like a drum roll.

We were harangued and harassed mercilessly, and fear was omnipresent—fear of making mistakes, fear of being ridiculed. If you screwed up, you might be called out in front of the platoon and made to do forty push-ups or sit-ups or, even worse, forty grunts, an exercise invented by someone who must have truly hated his fellow man. Grunts involve assuming a squatting position and raising yourself in half-aerial moves, during which your hands come up and you actually leave the ground. They are excruciatingly difficult, and all the while a sergeant would be yelling, "Faster! Faster! Faster! More! More! More!"

Eight hours of sleep were allowed at night, and we got one hour of free time during the day when we could write letters to or read them from the people at home, polish our rifles, or whatever. Our quarters were Quonset huts, and we had no weekend liberties. There were three meals per day, and for each one we marched to the chow hall and had twenty minutes to eat. We marched to the showers and moved in double-time to the parade ground. We did fourteen-mile field marches, carrying forty pounds of equipment on our backs.

Sometimes, tempers became frayed, and recruits got into fights. The drill sergeant might react by saying, "All right, you two SOBs! You two jerks! You want to fight, come out here in front!" The two men would stand in front of the platoon, and the sergeant would tell them, "Now, go at it! Don't fake this! Hit him!" And they'd really start belting each other. When they had beaten themselves to exhaustion, the sergeant would say, "Don't fight one another! Fight Japs!" (Oh, yes, I got into some fights, but never one that put me in front of the platoon.)

And there were the lectures, with us sitting in bleachers and a sergeant standing in front of us with a chalkboard. We learned about Marine Corps history. We memorized the Eleven General Orders of a Sentry—saluting officers, staying at your post until properly relieved, and so on. "BASSETT! GENERAL ORDER SIX! WHAT DOES IT SAY?"

"Sir! To receive, obey, and pass on to the sentry who relieves me all orders from the commanding officer, officer of the day, officer of the deck, and officers and petty officers of the watch only!" Get one word of it wrong, and you had to stand in a corner and say it correctly fifty times.

The second phase of boot camp involved a four-week period of intensive rifle training. We spent days learning how to assemble and disassemble our rifles. And we spent untold hours cleaning them—if you were caught with a speck of dust in the barrel, you were subject to all sorts of criticism and physical discipline. We were still doing close-order drills on the parade ground, but on the rifle range, we had to qualify from many different positions—standing, sitting, prone. At 500 yards, if you missed the target, a big pole with a pair of red drawers would be lifted up and waved. They were called "Maggie's drawers," and the whole line of shooters would know you had messed up.

But during this time, a tiny thread of confidence began to return. You began to think, "I can handle this. I'll be able to make it through." I recall writing my father a letter and telling him, "Believe me, Dad, I can do this."

One thing that did impress the sergeants about the Yale recruits was our 100 percent participation in a voluntary Red Cross blood drive. And 100 percent of us qualified in both rifle and swimming. We had all taken swimming classes at Yale, and when the noncommissioned officers tossed us in the water with our clothes on and laden with equipment, we all bobbed to the surface and swam to wherever they wanted us to go.

By the time the third phase of boot camp started, the finishing period, so to speak, we had bought into the culture. Instead of being in a perpetual state of panic—worrying, "Am I doing this right?" or whether the drill sergeant was going to "get on my ass"—each of us had learned to anticipate what was coming. Ultimately, there was the wonderful feeling of graduation from basic training.

Afterward, each of us carried a little chip on his shoulder. There was a somewhat arrogant feeling of superiority involved, the belief that we had done it, and not everybody could. We had survived. We had achieved. By far, we were in the best physical shape of our lives. And we were well-trained professionals.

§

Ten of us were selected to go to officer candidate school (OCS) in Quantico, Virginia. It was sort of a highly accelerated version of West Point for Marines. I still don't know why I was selected to go. The program lasted for three months, and we were treated like dirt. After finishing, we were commissioned second lieutenants. Then we were assigned to the reserve officers' class. After graduating OCS, I was sent to Camp Pendleton, thirty-five miles north of San Diego near Oceanside, California. Camp Pendleton encompasses 200 square miles of terrain, and there were nights we had to march fifteen to twenty miles. We also had to practice landing maneuvers in rubber boats, all the while freezing our butts off.

My father decided to visit me during Christmas week. He was en route from Kentucky to the West Coast when I suddenly got orders to go overseas. I explained the situation to the first lieutenant in charge of my platoon, and he said, "Where is your father? What train is he on?" The Red Cross got ahold of my father in Kansas City, Missouri, and told him what was going on. On December 26, I was put on the troop transport the USS *Sea Bass* in San Diego and shipped out—destination Guadalcanal.

There were 1,200 regular Marines and 26 second lieutenants aboard. The trip would take eighteen days, and the second lieutenants were housed in an area with double-decker bunks. A day after we left Southern California, what's referred to as the "offshore roll" began to affect us, and everybody became seasick, sicker than hell. Somebody advised me, though, that when I went on deck, if I avoided looking down and didn't look at the horizon, if I instead looked up, way up, the seasickness wouldn't be so bad. Try to get your balance, I was told, and breathe easy. It was good advice.

The worst duties on board involved being officers of certain parts of the *Sea Bass*. Once we sailed into the South Pacific, I had to inspect the ship's bowels. There must have been ten or twelve layers of bunks. All the men were sick, and the place smelled horrible. I kept thinking, "Thank God my bunk's not down there."

We landed at Guadalcanal on an old wooden dock, where a salty old Marine sergeant wearing a shirt with cut-off sleeves, a pair of shorts, and a campaign hat walked up to us. A classic old salt. He said to us, "All right you sons of bitches, line up alphabetically by height!" We were shuffling around, grins on our faces, trying to comprehend what he meant, and he said, "What's so goddamned funny?" I was six feet, three inches tall, which put me at the front of the line, and the sergeant said, "You first six assholes get into the truck. You're going to the Fourth Marines."

That was one of the luckiest things that happened to me, because the Fourth Marines (part of the Sixth Division) was one of the Corps' great regiments. Collectively, the Fourth Marines were called the "Shanghai Marines" or the "China Marines," because from 1927 to 1941, they were assigned to Shanghai, China, to protect American citizens and their property in the international settlement there. China was then immersed in internal conflicts, and Shanghai had a population of 3 million Chinese nationals. The Fourth Marines variously numbered from 1,200 to 1,600 men, but they did what they were entrusted to do, which was serve as unofficial American ambassadors and as a quasi-police force. They witnessed and had to deal with many of the Far Eastern events that led directly to World War II.

In the 220-year history of the Marine Corps, the Fourth Marines is the only regiment that ever lost its colors, which means surrendering in battle. Other regiments have been annihilated but have never raised the white flag. But the members of the Fourth Marines were forced to do that on May 6, 1942, on the island of Corregidor near the Bataan peninsula. They were surrounded, they had no air cover, and the Japanese blockade of the island had cut off all possibility of supplies and reinforcements. The Fourth Marines burned their colors, surrendered, and for a time ceased to exist.

The regiment was reborn at Guadalcanal in February 1944, and its members were determined that what had occurred at Corregidor would never happen again. The Marine Corps commandant, Brigadier General Keith T. Holcomb, merged three reinforced battalions into the reconstituted regiment: Carlson's Raiders, Edson's Raiders, and Shapley's Raiders. They were named for the officers who led them: Lieutenant Colonel Evans F. Carlson, Colonel Merritt "Red Mike" Edson, and Lieutenant Colonel Alan Shapley.

By the time the war concluded, the honors awarded to the Fourth Marines included the Presidential Unit Citation for the regiment's performance on Guadalcanal and Okinawa, the Army Distinguished Unit Citation (an example of one branch of the service saluting another) for the regiment's performance in the Philippines, and a Navy Unit Commendation for its performance in Guam. Decades later, General Randolph McC. Pate, who also served as commandant of the Marine Corps, would write, "The 4th Regiment, in its near half-century of service, has acquired a sense of tradition and esprit de corps distinctive even in a Corps noted for those qualities. . . . In its performance of duty, the 4th Marines has always been a 'second-to-none' outfit."

And here I was, a twenty-three-year-old second lieutenant, green as a gourd, assigned to the Fourth Marines, Baker Company, First Battalion. On the *Sea Bass,* I had crossed the equator for the first time in my life on January 6, and I participated in King Neptune's Court, an initiation ceremony into the Ancient Order of the Deep. They still do this on some military ships (and, I'm told, on some commercial passenger liners). As a "pollywog," I had my head partially shaved and smeared with some horrible mixture. I looked like a Mohawk Indian, somehow transported from General Wolfe's command during the French and Indian War to an island in the Pacific theater during World War II.

The officers' mess was a canvas tent full of holes. It included a bar made from wooden planks and mounted on top of fifty-five-gallon drums. The first time I went in there, I was in a group of six second lieutenants, all of whom had been through the King Neptune ceremony. Our heads were pale white except for the tuft of hair in the middle. We looked ridiculous, and all these tough-looking, battle-tested, veteran Marines were standing at the bar, staring at us with disdain. Drinks were served in dark green beer cans. "What'll you have?" said the guy behind the bar.

"Well, I'll have . . ."

"What'll you have?!"

"Whatever you've got." And he tossed one cube of ice into each drink.

It started to rain, and the water was coming through the holes in the tent. My group responded by sort of huddling together, but the other Marines just stood there. The only movements they made was to put their hands over their drinks. Each man was allowed only one cube of ice, and they wanted to get two or three drinks down before the ice melted.

Their attitude toward us was one of utter disgust, and I can't fault them for that, because by comparison, we looked and acted like wimps. A couple of days later, we went to the company barber, an old Italian corporal, and he worked on our haircuts, making us look somewhat human.

§

Our landing on Okinawa was scheduled for April 1, 1945. April Fools' Day, which seemed appropriate, considering the reception we expected to receive from the Japanese. Some of the briefing officers had told us we could expect casualties to be as high as 85 percent on the beach. But we swept ashore at Okinawa without opposition—piece of cake, or so we thought.

What we did not know was that the Japanese commander, Lieutenant General Mitsuri, had more than 100,000 troops waiting for us, and most of them were entrenched in the southern hills of the island. I can state this with assurance now, with more than sixty years of research by military historians to guide me. But at the time, we did not know where the Japanese were.

We were marching north from Yonton airfield, in double file up these little roads toward the Motobu peninsula, when we got the news that President Franklin Roosevelt had died on April 12 in Warm Springs, Georgia. I had never heard of Warm Springs. I did not know where in Georgia it was. I did not know who Roosevelt's successor, Harry Truman, was. Throughout our lines, there was a sense of unease—and for ample reason. During the following weeks and months, U.S. forces became engaged in a terrible battle. The famous flag raising on Mount Suribachi on the island of Iwo Jima had taken place on February 23. I have read that the photograph of that flag raising (or, perhaps more correctly, the photograph of the reenactment of that flag raising) is the most reproduced photo in history.

But more of our men lost their lives at Okinawa than at Iwo Jima. Okinawa is only 360 miles southwest of Japan. The Japanese were aware that, if taken, the island could be used as a primary Allied support and supply base for an invasion of the Japanese homeland. And even if the Japanese could not hold Okinawa, they could buy time to fortify their homeland defenses. Okinawa was a much bigger operation than Iwo Jima. It involved 180,000 American military personnel. One Marine described it as "hell's own cesspool," and I don't disagree with that assessment.

By the time the battle for Okinawa concluded, almost every Japanese soldier on the island had been killed. Well over 100,000 natives of Okinawa lost their lives. The Okinawa campaign resulted in more than 4,600 U.S. soldiers killed and 18,000 wounded. The U.S. Navy suffered nearly 5,000 dead and 4,900 wounded from kamikaze attacks. And the Marines had 3,200 killed and 13,700 wounded. One of those wounded was me.

We were attacking Mount Yaetake—the very center of Japanese resistance—on the Motobu peninsula along the western coast of Okinawa. This was before the fighting in the southern portion of the island had commenced. The Japanese had 2,000 soldiers entrenched on Yaetake, and it was our job to flush them out. It was very early on the morning on April 15, and my platoon was designated the "point," or lead company, of the patrol probing the Japanese defenses.

The Japanese were very patient and shrewd. When they had us in range, they would sometimes wait half an hour or even longer before opening fire. That allowed them to identify the officers and platoon leaders and concentrate on eliminating them first. Each platoon leader had forty-eight men under his command. The Japanese figured that the sooner they could take out the man in charge, the more advantageous it would be.

We were aware of this. On each side of the front of his shirt collar, a second lieutenant wore a pair of bars, identifying his rank. Each bar was about three-quarters of an inch long and one-quarter of an inch wide—not large displays of rank, by any definition, but any Japanese soldier with binoculars could pick them out. We were instructed before entering battle to reverse our collars, so the bars wouldn't show.

But the Japanese had other means of identifying us. Most of the orders we gave were unspoken, transmitted by hand and arm signals—a hand raised upward to order a pause in advancement, an arm extended forward to order a continuation of the advance. The Japanese would be watching to see who was directing movements. Hidden and silent within their caves and in the thick vegetation of the steep slopes and ravines, they would sometimes allow a line of Marines to pass without firing, all the while training their gun sights on the individuals who appeared to hold command rank. And when they figured they could not miss, the Japanese opened up.

The extremely rocky terrain made it nearly impossible for us to receive tank support. Meanwhile, the Japanese had set up machine-gun nests and mortars. Many of them had painted their faces green and wrapped themselves with leaves, for camouflage purposes. They were like phantoms, perfectly blended into their surroundings, suddenly appearing, suddenly disappearing. We did not have the same advantage. Indeed, it is interesting to compare the combat clothing worn by Marines in World War II with the gear worn by modern-day Marines. The green utility uniforms of yesterday, which offered zero protection, are a tragic contrast to the high-tech camouflaged body armor of today.

The initial step in capturing Mount Yaetake involved the seizure of a 700-foot ridge, or foothill so to speak, about 1,200 yards inland. It was the first area of high ground on Motobu, and the ridge dominated the coast road. Taking that ridge was an operation that, by itself, had cost two Marine companies more than fifty casualties. A long line of stretcher bearers provided testimony that success had been achieved at great cost.

Approaching the lower slope of Mount Yaetake, we went through an open area of several hundred yards where there were no depressions or other means of protection. And that is where a Japanese sniper shot me. His bullet went through my right hand, between the thumb and index finger. How it happened that he did not hit me in the stomach or the chest or between the eyes, I will never know. Perhaps it was the wind factor or the fact that I was moving. Or maybe I made a sudden move (I cannot recall if I did or not). Or perhaps a combination of two of these factors, or all three, made the difference.

Several minutes later, the Japanese zeroed in on us with their mortars, and the shells began coming down on us and exploding. A mortar fragment hit me in the right knee. It was a minor wound, not a major one. Our battalion called for artillery support, which arrived very quickly, and the salvos pretty much eliminated the immediate threat and allowed those of us who were wounded to be removed from the field of fire. I don't recall exactly what happened after that, but I do remember that I was never actually knocked off my feet.

I was put on the USS *Samaritan,* a 394-bed hospital ship, and then I was taken to Saipan and was in a hospital there for six weeks. For a while I thought I might lose the hand, but that did not happen, and the doctors and nurses eventually got me on my feet and walking again. I still have scars from both wounds, but otherwise, they have never bothered me. I have wondered on many occasions, over the years, over the decades, for well over a full half century, what would have happened if that enemy soldier's aim had been truer?

As it was, 500 officers and men of the Fourth Marines alone were killed during the Okinawa campaign. And more than 2,400 others were wounded. Those numbers will remain embedded in my mind forever.

With the defeat of the Japanese at Okinawa, the Sixth Marine Division, including its Fourth Marine Regiment, was shipped to Guam, where it regrouped, retrained, and resupplied with both manpower and weapons for the anticipated invasion of mainland Japan. I was discharged from the hospital in Saipan and was flown with a group of other Marines to Guam to rejoin our regimental outfits. We were combat experienced and ready for action. Some experts were predicting that the invasion would result in 1 million Allied casualties before it was over.

Then the atomic bombs were dropped on Hiroshima and Nagasaki on August 6 and August 9. To the world, they provided terrifying proof of the consequences if the Japanese refused to surrender unconditionally. On August 14, Emperor Hirohito, in a radio broadcast to the Japanese people, told them, "We have ordered our government to communicate to the governments of the United States, Great Britain, China, and the Soviet Union that our empire accepts the provisions [of the Potsdam Declaration]." This meant Hirohito would remain as emperor, but any authority he had would be subject to the Allied supreme commander (who turned out to be General Douglas MacArthur). The Japanese surrender, Hirohito told his radio listeners, was in accordance with "the dictates of time and fate. We must bear the unbearable."

On August 15, a group of some 1,300 occupation troops went aboard the 455-foot attack transport ship the USS *Lanier* and sailed as part of Task Force 31 of the Third Fleet. Our destination was Japan. Despite Hirohito's words, we all knew that no formal surrender had occurred, and we were fully combat prepared and loaded. On August 27, the *Lanier* anchored in the Sagami Gulf, which is situated between the Miura and Izu peninsulas. And on August 30, we steamed into Tokyo Bay.

I remember vividly a fellow officer saying to me, his voice filled with awe, "Look at Fujiyama."

I said, "Where is it?"

He said, "Look, don't you see it out there?"

I said, "No, I don't see it. I don't see it at all! Where? Where is it?" We were about three miles offshore, and I was looking for a mountain in the distance. But Fujiyama was this giant, good God, massive thing. I was looking right into the mountain's base without realizing it, unable to comprehend its majesty and beauty.

At that time, there were approximately thirty active Marine regiments, but the Fourth Marines was chosen to represent the entire Corps for the initial landing on Japan. The distinguished combat record of the Fourth Marines was one of the reasons for this honor. Another was what had happened exactly three years, three months, and twenty-four days earlier at Corregidor, when on command of higher authority the regiment had surrendered its colors.

We came ashore at Yokosuka Naval Base, which was in the middle of the Miura peninsula and faced Tokyo Bay on the east. It was about forty miles south of the city of Tokyo and had broad, concrete runways for naval seaplanes, runways that extended right out into the ocean. We did not know what to expect. The atomic bombs had been dropped on Hiroshima and Nagasaki only three weeks earlier. There still wasn't any formal peace. We had heard stories about what had happened to the captured American Marines during the Bataan Death March. Admiral Chester W. Nimitz had warned us to be on the alert for "Japanese treachery." The Japanese had fought to the death on Okinawa—we had taken very few prisoners there—and it still seemed like we were engaging some strange, alien being, completely unfamiliar to us.

At Yokosuka, we trooped up the seaplane ramps and were surprised that hardly anyone else seemed to be there. There were stacks of Japanese rifles, eight to ten feet high, in the square. There were two men in black uniforms, Japanese policemen, waving white flags. And that was it. Neither of the policemen spoke English. We moved cautiously and did not advance beyond the Yokosuka airfield that first day and night.

Every now and then, we would catch a glimpse of the slight movement of a shutter, a blind or curtain in the window of one of the houses. Inside one of the hangars at the base we found a blackboard, on which this message was scrawled:

Welcom Americans
To Japan
Treat a gallent
Enemy good. We will
Do the same.

It was very, very eerie. We found out later that a great deal of propaganda had been circulated about American Marines among the Japanese civilians —posters depicting us as beasts with claws and fangs that were dripping blood. Japanese women, particularly, had been warned of the atrocities we would allegedly commit.

The Japanese surrender took place on the deck of the battleship USS *Missouri* on September 2. We had no television, but we heard plenty about the surrender ceremonies on Armed Forces Radio. And I remember great masses of planes, B-29s, filling the sky. Five days later, we were ordered to put on a parade at a Japanese troop compound. Our initial reaction was

"God damn! What the hell! A parade? Whose idiotic idea is this?" But it turned out to be very moving. The surviving members of the Fourth Marines who had been prisoners of war—there were less than a hundred of them—were brought there as special guests. They were emaciated. They all were given new uniforms that just hung on them.

In addition to my other duties, I was the laundry officer. At the troop compound, there were these huge bowls, six feet deep and equipped with steam jets, into which we dumped the laundry. The goal of the parade was to put on a proper show for those ex-prisoners, those brave, wounded, half-starved men. Our commanding officer, Colonel Robert V. Bell, told me, "Bassett, I want these uniforms so goddamned stiff they'll stand up by themselves."

§

Half of our men were eventually sent to Tiensing, China, and the rest of us stayed on at Yokosuka. Every Marine who served overseas was assigned "combat points," determined by the number of months he had served overseas. The purpose was to have a logical rotation of people returning to the United States for honorable discharge. Our combat points were not up until March 1946, and during the winter months, we were still going out on patrol. The U.S. military remained concerned about Japanese factories that had been constructed during the war in underground caves. We were ordered to probe those caves to determine whether there was any activity still going on.

By this time, I had been promoted to first lieutenant and had been made the executive officer of Company B. One morning, we found a cave about a mile away from the base and decided to give it a thorough look. I entered the cave and saw a pile of wooden containers. Acting like a fool, trying to impress my men, I went up and kicked one of the containers to the side, then hit down on it with the butt of my carbine. The top of the container ruptured, and what seemed like a sea of mud flowed out. It turned out to be a composition of brown, sticky material used to lacquer wooden furniture and utensils. I stuck one of my hands into the stuff, smelled it, and then went on patrolling.

About two days later, my face began to swell. And my genitalia began to swell. And then my eyes began to swell shut. I went to sick bay and was told, "You've got some sort of rash," which was treated with calamine lotion. Another day passed and my mouth began to swell. I said to my Marine Corps driver, "Look, this has gotten out of hand. Take me to a Japanese hospital." What I didn't know, did not find out until later, was that the fundamental composition of the lacquer I had put my hand into was sumac oil. Sumac is a member of the same family as poison ivy, and as a boy, I could just about look at a field a hundred yards away and if poison ivy was in it, I would break out. I had some terrible bouts with poison ivy as a youngster, but my allergic reaction to the sumac oil was the worst I had ever experienced.

We drove about ten miles to a Japanese hospital. I was in a Marine Corps jeep wearing a Marine Corps uniform, so there was no mistaking who I was and what I represented. Physically, I was a mess—hurting, aching, swollen all over, and covered with a rash. A Japanese doctor looked at me very carefully, gave me a shot, and said, "Okay, okay," which might have been all the English he knew. I could feel the injection in my bloodstream, going round and round, and I suddenly had a terrible panicky feeling that I had done something extremely foolish, considering the hatred that existed among the Japanese people over the dropping of the atomic bombs, the surrender, and the continuing occupation of their country. The doctor wrote down something in Japanese, which I took back to our Marine Corps medical people. Subsequently, I had to be evacuated to a hospital ship. By that time, I could not open my mouth. I could not urinate. I could hardly breathe. On the hospital ship, they put me on a bed with a rubber mattress. The doctors totally wrapped me in sheets and cheesecloth, with a hole for my nose and another hole for my mouth. I was fed through a tube, and the doctors saturated me with some sort of solution to alleviate my allergic reaction. To this day, I don't know what the solution was, but it is not an exaggeration to say that my skin was a sea of blisters.

I was eventually discharged from the USS *Samaritan* and returned to the Yokosuka Naval Base, and about two weeks after that I received orders to return to the United States. I was to be shipped home in the company of thirteen other officers and forty enlisted men. We thought it was going to be a grand trip; we had heard about the grand voyages home enjoyed by other military personnel. When we inquired which ship we would be traveling on, we were told, "The USS *Yolo*." That did not sound as exciting as being on the HMS *Queen Mary* or *Queen Elizabeth,* which had been used to transport American troops from Europe to New York after Germany surrendered.

We asked, "Where is the *Yolo*?"
And we were told, "It's in Yokohama Harbor."
We asked, "Has anybody seen it?"
And we were told, "No, but it's going to be great. And what the hell do we care, as long as we were going home?"

We went up to Yokohama Harbor and there was the *Yolo*, and it was a goddamned LST tank landing ship. It was 328 feet long, with a beam of 50 feet and a draft of 11 feet 2 inches, and it had a maximum speed of ten knots. It was designed to carry tanks in the hold, which was about the size of a football field; the bow opened up, so the tanks could rumble out onto the beach or dock. For our convenience, a Quonset hut had been set up on the deck to serve as sleeping quarters for the officers. The enlisted men would be relegated to the hold. We kept complaining, "Is this the way they're transporting us after months of combat and patrol duty for our country?" But when the time came to go aboard, no one chose to stay behind. We were bound for Honolulu and from there to the Pacific coast; then on to our families, our friends, and normalcy.

We brought forty cases of beer with us on the *Yolo*. We put the cans of beer in fifty-five-gallon drums and packed it with all the ice we could get. The ration would be two cans of beer per man per day, and each time you took a can, you had to check your name off. Anybody caught taking an extra can would be dumped overboard.

During our trip to Honolulu, a series of tidal waves—or, more correctly, tsunami (a Japanese term that is both singular and plural)—rolled ashore at Hilo on the island of Hawaii. The waves then proceeded westward across the Pacific and almost capsized the *Yolo*. Maybe I am exaggerating a bit, but the trip to Honolulu was not entirely without peril.

Most perilous to me, though, was the sun. I was tired of playing cards and watching everybody get seasick, so I would take a book out on the deck and sit in the sun and read. I did that for a few days and got sunburned to a crisp. Remember, I had recovered only recently from that allergic reaction to the sumac-based lacquer, and all my skin was new. At night, when I could not sleep, I would sit on the bow of the *Yolo*, hoping the breeze might cool me off. I would sit there with a towel clenched in my teeth, trying to get relief from the burns. I was in terrible shape.

We finally got to Honolulu. From there, the USS *Shangri-La*, the aircraft carrier that served as the flagship of Vice Admiral John S. McCain's Second Carrier Force, brought us to San Francisco. That ship had nearly seven times the displacement of the *Yolo* and could officially do 32.7 knots; unofficially, it could churn through the ocean much faster if need be. We dubbed the *Shangri-La* the "Magic Carpet." The *Shangri-La* had been stripped of all its aircraft to make room for us. Those planes had been a major factor in the Okinawa campaign and had pummeled Tokyo several times. Prior to ferrying us home, the *Shangri-La* had participated in Operation Crossroads, which involved the atomic bomb tests at Bikini atoll. A lot of this I did not learn until later on, and although it did not mean much to me then, it does now.

§

A railroad Pullman car carried me back to Kentucky. It was a three-day trip, and I got there in time to go to the Kentucky Derby. Two of my college roommates, Fred Whitridge and Zandy Harvey (my partner in various crimes), went to the Derby with me. Both had become U.S. Army officers. Fred would later become an executive vice president of the Zellerbach Paper Company in San Francisco. And Zandy became a very distinguished federal judge; he presided over the John Walker Jr. spy case.

On Derby day, my father said to me, "I want you to take care of Helenita Kleberg today." She was the daughter of Robert J. Kleberg, who owned King Ranch. Mr. Kleberg was also a great friend of Major Louis A. Beard, who was in charge of Greentree Farm, with which my father was associated. My father's instructions were firm: "Conduct yourself like a gentleman, not like some wild Marine."

Robert Kleberg actually had a horse running in that year's Derby, a homebred named Assault. Initially, Assault had not appeared to be much of a racehorse. As a maiden two-year-old, he had been sent off at odds of 79–1 in a race and finished fifth. But he became a stakes winner before that year was over, and at age three he had won the Wood Memorial, which was and still is one of the most prominent Derby prep races.

Most people did not expect Assault to do much in the Derby, though. Maine Chance Farm, owned by Elizabeth Graham, had a three-horse entry consisting of Lord Boswell, Knockdown, and Perfect Bahram, and they were going to go off at close to even money. The *Daily Racing Form* had five of its handicappers make Derby selections, and four of them picked Lord Boswell to win—he was being ridden by Eddie Arcaro, which might have had something to do with it. The fifth handicapper picked a horse named Hampden, who raced for William DuPont Jr.'s Foxcatcher

Farm. Two of the handicappers picked Assault to finish second, and in a very unscientific poll conducted by the *Racing Form* of 119 jockeys, trainers, owners, and other nonparticipating racing personnel, 13 of them thought he would win. So Assault was not the longest of long shots; his odds were 8–1.

"I want you to be thoughtful and gentlemanly with Helenita," my father told me. "She's only seventeen."

We got to the box at Churchill Downs, and Helenita was already there. This was the first postwar Derby, and it was the first where a crowd of 100,000 was announced. Rather than focusing on being gentlemanly toward Helenita, I spent the afternoon hooting and hollering. I had a few drinks and was kind of wild in those days. The seventh race on the card was the Derby, and Assault came through on the inside to take the lead at the top of the stretch, then drew off to win by a record-equaling eight lengths. Helenita was all exited, jumping up and down, and then she went down to the winner's circle with her father and Assault's trainer, Maxwell Hirsch. Zandy, Fred, and I just stood there, not fully comprehending what had happened. The winner's circle ceremony concluded, and Helenita came back to the box bearing the garland of roses. She asked us, "Are you going back to Lexington?"

I said, "No, we're going to the Louisville Country Club. Do you want to go?"

She said, "Do you mind?"

I said, "No, come on." We loaded into Fred's car and headed for the country club, not having much of an idea where it was—somewhere on or near Brownsboro Road, we thought. Not surprisingly, we got lost, and after riding around for about forty-five minutes, we saw some big beautiful buildings adjacent to a parking lot and said, "That's it."

Fred escorted Helenita to the front door. She had the garland of roses draped over her shoulders, and they had no problem getting in. Then Zandy and I came up, and the men at the door asked us, "You fellows, you are guests of whom?"

I forget what our answer was, but we were told, "Sorry, you can't get in," and they slammed the door in our faces.

"Hey, I'm a Marine." I don't remember if I actually said that out loud, but that is what I was thinking. I do recall saying out loud, "Hell, we can get into this place." So Zandy and I went around to the back of the building, where we saw some latticework covered with roses that extended up the second floor. Above it, there were some open windows. I said, "Let's go," and boosted Zandy up onto the lattice. After he made his way up to the windows, I worked my way up too. We climbed through the windows, found a men's room, and washed up. We then starting walking down the stairs to the first floor, and coming up the stairs was Harry Miller of Barney Miller Radio, which had a store in Lexington. I said, "Hello, Harry, how are you?"

He said, "Hi, Ted, what are you doing here?"

I said, "Well, this is the Louisville Country Club, isn't it?"

Harry said, "No, it's the Standard Country Club," which was a private Jewish club. Within minutes we were ushered out again.

A few final notes: Assault went on to become North America's seventh Triple Crown winner, joining an exclusive club that at the time included Sir Barton, Gallant Fox, Omaha, War Admiral, Whirlaway, and Count Fleet and would subsequently include Citation, Secretariat, Seattle Slew, and Affirmed.

Helenita is now Helen Groves and owns Silverbrook Ranches near Baird, Texas. She comes to Kentucky often to visit her daughter, Helen Alexander, with whom she partnered (along with David Aykroyd) in breeding and racing Althea, who was North America's two-year-old filly champion in 1983. Mrs. Groves still attends the Keeneland sales and races, and many times we have reminisced and shared a laugh about Derby day in 1946.

In retrospect, of course, I did a lot of crazy, stupid things when I was young. The Kent School environment had been so strict that when I got to Yale, with the sudden freedom I had never experienced before, maybe I went a bit over the top. But getting shot on Okinawa and surviving it put some sense into me. Judge Harvey and I had a reunion at the Yale Club in New York City in March 2005. We talked about some of the things we had done, and he said, "If the FBI, when they were investigating me, had learned about some of our antics, I would have never gotten my judgeship." He may be right.

The Marine Corps—I have often wondered what my life would have been like if I had not been exposed to that culture and experience. For those of us who embraced the Corps' message—demanding a sense of pride, instilling a core of confidence, and realizing that uncharted waters are to be navigated, not avoided—it is a life-changing experience. Of course, that's if you buy into the Corps' philosophy, and not everybody does. But I did. *Sepius Extertus, Semper Fidelis, Fraters Infanitas.* These words, the hallmark of the Forth Marines, mean "Often Tested, Always Faithful, Brothers Forever." I accepted these beliefs with my heart and soul. What the Marines Corps does is change your mind-set, your outlook, and those changes remain a part of you forever. And in my case, at least, the Marine Corps took a nobody and tried its absolute best to make a somebody out of him.

[Editor's Note: On April 20, 1990, the U.S. Marine Corps Command and Staff College Foundation presented Ted Bassett with its ninth annual Semper Fidelis Award, "as a former Marine who has exemplified high principles and dedicated service to Country and Corps." Previous recipients of the award include former astronaut and U.S. senator John H. Glenn Jr.; former U.S. secretary of labor, treasury, and state George P. Schulz; and former U.S. secretary of the treasury and state James A. Baker III. And on November 11, 2007, Bassett received the Department of the Navy Superior Public Service Award, the second highest civilian honor, for his "contributions and unflagging support of the United States Marine Corps for 64 years."]

Chapter 4

Postwar Experience

FOLLOWING MY HONORABLE discharge from the Marine Corps in 1946, I wanted to attend Harvard University Business School. But my grades at Yale had not been spectacular, and Harvard put me on a waiting list—for a period of undetermined length. Without much else to do, I decided to take a cruise with some friends through the coastal waters of New England. My partners in this adventure were my old Yale roommates Zandy Harvey and Fred Whitridge and Endicott "Cotty" Davison, who was a former captain of the Yale football team. We rented a thirty-eight-foot schooner named the *Emily Morgan*. It had three sails. None of us knew anything about sailing, with the exception of Cotty.

We started at Essex, Connecticut, and sailed into Edgartown, Massachusetts, and then up the coast past the Massachusetts and New Hampshire shorelines and to the waters off York Harbor, Maine. In mid-June, I called my father. It was Father's Day, and his birthday was also coming up, and I wanted to give him my best wishes. But he wasn't particularly interested in receiving them. My father said, "When are you coming home?"

I said, "Oh, I think in about four or five weeks."

He said, "I want you to go down to Boston for an interview."

I said, "With whom?"

He said, "With the Great Northern Paper Company."

I told him, "Oh, Dad, I don't want to. I'll wait until I get into Harvard. There's plenty of time, there's no rush."

But he said, "I think you had better go down there right now. Jock Whitney's family owns the company."

I said, "Oh, Dad, gee whiz," but the language that was going through my mind was a bit stronger. I was twenty-four years old. I had been the leader of a Marine Corps rifle platoon. I'd nearly had my head shot off in the Pacific. And now I was being treated as the idiot son.

But I listened to my father. My friends were mad at me, but I paid them for my share of the cost of the cruise, said good-bye, and took the train down to Boston. An interview had been arranged for me with a Mr. Daniels (I cannot remember his first name) at the Great Northern Paper Company's offices at 201 Dorchester Street.

The Great Northern Paper Company manufactured newsprint. The primary source materials for newsprint, of course, like all paper products, are trees. In line with this, the company, at that time, owned one-ninth of the entire state of Maine. I'm talking about approximately 3,500 square miles of timber holdings.

Looking around inside the Dorchester Street offices, I saw rolltop desks and men wearing green shades as they did their work. Only a couple of days earlier, I had been sailing around the New England coast on a boat, with future destinations unknown. I thought, "What the hell am I doing here?"

Truth be told, Mr. Daniels did not seem to have any great interest in me, either. He was a down-easter, born and raised in Maine, and looked upon working for Great Northern Paper as the equivalent of receiving the Pulitzer Prize. In retrospect, he was probably pondering a question of his own—what the hell am I doing interviewing this kid? Mr. Daniels said, "We're going to start an apprentice internship program. We understand that you're interested, and we may—may—have an opening for you."

I said, "Okay," and called my father.

He said, "Come on home and we'll talk about it."

I got on a train and I went home, and my father said to me, "You've been roaming around long enough. I think you had better start work."

By that time, I had met Lucy, and I knew she was going to be a fresh-man that fall at Smith College in Northampton, Massachusetts. Still, I thought, "Hell, I'm going up to some town called Millinocket in the god-damned backwoods of Maine." This was after I had been in the South Pacific, halfway around the world.

But my father said, "Jock Whitney has taken an interest in you, and I think you had better take this opportunity while you can." My father also bribed me. He bought me a black 1946 Ford coupe. He said, "Go on up there. Spend some time on the job. Put some organization into your life. And, after a while, maybe Harvard will take you in."

Well, I drove to Millinocket. God, it seemed to take forever. The arithmetic worked out this way: Lexington is 950 miles southwest of Boston; Bangor, Maine, is 250 miles northeast of Boston; and Millinocket is 65 miles north of Bangor. And the interstate highway system had yet to be built. The only saving grace was that Lucy was at Smith. And while Northampton was hundreds of miles from Millinocket, it was still a lot closer to north-central Maine than it was to Lexington.

Millinocket was a company town—it had been founded by the Great Northern Paper Company in 1899. I had done a little bit of research and discovered that the average high temperature in Millinocket during the month of January was twenty-three degrees Fahrenheit; the temperature had gotten as low as forty-two degrees below zero in February. Snowfall during the course of a year in Millinocket sometimes totaled more than thirteen feet. During the winter months, the snow reached up to the eaves of buildings.

There was a train depot in Millinocket, operated by the Bangor & Aroostook Railroad (or BAR, as it was also known). The depot had a stationmaster, but I don't recall it having any other employees. Millinocket also had a taxi company—with one cab. And there was a movie theater that showed first-run films about eighteen months after their release.

I checked into the Hotel Millinocket, an old frame building that was also owned by the Great Northern Paper Company. In the dining room, I sat by myself because I didn't know anybody. I thought, "Well, I'll give it a month. But if anyone thinks I'm going to stay up here in the backwoods of Maine and deal with these down-easters on a long-term basis, forget it."

§

After the first week, it did not seem so bad. My sense of being marooned subsided. The Maine people did not accept me in a warm fashion, but they were genuine, and I thought, "There might be something interesting and challenging here."

My job was that of a mill hand. The factory had three shifts, and every three weeks, my shift would change. It would be from 8:00 A.M. to 4:00 P.M. in one section. Then it would be from 4:00 P.M. to midnight in another section. And then it would be from midnight to 8:00 A.M. in still another section. The purpose was for me to learn, step by step, the process by which newsprint was manufactured. First, I was taken into the forest to see the lumberjacks topping off and cutting down the trees and trimming them into gigantic logs. And I would see the logs transported by train and by truck to the factory in Millinocket. Huge sluices were utilized to transport the logs, too—they would come cascading down the hillsides. It was an awesome sight. Next, I would spend time in what they called the "wood section," where conveyor belts would put the logs through high-speed cutters, the mechanized knives converting them into wood chips. Then I would go to the section of the factory where the wood chips would be put into high-temperature vats and converted into pulp. And from there, I would go to the section where the pulp was made into paper by machines that were a hundred yards long.

From the paper-making section, the rolls of what was now newsprint were loaded into railroad freight cars. One freight car would be designated for the Louisville *Courier-Journal*. Another freight car would be designated for the *Washington Post*. And another for the *Boston Herald*. And still another for the *New Orleans Times-Picayune*. Locomotives from the BAR would be hitched to fifty or sixty freight cars at a time. The freight cars would then be taken to a hub such as Boston or New York, where they would be separated and transported by other railroad companies to their final destinations.

The executives who ran the mill never had me do anything that was dangerous. I was going through an apprenticeship—as were about six or seven other young men. We were learning the business from square one, with the possibility of eventually being promoted to executive positions. The mill executives did not want any of us to get hurt. Maybe more important, they also did not want some clod slowing down the process because of a mistake he made. The rank-and-file mill hands, many of whom had been there for decades, were always willing to explain to me in detail what they were doing and answer my questions. They knew I posed no threat to their jobs.

By the time the college football season started, I had made some friends, particularly among my fellow apprentices. I hadn't seen a football game in three or four years, and one Saturday we decided to go see Bates College play the University of Maine. I've long forgotten who won, but the game got my imagination going, and I said to my friends, "We ought to get up a football pool." So two other guys joined me in developing this thing we imaginatively called the "pool," although what it really constituted was bookmaking. Instead of having four-, five-, or six-point spreads or whatnot, we had something we called "five and two." For the life of me, I cannot remember what that involved—it was sort of a Rube Goldberg formula that required your team not only to beat the point spread but also to score two touchdowns, making it a lot tougher to win.

On Saturdays, we would work a half day. Then would come the call throughout the factory, "Lock up! Everybody lock up!" We would go into the office and turn in our time sheets and then slyly (or so we thought) stick a wad of paper in the door latch. This would allow us to enter the office on Sundays, when nobody else was there. In the office was an old mimeograph machine, the kind you poured purple ink into. We would sneak into the office on Sundays and run off copies of our football sheets. The sheets would include the Notre Dame game and some regional college contests—six games altogether. And we would each put $25 into the pot to cover any losses we might have from the scheme. Each of us would be responsible for selling twenty-five of the sheets.

We were pretty scared the first weekend that we were going to lose our shirts. But nobody won. And we thought, "Maybe we're on to something. Why not add a few more games next weekend?"

During the ensuing weeks, when we were on break time, we'd walk through the mill and say, "Do you like football?" If one guy had won six bucks, we'd say he had won sixty. Soon we were telling people that somebody had won $100. We got to the point where we were selling $150 worth of tickets each week. We'd put the money back into the pool, and it really began to swell.

Not surprisingly, the supervisors eventually caught us. And we nearly got fired. Thus ended my briefly held avocation as a college football bookmaker.

§

After eleven months, the Great Northern Paper Company transferred me down to its sales headquarters in New York City. They were at 342 Madison Avenue, old offices, nothing fancy. Really stark would probably be a better way of describing them. But they took up an entire floor. The vice president in charge of sales was Richard Casper. He was originally from Madison, Maine, and his outer demeanor was that of a craggy old New Englander. But he was a wonderful guy, once you got to know him, though possessed with an odd habit. He was a cigarette smoker. And when he was talking seriously or wanting to make a point, he would use one hand to grab the wrist of his other hand that was holding the cigarette. And he would draw the cigarette to his mouth in this manner and do what was called "French inhale." The smoke would go up in the air and around and then go in his nostrils and come out of his mouth.

At our first meeting, Casper inhaled his cigarette and said to me, "Where are you from, Bassett?"

And I told him, "Kentucky." Which, of course, he knew. My father's connection with the Whitney family through Greentree Stable may not have helped me much, but it certainly didn't hurt, and it was something he was aware of.

Mr. Casper then said, "What do you think about the months you spent at the mill?"

And oh, I was prepared for that question. All the old executives with Great Northern Paper had worked in the mill. The mill had been their entrance point to the company. They had all spent years there, learning from the ground up what it takes to be successful in the newsprint manufacturing business. To them, the mill was hallowed ground.

I said, "Well, Mr. Casper, I appreciate the opportunity to be here in New York. But I would hate to leave the mill. It has been such a wonderful experience being there. The production that takes place, the people who are there, the Maine woods. I have never had an opportunity like this before."

Mr. Casper inhaled his cigarette and said, "Yes, but we would like to have you down here. We want you to become one of our regional representatives. And we've been thinking about what region to assign you. You're from the South, you say?"

"Yes, sir, " I told him again, "I'm from Kentucky." And I'm thinking, "Great Northern Paper sells newsprint to the *Lexington Herald* and the *Lexington Leader*. The company sells newsprint to the Louisville *Courier-Journal*. The company supplies newsprint to the *Lawrenceburg Messenger*. And to the newspaper in Paducah, Kentucky."

"Well, Bassett," said Mr. Casper, as he inhaled his cigarette one more time, "we've been thinking about assigning you to southern territory."

"Oh, thank you, Mr. Casper," I said. "I really appreciate that so much. I won't disappoint you."

And then Mr. Casper said, "We're going to start you in South Philadelphia."

§

The Great Northern Paper Company provided newsprint for the *Philadelphia Bulletin* and the *Philadelphia Enquirer*. But my travels for the company soon took me well beyond the boundaries of the City of Brotherly Love. I became a regular on Piedmont Airways and Eastern Airlines; Trailway buses; and the Pennsylvania, Chesapeake & Ohio, Norfolk & Western, and Atlantic Coast Line railroads. In those days, most newspapers were not owned by chains, whose stock traded publicly on national exchanges. The papers were owned by great families, many of which had long histories in the newspaper publishing business.

Newsprint was always in short supply, so I was usually a very welcome visitor during my journeys. I would call on each publisher a minimum of twice a year, and they would take me out to dinner. As time went on, my territory expanded farther southward, encompassing the *Baltimore Sun*, the *Washington Star*, and the *Roanoke News*. Great Northern Paper eventually promoted me to the position of southern sales manager.

I served as the Great Northern Paper representative to newspapers of all sizes—from weeklies with circulations of 2,000 to 3,000 to dailies with circulations in the hundreds of thousands. In a state such as North Carolina, I would travel to the offices of the *Charlotte News* and the *Charlotte Observer* (which were separate papers back then), the *News and Observer* of Raleigh, the *Durham Herald-Sun*, the *Wilmington Star News*, the *Rocky Mount Morning Telegram*, the *Greensboro Daily Record*, and much smaller operations such as the *Daily Southerner* of Tarboro and the *High Point Enterprise*—along with various points in between. There weren't any big hotel or motel chains in the South in those days, and I often stayed in these little two- or three-story places that had no air-conditioning.

On the opposite end of the weather spectrum, I remember one winter morning when I left Raleigh to go I think it was to Wilson, about forty-five miles to the east. Wilson had a small newspaper called the *Daily Times*. Nowadays, you get from Raleigh to Wilson by way of a major state highway, Route 264. But back then, you traveled on a two-lane country road (one lane going in each direction). It had started to snow, and I was driving the black Ford coupe my father had given me when I went to Millinocket. (It was a rarity for me to drive during one of these sales trips. Usually I depended on planes, buses, and trains for transportation. I believe the reason was that it had become prohibitively expensive to keep the car parked in a New York City garage, and I was going to culminate this trip by driving to Lexington, leaving the car with my parents, and flying back to New York.) Anyway, I was trying to get to Wilson and the snow was becoming increasingly heavy. I fell in behind a long line of cars and trucks that seemed to be going only about five miles per hour. I was getting very frustrated by the slow progress, and when I saw what looked like a clearing on the side of the road ahead of me, I pulled out to the right, put my foot to the pedal, accelerated, and passed about eight to ten cars. And ran right into a snowbank. I was stuck and couldn't go any further. The cars I had passed were now passing me, and their drivers were grinning and waving and honking their horns at me, this smart guy who thought he could take some kind of a shortcut. I don't think I have ever felt more chagrined or embarrassed. It took a while for me to extricate myself from the snowbank. When I finally got to Wilson, the hotel there was full. So I pushed on to Rocky Mount, and the hotels there were full, too. And then to Tarboro— same story. By this time, the roads had become virtually undrivable. I pulled into a filling station and asked the owner if he knew of any place I could stay. He said, "Well, you can spend the night in a chair in my station."

I said, "How much will that cost?"

He laughed and replied, "Nothing."

The filling station had a chair, but no heat. I spent the night there with my hat on and my overcoat pulled around me, drinking and eating whatever my nickels and dimes could get from the vending machines. The following day, the highway department began plowing the roads, and I was able to continue my journey.

Air travel could be somewhat adventurous too. When I flew to and from Lexington, I always had to pass through Charleston, West Virginia, where the airport was on top of a mountain. The airplanes we rode on were DC-3s, which were propeller driven and had an aisle down the middle with single seats on each side. They were flown by two-member crews and could seat up to thirty-two passengers. There was one night when I was flying out of Charleston—I don't recall if I was heading to Lexington or back to New York—and it was so overcast and drizzly that I couldn't see anything beyond the sides of the runway. The pilot gunned the plane's engine, started accelerating down the runway, and then suddenly slammed on the brakes. He later explained to the passengers that because the runway was so wet, he hadn't been able to attain the speed necessary for the plane to obtain lift. But he did not give us a chance to get off the plane. We waited for a half hour and then the pilot tried another takeoff, and this time he was successful.

§

Living in New York City during the post–World War II period was wonderful. There was an incredible electricity in the air—New York just vibrated with life. I loved having dinner at Toots Shore's restaurant on West Fifty-first Street. The menu there contained "nuttin' fancy," as Shore used to say, but his restaurant was a great hangout for writers, professional athletes, and people involved in the performing arts.

Lucy and I would go to Radio City Music Hall and see the Rockettes perform their intricate, high-kicking dance routines. We would also go to the dinner clubs and nightclubs—not on a nightly or weekly basis, which wasn't within our means, but occasionally. Doing so was one of the great experiences of being a young couple in New York. One of our favorite places to dine was 21 on West Fifty-second Street. There was (and remains today) an array of jockey statuettes in front of the club painted in the silks of their owners, all of whom are patrons of 21. (Of course, we have the same sort of thing at Keeneland.) Such diverse figures as Ernest Hemingway and Alfred Hitchcock frequented 21, and I've read that Humphrey Bogart proposed to Lauren Bacall there.

The decor at 21 has always been intimate. It is not a large place and reminds you of a British club. As you went in, there were two very well-dressed men who gave you the once-over. These men had a remarkable ability to remember the faces and names of the regulars. But if you were unfamiliar to them, they could be very imposing, as you became locked in by their silent, inspective stares. If they didn't think you belonged, they would ask, "Do you have a reservation?" And if your answer was no, they politely but quickly ushered you aside. We were never denied entrance and never saw a ruckus occur, but it was nonetheless unnerving to wonder whether we would receive their nods of approval or glares of disapproval.

Another place we would go was the El Morocco on East Fifty-fourth Street. The El Morocco's trademark was its zebra-striped banquettes and chairs. This was the era when Lester Lanin and Meyer Davis were the kings of the society dance bands. Their music offered a café community blend of strict, quick tempos and light, bouncy two-steps. Several decades later, the bands of Cliff Hall from Palm Beach became famous for doing the same.

When I was a young man, dancing was something you did in time and in tandem with your partner—it was dramatically different from today's wild gyrations, acrobatic torso twisting, and windmilling of the hands and arms. The El Morocco would always have two bands playing, providing a continuous beat of rumbas, the cha-cha, and sophisticated fox-trots. The bands also played tunes from the great Broadway shows, sometimes fusing them in four-piece medleys. Lucy was an excellent dancer, and although I wasn't more than a left-footed hoofer, we spent our share of enchanted evenings dancing at the El Morocco.

Entertainment opportunities at the clubs were enormous. The Copacabana, on East Sixtieth Street, was one of our favorites, too. That's where we saw Johnnie Ray perform "Cry!" and he actually cried while he was singing it. The people in the audience would stamp and clap, and many of them would cry with him—including a few who would weep so inconsolably that Ray would hand them his handkerchief. At the Copacabana, Ray broke attendance records that had been set by Dean Martin and Jerry Lewis.

But our favorite nightclub of all was the Versailles on East Fiftieth Street. It was there that several times we saw the great French singer Edith Piaf perform. She was petite, gaunt, and always dressed in black, and she had a truly extraordinary voice. What began as a short engagement for her at the Versailles was subsequently extended to five months, and it was a sellout every night. Edith became widely popular not only among New Yorkers but throughout the country. She appeared on the *Ed Sullivan Show* something like eight times. Edith sang almost all her songs in her native French, and even though the majority of the people in the audience did not understand the lyrics, they were captivated by the power and emotion in her voice. Her most famous song was "La Vie en Rose," the lyrics to which were written by Edith herself. When she died at the age of forty-seven in 1963, her funeral procession in Paris lured hundreds of thousands of mourners and caused traffic in the city to come to a complete stop. A motion picture was made about Edith (also titled *La Vie en Rose*). I saw it during the summer of 2007 and I was so enthralled that I went back to see it a second time.

Our years living in New York also coincided with the era of the great Rodgers and Hammerstein musicals: *Oklahoma, Carousel, South Pacific, The King and I.* They were performed on Broadway in places such as the St. James and Majestic theaters. The best seats were in the orchestra, and they cost $6.60 apiece. By contrast, in the winter of 2007, I went to the theater in New York to see *Jersey Boys,* and the price of an orchestra seat was $122.50.

The original Broadway production of *South Pacific* starred Mary Martin, who was a tremendous talent. She also performed the title role in the subsequent musical *Peter Pan.* Her costar in *South Pacific* was the opera singer Enzo Pinza, who sang something like 800 times for the New York Metropolitan Opera and whose rich basso voice was known worldwide. The reviews were terrific. *South Pacific* eventually received the Pulitzer Prize for drama and played every night to houses that were sold out weeks and even months in advance.

From the time *South Pacific* first opened in April 1949, Lucy dearly wanted to see it. This was the year before we got married. She was a senior at Smith College, and our courtship was in full bloom. I wanted to do everything I could to impress her, but damn! it seemed impossible to get *South Pacific* tickets. However, on November 12 of that year, the University of Notre Dame and University of North Carolina football teams were playing each other at Yankee Stadium. Notre Dame was on its way to a national championship, and that game was a tough ticket too, even though Yankee Stadium seated 67,000 people. But one of my clients, the *Durham Herald-Sun,* had provided me with a pair of tickets to the game, and they were pretty good seats, somewhere around the thirty- or thirty-five-yard line. So I went to a broker who I had done some business with before and asked him if he would be willing to swap two orchestra tickets to *South Pacific* for two tickets to the Notre Dame–North Carolina game. He gave me a little song and dance and then said, "Well, Bassett, call me tomorrow or the next day." I went away thinking I was about to make a pretty good trade. And a day or so later he informed me, "I've got the two that you want." I gave him the two football tickets, and he gave me the two to *South Pacific,* which I expected to be in the orchestra. But they were in the third balcony! And I still had to pay list price for each of them, which I believe was $3.50. Notre Dame won the game 42–6. But we got to see and hear Mary Martin sing:

> I'm as corny as Kansas in August,
> High as a flag on the Fourth of July!
> If you'll excuse an expression I use,
> I'm in love, I'm in love,
> I'm in love, I'm in love,
> I'm in love with a wonderful guy!

To a young couple such as Lucy and me, this was magic. We also went to see the Irving Berlin musical *Call Me Madam,* with the original cast that included Ethel Merman and Paul Lukas. It was the time of Rosalind Russell's Tony Award–winning performance in *Wonderful Town,* and we went to that. There was always an outstanding play that everyone was talking about, even out in the hinterlands, and whenever Lucy's parents or my parents came to visit us, going to the theater was pretty much mandatory. It was an integral part of the New York experience.

Afterward, we would leave the theater amidst an immense crowd and walk up Broadway, humming the songs from the shows we had attended. The melodies and lyrics to these songs would become part of the national fabric. And seeing the shows would be looked upon as badges of honor. People would ask, "Have you seen *South Pacific?*" Yes, we have. "Have you seen *Call Me Madam?*" Oh yes, we went last month. Being able to respond in that manner brought feelings not only of self-satisfaction but of pride. They weren't just shows; they were blockbuster events.

§

After Lucy and I married, we lived at 277 Park Avenue. Our apartment had a bedroom, bathroom, living room and kitchen. In totality, it was about as large as the conference room that's adjacent to my office in the Keeneland Cottage. But we had a butler. His name was Joseph Carr. He and other members of his family had been longtime employees of Lucy's parents, and the Gays had sent him up to New York to work for us. We paid him something like $50 a week. Joseph was about sixty-five years old and was originally from Midway, Kentucky. But years earlier he had worked for a family in New York and was very familiar with the city. We housed him in the Harlem YMCA, and he would commute to our apartment six days a week. Joseph was black and had a distinguished air. He was actually a combination butler, cook, and houseman, and he taught us a lot about living in New York City. (Later, Joseph returned with us to Kentucky and remained in our employ for two decades.)

§

Having been in the Marine Corps, I had no particular admiration for General Douglas MacArthur. A lot of Marines shared that view, and I think part of it stemmed from interservice rivalry. We always felt that while we had the toughest battle assignments, the Army received preferential treatment with regard to materials and supplies. Looking back, whether or not there was any truth to these notions, I don't know.

But there also existed a strong feeling among us that MacArthur, in March 1942, had vacated the Philippines, choosing not to stick around for the fight. And although MacArthur had been ordered to leave by Franklin Roosevelt and had dramatically vowed, "I shall return," we kept thinking of those members of the Fourth Marine Regiment who had stayed on Corregidor and had no choice but to surrender and either subsequently died or spent years imprisoned by the Japanese.

Of course, what did it matter what I thought about MacArthur? He achieved the rank of five-star general, became the supreme commander of the Allied forces in the southwestern Pacific, received the Japanese surrender on the battleship *Missouri* in Tokyo Bay, and was in charge of the postwar occupation of Japan. I, in comparison, was a first lieutenant whose responsibilities included the regimental laundry.

During the years immediately following the war, my views on MacArthur had tempered, but only somewhat. Attitudes branching from the interservice rivalries can stay with you for a long time. But MacArthur had been in the Pacific during World War II, and I had been in the Pacific during World War II, and emotional bonds emerge from such common denominators that become part of you as well. He was, indeed, a great soldier, a brilliant military strategist, and in 1950, Harry Truman put him in command of the United Nations military forces in South Korea. By this time, MacArthur had become such a hero to Americans that there was serious talk about him running for the presidency.

Then on April 11, 1951, Truman relieved MacArthur of his command. I am not going to go into detail as to why this happened—there are many historians who have detailed and assessed the subject far more competently than I ever could. But I do remember the huge public outcry over Truman having humiliated MacArthur in this way. The public was appalled. And incensed. Newspaper columnists throughout the country, in the most furious words they could summon, condemned Truman's action. MacArthur headed home. On his schedule was an address to a joint session of Congress on April 19. But prior to doing this, he was coming to New York, specifically to the Waldorf-Astoria Towers, which was just one block from where Lucy and I lived.

Our apartment faced the inner courtyard, so we could not see the street. But I knew from newspaper and television reports that after arriving at Idlewild Airport, MacArthur would go by motorcade right up Park Avenue to the Waldorf. I had never seen MacArthur in person before. But now I had to! I just had to! Lucy was both mildly amused and perplexed. "You and your fellow Marines used to call him 'dug-out Doug,'" she said. "You've always been so anti-MacArthur, ridiculing him. And now, you want to run downstairs, run outside. . . ."

So yes, I rushed downstairs and out the front door in the main lobby and headed up toward the Waldorf. The crowd was fifteen people deep, and I had to stand in the back. MacArthur was in an open car, and as his motorcade approached, I began jumping up, again and again, trying to get a glimpse of his head. I was even willing to accept just a glimpse of that famous crushed general's hat he always wore. Jumping. Jumping. Jumping. Going up, going down. Literally like a puppet attached to a string. And then, there he is! I saw him! I saw him! I actually saw him!

We did not have a television set in the Great Northern Paper offices. On the day MacArthur addressed Congress, I came home at noon to watch his speech on our twelve-inch black-and-white TV. I would not be content just to hear it. I had to see it, just like I had to see MacArthur that evening his motorcade brought him to the Waldorf. There were questions about how he would be received by the members of Congress and what he would say to them.

Well, it turned out that MacArthur's speech was interrupted by ovations thirty times. His concluding words were mesmerizing: "Old soldiers never die, they just fade away. . . . I now close my military career and just fade away—an old soldier, who tried to do his duty as God gave him the light to see that duty. Good-bye."

In the ensuing decades, much has been written about MacArthur. His often controversial decisions have been subjected to a great deal of analysis, not all of it flattering. But I do feel that history eyes him well in at least one major regard: the powerful role he played in the successful occupation of Japan from 1945 to 1951. MacArthur's insistence on reestablishing the authority of the Japanese emperor was a classic act of statesmanship. It prevented what could have been a political disaster and led to the democratic reform of postwar Japan.

§

MacArthur died in April 1964. His widow, Jean Faircloth MacArthur, became a good friend of John and Edna Morris. John represented the fourth generation of one of the most prominent families in racing. The family's all-scarlet racing silks, registered in 1840, were carried to victory by Ruthless, who won the inaugural running of the Belmont Stakes in 1867. Until John's death in 1985, they were the oldest continuously used racing colors in the nation.

In 1973, John was a trustee of the New York Racing Association. At the time, I was rather insignificant in racing circles. A nonentity. But John had become one of my mentors, which was a very kind thing for him to do, because he was a director of the Fasig-Tipton Sales Company, which was a rival of Keeneland.

One day in late May 1973, John called me on the phone and said, "Ted, are you going to the Belmont Stakes?" When I told him I was, he invited me to have lunch with him in the Trustees' Room on Belmont day and to watch the race in his private clubhouse box, which was in the first row near the finish line.

I did not know until I arrived at Belmont Park that John and Edna had also invited Mrs. MacArthur to be their guest that day. They seated me right next to her, at both lunch and in the box, and she was a lovely, delightful lady, possessed of an intrinsic ability to make you feel that whatever you said was interesting to her. I told Mrs. MacArthur the story about how thrilled I had been to just briefly see her husband's face that evening in front of the Waldorf, decades before. She said, "I'm not surprised. Many people felt that way about the General. [She always referred to him as the General, never as Douglas or Doug.] The General would have understood that, certainly."

Through her friendship with Edna, Mrs. MacArthur had become an avid racing fan. She was not a bettor, but she enjoyed the atmosphere of the racetrack, the people, the spectacle of a major racing event. And that afternoon, she witnessed one of the greatest spectacles in the history of the sport—Secretariat's thirty-one-length victory in the Belmont in the world-record clocking for one and a half miles on the dirt of 2:24.

There have been many, many detailed descriptions over the years of Secretariat's performance that day, and I'll briefly add mine. Racing fans had been waiting twenty-five years for a Triple Crown winner, and as Secretariat began to increase his lead over the rest of the field, the Belmont crowd's roar of expectation, of appreciation, was deafening. Not only for the fact that he, indeed, was sweeping the Triple Crown, but for the manner and the powerful way he was doing it, the overwhelming dominance he was demonstrating—I am the champion, and be there no question about it!

People on the Belmont apron and throughout the grandstand were raising their fists and pummeling one another and jumping up and down. But in John Morris's box, we were simply standing and applauding. You see, that's part of the culture to which I had adjusted. One did not overly react to things. Twenty-two years earlier, in front of the Waldorf, I too had been jumping up and down when Douglas MacArthur arrived. Now I was John and Edna Morris's guest, as was Mrs. MacArthur, a circumstance that carried with it an unwritten requirement to behave accordingly. Despite my Kent and Yale background, it was an adjustment I was still continuing to learn. I am not suggesting that doing so was easy.

Forward to 1980. On February 1 of that year, the Eclipse Awards dinner was held in the Waldorf. Mrs. MacArthur was still residing there, and Lucy and I invited her to be the honored guest at Keeneland's table. John Y. Brown Jr., who was then governor of Kentucky, and his wife, Phyllis George, a former Miss America and CBS sportscaster, were also our guests, as were the Morrises and John A. O'Hara, the president of *Reader's Digest* magazine.

Over the years, whenever Lucy and I hosted a table at a dinner of this nature, we have been very careful about seating arrangements. One thing we generally do not believe in doing is sitting husbands next to their wives. Lucy and I do not want anyone to be left out of the conversation mix, and oftentimes the best way to ensure that is to put a space or two between spouses. At the Eclipse Awards dinner, we sat John Y. Brown immediately to the right of Mrs. MacArthur. But to my profound disappointment, throughout the evening John kept on leaving the table to greet and chat with various friends and political supporters. Mrs. MacArthur appeared unfazed by his absences, but I grew increasingly perturbed over John's behavior. I later, quite heatedly told him, "Here is one of the most distinguished ladies of our time. She was our guest of honor. You should have shown her more respect!"

§

The post–World War II period in New York City also constituted a tremendous era for sports. Baseball, especially. You pretty much couldn't live in the city without becoming an ardent fan of the New York Yankees, New York Giants, or Brooklyn Dodgers. This was the period when Joe DiMaggio, Yogi Berra, and Whitey Ford played for the Yankees; when Leo Durocher managed a Giants team that included Willie Mays, Sal "the Barber" Maglie, and Eddie Stanky; and when the Brooklyn Dodgers' team included Jackie Robinson, Pee Wee Reese (who was from Kentucky), Duke Snider, and Preacher Roe, who Roger Kahn would later celebrate in his best-selling book *The Boys of Summer*.

Yankee Stadium, of course, was the home of the Yankees. On the other side of the Harlem River, adjacent to an area known as Coogan's Bluff, the Giants played in the Polo Grounds. And the Dodgers' home was Ebbets Field. My friends and I would get aboard at Grand Central Station on East Forty-second Street and take the subway trains to see games in all three ballparks. We didn't care where we sat—we would just go to one of the general admission windows.

During my early days in New York, the Dodgers had an outfielder named Pete Reiser, who was enormously talented but kept running full tilt into the outfield walls while chasing long flies. Back then, the walls were made of brick or concrete. Reiser had a spectacular career, though, not surprisingly, it did not span a lengthy period of years.

There was a case one day when Lucy went to a Red Sox–Yankees game with a friend named Faye Caulkins. The sportscaster Bud Palmer was a good friend of mine, and I had introduced him to Faye, who he eventually married. Bud had obtained the tickets for Lucy and Faye. After the game, they were introduced to DiMaggio. Lucy was thrilled to death, and, not having the same opportunity, I was very envious.

College basketball was huge in New York in those days. Ned Irish, a former sportswriter for the *New York World-Telegram,* was head of basketball operations at Madison Square Garden. Just about every year, Irish would bring the University of Kentucky basketball team in to play teams from St. John's or Long Island University at the Garden, and those games would invariably sell out. This was back in the late 1940s and early 1950s, when Kentucky fielded three NCAA champion teams in four seasons and was represented by such consensus first-team All-Americans as Ralph Beard, Alex Groza, and Bill Spivey.

Professional boxing was huge, too. I had long been a boxing fan. After graduating from Kent School in the late spring of 1941, I stayed there for a few additional weeks, studying for my College Board examinations. On the evening of June 18, Father Sill invited me and several other Kent boys who were studying for their boards to his study to listen to the radio broadcast of the heavyweight title match between Joe Louis and Billy Conn. This was quite a treat, because Kent students were not allowed to have radios in their rooms. And pocket-sized transistor radios did not yet exist. We sat there listening as Conn, a former light heavyweight champion who weighed twenty-five pounds less than Louis, gave him all he could handle before being knocked out by a right hand to the jaw in the thirteenth round.

Ten years later, on September 12, 1951, I was actually attending a title fight. That was the night Sugar Ray Robinson regained the middleweight title from the British champion Randy Turpin, who had won a fifteen-round decision from Robinson two months earlier in London. The return match was at the Polo Grounds, and I remember looking at the seats that had been set up around the ring, near the second-base area of the infield, that cost over $100 apiece. I could not afford anything like that—I paid something like $20 for a seat back in the grandstand. The crowd that night was 61,370, and the place was full of Brits. My seat was surrounded by ones occupied by crew members from the transatlantic ocean liner the *Queen Elizabeth.* Turpin opened up a deep cut over Robinson's left eye in the tenth round. But in the eleventh round, Robinson knocked Turpin down, backed him into the ropes, and then unleashed an incredible torrent, something like thirty-one punches in twenty-five seconds. The referee stopped the fight, and, to my delight (though to the dismay of the *Queen Elizabeth* crew), Sugar Ray retained the title.

New York had something like fifteen daily newspapers back then. I regularly read the *Herald Tribune;* its sports page was edited by Stanley Woodward, and its primary sports columnist was Red Smith. I also loved the columns of Bill Corum, who wrote for the *New York Journal American* and in 1925 had coined the phrase "the Run for the Roses" to describe the Kentucky Derby. (From 1950 to 1958, Corum would serve as president of Churchill Downs.)

But all the city's newspapers had superb writers and offered outstanding sports coverage. From his midtown Manhattan office, Grantland Rice wrote sports columns that were syndicated nationally by the North American Newspaper Alliance. John Kieran was a sports columnist for the *New York Times.* As were Jimmy Cannon for the *New York Post,* Joe Williams for the *New York World Telegram,* and Ben Hecht and Barney Nagler for the *Morning Telegraph* (which was something of a sister publication to the *Daily Racing Form* but covered a wide array of sports and entertainment topics). These men were icons to sports enthusiasts. You really bought the newspapers to read their columns, devouring almost every word they wrote. And they weren't just sportswriters. They were accomplished, knowledgeable, articulate people, possessed of fascinating personalities. The respect and admiration I had for them carried on in later years—my exposure to their work as a young man had a lot to do with the excitement I experienced when we hosted the Blue Grass Stakes press dinners at Keeneland.

One thing I did not do, however, was go to the races, even though there were three tracks in the New York City area—Belmont Park, Aqueduct, and Jamaica—that, combined, offered six and a half months of Thoroughbred racing each year. I may have gone to Belmont once while I was living in New York, but if so, I do not recall anything about the trip. A reason might have been that I did not know how to get to the racetracks.

But I knew how to get to the other sporting venues. The subway trip to the Polo Grounds involved taking the Number 1 train from Grand Central Station to the Columbus Circle Station at 145th Street, then taking the D train to 155th Street. From there it was just a two-block walk to Eighth Avenue and 157th Street, which is where the Polo Grounds was situated. The trip to Ebbets Field involved riding the Number 4 train from Grand Central to Brooklyn, or taking the D train again (which also went to Brooklyn) and then walking a short distance to the ballpark, which was bounded by Sullivan Place, Bedford Avenue, and Montgomery Street. Knowing such things was part of the pride of being a New Yorker.

In regard to baseball, I was a Giants fan. I cannot remember why. Maybe it had something to do with my imitating Hank Lieber's method of catching fly balls during my baseball-playing days at Kent. I do recall my incredulous reaction in July 1948 when Durocher left his managerial position with the Dodgers to become manager of the Giants. Dodgers fans had loved him. Giants fans had hated him. Now the situation, virtually overnight, was being reversed.

The one date from this era that will always remain entrenched in my mind is October 3, 1951. A Wednesday, with an overcast sky. The Giants and Dodgers had finished the regular season in a tie for first place, and they were at the Polo Grounds, playing the final game of a best-of-three playoff to see who would go against the Yankees in the World Series.

Back then, the *New York Times* was headquartered in a flatiron, triangular-shaped building that pointed northward from Times Square. (In fact, Times Square is named for the *New York Times*.) There was an electronic scroll that ran across the upper portion of the building that faced the square, which kept track of breaking news events, and the people passing through Times Square would pause and look up to read the scroll. During the seven-year period from 1947 through 1953, at least one New York team was involved in the World Series six times. And during five of those years, two New York teams were involved. "Subway series" is what they were called. The scroll on the *Times* building would keep track of the games—not necessarily the play-by-play, but inning by inning—and the crowds watching the scroll would get quite large. And the same was true for those playoff games in 1951. A major portion of the city's population became engrossed by what was transpiring.

Television was in its infancy. The offices of Great Northern Paper were on Madison Avenue, between Forty-third and Forty-fourth streets, and when I was coming back from lunch that afternoon, the game had already started. There was a store that had a television set with what appeared to be about a fifteen-inch screen in its display window. The television was showing the playoff game, and people were gathered two and three deep on the sidewalk watching it. This was not an untypical scene for October back then.

Among the Great Northern staff there was a mix of Yankees, Giants, and Dodgers fans—which divided the staff into three passionate rooting sections. We had the radio tuned to WMCA-AM and were listening to the play-by-play by the Giants' announcer, Russ Hodges. And so it was that at 3:58 P.M. eastern standard time, in the last of the ninth inning, on a count of no balls and one strike, with the Dodgers' Ralph Branca pitching to the Giants' Bobby Thomson, I heard Hodges's famous call as it happened:

> Branca throws. There's a long drive! It's gonna be, I believe . . . The Giants win the pennant! The Giants win the pennant! The Giants win the pennant! The Giants win the pennant! Bobby Thomson hits into the lower deck of the left-field stands! The Giants win the pennant! And they're going crazy! They're going crazy!

A short time later, I went out on Madison Avenue, and the scene was incredible. People were clapping their hands, yelling, cheering, screaming. "Do you know what happened? Did you hear? Did you hear it?!" Drivers had stopped their cars in midstreet and were blowing their horns. It was a major eruption of sound. The next morning, Red Smith said in his *Herald Tribune* column, "The art of fiction is dead. Reality has strangled invention. Only the utterly impossible, the inexpressibly fantastic, can ever be plausible again."

Giants fans were elated. Dodgers fans were distraught almost beyond description. And Yankees fans . . . well, the Yankees went on to beat the Giants in the World Series, four games to two. You see (and this is something all Giants and Dodgers fans had to learn), in the early 1950s, every year was "next year" for the New York Yankees.

§

After spending three years as a married couple in New York, Lucy and I were getting a lot of pressure to come home. I was somewhat reluctant to do this. I loved the city. I loved my job. And our apartment was only about a seven-minute walk from my office. But I was a Kentuckian who had married a Kentucky girl, and the lure of returning to the region of our roots was tugging hard on both of us.

The Great Northern Paper people were polite but rather perplexed about the situation. I had been slowly making my way upward in the company, and they were pleased with my progress and pleased with my work. Lucy, herself, voiced no demands to go home. But I knew where her heart was. She would say, "Ted, if we're going to stay here, shouldn't we think about getting a home in Westchester or out on Long Island?" But I was aware of her unspoken message. And I understood.

So, at the age of thirty-two, I resigned from my position with Great Northern Paper, and Lucy and I moved home to Kentucky. From an occupational standpoint, I was starting all over again. Through Mr. Gay, my father-in-law, I was planning to get involved in farming. My own father had difficulty comprehending this. "You've got a Yale education," he said. "And you're going to trade that in to become a dirt farmer?"

What I really wanted to do was own and operate a newspaper. But I didn't have anywhere close to the financial backing needed to purchase the *Lexington Herald* or the *Lexington Leader*. But I did take a look at the *Danville Advocate-Messenger,* a daily that served the readership of the seat of Boyle County, about thirty miles south of Lexington. I made an appointment to meet with the editor, Enos Swain. But we did not talk for long. Swain told me the *Advocate-Messenger* was owned by the J. Curtis Alcock and J. S. Van Winkle families, and the family members didn't want any participation in the paper by outsiders. I was politely rebuffed.

I became a farmer—and literally got down into the dirt. Mr. Gay told me, "You can do two things, Teddy. You can be a windshield farmer, driving around in your truck, watching the farmhands toil in your fields. Or you can get out of the truck, put on overalls, roll up your sleeves, and learn how to grow crops and raise livestock." This was Mr. Gay's way of saying I could sit on my rear end or get off it and learn how to farm the hands-on way, which involved blisters on the hands, aches in the back, a sunburned face, and clothes bearing the odor of yesterday's sweat.

Mr. Gay made 250 acres of land available to me. I began raising bluegrass seed. And corn. Some cattle, too. And sheep. The sheep were the most prominent of my livestock ventures. I purchased 100 ewes for $38 each, and to service them, I obtained 4 rams (or bucks, as they are also called). The lambs that resulted from each breeding season were sold at the Lexington stockyards. I also derived income from the wool the sheep produced. I didn't shear the sheep myself—there were a couple of men in the area who were really good at it, and that's how they made their living, going from farm to farm.

My big market item, though, was tobacco. I annually raised twenty acres of burley, which is used primarily in the manufacture of cigarettes. In the mid-1950s, the planting and cultivation of tobacco were done almost entirely by manual labor. We set the plants in the ground by hand. We "chopped out" by hand, which involved clearing the weeds that grew around and between the plants with hoes, so they wouldn't compete with the tobacco for water. We cut the plants with specially designed tobacco knives by hand, and then speared them on sticks. And then we housed the tobacco by hand in gigantic barns that were six or seven tiers high. Accordingly, you had six or seven groups of men handing and pulling the tobacco up. The men in the lower tiers worked the hardest, but the ones on the upper tiers always faced the peril of falling from the barns and breaking their necks. The tobacco would be hung in the barns, allowing it to be air-cured.

From January until March, we would go around picking up the fallen dead trees and limbs in the nearby woods and would stack them like Indian tepees, four to five feet high and eight to ten feet wide. We would set the stacks on top of these wire apparatuses, which were about the size of the conference table I have today in the Keeneland Cottage, maybe thirty to forty yards apart in the tobacco fields. The apparatuses would be hooked to a tractor by cables, and we'd set the stacks on fire, have them sit atop a tobacco bed for twenty or thirty minutes, and then start the tractor and tow them on top of another bed. The purpose was to burn as much weed seed out of the ground as we could. Nowadays, chemicals are used to eliminate the weed seeds. But back then, if you drove out into central Kentucky's tobacco country, you would see those fires all over the place. Sometimes, we would stay up throughout the night burning the beds.

I was sent to tobacco grading school by Mr. Gay. The five-day course was offered at the University of Kentucky, and it was taught by Red O'Hara, a federal government employee who went around to land-grant colleges and universities in the region for that specific purpose. Being able to properly strip burley is an important skill. The "flyings" are the most valuable part of the plant. They're on the bottom. Next come the "lugs" or "cutters," as they are also called. Then come the "leafs," with the green also being separated from the red. And then, least in value, at the top of the plants, are the "tips."

Nowadays, burley is brought to the market in bales that are not divided into grades. But in those days, we carefully put the flyings, lugs, leafs, and tips into separate baskets. We would stand at long tables and do the stripping by hand—one person's job was to take off the flyings, another person's job was to remove the lugs, and so on. I would get up at 6:00 A.M. to participate in this chore. We would begin about the end of November or early December and try to be finished before February. The process culminated when we brought the baskets of flyings, lugs, leafs, and tips to a warehouse to be sold. There, the baskets would be marked in ways that only tobacco people understood: CF, C1F, C2F, B2F. A designation of B2FR meant "leaf red." MG indicated "mixed green."

Altogether, Mr. Gay grew about 350 acres of burley, and he knew most of the buyers. There would be representatives at the warehouse from the R. J. Reynolds Tobacco Company, Liggett & Myers, the American Tobacco Company, Brown & Williamson, and Philip Morris. They would all walk past a long line of baskets of tobacco, behind the auctioneer, who would usually start the bidding at whatever the federal subsidy was—58 cents a pound, or 59 cents, sometimes as high as 65 cents. We never sold our product directly to the tobacco companies. We always had to sell through the warehouse and its auctioneer.

You needed a strong pair of hands to do work like this. I was fortunate that my hands were always very strong. As were my father's. He was always insistent that when you shook hands with a man, you looked him straight in the eye and gave him a good grip. I still believe that's sound advice for any father to give his son.

There were many times during my tenure as a farmer, during those bone-tiring, physically and mentally exhausting days, when I thought back to years when I was an executive living in New York. The years that included dining at 21, dancing at the El Morocco, seeing the Broadway plays and attending Edith Piaf's performances, and watching the Giants play the Dodgers at Ebbets Field and the Polo Grounds. I learned a lot being a hands-on farmer, and I enjoyed it. But I cannot honestly say that I have ever in my later years longed to do it again.

Chapter 5

State Police

WHEN ALBERT BENJAMIN "Happy" Chandler became governor in 1955, he appointed Peter Arrell Widener III as commissioner of the Kentucky State Police. Pete Widener had married Louise Van Meter, one of Lucy's closest friends since childhood. He was a multimillionaire—his family had deep roots in the powerful financial and social circles of Philadelphia, Pennsylvania. Pete's father and grandfather had bred and raced champion racehorses for decades, and after purchasing Hialeah Park in south Florida, they had transformed it from a small track that conducted illegal betting into one of the most beautiful and prominent pari-mutuel operations anywhere on the globe.

After serving in the U.S. Army as a private first class with a combat engineers unit during World War II, Pete attended the University of Kentucky. He was a law enforcement buff—police work was both his hobby and his avocation—and he was appointed a deputy constable in Fayette County in 1948. Subsequently, Pete was named the county's chief of patrol, and that same year, upon the death of his father, he inherited Elmendorf Stable, which made for an interesting transition from top local cop to master of the turf.

Through Lucy, Pete and I had gotten to know each other fairly well. After he had been Chandler's police commissioner for a year, he inquired if I might be interested in becoming a member of his staff. I told him, no, I've never had any interest in doing police work. Besides, I was growing twenty acres of tobacco. It was a backbreaking thing to do, and I was still trying to learn how to do it.

But Pete was persistent. He would call me up and say, "It's a rainy day. You can't do very much. Come on down to Frankfort and have lunch with me. I want to show you the organization." I'd go, and we would head out to the State Police pistol range, and we'd see a new gun or firing technique

93

being demonstrated. A couple of weeks would pass, and Pete would call me again and say, "What are you doing? Come on down. I've got a new helicopter I want to show you." And another week or two would pass, and Pete would be on the phone again. "I want you to see something. We've got this new polygraph machine. You know what that is? It's a lie detector, it can reveal when people aren't telling the truth."

What Pete had done was put out the baited hook, and whereas I had first ignored it, I was now becoming more and more tantalized, while slowly, artfully, being drawn in by the angler. Finally one night, I think it was about the middle of August in 1956, Pete was having dinner at our farm and he said, "You've got to make a decision now. Come on down and give police work a try." I told him, all right, I'll try to get the crop harvested and will be down right after Labor Day.

Three or four days later, Pete came back to me and said, "Ted, it's off. It's all off." I asked him, rather astonished, what in the hell was he talking about? Pete said, "Well, I went in to see Chandler and told him what I wanted to do. And Chandler said, 'Who is that boy?' I told him, 'He's Gus Gay's son-in-law.' Chandler exploded. 'Gus Gay! He's fought me in every election I've ever been in! Gus Gay's the biggest Republican in Woodford County!'"

Chandler was originally from Henderson County, but Woodford County was now his home. According to Pete, Chandler looked very carefully at him and said, "Where was that boy in the primary?" This was an important question in those days, because it was in the primary where the governor really got elected. At the time, six of the last seven gubernatorial races in Kentucky had been won by Democrats. Chandler's real fight hadn't occurred in the general election, where he had trounced the Republican candidate, Edwin Denney, by nearly 130,000 votes. The election had really been decided in the primary, where he beat Bert T. Combs, who was the hand-picked choice of outgoing governor Lawrence Wetherby to be his successor.

Widener related to me what Chandler had said, then looked at me very seriously and said in a very measured tone, "Now, Ted, you voted for Chandler, didn't you?" I told him, well, no, I'm an independent. Pete sort of did this double take, or maybe something more along the lines of a triple take or even a quadruple take, and said, "Independent! Ted! You idiot! Go over to the Woodford County courthouse and get registered as a Democrat!"

So early the next morning, I drove over to the courthouse—or sneaked over might be a more accurate way of describing it—and did as Pete instructed. I had married into a Republican family. I had voted for the Republican candidate, Thomas Dewey, in the 1948 presidential election. I had voted for Dwight David Eisenhower in 1952. The reason why I had been registered as an independent was that it allowed me some choices in primary elections. In Kentucky back then, particularly in local elections, there often were no Republican candidates on the slate. Now here I was, registering as a Democrat. Pete phoned to confirm that I had done this and told me to "hang on."

A week went by, and I heard nothing. And I was getting pretty steamed. I kept telling myself, "I'm a Yale graduate. I'm a former Marine Corps officer, with a pretty good record." What didn't occur to me was that I was only thirty-four years old, and there were legions of guys out there who could match my résumé, page for page, three and four times over. Guys who were smart enough to realize from the outset that if you wanted to be appointed to a state position by any governor, it would be advantageous if you at least gave the appearance of being one of his political supporters.

In the end, the fact that I was now a fully certified Democrat cleared the way with Chandler. Pete called me and then came by the farm and said, "Things are now in order." We arbitrarily picked September 1 as the starting date for my appointment as director of driver licensing for the state of Kentucky. I never actually was interviewed for the job.

§

My first week as a state employee coincided with the infamous situation involving school integration in Sturgis, henceforth known as the little town that gave Kentucky a big black eye. And it gave me a huge awakening as to what was going on in our society. Sturgis is in Union County, in Kentucky's western coalfield region. In September 1956, with the assistance of the NAACP, 9 black children had enrolled in Sturgis High School, which had 310 other students, all of them white.

Let me add just a little bit of historical perspective. In 1954, the U.S. Supreme Court had issued its decision in *Brown v. Board of Education of Topeka,* making it unconstitutional for public schools to be segregated. But while the Supreme Court's ruling called for the full integration of schools throughout the country, it allowed for a transitional period of unspecified length. The underlying spirit of the Supreme Court's ruling was for educational jurisdictions and institutions to act quickly, and in many places in Kentucky, the city of Louisville especially, they did. Lawrence Wetherby, who was Kentucky's governor when the *Brown v. Topeka* decision came down, declared, "We will exert every effort" to make public school integration a reality. And after Wetherby left office, Chandler pledged to do the same.

According to the historian David L. Wolford, who has painstakingly researched the subject, within two years of the *Brown v. Topeka* decision, 92 of Kentucky's 160 school districts with biracial populations had integrated enrollments. This was not the case in Sturgis, however. Sturgis was a coal and, to a lesser degree, farming community of about 3,000 citizens, situated 170 miles west of Louisville. Black and white people worked side by side in the coal mines, and they both attended the town's only movie theater. But the blacks sat in the balcony, and the whites sat on the first floor. And although they both used the same public park, the blacks were restricted to one end of it, and the whites used the other.

Black students from Sturgis attended Dunbar Negro High School, which was in Morganfield, eleven miles away. Nobody of African American heritage had ever attended Sturgis High. But in late August 1956, nine black students registered for the upcoming school year. The reasons for their decision to do this were explained in the simplest of terms by the mother of one of the students, who told a *Lexington Herald* reporter, "It's closer, and they don't have to wait for buses. Besides, they can get better classes at Sturgis."

But a significant proportion of the white population in Sturgis was determined that this was not going to happen. On the first day of school, which was September 5, a yelling, shoving crowd of approximately 500 blocked the way of the black students into the building. The crowd was carrying shovels and pitchforks and picket signs that stated such things as, "Niggers, go home or get hurt!" One of the black students said a white man told him, "If you try anything else, we'll put you in a car, and you know what comes next."

Initially, the local police did nothing. That helped inspire Chandler to send in the Kentucky National Guard. Four units from Lexington, Henderson, Livermore, and Owensboro rolled into Sturgis. On the lead, standing atop an M-47 tank, was Major J. J. B. Williams from Somerset. It was one of four tanks that accompanied the units, which bivouacked on the grounds of Sturgis High School.

Meanwhile, Paul Smith, the acting director of the Kentucky State Police, and Don Sturgill, the newly appointed deputy safety commissioner, went down to Sturgis to assist in restoring order. After arriving, they were joined by forty state troopers, who were charged with the responsibility of keeping the roads open. But the State Police command was nowhere near the size of Williams's National Guard contingent, which ultimately numbered 600 National Guardsmen in the town. My job was to stay in Frankfort and man the phones, acting as a conduit of information between Smith and Sturgill and Chandler. The reports I received throughout the next week astonished me.

On September 6, National Guardsmen, equipped with riot guns and fixed bayonets, formed a protective barrier around the black students as they went to class. The hostile crowd had regathered, and people were shouting, "Let's hang them all tonight!" About 100 white students were willing to attend classes, and the crowd vented its anger toward them, too. "Go on back in you nigger lovers! Why don't you go home with those niggers?!"

That night, Smith and Sturgill discussed having the State Police put a protective cordon around Boxtown, which was the black section of Sturgis. But the next morning, a new crisis arose. In the town of Clay, eleven miles southwest of Sturgis, a black mother had attempted to have her ten-year-old son and eight-year-old daughter attend classes at the all-white elementary school. Theirs, like all black families in the Clay region, lived outside the city limits, and the automobile that was carrying them was stopped by a mob of white people and turned back.

By this time, news reporters and segregation proponents were descending on the area. Some of the reporters were being threatened—a group that had ventured into Clay was escorted out of town by men on motorcycles. The segregationists were holding rallies in Sturgis Public Park. A common theme of their rhetoric was, "If the National Guard and State Police don't leave, we will take care of them." Chandler threatened to declare martial law, and segregationist leaders such as Millard Grubbs, who had flown to Sturgis from Louisville, responded that the governor should be impeached.

All the while, I'm relaying the information back and forth—what a way to start a new job! But what was happening, of course, wasn't unique to Kentucky. A week earlier, Tennessee's governor, Frank Clement, had sent National Guardsmen and tanks into the town of Clinton, where attempts to integrate the high school had touched off riots. At about the same time, James E. Folsom, the governor of Alabama, stated that it was "going to take a long, long time" for public school desegregation to come to his state. And the following year, the so-called Little Rock crisis occurred, when Governor Orval Faubus called out the National Guard to prevent nine black students from entering the all-white Central High School. In doing so, he laid down the gauntlet before President Eisenhower, who responded by sending the 101st Airborne Division into Little Rock to ensure that public school integration would take place.

I don't know how many historians would consider Happy Chandler a visionary. But I do believe that when the Sturgis incident occurred, Chandler decided to make not just a local or regional statement but a national statement. He was actually serving his second tenure as Kentucky's governor, having initially taken office in 1935. Sandwiched between Chandler's terms as governor was a six-year stint in the U.S. Senate, a position from which he resigned to become commissioner of Major League Baseball. During Chandler's tenure as baseball commissioner, Jackie Robinson broke the color barrier with the Brooklyn Dodgers.

Chandler was shrewd. He was fifty-eight years old at the time of the situation in Sturgis and probably had aspirations for higher national office than the Senate. I believe he sensed that the civil rights issue was becoming a major political force, and if his record reflected strong support of desegregation, that would make him more attractive to the national leaders of the Democratic Party as well as to the national electorate. He wanted to dramatically show that he did not need to be prodded to enforce public school integration in Sturgis. He suspected the situation would receive national attention, and it did—the *New York Times* and newspapers as far away as London, England, covered the story—and Chandler knew the value of great scenic images, which was undoubtedly a major reason for the presence of the M-47 tanks.

But by the middle of the following week, the situation in Sturgis had calmed. The number of black students attempting to attend classes at Sturgis High School had dwindled to seven, and the angry mobs dwindled down to nothing. The National Guard and State Police pulled out. Kentucky's attorney general, Jo Ferguson, subsequently issued an opinion that the black students were attending Sturgis High illegally because the Supreme Court had given school boards the power to decide how swiftly integration would take place, and it was not the prerogative of black parents (or their sons and daughters) to make the decision themselves. The black students went back to Dunbar. And in September of the following year, Sturgis High was integrated—somewhat grudgingly, but without the presence of the National Guard or State Police.

What happened in Sturgis really changed me—all those reports I kept getting and relaying about the white townspeople yelling at and threatening those black children, some of whom were so frightened their eyes looked the size of Easter eggs. And those black mothers were so courageous, so dedicated, while seeing their children being subjected to the cruelty, the inexcusable, vitriolic hatred, merely because they wanted an equal opportunity for a good education. My entire background was as a member of white society. I had grown up in a white community. There were no black students at Kent School, none at Yale, and very, very few blacks in the Marine Corps (which was hugely different from the makeup of the Corps today). Kent, Yale, and the Marines had all emphasized that whatever you got involved in, it wasn't acceptable to be merely a passive participant—you should strive to make a difference. I came away from my first week working for the state more resolved than ever to be a person who takes stands—in a diplomatic manner, if possible, but I viewed it as critically important for myself and for others to set standards, to stick to them, and to be more sensitive to racial and human rights issues.

§

I think it's fair to say that when I was formally named deputy commissioner of the Kentucky Department of Safety in late March 1957, morale among the State Police was terribly low. The starting pay for troopers was only $179 a month. Their workweek involved six ten-hour days. They had no retirement benefits. The entire statewide force numbered only about 350, spread out over an area that encompassed 40,411 square miles, with a citizenry numbering approximately 1.1 million. Do the math, and you'll see that this worked out to one state policeman for every 115.46 square miles; one state trooper for every 3,143 Kentucky citizens.

During the next seven and a half years, the situation somewhat improved. "Somewhat," of course, wasn't enough. A trooper's professional life was grueling, largely thankless, and definitely devoid of the romanticized adventures depicted on the popular television series of the time, *Highway Patrol*, which had Academy Award winner Broderick Crawford as its star. A trooper I got to know very well, William O'Connell Bradley, was in the mid-1950s the only state policeman assigned to Magoffin County, in the eastern Kentucky coal mining region. There's a town in that county named

Salyersville, which back then, Bradley told me, had a single stoplight, and every Saturday night the local boys would shoot it out. New bulbs would be put in on Monday, which would last until the following Saturday, and then pow! pow! There went the light! It was a rough place, with the main problems being drunks and family squabbles, the latter of which consumed a lot of Bradley's time. "These old boys, miners most of them, would go out drinking, come home and start beating their wives," he said. "I'd have to go in, and get in the middle of a fracas, and haul the old boys off to jail. Half the time, before I made arrests, I had to fight them first. Then the whole family would come to court and testify against me, the wives included."

Don Sturgill, a graduate of Harvard and the University of Kentucky Law School, had become acting safety commissioner in the fall of 1956 and subsequently received a full appointment to the position. During our tenure as a team, Sturgill and I received legislative authorization to improve the strength of the State Police force by 105 uniformed men. The starting salary for cadet troopers was increased to $324 a month and rose to $376 a month once their training was completed. The workweek was reduced from sixty hours to fifty, and a mandatory retirement age of fifty-five was established, with accrued benefits. And a $500,000 State Police Academy and Laboratory was established in Frankfort.

But there remained a lot more to be done when on August 21, 1964, Edward T. "Ned" Breathitt, who was then serving his third year as Kentucky's governor, appointed me director of the Kentucky State Police. Troopers were still underpaid. The agency was still undermanned and underappreciated by the general public. I had a head full of ideas about how the overall situation could be dramatically improved.

To promote public awareness of the role of state troopers, we put up roadside billboards throughout the commonwealth, signs that depicted the smiling image of a trooper, with his patrol car in the background. In big red letters the signs stated, "IT'S MY JOB TO HELP YOU." Some of the billboards also provided the phone numbers of the nearest State Police posts. Others simply informed the public to dial the operator and ask for the Kentucky State Police. This was an attempt to improve relations with the general citizenry and to gain legislative support for more troopers and better pay. The idea was, instead of having a trooper with an outstretched palm that signified, "Stop! You are under arrest!" there was the concept of a trooper with an inverted palm that signified, "I'm here to be a good friend and neighbor." It may seem like a simple, even a simple-minded, thing, but people in every county told us those billboards were great, that they provided them with a deeper appreciation for what the State Police represented.

I also developed what came to be known as the "thin gray line" concept. I coined the phrase in reference to the gray uniforms the state troopers wore and the gray police cruisers (which had formerly been painted blue and white) they were now driving. One of my major goals was to further increase the State Police's manpower. I wanted to have at least one trooper assigned to each of the state's counties. While testifying before a legislative committee in Frankfort, I stated: "The only thing in Kentucky that separates law from lawlessness is the thin gray line." Very few things I've said over the years have had lasting effects. The "thin gray line" is one of the handful of exceptions. I wanted the State Police to catch the public's eye, and I used the "thin gray line" as a means of getting the attention of both the general population and the legislature. In the ensuing weeks, prominent Kentucky newspaper writers such as Sy Ramsey and John Ed Pearce frequently made reference to the phrase. Newscasters on radio and on television picked it up. Ultimately, the legislature gave us funding for 100 additional troopers.

And the effects have continued. In 1982, a decade and a half after I had left the director's position, a magazine called *Thin Gray Line* was created by the Kentucky State Police Professional Association. The first issue included the names and short biographies of the twenty-one troopers who had died in the line of duty during the Kentucky State Police's first thirty-four years of existence. Today, recruiting sites and posters for the Kentucky State Police say, "Join the Thin Gray Line." I don't mind telling you I'm very proud of that.

§

But it did not suffice to promote the State Police as an organization comprised of committed, concerned, dedicated citizens—we had to provide proof. That's one of the reasons why, in 1965, we founded Trooper Island Camp on Dale Hollow Lake, which is near the line that separates Clinton and Cumberland counties in southern Kentucky and extends over the border into Tennessee. The concept was to provide, without fees, a week-long recreational experience for underprivileged boys aged ten to twelve, most of them from urban areas. In doing so, we could dramatically improve the image these boys had of the State Police.

In the early 1960s, the property that was to become Trooper Island was owned by the U.S. Army Corps of Engineers. The state line between Kentucky and Tennessee cut right through the island. One of our State Police officers, Lieutenant John Ed Connors, would go fishing in the area, and he told me, "You know, this might be what we're looking for. This property is unused. It has great potential—the island in the middle of the lake is perfectly situated. The environment would be safe." John deserves a lot of credit for this, for I never would have had the imagination or the foresight to locate the right spot.

It took us several years of pushing paper, making phone calls, and going to Washington, D.C., Frankfort, and Nashville, earnestly politicking federal and state administrators and navigating through the monster bureaucracies of the federal and state governments (as well as the Tennessee Valley Authority), to finally get the property and the right to construct Trooper Island. We got a lot of help from the two U.S. senators representing Kentucky, John Sherman Cooper and Thruston Ballard Morton. Cooper was born and raised in the Somerset area and was a very close friend of Lucy's parents and would visit the farm. Morton was from Louisville and would later become chairman of the board of Churchill Downs. Both senators were Yale graduates. I knew them through the Yale Alumni Club of Kentucky, and having that educational bond among the three of us was an asset. The Corps of Engineers did not sell the land to us; they couldn't do that, and they couldn't just deed it to us either. So they leased it to us for a fee of $1 a year for a term of ninety-nine years.

The plan was for Trooper Island to be a nonprofit charitable corporation, funded entirely by donations from corporations and civic and business groups. The counselors and instructors on the island would be State Police personnel who volunteered their time. The boys would ride down to Trooper Island in State Police cars driven by troopers dressed in plain clothes.

FRIEND, not FOE. That was the image we wanted to instill in the minds of these boys about the State Police.

During its inaugural summer, Trooper Island was pretty much a bare-bones operation. The island had one small building, and tents were set up to house both the kids and the troopers. We had a sewerage problem to solve and almost got closed down because of it. We had to build a water purification plant. But swimming and canoeing instructions were provided. Archery instruction. Boys were taught how to fish. They loved it so much that some of the boys cried when it was time for them to go home. Many would return the following year.

Nowadays, Trooper Island is coeducational. Facilities have nearly doubled. The mission is now in its forty-fifth year of operation. And today there are state troopers patrolling the roads and serving the communities of Kentucky who will tell you that their first contact with the force occurred when they were campers at Trooper Island.

§

One of the things I was also determined to do was establish direct contact between myself and the troopers. If I was driving down the highway and saw a State Police cruiser parked on the side of the road, I would pull over, get out of my car, walk over with an outstretched hand, and tell the man what a great job he was doing. I did this once on Interstate 64 with a trooper named Alvie Dale Fortner, and decades later he told me he "felt nine feet tall that day." Fortner, himself, eventually became director of the State Police and did the same thing when he saw a parked cruiser on the roadside.

Something that needed correcting was the good-old-boy philosophy that existed at many of the State Police posts. I went to posts across the state and met with the troopers, without the command staff being present. I queried the troopers as to what they felt the State Police needed. I asked them, "What do you see as wrong within this particular post?" The troopers talked straightforwardly with me. They told me about the need for more manpower. They told me about the financial hardships caused by what were still inadequate salaries. But what really aggravated them was the preferential treatment certain post commanders gave to their buddies in the field—this was a cause of major morale problems.

I was endeavoring to improve the image and morale of the State Police, identifying them as members of a highly professional yet compassionate organization. At the same time, I was trying to distinguish their image from local law enforcement personnel and sheriffs' departments. One of the ways I sought to do this was with the use of blue emergency lights, instead of red ones, for State Police cruisers. I wanted to infuse in the public's mind that when they saw a blue light flashing, in a pull-over situation or otherwise, it signified that a well-trained and disciplined individual was on the scene and in control. At the time, red lights were used by wreckers, ambulances, school buses, highway department machinery, professional firemen, volunteer firemen, rural letter carriers, public utility vehicles, and local and county police chiefs, sheriffs, and their deputies.

Kentucky law was vague about who could and could not employ emergency red lights, and I was seeking legislation that would approve the blue lights, which would be restricted to usage by the State Police. Blue lights had become standard for the police in some European countries, particularly France, Germany, and Italy. By the mid-1960s, they were also being used by the Florida Highway Patrol and by the city police in Chicago and New Orleans. We had done some tests and discovered that blue lights are more effective than red ones in daylight, have comparable effects at night, and stand out more in foggy and misty conditions, regardless of what time of day it is.

Well, I had a blue-light bill introduced in the legislature. It wasn't any sort of a major measure, and I did not think it would generate any controversy or create any more problems than having the cruisers painted gray. But a few days after the bill was introduced, I received an urgent phone call from Fontaine Banks, who was Governor Breathitt's administrative assistant, telling me to report to the governor's office immediately. Banks said that, at that moment, there were about fifty sheriffs in Breathitt's office demanding that the bill be amended to allow them to use blue lights on their vehicles as well. Banks said, "Look, this bill is not going to go anywhere unless you satisfy the sheriffs' association."

I promptly went over to Breathitt's office. He was rather unhappy with me. He said, "What is all this?"

I told him, "Governor, the whole reason for the blue light is to distinguish our State Police, the dedicated, trained professionals, from the untrained people who tend to fill the ranks of local agencies." I was thinking particularly of sheriffs' department deputies, many of whom were no more than glorified tax collectors. Sheriffs were elected officials, and they appointed their own deputies, whose qualifications often consisted of being a relative or a friend, a friend's relative, or a relative's friend. If they had any training at all, it usually involved being assigned to older officers who took them on patrol for a couple of days and told them whose toes not to step on. This thinking did not endear me to the sheriffs. I did not want to modify the blue-light law and was diametrically opposed to any efforts to do so. But I quickly realized from Breathitt that if I was not willing to make concessions, I would, in effect, be sounding the death knell for the bill. So we had some public hearings. We made a concession to the sheriffs. And we also made one to the Jefferson County Police Department, whose jurisdiction included Louisville.

The legislature passed the measure, and Breathitt signed it into law. Through the years, the blue light did largely become identified with the State Police. Which gave me a partial victory, although not a complete one.

§

On a broiling hot day in September 1965, I received an urgent phone call directly from Governor Breathitt. He had been contacted from Washington, D.C., by Sargent Shriver, who at the time was serving as the first director of the Office of Economic Opportunity, a division of the U.S. Department of Labor. One of Shriver's duties was to administrate the Job Corps, an antipoverty program created the year before for disadvantaged youths and young adults aged sixteen to twenty-four from the inner cities. The purpose of the Job Corps was to provide them with vocational training, the opportunity to earn a GED or high school diploma, and, in the best-case scenario, prepare them for college. The Job Corps was the central program of the War on Poverty, a key component of the Great Society agenda of President Lyndon B. Johnson, who was Shriver's close friend and had appointed him to the Office of Economic Opportunity directorship.

Well, that September morning, Shriver had been informed that a riot was taking place at the Job Corps center located at Camp Breckenridge, which was a former World War II army post in Morganfield, Kentucky. Disorder. Fires. Chaos. The works. Shriver requested that the governor have the Kentucky State Police investigate the situation and report back to him about the severity of the problem. Breathitt, in turn, ordered me to immediately fly down to Camp Breckenridge to assess the situation, restore order, and report back to him.

While I was en route to Morganfield, the governor contacted me on the airplane radio and said that he had talked a second time with Shriver, who informed him that under no circumstances did he want the State Police to enter the camp and restore order among the thousand-plus Job Corps participants who were quartered there. Shriver was locked into the idea that the State Police had a collective storm-trooper mentality, that we would be overzealous and start knocking heads with billy clubs and that sort of thing. The police were not to enter the facility, Breathitt told me, until we were directly authorized to do so by Shriver.

Well, despite these mixed signals from Breathitt and Shriver, I took precautionary action by requesting the State Police posts at both Henderson and Madisonville to dispatch a half dozen troopers, equipped with riot gear, and have them take up a position on the perimeter near the main gate of Breckenridge. As our plane approached the camp, I remained mindful of the instructions not to enter the property, so the only alternative was to observe from the air, circling the area several times at a low altitude. Around we flew, and then around again. I kept searching for erupting flames and billowing smoke, mobs running rampant through the streets, buildings and other property being destroyed. But, much to my amazement, I didn't see any of this. There was a baseball game going on. And some other people were playing golf. The plane circled the area a third time. Nothing.

We landed on an adjacent airstrip and went to the camp's main gate to confer with the State Police officers who had arrived. But they didn't know what was going on. I went back to the plane and radioed the governor that, so far, we had not seen anything out of the ordinary, and he gave me Sargent Shriver's phone number and told me to get in direct communication with him. Cell phones did not exist in 1965, so we had to drive for some distance until we found a public phone booth. I pumped some quarters and dimes into the phone machine and managed to get Shriver on the line. I informed him of what I had found and, more to the point, what I hadn't found, and he replied that he could not believe that my report was accurate. Shriver said that he had been unable to communicate with the camp's authorities because the telephone lines had been cut. I told him I couldn't provide any more detailed information unless and until we were allowed to enter the camp.

As I was talking to him, I kept leaning out of the phone booth to see if any fire or smoke was erupting from the camp or if there were any other indications of disruption and/or destruction. Meanwhile, the operator kept cutting in, telling me I had to put more coins in the phone machine. I had to ask the people with me if they could lend me some change, while at the same time keeping the phone to my ear, with Shriver shouting over and over again that he would not tolerate any aggressive police action or physical abuse of Job Corps participants, and with the operator telling me every minute or so that another 25 cents was needed.

I do have something of a temper, and it began to go from a simmer to a low boil. Shriver went on a diatribe about what he called the "storm-trooper mentality" of police organizations, and I became incensed by his authoritative and dictatorial attitude and his comments implying that we were that type of organization, that because we were the police and because we were from Kentucky, we were racially insensitive to the Job Corps participants, the majority of whom were black. So I fought back. I told him we were a highly professional law enforcement agency with a long history of respecting individual rights. ("Please deposit 25 cents," said the operator.) If the State Police were to go in and restore order, we would do it in an acceptable and appropriate manner. There would be no indiscriminate cracking of heads or stomping on people. (Another 25 cents.) After a pause and more assurances from me, Shriver guardedly gave permission for the State Police to enter the camp.

We found no unruly mobs or major property damage—just a group of about forty Job Corps participants picketing and chanting at the headquarters of the camp director, whose windows had been stoned and broken. True, the director had barricaded himself inside his office. He had been frightened and concerned for his personal safety. But once we arrived, the Job Corps participants were quietly and quickly dispersed and sent to their dormitories without incident. The reasons for this quasi-rebellion turned out to be a six-week bureaucratic delay in processing their paychecks and dissatisfaction with the quality of their living quarters, coupled with the simple fact that the 1960s constituted an era of protest.

As I flew back to Frankfort, the opinion I had of Sargent Shriver was not complimentary. But it dramatically changed a few weeks later when I read an article in the October 15 issue of *Time* magazine. The article described a series of riots and disruptions at Job Corps centers across the nation and the obsessive use of police power to restore order that was prevalent in many of these areas. This article provided me with a much clearer understanding and a deeper appreciation of Shriver's frustration with police in general. And while I had felt personally wounded by his comments as they related to the Kentucky State Police, I could not deny that the excessive brutality he abhorred had taken place in similar situations in other jurisdictions. Through the ensuing years, my respect for Shriver grew, and I came to admire him for his service as U.S. ambassador to France and for his lifelong efforts to improve the quality of life for those less fortunate.

§

Dr. Joe Yokum is, today, the veterinarian for Overbrook Farm. But back when Joe was six years old, my grandfather, James Edward Bassett, and two of my aunts, Katherine Bassett and Frances Lee, lived at 436 Fayette Park, which was in an old enclave off North Broadway in Lexington. Yokum and his family lived on the other side of the street—their house was directly across from the home of J. D. Purcell, which in turn was next to the Widemann home, where lived J. D.'s daughter and her family. Her son, Jeff Widemann, was my closest friend when I was growing up.

During my days with the State Police, I would go there to see Jeff or to call on his mother. Sometimes young Joe would see me come and go. He had been told by his parents about my position with the State Police. To a young boy, that probably left a sizable impression. Well, following my visit one afternoon, Joe and one of his pals, a boy named George Lamason, were walking down the street when they came across a wallet lying on the ground. The boys picked it up and opened it. There, inside the wallet, was my police badge, along with about $20 in cash, which was a fair amount of money to a couple of young kids during the mid-1960s. Befitting their upbringing, the boys turned the wallet over to Joe's father, Tom Yokum, who promptly made arrangements to return it to me. A couple of weeks went by, and both Joe and George had pretty much forgotten about the good deed they had performed. Then, to their surprise, each of them received a large envelope in the mail bearing the seal of the state of Kentucky and marked "Official Business." The envelopes contained certificates naming them honorary colonels in the Kentucky State Police. This was a public relations tool we used to identify people who were good citizens or had performed a heroic act or did some other deed deserving recognition. A certificate would be accompanied by a letter from me stating, "In appreciation for your doing the proper thing as a citizen, we would like to extend the courtesy of issuing you an honorary colonelcy . . . ," and so on. I usually didn't know if the person I was writing to was aged six or sixty.

In this case, to me, it was a simple matter of rewarding a couple of boys for their honesty. To be completely truthful, I do not recollect this specific incident, but Joe does. Years later, he lost his certificate when his home was flooded, but my understanding is that George still has his.

And there is a postscript to this little story. The fact that Joe and George became honorary colonels also put them on a mailing list for a variety of things, including newsletters and invitations to policemen's balls. Joe would have to write a letter back saying, "Thank you very much for the invitation, but by mother says I am too young to attend."

§

Probably the most embarrassing thing that ever happened to me occurred on February 16, 1966, on Old Frankfort Pike in Woodford County. I was midway through my second year as director of the Kentucky State Police and was driving to Frankfort in my unmarked police cruiser. It was 7:15 A.M., the temperature was in the low twenties, and light snow was falling. I observed approximately 100 yards ahead a school bus, which had stopped to pick up a pupil. I slowed down and cautiously approached the school bus. The driver returned the bus's stop sign to its original position and turned off the blinking red lights. I kept slowly approaching the bus, expecting the driver to go forward. But the bus didn't move, so I gradually put more pressure on the brakes—and was dumbfounded to find that there was zero traction with the wheels. Try as I might, pumping the brake pedal again and again, the cruiser only gained momentum. The huge back bumper of the school bus (which was at the cruiser's hood level) loomed closer and closer, and despite my desperate efforts, I crashed into it. Upon impact, I pitched forward, and the hood of the cruiser came backward through the windshield, pushing the steering wheel into my face, hitting my teeth and cutting my lip. (Don't ask me if I had my seat belt on. I don't think I did. Anyway, in those days, seat belts consisted only of a lap belt around your waist. The shoulder harness had not yet come into use.)

What I did not realize until later was that the reason the school bus had not moved, initially, was because the adjacent stream had partially flowed onto the road, creating a sheet of ice, and the driver could not get any traction. Ironically, the impact of the collision provided the necessary push for the school bus to move forward. The bus driver never paused to look back, and to this day, I do not know who he was. But I was left stunned, mortified, embarrassed, shamed with my lip cracked open and bleeding. I was faintly relieved that, as the school bus disappeared into the distance, no one on board had apparently suffered any injuries. I radioed the State Police in Frankfort. "Unit 1 calling post 12. I'm involved in a 1088 [the code for an automobile accident] on Old Frankfort Pike. Please send a unit to investigate."

They radioed back, "Your location, again?"

I told them, "Old Frankfort Pike, Ducker Station, a quarter of a mile from the railroad tracks." They promptly dispatched H. C. Shipp, an old, seasoned trooper who regularly worked Woodford County and the surrounding area. Shipp was sort of a legend. Judges knew him. Constables knew him. Everybody seemed to know him. He was about forty years of age, very commanding and very strict—he believed in enforcing law by the letter. I can recall, both back then and in subsequent years, seeing

Shipp direct traffic at Keeneland's main entrance. There was no stoplight there in those days, and Shipp would direct traffic, east, west, going inbound to Keeneland, going outbound, all by himself. That was no easy chore.

Well, Shipp came to the accident site and got out of his cruiser and said, "Are you all right, Colonel?" I told him, yes, even though my teeth hurt and my mouth was bleeding. And Shipp said, "Well, can you drive this car?" I pointed out that the hood was smashed back into the windshield, but I could probably drive it if I stretched my head out the side window to see. Shipp said, "Why don't we call a wrecker and let me give you a lift to your office?"

So I took Shipp up on his offer, got to the office, and cleaned up. My teeth still hurt. I had gotten the number of the school bus, and I phoned the county's superintendent of schools to make sure no one had been injured and to find out if the driver had filed an accident report. He had not, the superintendent told me, and there had been no visible damage to the bus. I don't think the driver even realized I had hit him.

The next day, I called for a copy of the accident report filed by Shipp. It was delivered to me, and in big red letters across the top of the page Shipp had written the assessment, "APPARENTLY SOBER." I was infuriated. I called Shipp in and said, "Now, you came and investigated the accident. 'Apparently sober!' What's the idea? For God's sake, it was quarter past seven in the morning! Are you trying to embarrass me? I'm already embarrassed enough! The director of the State Police crashing into a school bus! Why did you say that? Why did you put . . . ?"

"Because that's the format we have, Colonel," Shipp said to me. "It comes from the Bureau of Records. It's our responsibility to indicate if and if not alcohol seemed to be involved. This is the easiest, simplest, most direct way of doing it, to put, 'Apparently sober.' So that's what I did."

He was right. And Shipp was following a policy I had helped design. We were involved in a program with the Harvard Medical School pertaining to the investigation of alcohol-related traffic accidents across the United States. Actually, the primary question we were trying to answer was, are suicidal motives involved in certain accidents? Some of them occurred in the bright of day, on safe road surfaces, devoid of heavy traffic. There would be no skid marks, but somehow, someone would nevertheless crash head-on into a concrete abutment. There were seminars I had attended at Harvard Medical School concerning this, and I had been a lecturer at the Harvard School of Police Science. Alcohol and suicidal tendencies can, indeed, be a deadly combination. To assist in evaluating causes of accidents, we had instructed our troopers in Kentucky to write in big, bold letters at the top of their accident reports whether or not someone had been under the influence. These reports were part of the packages we were forwarding to Harvard. Shipp had performed his job correctly.

Fortunately, the news media did not pick up the story of my accident. There may have been something small in the Frankfort newspaper, but nothing beyond that. There was never any question in my mind about doing an accident report. It was bad enough that I had crashed into a school bus. But the failure to report it would have made me a hit-and-run suspect. Imagine if the media hat gotten wind of something like that!

§

It was the practice of the Federal Bureau of Investigation to send out monthly bulletins to law enforcement agencies around the country, and I was aware from my reading of them that J. Edgar Hoover had a long-standing interest in the training of local police. Mr. Hoover had been the director of the FBI since 1924 and was an icon to law enforcement officials across the country. I sent Mr. Hoover a letter outlining the problems we were having in Kentucky and requesting his advice and counsel. I didn't know if I would get any response from him. Somewhat to my surprise, about ten days later, Robert C. Stone, the special agent in charge in Frankfort, called me to advise that Mr. Hoover—his agents always called him "Mr. Hoover," never simply "Hoover," and the same was true for me—would welcome the opportunity to directly discuss Kentucky's situation with me in his office on the fifth floor of the Justice Department building in Washington, D.C.

The appointment was set up for April 5, 1966, at 11:15 A.M. I arrived at the Justice Department shortly before 11 A.M., presented my credentials, and was ushered into a large, semicircular waiting room, where I was welcomed by two black FBI agents who escorted me to a seat. (The reason why I mention their race is because I later learned they were the only African Americans in the bureau at that time.) At 11:12, the agents beckoned me to stand in front of two massive oak doors. At 11:14, the agents opened the doors and escorted me down a long corridor that led to an almost cavernous office. At the rear of the office was a profusion of flags and presidential photographs and a large rectangular desk. Standing erectly at the right of the desk was J. Edgar Hoover. The clock on the wall behind his desk showed it was exactly 11:15. As I approached him, I felt the gaze of Mr. Hoover's dark, penetrating eyes evaluating me with every ponderous and quaking step I was taking. As I approached him, I hesitatingly offered my hand, and much to my relief, he greeted me warmly. We shook hands, and he gestured for me to sit down.

I had been informed by the two agents who had met me that my meeting was to last for fifteen minutes and not a second longer because Mr. Hoover had a heavy appointment schedule that day. I quickly brought up the reason for my visit—the need for his counsel in obtaining federal funds for the training of small, local police departments. He seemed genuinely interested in the progress we had made in improving the Kentucky State Police and in what we wished to do in expanding our training programs for supervisors and troopers alike to help them understand the magnitude and the complex maze of federal legislation emerging from the civil rights era. All the while, though, I was keeping a portion of one eye on the wall clock behind Hoover's desk. The hands on the clock moved to 11:27, then 11:28. At 11:29, I slowly began to stand up. But Mr. Hoover motioned me to remain seated. Our discussion continued. and step by step he gave me advice on how to go about submitting the federal grant proposal for the funds we needed.

Prior to going to Washington, I had done some background research on Mr. Hoover and had found out that he loved Thoroughbred racing. During the meets at Pimlico Race Course in Baltimore, he would reserve a private table every day in the clubhouse. In August of each year, Mr. Hoover would take a vacation trip to Southern California and attend the races at Del Mar. So I approached Alan Brewer, a distinguished equine artist in Lexington, and had him sign two of his prints and presented them to Hoover in appreciation of the time he had allotted me. The prints constituted a modest gift, but Mr. Hoover seemed sincerely moved. He said to me, "Would you do me the pleasure of having a photograph taken as a memento of your visit?" A photographer suddenly appeared and snapped several pictures of Mr. Hoover and me, including one as I presented him with the Brewer prints.

Later that day when I arrived back at my hotel, still in a happy haze over my meeting with Mr. Hoover, there was a message stating a package was awaiting me at the front desk. Inside was a copy of one of the photographs inscribed by Mr. Hoover. It was the sort of thing he did to create a reservoir of goodwill among the stream of law enforcement officials who clamored to see him. Mr. Hoover was a master of public relations. Sadly, some of the revelations that came out in the ensuing years about his professional and personal dealings have lessened his stature.

I cannot say that Mr. Hoover and I became close friends. But I would hear from him again in a letter dated February 6, 1970:

Dear Mr. Bassett:

Special Agent in Charge Baken has advised me that you were recently named President of the Keeneland Association and I want to extend my heartiest congratulations. This is certainly an expression of confidence in your ability and a clear indication of the esteem in which you are held by your associates.

Your friends in the FBI join me in wishing you continued success.

Sincerely yours,

J. Edgar Hoover

Six weeks following my visit with Hoover, I received notification from the officer of the FBI's law enforcement assistance agency that my request for funding of a pilot program to provide training for local police officers was approved. It was a spartan, bare-bones program for one day of training at sixteen Kentucky State Police posts for those local police officers who volunteered to attend. But it soon became obvious that this hastily organized effort lacked the necessary academic structure and legal professionalism that would provide credibility and stimulate interest for police officers. What was needed was a college-level law enforcement educational program, with associate's and baccalaureate degrees and complete academic standing. So I went to Governor Breathitt and said, "You know, we've got an opportunity here to dramatically upgrade the quality of law enforcement. We need to institute a rigorous training program that takes into account the Civil Rights Act of 1964, that makes the police more enlightened in dealing with the minorities within our population. Police officers need to learn to respect individual rights and to treat people from minority groups as the full-fledged citizens they are."

Breathitt said, "Well, fine, what do you want to do?"

I told him, "I want to approach University of Kentucky officials and see if they would embrace the idea of providing a police training curriculum."

I subsequently made direct contact with administrators at several institutions of higher learning in Kentucky, but the results were discouraging. At UK, I went to see Dr. John Oswald (Jack Oswald to his friends), who served as the university's president from 1963 to 1968. But Oswald expressed no interest. I knew he had a lot of other issues on his plate at the time, but still, I was rather astonished at his attitude. Racially motivated riots had been taking place in cities all across the country—in Harlem, Chicago, the Watts section of Los Angeles, Newark, Detroit, Philadelphia, Baltimore, and Memphis.

Television was becoming a major means of conveying the news, and it seemed that almost every evening the national broadcasts at 6:30 contained images of state and local policemen using police dogs and fire hoses to disperse black protesters. And the images that really awoke public sentiment and sympathy—and created enormous resentment toward law enforcement in general—were the ones involving the black children in Birmingham, Alabama. At the same time, the war in Vietnam was at its height, and there was a growing antimilitary movement in many parts of the nation. ROTC buildings were being damaged, in some cases even being torched, on college and university campuses. There was growing domestic discord on many fronts, and I wanted to avoid creating any more of it.

I next approached administrators at the University of Louisville but pretty much got the same reaction from them I had received at UK. The U of L was already the home of the Southern Police Institute, which was a three-month program designed to train not police officers but police supervisors. I again conferred with Governor Breathitt, and he encouraged me to go to Kentucky State College, which was an all-black institution in Frankfort. His rationale was that it would be beneficial for the police to be in an all-black academic environment, for it would demonstrate their willingness to listen, to share and be part of solving the problems of civil rights. But when I discussed this with Kentucky State officials, there was a great deal of reluctance from them, too. They had an inherent suspicion of white policemen, a lack of trust for what we stood for, and felt our motivations might merely be political ones and that we weren't genuinely concerned about the welfare of African Americans. I sensed their feeling of great relief when I departed. But I was far from relieved, because I still had the problem, where do I go with this concept? I kept running into a lingering prejudice among entrenched university faculty members against law enforcement personnel in general and police officers in particular.

We hit a home run, though, with Eastern Kentucky State Teachers

College (EKSTC) in Richmond. A few years earlier, the college's president, Dr. Robert R. Martin, had been very helpful. We had been trying to find a location for a new State Police post in the Richmond area. Our existing post was in an old house in a residential area in West Richmond. With our big antenna on the roof, police radio transmissions kept interfering with people's television sets. They would be watching *The Man from UNCLE* or *The Beverly Hillbillies,* and suddenly they would hear over their TVs, "Unit 444, report to post," or "Unit 444, there's a two-car accident on US 27." People were getting mad at us, so we were looking around for a place to relocate. We had no money.

I went to Dr. Martin and told him our problem. And he provided a solution. Construction on a new football field, Hanger Stadium (named for Arnold Hanger), had recently been completed on the EKSTC campus. Dr. Martin gave us a plot of land about a hundred yards from the stadium for a new post. He thought we could assist with traffic control on football Saturdays, and, of course, we did. It was an unusual arrangement, but it worked for both parties.

By 1965, Dr. Martin and his newly appointed director of research and testing, Dr. John D. Rowlett, had an ambitious and dynamic five-year strategic plan to double educational programs and enrollment and to achieve university status. New programs with the possibility of federal funding were high priorities on their list of goals, and they immediately saw the opportunity that existed with the police training concept. So Dr. Rowlett and I embarked on an intensive campaign to gain support from the EKSTC Board of Regents and the Kentucky Peace Officers Association, which was comprised of police agencies from across the state. We made numerous trips to Washington, D.C., seven or eight of them, presenting our plan to the agencies overseeing the allocation of federal funds, almost getting down on our hands and knees as we made our requests. And finally we obtained our initial funding—$38,844, made possible by the Law Enforcement Assistance Act of 1965, which had been signed by President Lyndon B. Johnson on September 22 of that year.

Two and a half months later, on December 6, the Kentucky Council of Higher Education approved EKSTC's law enforcement degree program. And in February 1966, twenty-three state troopers, thirteen men from county and municipal police forces, and thirteen EKSTC undergraduates who had declared law enforcement as their major field of concentration enrolled in Law Enforcement 101. Officially titled Introduction to Law

Enforcement, it was the first course offered by what, four decades later, has matured into the College of Justice and Safety at Eastern Kentucky University (EKU).

When we started, our facilities consisted of a single classroom. Today, the 59-acre Robert R. Martin Complex at EKU includes the College of Justice and Safety and the Kentucky Department of Criminal Justice Training. There are dozens of buildings, a 350-seat theater, and a fitness training center that is also used for instruction in physical arrests, physical searches, and accident investigations. A 7.03-acre asphalt facility is used for driver and pursuit training, and a 2.58-acre lake and 25- by 60-foot tank are used for aquatic training, rescue training, training for water accident and salvage operations, and the testing of aquatic equipment. There is a firing range, a cafeteria, a library, and a 23,000-square-foot fire and safety laboratory. The whole program has evolved into a model for college-level law enforcement education. It offers fully accredited degrees at the bachelor's and master's degree levels, and a doctoral curriculum is now in the planning stages.

§

In early 1967, Governor Breathitt summoned me to a meeting, during which he said, "While I agree with your efforts to promote the State Police to gain wider public acceptance and legislative approval to increase salaries and manpower, I think you will always be limited until you understand how important it is to be an organization that reflects the entire citizenry of the commonwealth. And as long as the State Police maintains a lily-white identity, conveying the message that blacks are not welcome within the ranks, there will be those who continue to oppose your achieving your goals."

Breathitt was telling me he wanted the Kentucky State Police to be integrated, and I did not offer any resistance. It was something that needed to be done, should be done—indeed, had to be done. During the early and mid-1960s, racial riots had exploded across the country, and the images of all-white police forces using fire hoses and tear gas and guard dogs to subdue black activists, again and again, occupied the front pages of newspapers and constituted the lead stories on national evening newscasts. The criticism that resulted from these situations, not only from the media but also from political leaders and the general public, was voluminous, and for good reason.

I cannot say that our search for a candidate to become Kentucky's first black State Police trooper was as brilliantly done as Branch Rickey's in his quest to integrate major league baseball. The candidate Rickey eventually chose, Jackie Robinson, who began playing for the Brooklyn Dodgers in 1947, had lettered in four major sports at UCLA, was a World War II veteran, and had been a star for the Kansas City Monarchs in the Negro American League before Rickey signed him. In contrast, we really did not know where or how to begin our search. We sent recruiting teams to college campuses. We set up recruiting booths at athletic events and at the State Fair in Louisville. We sought recommendations from community leaders. We conducted intensive background investigations And through these means, we came up with a list of candidates.

But there were other aspects involved. Remember, after a candidate completed his training program at the State Police Academy, it was our policy not to assign him to his home district. And again, in those days, sometimes there was only one state trooper assigned to a given county, which meant the thin gray line consisted of only a single man. Going to a county far removed from one's home area, say in eastern Kentucky, where the overall black population was very minimal, would be a daunting challenge to any trooper who wasn't white.

Salary did not serve as much of an incentive—as I told you before, the starting pay for a recruit back then was still only $324 a month for recruits, and it rose to only $376 a month after the completion of training. Yes, being a state policeman was more prestigious than being on a municipal police force. But in a municipality such as Lexington or Louisville, a black officer could perform his law enforcement duties within an environment that made him much more comfortable.

We finally did select a candidate, Millard West, who was from Lexington. He entered the State Police Academy as a trooper cadet on September 18, 1967. West was twenty-five years old, had completed one semester at Kentucky State College, and was the sole black member of his academy class of thirty. He graduated on January 26 of the following year and, contrary to normal procedures, was assigned to Fayette County. West's tenure with the Kentucky State Police extended through four years and nine months. He left the force on June 26, 1972, because of personal reasons.

§

In the spring of 1967, the Reverend Alfred Daniel Williams King, who was Dr. Martin Luther King Jr.'s brother and pastor of the Zion Baptist Church in Louisville, threatened to disrupt the Kentucky Derby. His group of activists was championing an open housing ordinance in Louisville, and Reverend King believed attention would be drawn to their cause if they could somehow link their activities to the big race. In the months immediately prior to the Derby, they had organized frequent marches in the southern part of Louisville, where Churchill Downs is located. Two weeks before the Derby, nineteen of the marchers had been arrested during a protest in the Churchill Downs parking lot. More dramatically, on the day of the Derby Trial Stakes, which was Tuesday of Derby week, five protesters, all of them young men, had leaped over the grandstand rail and run across the Churchill racing surface as the field of ten horses in the first race neared the midpoint of the stretch run. It was a startling thing to behold, and frightening. The protesters dashed to a point near the sixteenth pole and dived either under or over the inner railing. None of the horses altered course, the outcome of the race wasn't compromised, and, most important, nobody—neither human nor equine—was hurt. The five protesters, along with three others, were arrested by the Louisville police and charged with disturbing the peace, disorderly conduct, and trespassing. Twelve other young men from the group were escorted off the grounds. They had gone through the Churchill turnstiles singing civil rights songs, Al Schem, the track's director of security subsequently said, but no one had anticipated their actions. Reverend King let it be known, though, that what had happened was just a prelude to what he was planning for Derby day.

I promptly got a phone call from Governor Breathitt. He said, "Bassett, I'm giving you a direct order. The Derby must be run. It is our state's showcase. We're on national television. We're going to have 100,000 people coming through the gates at Churchill. The race is a huge economic entity. Tell me what you need, and we'll get it for you."

My reply was, "Well, governor, we'll do everything we can. But first of all, we do not have the power of arrest in Louisville. It's a Class 1 city, and by statute the State Police are denied jurisdiction unless we're invited in. We also have a manpower shortage. We can't station every state policeman we have at the track while ignoring the entirety of the rest of the state. I need some help from the National Guard, if you can get it."

Breathitt said that he would, that it wouldn't be a problem. And he came through on his promise. Arthur Y. Lloyd was the state National Guard's adjutant general. He was married to my wife's aunt (who was also named Lucy). I knew Arthur well. He came into Churchill with 2,000 men. We set up a command post in the infield cupola at Churchill and divided the surrounding area into a clock, with the finish-line pole representing the hour of twelve. At every other hour, one, two, three, four, etc., we set up a tent with one or two State Police officers, fifteen National Guardsmen, and a radio operator. We got a big tractor-trailer cattle truck and stationed it at the tunnel that leads into the Churchill infield at the five-eighths pole. If trouble arose, we were going to herd the troublemakers into the truck. (Today, with the human rights situation the way it is, we wouldn't have gotten far with this part of the plan.) We also set up a closed-circuit video camera to monitor the infield and the grandstand crowd along the stretch. This was the brainchild of Spercell Fayne, who was the State Police's chief photographer. Spercell was a guy who had lied about his age when he was seventeen to get into the Marine Corps and, after serving and being honorably discharged, became an expert in law enforcement surveillance. He had a black Plymouth station wagon and would set up his cameras on the luggage racks on the top, go to the areas where coal strikes and disputes among mountain people were breaking out, and document everything. The footage he gathered often proved very valuable in court.

On the Friday evening before the Derby, Lucy and I attended Marylou Whitney's Derby party. I left early to go home, which was an unusual thing for me to do in those days, but the possibility of a disruption of the state's signature event was crowding out every other thought in my mind. About midnight, I received a call from the Frankfort State Police post, informing me that the Detroit police had contacted them about a tip they had received from a Mafia connection—that the Derby was going to be disrupted by black protesters, who were going to gather in the Churchill Downs infield near the proximity of the starting gate armed with dog-training whistles, intending to blow them in unison and create such havoc that the horses wouldn't load into the gate.

A portion of my brain said, "All right, now we know what to expect." And another portion of my brain asked, "What are we going to do about it?" I didn't know anything about dog-training whistles. Back then, the Kentucky State Police didn't have any police dogs. So I called Dr. Charles Hagyard, the senior member of the Hagyard, Davidson & McGee veterinary clinic. "Dr. Charlie" is what most people called him. He had been a longtime friend of my father and had become a good friend of mine. But remember, it was now around one o'clock in the morning, and I woke him up. I said, "Dr. Charlie, I hate to call you, but I've got a serious problem about the Derby. We've received a very reliable tip from Detroit that the way they're going to stop the Derby is with dog-training whistles . . . to prevent loading at the gate. Uh, . . . does a dog-training whistle affect a horse?"

There was a brief silence on the other end of the line and then Dr. Charlie said, "Ted, I'll be damned if I know. Good night!" And he hung up the phone.

On Derby morning, I left Frankfort about six o'clock and drove down to Churchill. It was foggy. A light rain was falling. By 8:00 A.M., we had everybody and everything ready. If you look at a photograph of the Churchill infield that day, you'll see the series of small tents and all the men in khaki uniforms. At 11:00 A.M., a formal announcement was made by Dr. Martin Luther King Jr. himself that there would be no demonstrations at Churchill. Nonetheless, we decided to remain vigilant. I didn't question Dr. King's integrity, but it was possible that some protesters might go ahead with their plans anyway, even without his support. For me, the most moving part of that whole day occurred just before the Derby horses left the saddling enclosure and went out onto the track. Our men—the 2,000 Guardsmen, 100 state troopers, and 100 Jefferson County policemen—went into position, forming long, shoulder-to-shoulder lines, one state trooper, twelve National Guardsmen, a Jefferson County policemen, another state trooper, twelve more National Guardsmen, and so forth—on both rails for the entirety of the quarter-mile Churchill Downs stretch. No intruders were going to be allowed to get near the horses.

As soon as the men started dressing the lines, the applause began. It was a wave that gathered momentum, section by section, through the grandstand and clubhouse. People knew what we were doing, and they knew why we were doing it, and they were showing their appreciation. My mother-in-law, Elizabeth Sims Gay, was a wonderful lady who was interested in racing but not a great aficionado of the sport. And she didn't particularly like large crowds. She was not feeling well. But because of my involvement as director of the State Police and her brother-in-law's responsibility within the National Guard—and our commitment to keep Churchill open and run the Derby—she was determined to be present and show her confidence in what was being done. Elizabeth Simms Gay was one of the people at Churchill applauding.

Fortunately, nothing happened beyond what was supposed to happen. The Kentucky Derby went off at 4:31 P.M. as scheduled, without incident. The winning horse was a 30–1 shot, Proud Clarion, bred and owned by John W. Galbreath, ridden by Bobby Ussery, and trained by a Kentucky hardboot named Loyd Gentry, who went by the nickname "Boo."

Barney Nagler, a columnist for the *Daily Racing Form*, later noted that he observed only a single sign-carrier all day. The sign stated, "Wallace for President!" Nagler had no idea who the guy carrying the sign was. Neither do I, but I think it is safe to assume he was not a member of the Zion Baptist Church congregation.

§

In early December 1967, I resigned my position as Kentucky State Police director. I did it about a week before the December 12 inauguration of the state's new governor, Louie B. Nunn, who was the first Republican elected to that office in two decades and only the second member of his party to hold the office since the early days of the Great Depression.

The timing of my resignation was not coincidental. Whenever a changing-of-the-guard ceremony takes place in Frankfort, an enormous crowd is on hand to witness it, and the State Police have important responsibilities in regards to security, traffic control, and so on. I was not going to vacate the ship until all the necessary safety measures were in place. Still, I had to understand the political realities of what was occurring. It had been a whole generation since Kentucky had last had a Republican governor. The directorship of the Kentucky State Police was a high-profile job. And while I staunchly supported the provisions of KRS Chapter 16, which restricts any member of the State Police from participating in political activity, I was acutely aware that the director served solely at the pleasure of the governor in office. I was on record as a registered Democrat. I had initially been hired as a state employee by Happy Chandler, a Democrat. I had subsequently served under Bert Combs and Ned Breathitt, both of whom were Democrats. But Nunn was a Republican, and the pressure upon him to appoint one of his supporters director of the State Police was undeniable. My father-in-law was a very prominent Republican too, but I was unwilling to ask him for support. I felt that if I stayed, it should be on account of my record and not because of political influence.

One of the people who influenced my decision to leave was Major Leslie Pyles. He was in charge of field operations for the State Police (and years later would himself become director). While Pyles was a totally dedicated police officer and fearless when a dangerous situation or crisis arose, he was also a humble fellow, very considerate of his fellow man. He visited me at our farm shortly after Nunn's election and was concerned about the future of the State Police and the direction the organization might take. Pyles was subject to a very strict merit system, but he was not worried about his own future. He was more concerned about continuing the momentum the State Police had gained with the public and the legislature. Pyles asked me, "What are your plans?" I told him that, honestly, I did not have any specific plans regarding what I was going to do. He said, "Well, during your eleven years of working for the state, you've had a wonderful ride. You've done a lot to assist the State Police in getting wider public support. Maybe you ought to look elsewhere and start anew, and maximize what talents you have." And, Pyles further said, "Under the new Republican administration, any Democratic appointee occupying a position of major influence is going to be subject to a microscopic examination. This is inevitable. The new people in power will be trying, almost desperately, to find some sort of defect or shortcoming in your job performance that would result in the governor replacing you. In other words, they will be looking for reasons to disapprove of you, rather than reasons to approve or be supportive."

The ironic thing about this, of course, is that although by registration I am a Democrat and by personal philosophy an independent, I have always leaned Republican. In presidential elections, I twice voted for Eisenhower. I voted three times for Richard Nixon. I twice voted for Ronald Reagan. I twice voted for George Herbert Walker Bush, and I twice voted for his son. "Kentucky politics" remains Lucy's two-word explanation for the situation I found myself in, and it pretty well sums things up.

What Pyles said made a very deep impression on me. He and I had worked together very closely and very effectively, and I valued his opinion. His compelling words constituted a motivating factor to cut the cord.

Once the news of my resignation got out, the media people were very kind—to the point of being unduly flattering. John Ed Pearce wrote an editorial for the Louisville *Courier-Journal,* a Democratic-leaning newspaper, that read in part:

The name of Ted Bassett has become synonymous with that of the State Police with good reason, for he has been largely responsible for the status and respect that the troopers have achieved. He has served under [three governors], an indication not only of his ability but of his success in keeping the Police free of politics. He has been able to assure his uniformed men freedom from political placement or promotion, hiring or firing, and it has proved a major factor in the division's consistently high morale.

Under Colonel Bassett's direction, the Police have served in tense strike and racial situations where a wrong move could easily have damaged their reputation and future usefulness, and have emerged with increased public regard. The Division has managed, despite tight budgets and increasing hazards, to attract an unusually high caliber of man into uniform, and the State Police trooper today enjoys a healthy public respect. Every man in uniform has been trained in the latest law-enforcement methods, in mob and riot control and speed driving. They have been kept conversant with all court rulings concerning police and arrests, and required to meet strict physical standards.

An editorial that was published in the December 8 issue of the *Lexington Leader*, a Republican-leaning newspaper, under the headline "Gov. Nunn Should Keep Ted Bassett," read as follows:

State Police Director James E. "Ted" Bassett should not be allowed to resign his office to return to his Woodford County farm and business interests: He is too good a man for the state to lose.

In little more than three years, this 45-year-old ex-Marine has turned our State Police, which he dubbed "the thin gray line," into one of the nation's model forces. Battling against firmly entrenched opposition from the legislature and the voters, Mr. Bassett worked hard for adequate salaries and sufficient manpower to do his job well.

His key role in the successful passage of the motor vehicle inspection program, which starts next month, is but one of many safety programs he has fought for in an effort to cut down highway accidents and deaths in Kentucky.

Throughout his term in appointed office, Ted Bassett has been dedicated to the simple task of making Kentucky State Police the best in the nation. Aggressiveness and discipline which he gained in the Marines have aided him greatly in turning our police force into a team deserving of state pride.

We believe it would be a great mistake for Gov.-Elect Louie B.

Nunn to let Mr. Bassett slip away from his department. Gov. Nunn, who has pledged himself to a government of efficiency, economy and hard work, will have a difficult time finding anyone who can replace Mr. Bassett as director of Kentucky State Police.

We think Gov. Nunn should refuse to accept Mr. Bassett's tentative resignation.

Actually, my resignation was not "tentative." Being director of the State Police was a fascinating experience. But after eleven years in public service, I was interested, truly, in exploring new, totally different opportunities and career paths. About eight weeks after my resignation, Governor Nunn named Lieutenant Colonel William O. Newman to succeed me. He had been my deputy director, and Newman's appointment, I like to think, reflected favorably on the administration of the State Police during my term as director.

Chapter 6

Growth of Keeneland

THROUGH THE YEARS, Keeneland has often been branded as conservative, stodgy, and resistive to change. However, closer observation would reveal that the Keeneland Association is anything but an elephantine organization. Indeed, Keeneland has long been an innovator and views the past as a guidepost rather than a hitching post.

I will provide a couple of examples. In the fall of 1961, Keeneland was the first Thoroughbred track in North America to use a Visumatic timer, a device that posted both the fractional times of races and the final time, automatically, on the infield tote board. In the spring of 1979, Keeneland became the first track in Kentucky, and only the fourth in the country, to use the AmTote 300 Series Totalisator System, which allows patrons to buy and cash pari-mutuel tickets at the same window. And Keeneland has been an innovator in regards to carding races, too. In the fall of 1956, the inaugural running of Keeneland's Spinster Stakes was the first "weight-for-age" event ever carded for fillies and mares in this country. The conditions of the race called for three-year-old fillies to carry 119 pounds, while fillies and mares aged four years old and upward carried 123 pounds.

The Spinster was the brainchild of Hal Price Headley, who back in 1935 had been the first elected president of the Keeneland Association. Headley served in that position for sixteen years and then continued to be a guiding force at Keeneland until his death in 1962. Headley wanted Keeneland to have a major event that focused attention on breeding. He also wanted to provide an opportunity for central Kentucky breeders to race their best fillies and mares before the home crowd. So he created the Spinster.

In 1956, the inaugural Spinster had a purse of $70,400 (which was more than twice what the Blue Grass Stakes offered that year). The race lured a field of fourteen, the maximum number of horses the main oval at Keeneland can accommodate. It was won by a Claiborne Farm homebred, Doubledogdare, who was crowned champion three-year-old filly in North America at the end of the season. At the time, that inaugural Spinster field was arguably the finest group of fillies and mares ever assembled for a race in Kentucky.

During the first twenty-three years it was run, thirteen winners of the Spinster were honored as either champion three-year-old filly or champion handicap mare in North America. One of the Spinster winners who really stands out in my mind is Summer Guest, who at age five, the oldest runner in the field, upset that year's champion handicap mare, Desert Vixen, by a head in 1974. Summer Guest was owned by Paul Mellon and trained by Elliot Burch. The Spinster was the highlight of Keeneland's fall meet, the closing-day feature, and Mellon and Burch were so excited about winning that during the post-race celebration in the Keeneland Library they kept asking to see a replay of the Spinster again and again. Galjour Electronics, which handled our in-house video, accommodated them. And when I was finally able to call the Galjour crew and tell them, "Okay, we're done," they ran a scroll across the screen that said, "Good night, Mr. Mellon, wherever you are."

§

The major imprint that George Alexander Swinebroad left on Keeneland sales remains noticeable today. He was originally from the Lancaster, Kentucky, area, about twenty-five miles due south of Lexington. George began his career as an auctioneer while he was a sophomore at Centre College in Danville. He subsequently took singing lessons to help him with his voice control and his breathing. Before he came to Keeneland, George had spent a quarter century selling tobacco, real estate, purebred cattle, purebred dogs, hogs, sheep, farm machinery, antique furniture, fighting chickens, and mules. He had also sold horses of varying breeds in both the United States and Canada.

George was a protégé of George A. Bain, who from 1890 until his retirement in 1936 was considered America's premier horse auctioneer. Among other accomplishments, Bain sold Man o' War as a yearling for the then-hefty price of $5,000 at Saratoga Springs, New York, in 1918. Swinebroad initially dealt with Standardbred and saddlebred horses and added Thoroughbreds to his repertoire in 1939. He was an auctioneer at the first yearling sale ever held at Keeneland in August 1943, and the following year, he was hired by the newly created Breeders' Sales Company. From that point, George handled auctions at Keeneland until his death in May 1975. During his tenure, he sold eight yearlings that went on to be Kentucky Derby winners. Their names, the prices they sold for, and the years they won the Derby are as follows:

Horse	Sale Price	Year of Derby Win
Hoop Jr.	$10,200	1945
Jet Pilot	$41,000	1947
Dark Star	$6,500	1953
Determine	$12,000	1954
Venetian Way	$10,500	1960
Majestic Prince	$250,000	1969
Dust Commander	$6,500	1970
Canonero II	$1,200	1971

A firm believer in keeping the momentum of a sale going, George was the originator of what has come to be known in the auctioneering world as the "Keeneland chant." A writer for the *Blood-Horse* once described it as "a rhythmic admixture—a little sing-song from the tobacco market, a tad of number-mumble and gavel wrapping from cattle auctions—broken by dramatic pause and interlocutory comments on the inattention of buyers to [the] potential value of 'this yearlin' right hyere.'" The methodology of the chant has remained pretty intact over the years, and for those of you who can make neither hide nor hair of it, I have asked Keeneland's present-day senior auctioneer, Ryan Mahan, to provide us with a sample of it in considerably slowed-down form:

At three million, three million one, three million, you want to bid one, one, two, at three million one, two, at three million one, two, three! Three million three, four! Three million three hundred, anybody bid three million three hundred, how about four? Four! At three million three, three million four, three million five! Three million four hundred, anybody give more than five? Six hundred! Nope! Nope! Six? At three million six, seven! At three million six hundred, anybody give seven, anybody give seven? Eight! Three million eight? At three million seven, three million eight. Now nine! Eight here, you wanna go nine? You wanna go nine! At three million nine. Four million! Three million nine, four. At three million nine, you wanna bid four? You wanna bid four? You wanna bid four? At three million nine. We got four! Four million one. . . .

At times, George was accused of having a quick hammer, which is something that does not please consignors. His attitude was, "You had better get in now, brother, because I'm going to sell this horse." And he possessed tremendous insight regarding a horse's true value. He knew exactly what was standing in the ring in front of him, from the standpoints of both pedigree and conformation. And George knew the pool of potential bidders for a particular horse. His chant could be slow and even soothing, or it could be fast and intense. At his auctioneer's stand, with his cherrywood gavel in hand, he could be polite and personal or curt and dictatorial, whatever he felt the circumstances required.

My good friend, the Hall of Fame trainer Ron McAnally, tells about an incident involving George that I do not myself recall, but I have no doubt that it happened. We were having an auction at Keeneland, and there was a fellow in the crowd who had bid on a lot of the horses. Suddenly, one of the bid spotters yelled to George, "Hey, that man is drunk!" George looked down from his stand and said, "He's drunk?" The bid spotter replied, "Yeah, he's drunk!" So George said, "Throw him out!" The ushers began to lead the fellow up the aisle, and then George said, "Has the guy got any money?" The bid spotter replied, "Yeah!" George said, "Okay, bring him back!" McAnally contends that during auctions, George himself would sometimes turn around to one of his assistants and signal for a scotch or a martini. Auctioneering can be trying work.

By 1969, the year we opened the new sales pavilion, European buyers were participating with more and more frequency at Keeneland auctions, and some of the horses they purchased were winning impressively in England, Ireland, and France. After one of our sales that year, I believe it was the one in July, two prominent horsemen from France, Alec Head and Roland de Chambure, came to see me to complain about George. They said, "We can't understand what your auctioneer is saying. He's going too fast." Now, if you have ever been to a horse auction in Europe or Australia, you know the pace at those venues is considerably slower. Head and de Chambure pointed out that the two premier equine auction houses in England, Tattersalls and Goffs, had boards in their sales pavilions that kept track of bids as they increased. They told me, "At Keeneland, we don't understand where the bidding is. Why don't you display each and every bid you get on the pavilion board?"

Well, the reason was George. He did not want to use the board for running bids; he wanted to use it only for the horses' hip numbers and the final prices for which they sold. So I told Head and his colleague, "Our auctioneer has some reservations about doing that. He's concerned, among other things, about the board's accuracy. But I hear your point. Please allow me to think it over." Then I went to George and told him that foreign buyers were having problems understanding his chant. One of the factors was his accent. I told him, "There is nothing wrong with your accent, George. It's a good southern accent. You're a Kentuckian. But I wish you would speak with these people. They're prominent European horsemen. They purchase horses for Jacques Wertheimer [for whom Head subsequently trained a pair of Prix de l'Arc de Triomphe winners]. I wish, just out of general courtesy, that you would talk to them and . . ."

"All right, Teddy, I'll speak to them," George said. And he did.

Afterward, I asked him, "How did you do?"

George said, "Well, they've got a point. But listen! I know how to run an auction. I'm not going to have some operator handling a bid board who's not keeping up with me. I don't want to have to keep looking back at a board, checking to see if it's accurate."

I said, "No, no, George, that's not the issue. You run the auction exactly as you always have. It won't be your responsibility to check the bid board. It will be the board operator's responsibility to keep up with you. If he makes a mistake, he'll have to back up or change. But you maintain your total attention and focus on what you need to, with confidence, the way you always have."

George said, "All right, I'll try it and see."

The following year, we began recording all bids on the board. George seemed generally comfortable with it. And it has been our practice to do this at Keeneland sales ever since. But it was Head and his colleagues who made an issue of it and forced us to address that issue and thereby helped get the bidding process at Keeneland in tune with the twentieth century.

§

You might be amazed to know that during the past thirty-three years, 587 yearlings have been sold at Keeneland auctions for seven-figure prices or higher. The first was at the 1976 July Selected Yearling Sale—Hip Number 279, a colt by the Triple Crown winner Secretariat out of the multiple stakes-winning mare Charming Alibi. The colt was consigned by Bluegrass Farm, owned by the Texan Nelson Bunker Hunt. At the time, Hunt was rumored to be the wealthiest man in the United States, perhaps in the world.

The buyer was a six-member Canadian syndicate that included brothers Jack, Joe, and Ted Burnett, who owned Blue Meadow Farms near Toronto; one of their business associates, Henry Federer; Dr. Harold Potash, who was a dentist in Toronto; and John Sikura Jr., master of Hill 'n' Dale Farm in Ontario. The price was $1.5 million—more than twice the previous world record of $715,000 that had been paid by Mr. and Mrs. Franklin Groves for a Raise a Native colt consigned by Spendthrift Farm at Keeneland in July 1975. But Hip Number 279 was from Secretariat's first crop, and he was also a half brother to a filly named Dahlia, who had twice been Horse of the Year in England and champion grass runner in North America, and who at the time was the world's leading money-earning race mare.

One of the more fascinating aspects of the situation involving Hip Number 279 involved the "underbidders," those who engaged in battle with the Canadian syndicate in our Keeneland sales pavilion. A least three other syndicates were bidding on the horse. One included the California-based trainer Charlie Whittingham and Thoroughbred owners Aaron U. Jones, Lou Doherty, and Harold Snowden. Another included William S. Farish, who at that time was based in Houston, and race-car driver A. J. Foyt. And a third included a group of investors from Australia headed by Bart Cummings, who is universally acknowledged as the greatest trainer in the history of that country—Cummings has won Australia's greatest race, the Melbourne Cup, twelve times.

The syndicate comprised of Whittingham, Jones, and their partners bid as high as $1 million for Hip Number 279, then bowed out. This happened no more than half a minute into the bidding. In short order, Cummings and his group reached their limit at $1.1 million. That left the Farish-Foyt syndicate to duel with the Canadians. The former raised the bidding to $1.45 million. The latter countered with a bid of $1.5 million. Tom Caldwell, our head auctioneer, said "Yes, sir! That's a million and a half!" And then he raised his gavel. The Farish-Foyt syndicate would go no further. Caldwell brought his gavel down and said, "He's Canadian bound."

And, as it turned out, that is what the group named the colt—Canadian Bound. But he never raced in Canada. At age two, he was sent to France, where he made his career debut in September at the Evry course, finishing second. Canadian Bound did not compete again until the following July, when, at age three, he finished fourth and sixth in a pair of races at Maisons-Laffitte. Later that year, Canadian Bound was returned to the United States, and his training chores were turned over, interestingly, to Whittingham. Canadian Bound went on to make one more start, at age four, in July 1979 at Hollywood Park. As the 2–1 favorite, he finished fourth. He never graduated from maiden company. His career earnings as a racehorse totaled $4,770. He began doing stud duty in 1980, and by 1985, Canadian Bound's live foal fee was down to $1,000.

A little sidelight to this segment of Keeneland history: When bidding got up around the $1.4 million mark that evening in July 1976, I remember Caldwell saying aloud, "How am I doing, George?" The reference was to Swinebroad, who had died the previous year. George had long expressed his desire to be the first auctioneer to sell a million-dollar horse. He and Caldwell had been very close, and Tom always said that his one regret about selling that son of Secretariat, the colt eventually named Canadian Bound, is that George was not there to participate.

§

The first yearling to ever sell for an eight-digit price at Keeneland, or anywhere on the globe, was a colt by Northern Dancer out of a mare named My Bupers. This was Hip Number 308 at the 1983 July Selected Yearling Sale. He was consigned by Crescent Farm, which was owned by a man named Donald T. Johnson, who was originally from Hazard, Kentucky, and was the former owner of the Crescent Coal Company. The bidding duel that ensued was stirring—indeed, almost confrontational—and primarily involved two groups that were gathered in the back of the sales pavilion auditorium, no more than forty feet apart. One group was comprised of Robert Sangster and his colleagues, who included the great Irish trainer Vincent O'Brien and Tom Cooper. All were major partners in the Ireland-based division of the British Bloodstock Agency. The other group was comprised of Sheikh Mohammed bin Rashid al Maktoum and his entourage, which included Colonel Richard Warden, his principal bloodstock adviser.

It was a duel that had been anticipated, by participants and spectators alike, for the two groups had battled each other for top-of-the-line yearlings before. In July 1981 at Keeneland, Sangster and his partners had outbid the sheikh for a $3.5 million colt by Northern Dancer. And in July 1982, they had outbid the sheikh again for a $4.25 million colt by Nijinsky II. Both prices had set new world records for a horse sold at public auction.

Robert Acton was the manager of Sheikh Mohammed's Ashton Upthorpe Stud operation. By happenstance, he was standing next to Sangster and his group when Hip Number 308 was brought into our sales ring. It was reported in the *Blood-Horse* that Acton matter-of-factly said to them, "There's no use in your bidding, actually. We're going to get the colt."

Bidding started at $1 million. Initially, other participants were involved, including a group made up of D. Wayne Lukas and his clients. But by the time the $6 million plateau was reached, it was just Sangster and his partners versus the sheikh. Cooper was handling the bidding for Sangster's group, while Colonel Warden was handling that responsibility for Sheikh Mohammed. The bids rose largely in $100,000 increments. At $8 million, Acton turned to the Sangster group again. "You're never going to beat us," he was quoted as saying by the *Blood-Horse*. "Why try?"

One of the telling memories I have of that duel is that whenever Sheikh Mohammed raised the price, Sangster, O'Brien, and Cooper would pause, huddle, converse, discuss things back and forth, and evaluate their position. But as soon as they bid, the sheikh would immediately nod to Warden to go higher. Otherwise, Sheikh Mohammed's eyes were focused on either the bid spotter or the bid board in what I can best describe as a magnetic glare. His gaze reflected a position of enormous financial strength, and I will never forget it.

There was something else I will never forget, either. When the bidding reached $10 million, all that showed up on our bid board was a line of zeros. This brought a gasp from the people sitting in the pavilion. Was that a bid? Well, no, the problem was that our board only went to seven digits. When Sheikh Mohammed nodded to Warden to go to $10.2 million, it came up on the bid board as $200,000. But Tom Caldwell announced what the sheikh's bid actually was, and Sangster and his partners knew what it meant—there was no sense in engaging in the fight any longer.

Caldwell's hammer came down. "Sold, for $10.2 million!" The sheikh left the auditorium, walked quickly through a large gathering of reporters and photographers without stopping or saying a word, and got into a limousine that was waiting for him outside the pavilion. The limousine took him to his private Boeing 727 that was parked at the end of the runway at Blue Grass Airport across the street. Within half an hour, the sheikh was in flight, headed back to his homeland of Dubai.

Sheikh Mohammed subsequently named the colt Snaafi Dancer. He never raced and was close to being infertile at stud. Of the few horses Snaafi Dancer sired, the best was a filly named Winloc's Dancer. She was sold as a yearling for $20,000 at the 1989 January Horses of All Ages Sale at Keeneland. Winloc's Dancer was victorious in just one of her sixteen career starts and earned purses totaling $5,658.

And as you probably expected, following the 1983 July sale, we had an extra digit placed on our bid board.

§

The auction duel that stands out the most in people's minds, of course, is the one that involved Hip Number 215, a colt by Nijinsky II out of a mare named My Charmer, at the 1985 July Selected Yearling Sale. During his own racing days, Nijinsky II had been Europe's Horse of the Year. My Charmer was the dam of the 1977 Triple Crown winner and Horse of the Year Seattle Slew. Hip Number 215 was consigned by a partnership that included Warner Jones, Will Farish, and William S. Kilroy, and there was a good deal of speculation the colt would sell for another world-record price.

When Hip Number 215 was brought into the sales ring, every seat in the pavilion had an occupant. The press box, situated to the auctioneer's right, was overflowing, and numerous other reporters and photographers were standing in the aisles. The bidding started at $1.25 million, quickly increased by increments of $500,000, and within one minute shot past $8 million—which remains the most rapid ascent in price I have ever seen for any horse at Keeneland or anywhere else for that matter. Once the bidding climbed beyond $9.8 million (which took only about another forty seconds), only two groups remained in the battle. One was comprised of the Europeans Robert Sangster, Vincent O'Brien, John Magnier, and Stavros Niarchos and a California businessman named Danny Schwartz—they, once again, were formally bidding under the name of the British Blood-stock Agency. The other group was comprised of D. Wayne Lukas and a team of his investors, which in this case included Lloyd R. "Bob" French Jr., Eugene V. Klein, and Melvin Hatley.

Sangster and company were doing their bidding from the holding area at the rear of the sales pavilion. This is where the horses are kept just before they are brought into the sales ring, and we have spotters and a board that keeps track of the bids there, too. The Lukas group was sitting in the pavilion's main auditorium—there were five of them, from right to left (from the auctioneer's view), French; Klein's wife, Joyce; Klein; Lukas's wife, Shari; and Lukas (Hatley was not present).

From this point onward, the volume of bidding slowed somewhat, as each group would caucus before deciding to one-up the other. Bidding reached $10 million, then $10.3 million, which broke the old record. Our head auctioneer Caldwell, with a big grin on his face, then said to the crowd, "Oh, ho, ho! You ain't seen nothin' yet."

Lukas later told me that at the $10.5 million point in the bidding, Klein, who was a former owner of the San Diego Chargers football team, turned to him and said, "Wayne, I'm out. This is ridiculous. I'm out of here." Klein was a little hard of hearing, and he said it rather loudly. But the battle continued, with the bidding surpassing $11 million. Lukas, himself, began to get very hesitant. "I was in for a big chunk, and I don't have that kind of wheel base financially," he later said. Regardless, on went the battle, with the bidding reaching $12 million, then $12.5 million.

Something then occurred that I have watched time and again over the years, for Keeneland captured it on videotape. French, who was an oil company owner from Midland, Texas, tore out a page from his sales catalog, wrote something on it, folded it, and passed it to Klein's wife. She unfolded it, read it, and passed it to Klein, who read it, then raised his head in shock and amazement. He then passed the note to Lukas's wife, who in turn passed it to Lukas. What did the note say? I did not ask Lukas that question immediately, for I thought it would be improper. But I finally did query him about it a few years later. He told me that note said, "Go to $15 million!"

Lukas and his group did not, however. He made one final try at getting Hip Number 215 with a $13 million bid. But after Sangster and his partners bid $13.1 million, Lukas had a short conversation with the members of his group, then told Caldwell no when the latter asked if he wanted to try them one more time. Caldwell lifted his gavel, looked at Lukas, and Wayne shook his head. Down came the gavel, concluding a battle that had spanned nearly eight minutes. Those assembled in the auditorium broke into applause. Caldwell congratulated the winning bidders and noted that a representative of the British Bloodstock Agency (Ireland) had signed the sales ticket for the world-record $13.1 million yearling colt. And then Tom did something very unusual—he requested a second round of applause for Lukas and his group. The audience generously complied.

Lukas left his seat and began walking up the aisle. He was thinking to himself, he later told me, "Wow! We really ran the red light! And I was in this thing as a full-blown partner!" And as this was going through his mind, French said to him, "Wayne, why did you give up? We had them on the ropes."

Sangster later said he was surprised that it was an American group bidding against him, that at first he thought his opponents represented other European or Arab interests, specifically the Màktoums. "Most of the best horses bought here go to Europe, and I wouldn't like to see this one in an opposition camp," Sangster said. "I didn't want to see him in Europe taking on our best colts. Wayne Lukas was a very brave bidder. I was surprised a group of Americans were in for that price." (When he considered his actions in retrospect, I think Lukas was more than a little surprised, too.)

But I do think Wayne delivered a message that day. In the years immediately leading up to 1985, bidding on the most expensive yearling colts at Keeneland in July had pretty much been dominated by the Europeans and Arabs. However, Lukas had now shown that his organization had gathered enough strength where he could participate in the fray at the uppermost level.

In 1988, Lukas was the leading buyer (in terms of gross expenditures) at the Keeneland September Sale. When I say "leading buyer," I am really talking about the collective group of clients he represented. Wayne had a very large clientele back then, and he would sign all the sales tickets and then work it out with his clients as to who would pay for which horses. Well, shortly thereafter, I received a letter from Wayne. In it, he stated that in light of his becoming "Keeneland's leading buyer," he had some requests. He said that in regard to future sales, he wanted me to arrange for the Maktoums' jets to be removed from their traditional parking spots at the end of the Blue Grass Airport runway so that the private plane utilized by Wayne and his clients could have the spot. Further, Wayne requested that a stretch limousine be on call to meet him on all occasions he came to Keeneland, and that it be completely air-conditioned and be driven by a man in uniform, preferably one who spoke fluid English. Wayne wanted a private room at Keeneland, where he and his clients could bid on horses, and he wanted "soft, soothing music to be continually piped into the room, because spending millions of dollars on these animals can be very stress-ful." Wayne wanted food in the room, too. "Lump crabmeat would be good," he wrote. "Maybe some lobster. Some hors d'oeuvres, of course. And some of my Texas clients might like some meatballs." He signed the letter, "Sincerely, D. Wayne Lukas." He was joking, and Wayne and I have laughed about that letter ever since.

And, oh yes, how did Hip Number 215, the $13.1 million yearling, fare as a racehorse? Sangster and his partners named him Seattle Dancer. He made five career starts and won two of them—the Derrinstown Stud Derby Trial and the Gallinule Stakes, both of which were run in Ireland. Seattle Dancer's career purse earnings, when converted to U.S. currency, totaled $189,068.

His career at stud was itinerant. Seattle Dancer stood at the North American division of the Coolmore stallion empire, Ashford Stud, and subsequently was moved to Coolmore's main complex in County Tipper-ary, Ireland. In 1995, Seattle Dancer was what is referred to as a "shuttle stallion," as he stood for a full breeding season in the Northern Hemi-sphere and also for a full Southern Hemisphere breeding season in Austra-lia. In 1996, Seattle Dancer was sold to East Stud on the island of Hokkaido in Japan, where he stood until 2003. Then he was sold to a syndicate that transported him to Gestut Auenquelle in Rodinghausen, Germany, where he stood for an annual live foal fee of 6,000 euros. Seattle Dancer was not an outstanding stallion, but he was far from a dud. Pike Place Dancer, who won the 1997 Kentucky Oaks, was one of the thirty-seven stakes winners he sired. Seattle Dancer was twenty-three years old when he died of a heart attack on June 2, 2007.

§

On the morning following the culmination of the 1984 spring meet, Keeneland began installing a turf course. Our fiftieth anniversary was nigh, and we wanted to do something in conjunction with it that would draw attention. We also felt it was time to further diversify our racing program. Keeneland's purse structure had grown to the point where (on a daily distribution basis) it ranked eighth in North America. We also had a very competitive stakes schedule—eight of our stakes bore graded status, and both the spring and fall meets were anchored by grade 1 events, the Blue Grass and the Spinster.

At that point, none of Kentucky's tracks were offering turf racing. We made contact with a Canadian firm, Read, Voorhees and Associates Limited, that had developed a concept involving turf courses built on fifteen inches of sand. The concept provided excellent drainage, and races could still be run on the course when it had rained heavily. The only time a switch to the main track would be necessary is when it snowed, which on rare occasions happens at Keeneland during the early portion of the spring meet, but never in the fall.

Read, Voorhees and Associates had already installed turf courses at Bay Meadows in northern California, Turf Paradise in Arizona, Fair Grounds in New Orleans, and Woodbine in Toronto. Bill Greely and I made a trip to all these tracks. We talked extensively with horse owners and trainers, obtaining their opinions and valuations, and the feedback we received was almost unanimously positive.

Putting a turf course in at Keeneland, though, presented special challenges. Paul Semens, the lead engineer for Read, Voorhees and Associates, had to spend many weeks figuring out how to fit its seven-and-a-half-furlong dimensions inside our one-and-one-sixteenth-mile dirt oval. The latter, itself, had been squeezed in when it was originally installed. Keeneland's infield has many variances in elevation. Also, many years ago, there was an infield lake at Keeneland, adjacent to where the run into the backstretch is located now. There was a deep depression there, and further on (as you moved down the backstretch), there was an undulating slope in the infield, with an eight-foot drop in elevation from front to back.

We were deeply concerned about the viewpoints of jockeys—after all, they were the ones who would ride the course. Lester Piggott, one of the all-time greats from England, came to visit Alice Chandler, who is the daughter of Hal Price Headley, a Keeneland director, and a very prominent central Kentucky breeder. We called Alice and asked her if she would bring Lester over so we could walk around the proposed layout and get his reaction. In the company of Alice, Bill, and me, Lester walked over the course. Fifteen minutes went by, and Lester said nothing. Twenty minutes. Total silence. Twenty-five minutes. We completed our walk, and he still hadn't said anything. I thought, "Oh my, he must have serious doubts about the practicality of what we want to do."

And then Lester Piggott turned his head toward me, and with a wry smile in his Berkshire, England, accent said, "Pyce of cyke." That's all he said. And that was all we needed to hear him say. Lester Piggott had given our proposed turf course his unqualified endorsement.

We allowed the course to root deeply for a year and a half before we used it for racing. The first turf race in Keeneland's history was a one-and-one-sixteenth-mile allowance. It was run on October 5, 1985, the opening day of the fall meet. The winner was a three-year-old filly named Ogama Bay, trained by Joe Bollero. (Many years earlier, Bollero had been a jockey and claimed to have ridden for Al Capone on the Chicago circuit.)

Many of the turf courses in Europe go up and down hills, but this is an unusual concept for a North American course. If you are standing at track level on the clubhouse lawn at Keeneland watching a turf race, the horses and their jockeys, as they're going down the backstretch, seem to briefly disappear. What's happened is that they have gone down the hill. Then they reappear—first the jockeys' caps, then their heads, then the horses' heads, and so on—as they come up the hill. The effect is like seeing a race that's simultaneously being run forward and upward on a moving elevator.

In the years since we constructed Keeneland's course, Manila, Steinlen, Itsallgreektome, Possibly Perfect, Chief Bearhart, Ryafan, Fiji, Perfect Sting, Golden Apples, Intercontinental, and Miesque's Approval have all been honored as North American turf champions. And all eleven of them either won or placed in graded turf stakes at Keeneland.

§

Sunday racing at Keeneland is something that initially required a hard twisting of our arms. We had reservations about it. Well, actually, we approached the idea with what could best be described as overwhelming reluctance. There were heated differences among local religious groups about the appropriateness of racing on the Sabbath. Catholic leaders tended not to mind, but a number of Baptist ministers were appalled.

Prior to 1991, Keeneland conducted live racing on Tuesdays through Saturdays. But Thoroughbred tracks across the nation and throughout the rest of Kentucky had raced on Sundays for years, and we were being pressured by horsemen, patrons, and members of the Kentucky State Racing Commission (which was then chaired by Lyle Robey, a Wallace Wilkinson appointee) to give it a try.

Bill Greely played a huge role in handling this situation. He met face-to-face with several of the most vocal clergymen who opposed Sunday racing, including the Reverend Wayne Smith, who was founder and senior pastor of the Southland Christian Church in Jessamine County, just south of the Lexington city limits. With a Sunday attendance that averaged around 8,000, Southland Christian had the largest congregation of any church in central Kentucky. Dr. Smith had a voice that was heard. Bill promised him that Keeneland would introduce Sunday racing without fanfare. He further promised that we would continue our tradition of not racing on Good Friday, and we would not race on Easter Sunday either.

During the spring meet of 1991, Keeneland eliminated racing on Tuesdays and offered a trio of Sunday cards. Our on-site attendance on Sundays averaged 13,363, and our on-site wagering handles averaged $1.34 million. Those figures were up 48.3 percent and 26.8 percent, respectively, from the ones that had been generated the prior spring on Tuesdays. This was also back when we were first beginning to stick our toes into the simulcasting waters, and with off-site wagering added in, our Sunday handles averaged $1.9 million.

From that point, Sunday racing became a Keeneland staple. It is now our second biggest day of the week, and if you go out on the grandstand apron on a typical Sunday afternoon during the race meet, you will find it jam-packed with families. And to this day, we continue to honor our pledge not to race on Easter Sunday. I will confess, though, that if Good Friday occurs during the race meet, as it does in 2009, we do conduct a live race card.

§

For sixty-one years, Keeneland was the only pari-mutuel racetrack in the world (or at least the only one I was aware of) that did not have a track announcer. When queried about this, the longtime response of management personnel, me included, was that Keeneland wished to feature the beauty of the horse, the spectacle of racing, with emphasis on the sporting nature of the event rather than the commercial and wagering aspects.

One of the founders of the Keeneland Association (it may have been Hal Price Headley) was once quoted as saying that he was turned off by racetrack announcers constantly urging patrons to go to the mutuel windows, reminding them again and again there were only so many minutes to post time, and warning, "Don't be shut out." But the real reason Keeneland did not have a public-address system when it began racing in 1936 is there wasn't enough money left over after land purchase and construction costs to install one. And as the years went on, the absence of a track announcer made Keeneland unique, it created a mystique about the track. The great turf writer Joe Palmer assessed the subject thusly:

With no announcer to prompt them, Keeneland's patrons learned to look for themselves. They began to actually see racing, to pick out colors from a flying, close-packed field, to perceive one rider hug the rail for an opening on the turns, another swing wide to take the "overland," a third pick his way through a scattered field, grazing disaster with every dexterous swerve. They learned to know when the leader was laboring and when he was running under a comfortable hold. They began to distinguish between a horse which was being outrun and another which was being held off the pace. They learned, in short, to appreciate horsemanship in a jockey and performance in a horse. Having learned this, they will continue to go to the races—as long as the races remain good—for the rest of their lives.

Periodically, Keeneland conducted polls among its racetrack patrons. These polls sought reactions and comments involving various aspects of our operation, such as the prices of seats and food, parking, and the quality of the race cards. Sometimes, the issue of not having a track announcer was included in the questionnaire. The response was never overwhelmingly for or against a track announcer—rather, it was always pretty evenly split, never varying more than a few percentage points between the pros and cons. The older, long-standing patrons were used to not hearing a track announcer at Keeneland and tended not to want one. And the younger patrons, particularly those who frequented our grandstand areas, tended to believe a track announcer would be a great addition whose time had arrived.

When we decided to bring in a track announcer in the spring of 1997, the motivating reason was the expansion of simulcasting. By that time, Keeneland was regularly sending its signal to 500 to 600 outlets across the country. Mike Battaglia had for years been providing calls of Keeneland races for our simulcast customers, and we felt it was inconsistent and indefensible not to have race calls on-site. People were now being introduced to racing at the simulcast outlets. They would come to Keeneland expecting to hear race calls, and when they did not, their reaction was a bewildered, "Hey, what's going on?"

Finding a track announcer was another responsibility taken on by Bill Greely. He listened to dozens of tapes from applicants. After interviewing each of the finalists, Bill selected Kurt Becker, who had a substantial background calling harness races. Kurt's father, Carl Becker, is one of the most respected Standardbred announcers in the sport; for many years, he was the voice of the Hambletonian at the DuQuoin State Fair in the family's home state of Illinois. And Kurt had called Thoroughbred races on the Chicago circuit, including a pair of renewals of the Arlington Million. But Kurt had gained his most pronounced acclaim, believe it or not, as a NAS-CAR race caller. He possesses a calm, modulated voice, and we figured that if Kurt could accurately identify NASCAR automobiles going from 150 to 200 miles an hour, he should have no problem accurately calling horses who were traveling a mere 30 to 40 miles an hour.

Kurt has now been calling the races at Keeneland for twelve years. He will spend hours researching the proper pronunciation of the names of horses, their owners, jockeys, and trainers. Kurt does not needlessly embellish race calls; he simply describes what he sees, accurately and authoritatively. He is exactly what we wanted in a track announcer.

§

During the past forty years, Keeneland has spent over $100 million on capital construction and expansion of facilities. And this has been done, I truly believe, without compromising Keeneland's charm and ambience. A major reason for this preservation is that for many decades we dealt with the same firms: the same building designers, Froehlich, Kow and Gong Architects Inc. of Los Angeles, California; the same interior decorating firm, William Hodgins, Inc. of Boston, Massachusetts; the same landscape design firm, Innocenti & Webel of Locust Valley, New York; and the same project management firm, Denham-Blythe Company, which has a major branch in Lexington.

Individuals from these firms—I am talking about immensely talented people such as Morio Kow and Bill Hodgins, George Betsill of Innocenti & Webel, and Larry Hay of Denham-Blythe—were familiar with and respected Keeneland's uniqueness. They did not feel compelled to reinvent the "Keeneland look" every time we undertook a new project. Granted, they did not always voice immediate unanimity. But they always reached a consensus on how to best maintain Keeneland's appearance.

An excellent example of their efforts is the new Keeneland Library. Allow me to incorporate just a touch of historical perspective here. The library at Keeneland has long been a special treasure. It was established in 1939 when Arnold Hanger acquired a 2,300-volume collection of racing-related books from New York attorney Robert James Turnbull. Arnold's concept was to have a library filled with literature of the turf that was accessible to the public. For decades, it was located on the second floor of the administration building. Its holdings kept increasing, and in 1958, Amelia King Buckley, who was the association's first head librarian, wrote a book detailing the entirety of what was on Keeneland shelves. The book was 206 pages long.

As time passed, the holdings of the library continued to expand. Books, magazines, files of newspaper clippings, photographs, and photo negatives. And some of the holdings were a bit beyond the scope of Thoroughbred racing and breeding. I'm about to tell you something only a few people know. The Keeneland Library has one of the largest photographic collections of the heyday of the Ringling Brothers Barnum & Bailey Circus in existence. Here's how this came about: Charles Christian Cook was one of the great racetrack photographers of the first half of the twentieth century. From 1901 to 1951, he took photographs of major racing events and personalities at tracks throughout the eastern United States, the Midwest, and the South. Cook's only hiatus from this occupation was during World War I, when he was a combat photographer. Cook's avocation was photographing Ringling Brothers circus acts. He did this for fourteen years, often traveling from Hialeah during the winter months to take photos at the Ringling Brothers' off-season headquarters in Sarasota, Florida. Many of these photos were preserved on glass plates. When Cook donated his racing collection—prints of photos, negatives, and glass plates—to the Keeneland Library in 1954, he also donated some of his aerial shots of European battlefields. And he donated his collection of circus material as well. All have now been in Keeneland's possession for over half a century.

Hippiater Expertus, which is Latin for "The Well-Trained Horse Doctor," is the oldest book in the library. It was published in Nuremberg, Germany, in 1678. Four inches thick, the book is an encyclopedia of equine medicine and training practices. The text of each half page is written in Latin, next to a corresponding half page written in German. The book further contains detailed illustrations made from wooden engravings, which detail conformation of the horse, proper use of equipment, and battle maneuvers (which are depicted against a detailed background of Renaissance architecture). I do not read either Latin or German, but I can still tell you that *Hippiater Expertus* is a treasure chest of content.

Nine years ago, an agreement was reached for the *Daily Racing Form* to donate its archive to Keeneland. This involved more than a century's worth of bound *Racing Forms* and other materials. Back then, our library contained only 3,300 square feet of floor space. So we decided to build a new, much larger, state-of-the-art library facility.

On July 15, 2002, the new Keeneland Library opened its doors to the public. Its construction and furnishing cost $4.5 million, and it encompasses 15,000 square feet of floor space. It is the permanent home of the *Racing Form* archive, the archive of the *Form's* sister publication the *Morning Telegraph,* and complete collections of such magazines as *Blood-Horse, Thoroughbred Record,* and *Thoroughbred Times.* And it further contains thousands of racing-related books, other magazines, thousands of files of newspaper clippings, thousands of videocassettes, and hundreds of thousands of photographs and negatives—all pertaining to Thoroughbred racing and breeding.

For me, it is always a treat to step through the doors of the Keeneland Library. It was classically designed by Morio Kow, with an entrance featuring the Froehlich arch, which can be found in buildings throughout the Keeneland grounds and was originally designed by Morio's mentor, Arthur Froehlich. The exterior of the library is made of hand-chiseled stone, and the interior includes black walnut cabinetry, hone-finished granite countertops, and paneled cathedral ceilings. In the event of a fire in the rare periodicals room, water would not be used to douse the flames—rather, a system would engage that would force out the oxygen, extinguishing the fire quickly while leaving the periodicals dry and undamaged.

Fully wired for computer access at every work table, the Keeneland Library would be a jewel on any college campus and a prize for any community. And, in accordance with Keeneland's mission and the vision of Arnold Hanger, it remains fully accessible to the general public.

§

Throughout my presidency of the Breeders' Cup, I was frequently criticized for not demonstrating more enthusiasm regarding Keeneland submitting a bid to host the event. I will admit the idea did not interest me very much. It wasn't that I thought Keeneland would fail to provide a beautiful and picturesque venue for the Breeders' Cup. Of course it would. Nor did I believe that Keeneland's staff would be incapable of handling the task. They would have done a wonderful job. But in my view, Keeneland did not have then, and does not have now, the necessary facilities to properly accommodate the public, the horsemen, and the media for the Breeders'

Cup. And I think this should be obvious to anyone who considers the basic requirements of what a host track needs to provide.

First of all, the Breeders' Cup, commencing in 2007, became a two-day event. Pretty much everything that had to be provided on Saturday during the first twenty-three years of the Breeders' Cup now has to be provided on Friday too. The Breeders' Cup requires 20,000 seats for each of those days. And 13,000 of those seats must be for VIPs in prime locations, with dining capabilities. Keeneland's total seating capacity—stadium seats, clubhouse, dining room, corporate boxes, everything combined—is 8,535. To date, the record on-site attendance for a Breeders' Cup Saturday is 80,452, achieved at Churchill Downs in 1998. The lowest on-site attendance figure is 37,246 at Belmont Park in 1995. Currently, the Breeders' Cup has target attendance figures of at least 40,000 for Friday and at least 45,000 for Saturday. But the record attendance for any day at Keeneland is 33,821, which we drew for the 2007 Lexington Stakes. Elementary arithmetic therefore reveals that the smallest crowd for a Breeders' Cup Saturday is still bigger than the largest crowd that has ever attended any race day at Keeneland. And a targeted attendance of 45,000 is nearly 34 percent larger than any gathering Keeneland has ever accommodated.

Further, the Breeders' Cup looks for on-track handles in the proximity of $13 million on Friday and $14.6 million on Saturday. But the record on-track handle at Keeneland, achieved on Blue Grass day in 2005, is $3.6 million. On its biggest days, Keeneland has a maximum of 553 pari-mutuel machines in operation. The Breeders' Cup would require 1,500. And further still, the Breeders' Cup requires a Totalisator operation capable of processing a pari-mutuel handle from all sources of $100 million per day. The prevailing record handle from all sources for a Keeneland card is $19.25 million, achieved on Blue Grass day in 2007.

The Breeders' Cup annually issues 700 to 800 media credentials and requires 275 electronic positions to accommodate the press. Keeneland has a very nice press box, but it has capacity for only about 75 reporters and photographers—and that's if we really jam people in. The Breeders' Cup requires 1,000 preferred parking spaces for its staff, guests, and participating horsemen. But Keeneland's preferred parking area has room for less than 400 automobiles.

Still, the concept of a Breeders' Cup at Keeneland has never been rejected out of hand. It actually dates back over two decades. Shortly after the inaugural running of the event at Hollywood Park, the Breeders' Cup

James Edward Bassett III at age four.

My father,
James Edward Bassett Jr.

My mother,
Jane Brooker Bassett.

Reverend Frederick Herbert Sill, founder and head-master of Kent School.

(Right) That's me on the right, playing center for Kent's varsity basketball team.

(Below) At Yale, I was on the cheerleading squad – I'm third from the right.

(Left) Lighting up during the initial landing in Japan – this photo appeared on the front page of *Stars and Stripes*.
(Below) Lieutenant Bassett—amidst the wreckage of postwar Japan.

(Above) When the Fourth Marines landed at Yokosuka Naval Base, we were greeted by this sign.

(Right) The pose is dramatic, but when I left the Marine Corps following the war I really had no idea what I would do with my life.

Lucy and me as a young married couple.

(Above) Don Sturgill (left) and I watch as Kentucky governor Albert "Happy" Chandler signs a bill for a State Police retirement program into law.
(Below) At age forty-two, I was appointed director of the Kentucky State Police.

(Left) "Protest, yes! Defiance, no! The law will be enforced!"

(Below) Shaking hands with FBI director J. Edgar Hoover at the culmination of our meeting in early April 1966.

With Louis Lee Haggin II, my boss and mentor during my early years at Keeneland.

Major members of the Bassett team at Keeneland—from left to right, Bill Greely, Rogers Beasley, me, Jim Williams, and Stan Jones.

Ronald Reagan was governor of California when he visited Keeneland in the early 1970s.

Walking the proposed layout of the Keeneland turf course with the great English jockey Lester Piggott and Alice Chandler in 1983.

An awkward (but oddly fortuitous) moment—the Aga Khan and I have just dropped the King George VI and Queen Elizabeth Diamond Stakes trophy on my toe.

With Queen Elizabeth II, Lord Porchester (her director of racing) and Lucy during the Queen's visit to Keeneland in October 1984.

Lucy and me, guests of the Queen, on our way from Windsor Castle to the races at Ascot.

site selection team made a trip around the country, checking out the various tracks that might be interested in being future hosts. One of their stops was Keeneland—this occurred in 1985. We met in the directors' room, with Bill Greely, Stan Jones, Jim Williams, and me representing the Keeneland Association. Among the Breeders' Cup team were Michael Letis and Michael Trager, who together headed Sports Marketing Television International Inc., a New York firm the Breeders' Cup had retained. Letis and Trager were very professional. But I received the impression that their presence was basically a courtesy call for the purpose of being polite to central Kentucky breeders.

We quickly became aware of the enormous disruption of "business as normal" that we would be facing, as the Breeders' Cup group outlined one prerequisite after another. In order for Keeneland to host the event, we would have to displace every corporate box holder, clubhouse and grandstand box holder, and longtime patron we have. True, every racetrack that hosts a Breeders' Cup has to deal with this. But at the same time, most of those tracks have the capacities to relocate their regular customers elsewhere. At Keeneland, that was not the case and is not the case. We would have to tell all our box holders, including those with the corporate suites, that for the Breeders' Cup, their regular accommodations would not be available to them. And we would do that because we would have no other choice.

You see, when you host a Breeders' Cup, you cannot expect horsemen—breeders, owners, trainers—along with their guests to venture in from various parts of the world and sit in temporary bleachers adjacent to the backside. You have to put them in a place where they have a good view of the races. This is a fundamental requirement when staging the event. And the same is true for sponsors. For the 2008 Breeders' Cup, they included Grey Goose vodka, Sentient Flight Group, Emirates Airlines, Bessemer Trust, John Deere, and UPS. Dos Equis has become the official beer for the event. Each of the corporations involved will bring 50 to 100 people to the Breeders' Cup. These are VIPs, and they include executives, their spouses, guests, and other business clients. And if you want to host the Breeders' Cup, you have to provide quality space for these people. All of them.

We do have sufficient stabling at Keeneland for a Breeders' Cup. The 57 barns contain 1,951 stalls. On Rice Road we have a quarantine facility, which is something the U.S. Department of Agriculture requires if horses are brought in from overseas. But ours is small; it has only 16 stalls. A much larger one would have to be constructed.

The main track at Keeneland has been widened in recent years, allowing for fields of up to fourteen horses. Keeneland's turf course is wide enough for a field of fourteen at most distances, but not all. And the distances of some of the races would have to be changed. The Breeders' Cup Marathon would probably have to be run at one and five-eighths instead of one and a half miles; the Breeders' Cup (dirt) Mile would have to be run at either 7 furlongs, 184 feet (which is known at Keeneland as the Beard Course) or one and one-sixteenth miles; the Breeders' Cup Turf Sprint would have to be run at five and a half instead of six and a half furlongs; and the Breeders' Cup Filly and Mare Turf would have to be run at one and three-sixteenths instead of one and a quarter miles, and since it would start at the bend of the turn into the stretch, it could only have a field of twelve.

Properly accommodating the media is something that really worries me. We have spent nearly three-quarters of a century fostering Keeneland's image—this pristine jewel located in the bucolic, rolling meadows of central Kentucky. This splendid place where the traditions of the sport are forever to be maintained. And we rely on the media to help us convey this image to the public. We see the press as our partners in the continuation of the Keeneland tradition. But if our press box can only accommodate a small fraction of the working media who would be on hand, what about the remainder? Should we stick them in a tent beyond the first turn, where they will hardly be able to see anything? And what happens if the weather is bad? The possibility that after spending decades building up our reputation at Keeneland within the media, we could put it in jeopardy during the course of one weekend is frightening. I was personally involved as an administrator for nine editions of the Breeders' Cup and have been to nearly twenty of them. The power of the media is a key component to the success of the event. It is absolutely essential to make the members of the press feel welcome and comfortable and to provide them with access to the information they need (the latter is especially true for reporters working on tight deadlines). To me, taking care of the press is as important as the proper handling of VIP seating. General parking is something I don't have any reservations about. Large sections of the 997 acres that now comprise Keeneland are open land, and we have room for 15,000 automobiles. An area about one and a half acres in size would have to be utilized for a television compound—the trucks, satellite senders and receivers, and other equipment involved in broadcasting the event.

Turf Catering has been the concessionaire at Keeneland since the inaugural race meeting in 1936, and I have no reservations about its ability to serve a Breeders' Cup crowd. Mike Wolken and his staff would meet the challenge.

Lodging—in the Lexington area there are over 100 hotels with 10,250 rooms, about 8,400 of which we would deem adequate. We would have to block out just about everything that is available within a twenty-five-mile radius of the city. A Breeders' Cup could not be held at Keeneland on any weekend when the University of Kentucky football team is playing a home game, but that's something that could be worked out with UK.

Getting to Lexington would not be a problem. Blue Grass Airport easily handles the air traffic that our big racing days and September sales generate. Michael Gobb, the airport's former executive director, told me they have twenty corporate jets there at a time. The airport is right across the street from Keeneland. And Lexington is directly connected from the east and west by Interstate 64 and from the north and south by Interstate 75.

Lexington and its surrounding countryside constitute the heart of the Thoroughbred industry. And it is my belief that this community deserves a Breeders' Cup. But it would be a terrible thing for Keeneland to host the event and exclude all our regular, loyal, long-standing patrons. This does not mean the quest to host a Breeders' Cup here should be abandoned. Modestly sized racetracks have done it before. I am thinking particularly of Lone Star Park in Grand Prairie, Texas, a city equidistant between Dallas and Fort Worth. I have either participated in or sat in on dozens of presentations by track management and civic teams about hosting the Breeders' Cup, and Lone Star's was one of the most compelling I ever witnessed. They had an excellent team headed by Corey Johnsen, who was Lone Star's president and general manager. The team further included a representative from the Texas governor's office, the mayor of Grand Prairie, and the heads of the city council and chamber of commerce—a highly impressive group. They came armed with computer modules. Instead of flipping cards or displaying diagrams, they were able to overlay on a big screen where all the temporary facilities would be set up to serve the extra volumes of people. This allowed us to visualize the whole layout. We felt we were actually at Lone Star, seeing the changes getting made.

Lone Star ended up hosting the 2004 Breeders' Cup. Prior to that, the largest crowd the track ever had was 33,805, and the largest on-site handle it had ever generated was $3.13 million. But on Breeders' Cup day, a crowd of 53,717 came through the gates at Lone Star, and they wagered $13.33 million. It could be done. And it was done.

If Keeneland approached the planning of a Breeders' Cup with the same diligence that Lone Star's management did, the event could be hosted in Lexington. Granted, it would not be the Keeneland you are normally used to seeing. There would be an ocean of temporary facilities set up—bleachers, lots of tents, and so on. I am not talking about a NASCAR setup, with facilities looping the entire track. The sales pavilion would have to be utilized, as would the Keene Barn and Entertainment Center. The Keeneland infield is not flat like the one at Churchill Downs; it is hilly. But we do have a tunnel that stretches in there and could construct another one. Part of the infield could be used for patrons. It would be crowded everywhere you went, but large crowds help make racing's major events all the more memorable. The Derby at Churchill. The Preakness at Pimlico. The Travers Stakes at Saratoga.

So then comes the question: Will we eventually see a Breeders' Cup at Keeneland? I do believe that the answer is yes.

Chapter 7

Queen Elizabeth II

THE IDEA OF inviting Her Majesty Queen Elizabeth II to visit central Kentucky was born in the mind of David Hedges, who was Keeneland's representative in England during the 1970s and 1980s. In those days, particularly because so many British horsemen were active at our sales, we felt we had to have a representative over there to advise us on catalog distribution, publicity, and collections.

David saw the proposed visit as a wonderful way to strengthen the ties between the North American and European segments of our industry. The Royal Family has a long heritage of breeding and racing Thoroughbreds. King Charles II, who reigned from 1660 to 1685, is often credited with being the first royal participant in what long ago was dubbed the "Sport of Kings," and the Queen's great-grandfather King Edward VII campaigned the 1909 Epsom Derby winner, Minoru. One can cite numerous other examples of the Royal Family's active participation in racing over the centuries, a task that I think rests best in the hands of British racing historians. I will mention, however, that the Queen's father, King George VI, bred the 1946 English One Thousand Guineas winner, Hypericum.

Now, Hypericum's dam, Feola, was also the mother of a filly named Knight's Daughter, who was sold by Captain Charles Moore, manager of the Royal Stud, to Arthur Boyd "Bull" Hancock shortly before the Queen's coronation. Hancock, whose family owned Claiborne Farm, bred Knight's Daughter to Princequillo, and the resulting foal was Round Table, who set or equaled sixteen track and course records during his racing career and is universally considered one of the all-time greats in North American racing.

When George VI died in 1952, Queen Elizabeth II ascended to the throne already possessing a special love for the sport, and she has been an active racing participant ever since. In the mid-1980s, she had some mares at John W. Galbreath's Darby Dan Farm, and David Hedges envisioned a royal visit where she would tour our major stud farms and see the top stallions and, indeed, arrange for some of her mares to be bred to them. The Queen could also spend an afternoon at Keeneland enjoying the races. David was more than enthusiastic—he implored us to understand how important this all could be.

Of course, we didn't need any arm twisting. Will Farish III, who is an heir to the family that founded Humble Oil and a longtime director at Keeneland, had met the Queen before at a polo match in England. We asked Will to contact Lord Porchester, who is the Queen's racing manager in England, and the initial details began to be worked out. A visit by the Queen, especially to a foreign country, is not something that can be arranged within weeks. It took about a year before everything was in place. Will and his wife, Sarah, very graciously offered to host the Queen at their Lane's End Farm in Versailles. Obviously, it's a unique honor to have the reigning monarch of the British Empire as a houseguest. But from the moment the plan to do so becomes publicly known, your privacy ends. Reporters from all over the world will deluge you, day and night, with questions about her stay and your background.

It was to be the Queen's sixth visit to the United States but her first ever to our Bluegrass State, and her afternoon at Keeneland was to be her first time at a racetrack in this country. Six or seven weeks before her visit, the British Secret Service came to see us and explain the procedures of her visit and to work out such plans as where she would dine and where the trophy presentation would take place for the race we were inaugurating in her honor, the Queen Elizabeth II Challenge Cup Stakes. Back then at Keeneland, we did not have a winner's circle. For regular races, we'd simply have the clerk of scales draw a chalk circle on the track surface, and the brief congratulatory ceremony would take place there. But after a stakes race was run, people were to walk across the track for the trophy presentation, and it didn't matter whether rain, snow, or sleet was falling or how thick or gooey the track surface was. If you were the winning owner or trainer or had been invited to make the trophy presentation, you had to walk across, even if it meant wading through a swamp.

Well, the British and U.S. Secret Service, not surprisingly, suggested to us that it wouldn't really be appropriate for the Queen to do something like this and said that, for a number of reasons involving security and so forth, they'd prefer to have her present the trophy on the grandstand side. And this is why we finally, in Keeneland's forty-ninth year of existence, constructed a winner's circle. We did it so Queen Elizabeth II would have the proper setting to present the trophy for the stakes race that was named in her honor.

The Queen arrived at Keeneland at 12:35 P.M. on Thursday, October 11, 1984, the fourth day of our fall meeting. Her motorcade was escorted by state and urban county police. If you add together all these officers and Secret Service people assigned together, the total would come to about 100. Keeneland's general manager Bill Greely; his wife, Norma; and Lucy and I were standing at the clubhouse entrance to meet and welcome her, and I felt as stiff and rigid as a board. I can still see in my mind's eye the Queen getting out of the car—she was accompanied by the Farishes—and my thoughts kept repeating the very polite but strict instructions the British Secret Service had given us regarding appropriate protocol.

You were not to offer your hand in greeting but had to wait until the Queen extended hers and then, but not until then, were you to extend yours in turn. You were never, never to reach. And otherwise, you were never, ever to touch her. In 1992, the American trainer Ron McAnally brought a horse named Dr. Devious to Epsom Downs and won the Epsom Derby with him. In the winner's circle, McAnally was so excited that he put his arm around the Queen Mother, which inspired the headline in several British newspapers, "KING-SIZED GAFFE!" McAnally's wife, Debbie, said she was as shocked as anybody when she saw her husband do this.

When escorting the Queen, we were told, you were always to walk to her right. The address "Your Majesty" is used only for formal occasions. Her formal title is actually "Elizabeth II, by the Grace of God of the United Kingdom of Great Britain and Northern Ireland and Her other Realms and Territories Queen, Head of the Commonwealth, Defender of the Faith," but by the time you got all that out, half the day would be over.

The Queen does have a sense of humor, and one of the stories I've always enjoyed involves those highly unusual occurrences when one of her subjects inadvertently penetrated her ring of security, came face-to-face with her, stuttered and stammered and ultimately said, "You look awfully like the Queen." She quickly responded, "That's reassuring." Nothing like that exchange, however, was going to occur at Keeneland. We were instructed to respond to her observations and questions with "Yes ma'am" and "No ma'am." Everything was to be done in a low-key, subtle, dignified way. The Greelys and Lucy and I had memorized these instructions, and I kept repeating them in my head.

We welcomed the Queen and walked into the clubhouse by way of a pathway that had been set up with velvet rope. All our directors and their spouses and children were there to see the Queen. We went through the lobby and from there to the paddock outside. It was the shortest route and, therefore, in line with Secret Service concerns, the best one. It was one of those Indian summer days with bright skies, warm temperatures, and gentle breezes. Absolutely perfect. The afternoon at Keeneland had been designated the Queen's only public appearance during her six-day stay, and the crowd numbered 12,666. Among them was a little girl who suddenly ducked under the ropes and walked up to the Queen and extended a small spray of mums as a gift. I didn't know this at the time, but this gesture is rather a usual circumstance at public gatherings for the Queen, for a child to approach her with a bouquet. But in this case, it was totally unrehearsed, totally unexpected, one of those things that selects its own little place in your memory and will forever reside there. The Queen smiled and stopped and leaned over to accept the flowers and spoke to the little girl. That unforgettable moment humanized everything; it allowed everyone to relax.

From the paddock, we were to go through the clubhouse to the Lexington Room for a luncheon in the Queen's honor. As we passed the crowd, people, one after another after another, spontaneously began applauding. This happened with every step we took. There were small children sitting on the shoulders of their parents, and many of them were waving little British flags. I found out later that many of the parents were British born, had married American citizens, had relocated to this country, and had journeyed in from Atlanta, from Chicago, from cities throughout the South and the Midwest. At Keeneland, we hadn't distributed the little British flags, but these people had brought them on their own, hundreds or maybe even thousands of them. (Keeneland, as you can surely understand, had a much larger representation of the Union Jack flying from a flagpole in the infield.) Some of them called out, "God save the Queen," and I think a few of them even started singing the song that bears that name.

At the luncheon, Lucy and I sat with the Queen. Our table also included the great banking magnate, horse breeder, and art collector Paul Mellon, who was a friend of hers, and Keeneland trustees W. C. Smith and Charlie Nuckols Jr. The Queen was on my immediate right, and on her immediate right was Charlie, and at one point during the luncheon, when there was a lull in the conversation, I leaned over and said to Nuckols, "Charlie, did you ever think that two old rednecks from Woodford County would ever be sitting next to the Queen of England?" The Queen chuckled, but Charlie wasn't quite so amused and replied, "Speak for yourself, Ted."

Keeneland scheduled eight races per day back then, and the Queen Elizabeth II Challenge Cup Stakes was the fourth event that afternoon. It was a newly created race—we didn't take a stakes that we had been offering for years and merely rename it. And the exact name we gave the race was Lord Porchester's idea. We could have simply called it the Queen Elizabeth II Stakes, but there were already several of those around the globe. There's a race bearing that name that's run in England each year, and there's also one that is run every April at Sha Tin Race Course in Hong Kong (keep in mind that Hong Kong was a British colony until 1997, and there is still a very strong British influence there).

Anyhow, we thought the name Queen Elizabeth II Challenge Cup had a powerful resonance—its name alone would provide notice it's something special. The inaugural running had a $75,000-added purse, along with a $25,000 supplement from Breeders' Cup Limited (to be awarded to finishers in the top four places who were Breeders' Cup eligible), which was substantial in those days, and it was carded for three-year-old fillies at one and one-sixteenth miles on the main track (our turf course would not be ready for use for another year). We dearly wanted a big field to go postward, and that's what we got—twelve fillies, ranging from the odds-on 3–5 favorite Sintra to the 229–1 long shot You Darling You.

Prior to the race, the participating jockeys, standing in perfect straight-line formation, with their riding caps removed, were introduced to the Queen. They had been carefully advised as to the proper protocol as well. The Queen watched the race from the big window in the Lexington Room that overlooks the track. As we had hoped, it was a terrific contest, with Sintra, who was ridden by Keith Allen, staying in the middle of the pack early on, making a huge move on the far turn, taking the lead in the final furlong, and then holding off the gate charge of the 7–2 second choice Solar Halo, who had Pat Day aboard, to win by a nose.

Keeneland had all intentions of providing a fine trophy to commemorate the race, but we were informed that this was something the Queen wanted to do herself. The trophy she had brought was a beautiful silver cup of Georgian design from the English jeweler Asprey's of London, appropriately engraved, and we've continued to use it each year—engraving the name of the winning horse upon it with each running of the Queen Elizabeth II Challenge Cup. Sintra was co-owned by Bill Lickle and Seth

Hancock's Cherry Valley Farm, where the filly had also been bred. They were the first recipients of the trophy. Keith Allen was asked by the Queen in the winner's circle if he enjoyed riding at Keeneland, and Allen replied, "Oh, I do, ma'am," and didn't elaborate beyond that. Allen, a boy from Beaumont, Texas, was only nineteen at the time, and there's no way I can fault him for being a bit tongue-tied.

From the winner's circle, we walked down to the sales pavilion. We had been told that the Queen had read a great deal about our sales and wanted to see one in operation. Well, we sold yearlings in July and September and breeding stock in November and January, but unfortunately, Keeneland only raced in April and October. So we put on a mock sale, had the auctioneers and bid spotters go through their actions, with the bids flashing up on the sales board and Tom Caldwell doing the Keeneland auctioneer's chant that George Swineboard had originally developed. We also decided to add some historical context to the mock sale, re-creating the auctioning of Sir Ivor, who sold for what was then a record price of $42,000 at Keeneland in 1966; The Minstrel, who sold for $200,000 in 1975; Storm Bird, who fetched $1 million in 1979; Sharif Dancer, who sold for $3.3 million in 1981; and Snaafi Dancer, who brought what was then the all-time record for a yearling of $10.2 million in 1983. To play the equine parts, we recruited five horses that Carl Nafzger was training at Keeneland: Kamino Princely, Kamino Shine, My Earl, Real Handsome, and Sunshine Today. If you look at Kamino Princely's career race record, you'll see that he made twenty career starts, won three of them, came in second once and third three times, and earned purses totaling $37,570. But for one brief period on the afternoon the Queen was here, Kamino Princely was a $10.2 million horse.

Afterward, we walked down to the stable area and went through two or three of the barns, and the Queen stopped and spoke to some of the trainers and grooms. A few days earlier, one of the horses trained by Nafzger, Star Choice, had equaled the Keeneland track record for one and one-eighth miles—a time of 1:47⅖ when winning the Fayette Handicap—and the Queen took a particular interest in seeing him. Carl also brought out a filly named Mr. T's Tune, who had run third in the Queen Elizabeth II Challenge Cup and was still wearing the gold tassels her groom had put in her mane to celebrate the occasion. We went to the barn of Harvey Vanier, who the previous year had trained the Blue Grass Stakes winner Play Fellow, a colt whose name was familiar to the Queen.

Then we went back to the sales pavilion, and we had the entire Keeneland staff lined up, all the men and the women, the engines who make the place go, and the Queen went by and spoke to each one of them. One of her assistants presented Bill Greely and me with autographed photographs of the Queen in beautiful frames. Her motorcade picked her up in front of the pavilion, and she departed, I think, sometime after four o'clock. It was the final full day of her Kentucky trip, and the Farishes were hosting a farewell party for her that evening.

Within a day or so, Lucy and I received a note from Philip Moore, the Queen's private secretary, and the first two paragraphs read as follows:

As soon as The Queen returned to Lane's End . . . Her Majesty instructed me to write to you to say how very greatly she had enjoyed her day at Keeneland. The Queen is most grateful for your kind hospitality and for enabling her both to see the racing at Keeneland and also the remarkable sales complex. Her Majesty had heard so much about Keeneland over the years and it was a great pleasure for her finally to be able to see for herself that Keeneland more than warranted its reputation.

The lunch was excellent and The Queen was particularly pleased to have the opportunity of meeting so many people involved in racing in Kentucky. The Mock Auction was a new and fascinating experience for Her Majesty and was beautifully staged. I should be grateful if you would Convey The Queen's appreciation to Mr. Greely and all the staff at Keeneland who did so much to ensure the success of her visit.

The note went on to tell of the Queen's delight at receiving a watercolor by the equine artist Jenness Cortess and a print by Peter Williams of Secreto winning the Epsom Derby. You might want to ask Williams about this sometime—to this day you can find him most afternoons during the race meets in the Keeneland paddock, working on his paintings underneath the sycamore tree.

And for me, the Queen's visit was a wonderful, fascinating occasion, and we felt so privileged and proud that she would come to Keeneland.

§

In the spring of the following year, Lucy and I received a communication from Buckingham Palace inviting us to have lunch with the Queen on a Thursday afternoon at Windsor Castle. Following lunch, the communication stated, the Queen and her guests would attend the Ascot Gold Cup, one of England's premier and most historic races, at the Ascot Heath racecourse (popularly known as Royal Ascot) at Berkshire in Surrey County.

Notice how I've phrased this—we "received a communication from Buckingham Palace." You see, the Queen rarely, if ever, writes anyone directly, never invites anyone directly. That duty is always, invariably left to her private secretary or others who attend and assist her. The initial letter will read, "Her Majesty has commanded me to extend to you an invitation to attend lunch. . . ." It comes by mail. Later, when arriving at your hotel in England, there will be another, more formal invitation awaiting you, with a wax seal on the envelope that bears the Queen's royal crest. This one informs you of the time and place of the royal function you'll be attending and provides a telephone number to call if you have any questions or need further instructions.

Lucy and I arrived on Monday and checked into Claridge's, which is on Brook Street in the Mayfair section of London, a short stroll from Hyde Park. One of the first things I did was go to Moss Brothers, a tailoring firm with a rental history that dates back to 1851, to be measured for my top hat and morning coat. One may have grand visions beforehand what this is going to be like, but it turned out to be sort of an assembly line, so many men were there for the same purpose.

Thursday came, and Lucy and I were advised to allow an hour and fifteen to an hour and thirty minutes to go from Claridge's to Windsor Castle. It was the first time I had ever worn a top hat and morning coat, and going down in the hotel elevator, I felt foolish to the point of ridiculous, thinking how silly I must have looked. But when I got to the lobby of Claridge's and saw all the other male guests dressed the same way I was, my self-consciousness eased.

We departed the hotel by limousine at 10:15 A.M., and it was eye-catching during the journey up and down the streets, watching the people getting into limos and taxis, the men all wearing top hats, their elegantly dressed ladies carrying parasols. I felt like I was a character in *My Fair Lady* and half expected to see Rex Harrison suddenly materialize, dressed to the nines and on his way to races, just like in the play and movie.

Then we got into a serious traffic jam. Our limousine slowed to a walk. Then the walk slowed to a crawl. And subsequently to something even slower than a crawl. In the distance, the tower of Windsor Castle came into view. And at that moment, our limousine came to a halt. I could see by the great Windsor Castle clock that it was fast approaching noon. Our invitation had told us our arrival should be precisely at 12:15. We were half a mile from the Windsor main entrance, with the hands of the that huge clock inching along, and with the limo inching along, and I was about to have a heart attack.

Lucy turned to me and said, "Do you have that invitation?"

I said, "Yes," and handed it to her. She read it and abruptly opened the rear passenger door of the limousine and stepped out. Half bewildered and half panicky, I said, "Where are you going?"

She replied, "Please, just sit there."

So I sat in the back of the limousine and watched her stalk up to the head of the traffic jam, where there was a British bobby directing traffic. I leaned out the window to look and saw Lucy having a conversation with him. The bobby, very erect, was looking at her in an austere manner. She showed him the invitation, he looked at it, and then he quickly put his hand up, with his palm at a ninety-degree angle, stopping all the other cars and trucks and at the same time waving and beckoning with his other hand toward our driver and me. Our driver looked out the window and said, "What does he want us to do?"

I replied, "I don't know." At that point, Lucy began to wave us on.

We pulled out of the traffic, Lucy got back in, and the bobby, with an impressive flourish, directed our limousine onto the wide, broad, pedestrian passageway to Windsor Castle. It is called the Long Walk. There are signs stating, "No Vehicles Permitted Beyond This Point." The Long Walk is about fifty yards wide, and its surface is composed of pebbles, which made the limousine bounce up and down—with me, mind you, adorned with my top hat. I was very apprehensive as our limousine ride neared its completion. I kept thinking that some sort of security team, maybe even James Bond himself, was going to emerge from the trees lining the passageway to stop us. But on we went, uninterrupted, until we reached the main entrance of Windsor Castle, where we were met by two men in livery uniforms. We showed them the invitation, and they said, "Welcome."

When we started to ascend the circular stairs at Windsor Castle, the clock stood at 12:14. Lucy and I entered a room and immediately saw two people we knew, Will and Sarah Farish. But as we looked around, it was like we had been transported to Madame Tousseau's Wax Museum. Familiar faces, yes, but not ones we ever expected to see in real life. There was Prince Philip, Duke of Edinburgh, Earl of Merioneth, and Baron

Greenwich. There was Prince Charles, the Prince of Wales, successor to the royal throne. There was Princess Diana. There was the Queen Mother. Lucy and I were given glasses of white wine. The Duke of York and Sarah Ferguson arrived ten minutes later, complaining about being held up because of a terrible traffic jam. I guess they did not have the fortune of encountering the same bobby that Lucy did.

Soon afterward, the Queen entered the room, offered her welcome, and chatted briefly with everyone. Then we all sat down to eat at a round table set for eighteen. I was seated immediately to the Queen's right, at the place of honor, between her and the Queen Mother. Lucy was sitting directly across the table on Prince Philip's right. My self-consciousness, though, was threatening to overwhelm my brain. I kept fearing I was going to pull some awful gaffe, something that would induce silence and stares from the assembled guests and maybe even make its way into the London newspaper gossip columns under the headline: "Kentuckian Displays His Backwoods Traits at Royal Gathering."

Well, there were four waiters in livery outfits serving us. The Queen, of course, was served first. One of the waiters was carrying a golden tray with four small fish fillets. He offered to serve the Queen, but she declined. He then turned to me, and I had a sudden premonition that a blunder of catastrophic proportions was about to unfold. I sat there, my hands on the fork and the serving spoon, frozen into indecision—should I take one of the fillets or two? I know this may sound slightly ridiculous, but here I was, the Queen to my left, the Queen Mother to my right, and I'm paralyzed, almost on the verge of collapsing from embarrassment. I looked across the table and saw another of the waiters serving Lucy. I saw her take one fish fillet, so I took one. Relief flooded over me, but I'll never forget how awkward I felt at that moment.

Overall, the luncheon was lovely. Afterward, we walked out into the Windsor Castle courtyard, where there awaited a fleet of old but very elegant Rolls-Royces, all beautifully conditioned and painted, with high roofs. There were ten of them, each driven by a livery-costumed chauffeur. The Queen, Prince Philip, the Queen Mother, and one of the guests were in the lead car. The Farishes, who were staying at Windsor Castle, were in the second car. Prince Charles and Princess Diana were in the third car. Lucy and I were in the fifth car, with Sarah Ferguson and Lady Fairhaven, who was the wife of the senior steward of the British Jockey Club.

The trip took about twenty-five minutes, and we rode down the tree-shrouded lane that leads from Windsor Castle, and then down the little rural roads that were crowded with people on both sides, waving to the Queen as she went by. We arrived at Ascot at the head of the one-mile stretch run, disembarked from the Rolls-Royces, and were led to the carriages in which we would complete the trip. There would be four people to a carriage, and each was to be drawn by four beautifully matched coachmen's horses, with a livery-costumed coachman riding the lead horse, and another elaborately attired coachman with a top hat sitting directly behind the passengers. We were in the fifth carriage.

Way in the distance, a mile away, I could see the magnificent Ascot grandstand. As the carriages moved on, the crowds lining both sides of the track began cheering and waving to the Queen. Lady Fairhaven said to me, "Mr. Bassett, I suggest that you wave and show some sign of recognition to the people who are lining the Ascot course." So I gave this little, timid, subtle wave of the hand. It wasn't anything even vaguely resembling a grand gesture. We went along about another hundred yards, and Lady Fairhaven said to me, "Mr. Bassett, I suggest you take off your hat, for they are playing our national anthem." I looked up at the carriages ahead of ours, and Prince Philip and Will Farish and the other men had removed their top hats from their heads. But I could barely hear the anthem; there was just a faint sound from the orchestra, which was still a good half mile in the distance. We went on a little farther and Lady Fairhaven said, "You may put your top hat back on Mr. Bassett." I had not been aware that the orchestra had stopped playing.

In a sense, I felt like I was again a student back at Kent School, with the stern headmaster saying, "Bassett, you may do this. Bassett, you may to that." But protocol is taken very seriously in England, and I wasn't about to be the redneck from Kentucky who had his own idea or agenda as to what constituted proper behavior.

Arriving at the grandstand, the carriages took us to the Royal Enclosure, and we got out and went to the Royal Box. I had been in there once before, at a time when Ascot was not running and an English friend had arranged for me to get a tour. The Royal Box is beautiful, right on the finish line, with a terrific view of the entire racecourse, which has right-hand turns and is exactly 1 mile, 6 furlongs, and 148 yards in length. The opening half of the course is almost entirely downhill, and the major portion of the closing half requires horses to go uphill. It's about as demanding a course as you'll ever see. In the mid-1980s, the four-day Royal Race Meet at Ascot generated a cumulative attendance as high as 183,000, which worked out to nearly 46,000 people per day, topped in North America only by the crowds that came to Churchill Downs on the culminating afternoons of Kentucky Derby week.

The Royal Box is furnished with easy chairs, four or five rows of them, with five chairs per side. The box does not contain anything resembling a throne for the Queen. She sits in an easy chair too, in the front row on the right. In front of her is a bay window, maybe thirty yards wide, flanked by other windows that all make for a concave crescent. And there is a set of levers that allows the Queen to move the windows up and down to whatever position she wishes them to be in, depending on the day's climate, whether it's warm or cold outside, whether the sky is clear or it's raining.

She is very conversant with her guests, and I sat down to chat with her and remember asking, "If you had a choice to breed one of your mares to any North American stallion, who would it be?" The Queen answered without hesitation, "Nijinsky II," who was standing at Claiborne and had won the Epsom Derby in 1970. We chatted briefly and then I excused myself, for I didn't wish to monopolize her time. The Queen is exceptionally knowledgeable regarding pedigrees and conformation and is always courteous and cordial. But you are always aware of who she is.

§

The Royal Race Meet at Ascot is traditionally held during the latter portion of June each year. There is also another meet at Ascot in late July, with six races each day, three or four of which are stakes events. The one I've attended with fair frequency in recent years is the King George VI and Queen Elizabeth Diamond Stakes, which is part of the World Series Racing Championship, a group of major international stakes that also includes such events as the Dubai World Cup, the Arlington Million in Chicago, the Prix de l'Arc de Triomphe at Longchamps near Paris, the Cox Plate in Australia, the Breeders' Cup Turf and Breeders' Cup Classic, the Japan Cup in Tokyo, and the Hong Kong Cup.

As chairman of the board of the World Series Racing Championship, I'd go to Ascot each year to present the WSRC trophy to the owner of the horse that won the King George VI and Queen Elizabeth Diamond Stakes. You don't need to wear a top hat and morning coat when attending this race, but there is a very strict protocol regarding the awarding of trophies. It's not like it is at U.S. racetracks, at Keeneland or Churchill Downs or Belmont or Saratoga, where a mob of people rushes into the winner's circle as though they are trying to establish a niche in the *Guinness Book of World Records,* with everyone pushing and jumping and yelling. At Ascot, there is a specific routine, and everything is always very carefully orchestrated and organized.

A canopied platform is set up in the paddock at Royal Ascot. The Queen is there, as is Robert Oppenheimer, who is chairman of the board of De Beers Diamonds, which sponsors the King George VI and Queen Elizabeth Diamond Stakes. Once the race is run, a designated attaché for the Queen indicates for the winning owner to come forth. He comes up to the platform and the Queen presents the stakes trophy to him. Then the victorious trainer comes up, and the same procedure takes place. After that, the winning jockey comes up and is presented with a small replica of the stakes trophy. All very formal, all very proper, all very dignified. And then they designate me to come up, and I present the World Series Racing Championship trophy to the winning owner. The procedure is that the Queen gently picks up the trophy and slowly forwards it into my hands. Under no circumstances should one appear overly eager to grasp the trophy.

In 2003, the winning horse in the King George VI and Queen Elizabeth Diamond Stakes was Alamshar, who was bred and owned by the Aga Khan. Alamshar pulled clear of his rivals to win by three and a half lengths, and British turf writers subsequently wrote that his was the most dominating performance in the race in at least a decade. The Aga Khan, no stranger to winner's circles in the United Kingdom, well knew that he wasn't to reach out and grasp the trophy either. So he patiently waited as the Queen politely, properly moved the trophy from her hands to mine. But as the exchange took place, neither of us had a good grip on it, and it slipped and fell to the ground, hitting me on the big toe of my right foot. I reached down and, with the Aga Khan's assistance, picked up the trophy, and I could hear the sigh of amazed dismay, a long, half-horrified "uhhh-hhhh!" that went through the assembled multitudes. Thankfully, Lucy wasn't there to see this. She would have said, "Ted, what did you think you were doing?" (or maybe something a bit more stringent). The Queen, of course, maintained her royal demeanor. She was unfazed. We did the trophy presentation without further mishap.

But several weeks later, I was back in Kentucky having my annual physical examination. I told Cary Blaydes, who had been my doctor for thirty-odd years, that I had a spot on the big toe of my right foot I wanted him to look at. In the days after the trophy had landed on it, the toenail had turned a deep black color. Dr. Blaydes asked me, "How long have you had this?" And for some reason, I purposely misinformed him and replied, "Oh, for a couple of weeks." Actually, I'd had a bruise on the toe for about six months. I do a lot of walking every night, about two miles, accompanied by my dogs. I initially thought it was just a matter of my shoe being too tight. I'd been soaking the toe in a basin of warm water once or twice a week, and it didn't hurt. But it had taken on that deep, dark change of color.

Well, Dr. Blaydes looked at the toe and expressed some alarm, and he sent me over to see Dr. John Cronin, an oncologist (a specialist who deals with tumors) at St. Joseph's Hospital in Lexington. Dr. Cronin took a slice for a biopsy. Several days later he phoned me and said, "You've got a problem, and we're going to have to put you in the hospital. You've been diagnosed with a severe melanoma, and we're going to have to amputate the toe."

I still wonder how in the world I developed a melanoma on my toe. Through the years I'd had severe sunburns on my face, hands, arms, neck, chest, stomach, and legs, after spending time at beaches. But I had never had any problems with my feet, with the exception of my experience in the Marine Corps, when I got sunburned so badly on the voyage from Tokyo to Honolulu at the end of the war.

About six months after I had the operation, I met with my old Yale roommate, Judge Alexander Harvey from Baltimore, and he said to me, "I heard you had a little bit of a problem. What happened?" I told him about the failed juggling act with the trophy at Ascot, and Harvey said, "Oh, come on, Bassett. That's the biggest cock-and-bull story I ever heard. Don't tell me the Queen dropped a trophy on your foot and you had to have your big toe cut off." I still don't think Harvey believes it happened that way.

I view the Ascot mishap as fortuitous. If it hadn't happened, I probably would not have mentioned the toe problem to Dr. Blaydes, and he wouldn't have brought it to the attention of Dr. Cronin. And in the long run, I might have ended up losing much more than a toe. I was in the hospital for a week, and after coming home was on a walker for two weeks, on crutches for two more weeks, and had to use a cane for an additional three weeks.

That fall, the filly Lucy had bred, Adoration, was a Breeders' Cup

Distaff winner at Santa Anita. I spent much of the early part of Breeders' Cup day hobbling around with the cane. Lucy told me, "You know, you're making this tougher than it is. Look, it's very easy. Act like you're dancing. Put your foot out. Don't try to walk on the balls of your feet; walk on your heels." Her advice helped, but not as much as Adoration's victory did. In our excitement to get up from our clubhouse table to go and congratulate the winning owners, John and Jerry Amerman, I forgot all about the cane and walked without it.

Two years later, on July 23, 2005, I was again in England to do the World Series Racing Championship trophy presentation at the King George VI and Queen Elizabeth Diamond Stakes. That year, it was run at Newbury Race Course (Ascot was undergoing a major renovation). The Duke of Devonshire, who is the Queen's representative to Ascot, invited me to attend a luncheon being held in honor of the Queen at Newbury on the day of the race. There were approximately twenty people at the luncheon, and I was fortunate enough to know about half of them, having met them previously at other events in England.

After lunch, the group moved to a viewing room that overlooked the finish line. From time to time, the Queen would join in the conversations or sit down and chat with someone. The atmosphere was very relaxed. About an hour or so before the race, I went over to sit by her, and we talked about Keeneland and about her racing stable. In filling in a moment of conversation, I said, "I know, ma'am, you've presented many trophies during your life. Do you recall the presentation two years ago when I dropped the trophy?"

"Oh, I do indeed, Mr. Bassett," she said. "I have a photograph of you on your hands and knees picking it up." We both laughed.

I said, "The Aga Khan's horse, Azamour, is the 5–2 favorite in this year's King George VI and Queen Elizabeth Diamond Stakes. Wouldn't it be a coincidence if he won it again?"

The Queen looked at me and said, "If he does, please hold the trophy firmly, Mr. Bassett."

In the stretch, a 50–1 shot made a game try at getting the victory, but at the finish it was Azamour prevailing by a length and a half. The Queen presented the Aga Khan with the stakes trophy. The winning trainer was summoned to the ceremony, and after him the winning jockey, and then I was given my cue. I shook the hand of the Aga Khan, and he grinned at me and said, "Let's keep a firm grip on it this time." And I did. Losing my right big toe was enough. I had no desire to lose my left one.

§

In the years following her visit to Keeneland, the Queen has made several additional trips to Kentucky, with the Farishes always serving as her hosts. But a return to Keeneland has not been on her agenda. Primarily, her interest has been visiting the stud farms and inspecting the stallions. Also, her trips have been made in the middle of the summer, when Keeneland doesn't race, and we no longer have the July Yearling Sale, so that would not fit into the schedule either. Certainly, if she ever chose to journey here when our April or October race meets were in progress, it would be a great privilege to have her visit Keeneland again.

Other members of the Royal Family have spent some time with us, though. The Queen's daughter, Princess Anne (whose formal title is "Princess Royal") has twice visited Keeneland for the Royal Chase for the Sport of Kings, which is a $150,000 steeplechase event we've hosted every year beginning in 1998. It is currently run at a distance of two and a half miles on the grass over hurdles, and because Keeneland's turf course goes slightly downhill and then uphill for the run down the backstretch, the Royal Chase is somewhat akin to steeplechase races that are conducted in England and Ireland.

The first time Princess Anne came here was for the Royal Chase's inaugural running, which was the one time it was contested at two and a quarter miles, and the winner that year was a horse, or, more precisely, a six-year-old gelding named Clearance Code, who returned $44 for a $2 win ticket. Princess Anne presented the trophy. It was a Friday, the closing day of the meet, and we drew an unusually large crowd of 17,089. Many people don't seem to want to miss the opportunity to see a member of the Royal Family.

During the afternoon, Princess Anne had an opportunity to tour the Keeneland Library, which was then a 3,200-square-foot facility on the second floor of the administration building. The English author Dick Francis, who is a former jockey for the Queen Mother and has written a host of mysteries with horse-racing themes, was a member of her entourage that day, and the librarians had put some of his works on display. Princess Anne also expressed special interest in books that traced the bloodlines of racehorses and in the historical photographs of Keeneland. She was on a tight schedule, she only had about fifteen minutes to spend in the library, and I got the impression she would like to have stayed there longer.

Princess Anne returned for the 2003 running of the Royal Chase, which was won by McDynamo, who went on to receive the Eclipse Award as that year's champion steeplechase horse. Our new library facility had opened at Keeneland nine months earlier, and a reception was held there for Princess Anne the day after the meet closed. Keeneland did not host the reception—a group called the English Speaking Union Club did. But Keeneland's head librarian, Cathy Schenck, was there to meet her, and Princess Anne remarked to Cathy that she was delighted with the new facility.

§

The Queen does not send Christmas cards. But we usually send Christmas cards to her. She probably gets thousands of them from her subjects and other people each year. Occasionally, we may send a gift to the Queen, usually a Hermes scarf. You may notice from photographs you've seen of her that when she's enjoying a light moment with her dogs or inspecting horses, she is often wearing a scarf on her head. Never does the Queen acknowledge a gift with a note written in her personal hand. This would be considered highly inconsistent with the appropriate protocol. But one does hear from one of her assistants. I'll give you an example. In April 1993, Lucy and I sent the Queen an Easter bouquet of flowers, and a few weeks later we received a typewritten note on Buckingham Palace stationery, over the signature of Robin Janvrin. It read:

> I am commanded by the Queen to thank you for your spectacular display of flowers which arrived for the Royal Family over Easter. These were much appreciated by Her Majesty and all the members of the Royal Family. The Queen has asked me to thank you both for this very kind gift, and to send her warm good wishes to you with this letter.

It's always a brief letter that begins, " I am commanded by the Queen" or "Her Majesty has commanded me to thank you" or "The Master of the Household has received Her Majesty's Command to. . . ."

In 1991, Lucy and I received an invitation to a reception at the British embassy in Washington, D.C., for the Queen and Prince Philip. The exact wording was as follows:

On the occasion of the Visit of
Her Majesty Queen Elizabeth II
and
His Royal Highness The Prince Philip, Duke of Edinburgh
The British Ambassador
is commanded by The Queen to invite
Mr. and Mrs. Bassett
To a Garden Party at the British Embassy

In the lower left-hand corner of the invitation, it was noted, "The Band of Her Majesty's Royal Marines will Beat Retreat at 5:00 P.M." In the lower right-hand corner of the invitation it was noted that men should wear either business suits or white dress uniforms. I chose the option of the business suit.

Regarding the Christmas cards, I always write a few notes, short ones, three or four paragraphs at the most, mentioning the results of that year's running of the Queen Elizabeth II Challenge Cup, saying something about the filly who won, perhaps mentioning what the horses in the field went on to do in their subsequent races. The Challenge Cup was elevated to grade 1 status in 1991, which put it in the top echelon of all stakes annually run in North America, and I remember devoting several lines in our Christmas card to the Queen about that.

In October 1985, Keeneland's turf course was ready, and we transferred the Queen Elizabeth II Challenge Cup from the main track to the grass. In 1990, we increased its distance to one and one-eighth miles (over what we call the Haggin course), and it now has a $500,000 purse.

But the Queen Elizabeth II Challenge Cup has really become the showcase event of Keeneland's fall meet. For decades, the Spinster Stakes possessed that status, but with the Breeders' Cup having been run in late October during recent years, Keeneland has been scheduling almost all its major fall stakes on the opening three-day weekend to allow a three-week break between those races and Breeders' Cup day. This has been true for the Breeders' Futurity and the Alcibiades as well as the Spinster, all of which have histories that date back to at least the mid-1950s.

It is not true, though, for the Queen Elizabeth II Challenge Cup. It is not a prep race for any other event; it stands alone and is run on a Saturday in mid-October. In 1997, it was won by Ryafan, bred and owned by Khalid Abdullah's Juddmonte Farms. Although she was bred in Kentucky, this was her first start in America. She had spent the previous sixteen months winning major stakes at courses such as the Curragh in Ireland, Longchamps, and Newmarket and Goodwood in England.

In the Queen Elizabeth II Challenge Cup, Ryafan was sent off as the 5–2 second choice. I can still see her jockey, Alex Solis, using a right-handed whip deep into the stretch and Ryafan edging ahead to win by a length and a half. Ryafan went on to also win the Yellow Ribbon Stakes at Santa Anita and the Matriarch Handicap at Hollywood Park in November. And two months later, Ryafan received the Eclipse Award as North America's outstanding female grass specialist. Mention of this was made in one of the Christmas cards we sent to the Queen, too.

Chapter 8

The Blue Grass Stakes

A LOT OF racing people do not realize this, but the Blue Grass Stakes was first run not at Keeneland but at the old Kentucky Association track at Fifth and Race streets in Lexington. The date was May 10, 1911, and the winner was a three-year-old gelding named Governor Gray, who set a track record for one and one-eighth miles of 1:51⅕.

While Governor Gray's name is not mentioned with frequency in the annals of the sport, he was a pretty good racehorse. Just three days following his Blue Grass triumph, Governor Gray finished second to Meridian in the Kentucky Derby, closing aggressively in the final eighth of a mile to miss by only three-quarters of a length. Governor Gray had actually gone postward as the Derby favorite, and one can argue he laid the cornerstone for the Blue Grass as a major Triple Crown prep race.

If you combine the twelve editions of the Blue Grass run at the Kentucky Association track and the sixty-nine that have been run to date at Keeneland, you will see the race has produced twenty-three winners of the Derby, thirteen winners of the Preakness Stakes, and thirteen winners of the Belmont Stakes. The Kentucky Association track discontinued the Blue Grass in 1926, and it wasn't until 1937 that it was renewed during Keeneland's first spring meeting. Back when Governor Gray won the race, the Blue Grass had a purse of $3,150. In 1937, when a gelding named Fencing was the winner, the purse was $9,475, which was fairly impressive for the time but roughly equivalent to what horses earn for finishing second in the maiden allowance races we have at Keeneland today.

In 1941, Whirlaway ran in the Blue Grass and surprisingly got beat—by six lengths, no less—by a colt named Our Boots. I was in my final year at Kent School, so I wasn't in Kentucky when the race was run, but I have since seen the chart, which, among other things, tells us that the Keeneland surface was muddy. The *Daily Racing Form* used to publish what handicappers called "mud marks," and the one in the *Form* next to Our Boots's name was comprised of a circle with an *X* in the middle of it, indicating that he was a superior runner when the track surface was wet and thick. But the same mark accompanied Whirlaway's name, and he was a Calumet Farm homebred—he had been born, raised, and received his early training only a short walk down the road from Keeneland. So Whirlaway had exited the starting gate in the Blue Grass as the 1–2 favorite under a jockey named Warren Eads. Keeneland had an infield lagoon back then, and legend has it that bodies were being combed out of that lagoon for the next week. Eddie Arcaro subsequently got the mount on Whirlaway and rode him to a Triple Crown sweep.

Being from central Kentucky, I certainly knew about the significance of the Blue Grass, although I'm pretty sure it wasn't until I was thirty-one years old that I attended the race. It was 1953. Lucy and I had moved from New York back to Kentucky, and the winner that year was a colt from California named Correspondent. He had registered his initial career win at Santa Anita during the winter and had scored in a pair of allowance sprints at Keeneland earlier in the meet. Correspondent was ridden by Eddie Arcaro, and one of the things that sticks out in my mind about that Blue Grass is he took the lead with his first stride out of the gate and was gone—he was a length in front after a half mile, two lengths in front entering the far turn, three lengths in front at the eighth pole, and his final margin was a widening five lengths. Correspondent's final time was 1:49, which broke the track record set in the 1948 Blue Grass by Coaltown, a stablemate of Calumet's Triple Crown winner Citation.

Keeneland's crowd that day was estimated at 11,000, and wagering totaled $586,904. Numbers like those would be apocalyptic for the Blue Grass nowadays, but back then they were big, reflecting the electricity that coursed through the whole of the Lexington community concerning the race. The Blue Grass was traditionally run on a Thursday afternoon, just nine days before the Derby, and simply knowing one of the participating horse owners was an immensely exciting thing. Correspondent was owned by Gordon Guiberson and his wife, who were associated, if I recall correctly, with A. B. "Bull" Hancock of Claiborne Farm. Lucy and I were invited to several parties the Guibersons attended, and it was like being on the outskirts of Camelot. I know it may be hard to comprehend, but this was an era when television was in its infancy and the Internet did not exist, and there was a certain mystique about the owners who had Derby horses that made them akin to knights on quests for Holy Grails. For most, of course, the quests had the stability of Cinderella's pumpkin coach. In the 1953 Derby, Correspondent finished a tiring fifth, as a 25–1 long shot named Dark Star handed heavily favored Native Dancer his only career defeat.

Round Table won the Blue Grass in 1957, setting a new track record for one and one-eighth miles of 1:47⅖. If you look at Round Table's career record, you will see that during his racing days he either set or equaled sixteen track and turf course records, which in that regard accords him a résumé unmatched by any other North American Thoroughbred before or since.

But I think where the Blue Grass truly gained its credibility was in 1959, when an English-bred horse named Tomy Lee came in from California. He had run well that winter at sprint and middle distances at Santa Anita, and in the Blue Grass he stretched out his talents for the first time at one and one-eighth miles and won by half a length over a Claiborne Farm homebred who was oddly named Dunce. Tomy Lee's jockey was Bill Shoemaker, and on the first Saturday in May, they teamed up again to win the eighty-fifth running of the Derby by a nose.

Thirty-one years earlier, during the Kentucky Association era, a colt named Bubbling Over, one of Colonel Edward Riley Bradley's homebreds, had won both the Blue Grass and the Kentucky Derby. In 1942, a Greentree Stable colt named Shut Out had done the same. But for whatever reasons these things happen, Tomy Lee's victory in both races started a trend that would continue throughout the following decade, during which the Blue Grass matured into the preeminent Kentucky Derby prep race.

You look at what happened and it is astonishing. In 1963, Chateaugay won the Blue Grass and the Derby. The same was true of Northern Dancer in 1964 and Lucky Debonair in 1965. That's three years in a row. Forward Pass won the Blue Grass and the Derby in 1968. Further, Decidedly, who finished second in the Blue Grass in 1962, went on to win the Derby. The same happened with Proud Clarion in 1967. Sherluck, who won the Blue Grass in 1961, was victorious in that year's Belmont Stakes, which is what also happened with Arts and Letters in 1969. Northern Dancer and Forward Pass also won the Preakness, and Chateaugay was a Belmont winner. Let's add it all up. During the 1960s, horses that finished either first or second in the Blue Grass registered six Kentucky Derby victories, along with two in the Preakness and three in the Belmont. They therefore accounted for 36.7 percent of the Triple Crown races run during that decade. I'm putting particular emphasis on this, because almost all the success occurred before I became affiliated with Keeneland. While I, indeed, had the privilege of witnessing many of these historic Blue Grass renewals, almost all of them did not take place during my watch.

§

I wish I could tell you I have strong recollections of the 1968 Blue Grass, which was the first during my tenure as a Keeneland administrator. But truthfully, I do not. Forward Pass went into the starting gate as the 11–10 favorite, and he ran like one, leading from start to finish and winning by five lengths. He was a Calumet homebred trained by Henry Forrest, who had also been the trainer of the 1966 Kentucky Derby winner Kauai King. In the late 1960s, Henry was the all-time leading trainer at Keeneland and at Churchill Downs, too, although most of his victories had come with claiming horses. In 2007, a full thirty-two years after his death, Henry finally gained the recognition he long deserved when he was inducted into the National Museum of Racing's Hall of Fame in Saratoga Springs, New York.

Forward Pass was a splendid racehorse. I would have to say he was the best Forrest ever trained. If you examine the career record of Forward Pass, you will see that he also won a total of eight other stakes, the Kentucky Derby, Preakness, Florida Derby, and American Derby among them. And he finished second in the Belmont and the Travers Stakes. But his Kentucky Derby triumph was earned by way of disqualification. Forward Pass actually finished second, a length and a half behind Dancer's Image, at Churchill, but post-race testing revealed Dancer's Image had the painkilling drug Butazolidin (commonly referred to as "Bute") in his system. The victory by Dancer's Image was voided by the Kentucky Racing Commission, which resulted in a legal case that dragged on for nearly four years. It was not until late April 1972 that the Kentucky Court of Appeals made a final ruling—the disqualification of Dancer's Image was upheld, and Forward Pass was the official winner of the 1968 Derby.

One of the things I do remember about the 1968 Blue Grass is how immediately taken I was by the camaraderie of the press party that Keeneland hosted. It was annually held the evening before the race in the clubhouse, and as the years went on, it became something I looked forward to with great anticipation. Decades before I came to Keeneland, the party had been a stag affair, attended by men only. But the gender line was broken in 1953 when Mary Jane Gallaher, whose career achievements included covering racing for the *Lexington Leader,* the *Thoroughbred Record,* the *Cincinnati Enquirer, Esquire, Newsweek,* and United Press International, crashed the party. (Mary Jane was also the first female reporter to be assigned a seat in the Churchill Downs press box during Kentucky Derby week.) And I've been told that gender equality took another huge step forward in 1960, when Cornelius Vanderbilt Whitney brought his colt Tompion to the Blue Grass. Whitney told Keeneland officials he wouldn't attend the press party unless his wife, Marylou, was invited too.

With the Blue Grass and the Derby being separated by only nine days, many newspapers and magazines allowed their columnists and turf writers to come and cover our race, then go directly to Churchill for Derby week. For me, a racing neophyte, the excitement of having all those great journalists at Keeneland, meeting them, sharing drinks and dinner, was exhilarating, enthralling. These are people whose stories I had been reading for months as they followed the horses along the Triple Crown prep trails. And now we had them in one huge, collegial gathering at our press party.

I'm talking about columnists and reporters such as Red Smith, Joe Nichols, Steven Crist, and Joe Durso of the *New York Times;* Whitney Tower, Bill Leggett, and Bill Nack of *Sports Illustrated;* Jim Murray and Bill Christine of the *Los Angeles Times;* Fred Russell of the *Nashville Tennessean;* Sam McCracken of the *Boston Globe;* Ed Pope of the *Miami Herald;* Furman Bisher of the *Atlanta Constitution-Journal;* Andy Beyer of the *Washington Post;* Dale Austin of the *Baltimore Sun;* Tom Siler of the *Knoxville Daily News;* Neil Milbert of the *Chicago Tribune;* Al Coffman of the *Detroit Free Press;* Pat Harmon, Bill Anzer, and Jack Murray of the *Cincinnati Post;* Sy Burick of the *Dayton Daily News;* Dean Eagle, Marvin Gay, Bob Adair, and Billy Reed of the Louisville *Courier-Journal;* and Charles Hatton, Oscar Otis, Bud Lyons, Barney Nagler, and Joe Hirsch of the *Daily Racing Form.* It is not an exaggeration to say that their reporting was of a quality that mesmerized the racing public.

One year at the press party, Whitney Tower, who was then with *Sports Illustrated* and later helped found a marvelous albeit short-lived magazine called *Classic,* came up to me and said, "Let's pep things up a bit. Joe Nichols loves to play the piano. We need to have a piano brought up. Come on, Bassett, don't be such a square."

Okay. I told Jim Williams, our media director, that we needed a piano, and judging from Jim's immediate reaction, you would have thought I had asked him to bring in a herd of elephants. But we got the piano. Nichols sat down and played it, and the clubhouse became filled with the voices of turf writers singing along. (That's something that just doesn't ever happen anymore.) One year, we asked Joe Hirsch to serve as our master of ceremonies, and he was so good at it that he went on to fill that role at our Blue Grass press parties for over thirty years.

These things opened up even more avenues of conversation and conviviality. We got into the tradition of ending the press parties by saying, "Good luck, good evening, good racing—and the bar awaits!" And dozens of reporters would stay for hours at the clubhouse bar, sharing rounds of drinks and stories and getting into friendly arguments about which horse would win and which horses wouldn't. I was an active participant in these post-dinner gatherings, and there were many Blue Grass mornings when I would come out to Keeneland rather bleary-eyed but so grateful for the friendship that had been manifested the night before.

But the whole atmosphere surrounding the Blue Grass Stakes was different back then. It was run on the next-to-last day of the Keeneland spring meet, and the social calendar of the meet slowly, steadily led up to it. Hotels became fully booked, restaurants became packed, and discussions involving the Blue Grass crowded out almost every other topic of sporting conversation. Radio talk shows devoted hours to fans calling in with their Blue Grass selections and the reasoning behind how they made those selections.

And the region's great horse farms—Calumet, Claiborne, Spendthrift. The Kentuckians who owned and worked at them took pride in supporting Keeneland, in running their stables here, and in nominating horses to the Blue Grass. And once Blue Grass day was over, it was time—time to go to Louisville for the greatest show of all.

It all reflected a sprit of support on the part of the press and on the part of the Lexington community that was so important to the development of the Blue Grass Stakes and to the development of Keeneland.

§

The winner of the 1969 Blue Grass was Arts and Letters. He was bred and owned by Paul Mellon's Rokeby Stable and was trained by J. Elliott Burch, who was a third-generation horseman. Elliott's grandfather, William Preston Burch, and his father, Preston M. Burch, had both been inducted into the racing Hall of Fame. And Elliott himself would become a Hall of Famer in 1980. He had been a teenage friend of Lucy's and had attended Yale before transferring to the University of Kentucky.

There was a great deal of excitement that year surrounding a quartet of Triple Crown candidates. The most prominent was Majestic Prince, who was the toast of the West. He was owned by an oilman from Vancouver, British Columbia, named Frank McMahon and was trained by the great former jockey John Longden. Majestic Prince had been purchased at Keeneland in July 1967 for $250,000, which was then a world-record price for a yearling. He had won the Santa Anita Derby by eight lengths and would go into the Kentucky Derby with an undefeated record in seven career starts.

In the East, there were three colts viewed as prime Kentucky Derby candidates. One was Top Knight, who had been North America's two-year-old champion the season before and at age three had won the Flamingo Stakes at Hialeah and the Florida Derby at Gulfstream Park. Another was Dike, who won the Wood Memorial at Aqueduct. The third was Arts and Letters, whom Mellon had bred at his farm in Virginia and had finished second in both the Flamingo and the Florida Derby, following a victory over Top Knight in the Everglades Stakes at Hialeah. We were very impressed that Mellon, such a distinguished breeder and owner, was going to be present at the Blue Grass. He, too, was a Yale graduate, a very erudite gentleman and a true sportsman. We entertained him at the Blue Grass luncheon—in those days it was held in the library at Keeneland—just a small gathering, a dozen or so people.

Bill Shoemaker rode Arts and Letters in the Blue Grass. They were favored at the prohibitive odds of 3–10 in the six-horse field. Through the opening half mile, they were in front by three lengths. They widened that margin to seven lengths through three-quarters of a mile. With an eighth of a mile remaining, they were in front by eight lengths. And they won by fifteen lengths, which remains the largest margin of victory in the history of the race. The reaction of the crowd was tremendous—its collective roar had increased with each length that Arts and Letters had widened his margin.

But I also remember how diplomatic and courteous Mellon was during the winner's circle presentation, as Governor Louis Nunn presented him with the trophy. Mellon was particularly gracious with his comments about the horse that finished second, Traffic Mark, saying he was a very nice colt and that his owners would experience a lot of enjoyment from his future efforts. When you win by fifteen lengths (which is roughly equivalent to fifty yards), it takes a good person to understand how difficult it is for the people whose horses lose.

In the Kentucky Derby, Majestic Prince was the 7–5 post-time favorite. Top Knight was second choice in the wagering at 2–1, and Dike was the third choice at 4–1. Three days before the Derby, Shoemaker had been injured in a paddock accident at Hollywood Park, and Braulio Baeza had replaced him on Arts and Letters, who was fourth choice at odds just short of 9–2. A terrific three-horse stretch battle ensued in the Derby, and Majestic Prince finished a neck in front of Arts and Letters, with Dike just a half length farther back in third.

Then, in the Preakness, Majestic Prince and Arts and Letters engaged in a stretch duel again—with Majestic Prince prevailing this time by a head. But in the Belmont Stakes, Arts and Letters went to the front early, was allowed by his competitors to set slow fractions, and drew off to beat Majestic Prince by five and a half lengths. It was the only defeat of Majestic Prince's career, and he never raced again. Arts and Letters, however, went on to win the Jim Dandy and Travers Stakes at Saratoga, and he defeated older horses that fall in the Woodward Stakes and Jockey Gold Cup Stakes at Belmont Park and Aqueduct, respectively. It was Arts and Letters who ended up being crowned both three-year-old champion and Horse of the Year.

Arts and Letters ended up being elected to the Hall of Fame. Shoemaker's victory aboard him was Bill's fifth of his record six in the Blue Grass. Shoemaker, of course, is in the Hall of Fame as well. As is Elliott Burch. There are no criteria for electing breeders or owners to the Hall of Fame, but five exceptionally prominent men have been inducted as "Exemplars of Racing": George D. Widener, Walter M. Jeffords, John W. Hanes, Cornelius Vanderbilt Whitney, and, yes, Paul Mellon.

And at Keeneland back in 1969, their were four Hall of Famers in our Blue Grass winner's circle: Arts and Letters, Shoemaker, Burch, and Mellon. Horse, jockey, trainer, and breeder-owner, a perfect foursome. I was new to the job back then, new to racing, and still a relatively young man. Looking back on it now, nearly forty years after the fact, what occurred that day has become much more meaningful.

§

Dust Commander, the 1970 Blue Grass winner, was owned by Robert E. Lehmann. The favorite in that year's race was Naskra, who had won the

Everglades Stakes. The Blue Grass field also included Hard Work, a colt who at age two had won the Breeders' Futurity at Keeneland, which in those days was a seven-furlong event. And the field further included a California-bred colt, Corn off the Cobb, who may not have borne the most prepossessing name for a racehorse but had finished a strong second in both the Flamingo Stakes and the Florida Derby.

Corn off the Cobb also had a very flamboyant trainer, Arnold Winick, around whom the press was always gathering for quotes. Winick had been saying he'd run his colt in the Derby and the Preakness but not in the Belmont, even if he was poised to sweep the Triple Crown, because the racing surface at Belmont Park "was like a plowed field." This did not endear him to the New York Racing Association.

We weren't sure whether or not Lehmann would attend the Blue Grass Stakes. He had an unorthodox background. Lehmann was born in a log cabin in the small town of Rising Sun, Ohio, started off his professional career as a tenant farmer, then got a Ford tractor dealership, and eventually got into construction. At age twenty-seven he was a millionaire, and within the next dozen years he added factories, warehouses, shopping centers, and the 650-acre Golden Chance Farm to his portfolio. Lehmann had also developed some exotic pursuits, and prior to the Blue Grass, he had been on safari in either Asia or Africa, hunting tigers or lions—I've forgotten which.

Lehmann did come to Lexington, though, arriving the day before the race. He was accompanied by a black Anglican African bishop, who came to Keeneland appropriately dressed for the role, complete with white collar and purple vestments. Lehmann had met the bishop on an airplane flight and brought his new friend to the clubhouse and to the paddock. These things did not exactly cause an incident, but there is no denying the bishop stood out. At the very least, he was a point of interest. The bishop's function was to bless Dust Commander, which he did in the walking ring, performing a short, informal ceremony that including making the sign of the cross.

Dust Commander then went out and delivered one of the most disciplined performances I have ever seen in the Blue Grass. Under a jockey named Mike Manganello, he was third through the opening quarter mile, third through the opening half mile, third entering and exiting the far turn, and third at the eighth pole; he then used a perfectly timed closing kick to win by three-quarters of a length. The longest shot on the board, he returned $72.80 for a $2 win ticket, and that remains the highest payoff ever for a Blue Grass winner.

Nine days later, Dust Commander went postward in the Derby, and his odds were a still very generous 15–1. Apparently, the bettors thought his Blue Grass victory was some sort of aberration. I don't know whether the bishop was at Churchill to provide another blessing, but Dust Commander prevailed by five lengths. I've since read that only one sportswriter, a columnist named Joe Falls from the *Detroit Free Press,* picked him in print to win. When asked in the winner's circle if he was thrilled, Lehmann replied, "Well, yes, but it doesn't compare, of course, with the rush one gets when bagging a tiger."

§

Memories of the 1975 Blue Grass remain vivid, but again for rather unusual reasons. As noontime approached, I was looking out my office window toward the Keeneland sales pavilion, and there was an absolutely torrential volume of rain pouring down, so great that the pavilion was literally obscured. Yet, walking up the hill toward the grandstand were thousands of people, their torsos bent over against the driving rain. They seemed to emerge, almost mystically, right out of the curtain of water. In my decades at Keeneland, this remains one of the most extraordinary things I have ever seen—the will, the zeal of the racing public to overcome the incredibly stormy conditions because they were determined to spend Blue Grass day at the races. Wind and water notwithstanding, they wanted to be here.

And believe me, that was an outstanding Blue Grass field. John W. Galbreath, the owner of Darby Dan Farm, had a two-horse entry consisting of Prince Thou Art and Sylvan Place. In late March in the Florida Derby, Prince Thou Art had been a three-and-three-quarter-length winner, and Sylvan Place had finished second.

Arthur A. Seeligson Jr., a fellow Yale man, had entered his homebred Avatar, who had won the Santa Anita Derby on the same day Prince Thou Art had won the Florida Derby. Robert F. Roberts and his wife had a colt in the race named Honey Mark, who a week earlier had won a seven-furlong allowance event at Keeneland.

Lehmann had passed away the previous year. Leukemia had taken him, and he was only fifty-two when he died. His widow, Verna, had taken the reins of Golden Chance Farm, and she entered her homebred Master Derby, an appropriate name for a colt on the Triple Crown trail. In late March, Master Derby had won the Louisiana Derby at Fair Grounds in New Orleans, and he had been a five-length winner in a one-and-one-sixteenth-mile allowance race at Keeneland nine days before the Blue Grass.

Of the nine horses entered, only Avatar and Honey Mark had mud marks next to their names in the *Daily Racing Form,* and there were questions pertaining to how well the remainder of the field would do on a surface that was threatening to turn into a swamp. But I had other concerns, too. The governor of Kentucky was then Julian M. Carroll. He had succeeded Wendell Ford, who had resigned the previous December to take a Senate seat. Well, Governor Carroll's wife, Charlann Harting Carroll, was expecting a baby. (The child, a daughter named Ellie, would become the first child born into a governor's family while residing at the present-day governor's mansion at the state capital in Frankfort.) So, along with everything else, I was worried about Mrs. Carroll. Keeneland traditionally hosts a VIP luncheon on Blue Grass day, and whereas in previous years it had always been held in the library, which was located on the second floor of the general office building, we decided that this time in would be in the sales pavilion. We thought everyone would be more comfortable there. And the governor and his wife were to be the special guests.

What we failed to anticipate was a typhoon. Also, despite all our planning, we had forgotten to inform the State Police about the luncheon's new locale. So the police escort dropped Mrs. Carroll off at the general office building, which, considering the weather, provided quite a challenge—well, not quite as daunting as the one facing Moses when he was on the Egyptian side of the Red Sea—a rather substantial volume of water was separating Mrs. Carroll from the luncheon site. Fortunately, Lucy was strolling through the general offices looking for an umbrella, and she saw Mrs. Carroll standing there. Lucy went and got her own car and drove it underneath the canopy at the front of the clubhouse entrance, where Mrs. Carroll got in. Lucy then drove Kentucky's first lady seventy-five yards, slowly, carefully maneuvering her way around and past the patrons braving the storm, to the sales pavilion entrance.

As this was taking place, the rain was cascading down the backside of the pavilion. A pond that had not been there before—and not a shallow pond, either—had suddenly materialized in the adjoining stable area. Arthur Seeligson always seemed to be smoking a cigar, and he was now. He had a cigar in one hand, a drink in the other. Arthur came up to me and said, "Ted, we've got to put the Blue Grass off. You can't expect these horses to run over this track, or expect the public to bet on them. You've got to postpone this race."

This may be the closest I ever came to having a heart attack. I said, "Arthur, we are not going to put this race off. There are thousands of people out there who have struggled and straggled through the rain to get here. This is not a baseball game, where we can pass out rain checks and play a doubleheader on Friday. In my memory, we've never put off a race on account of rain at Keeneland, and we are not going to do that now."

Well, Arthur then went to John Galbreath and said to him, "Ted's attitude is terrible. I think Keeneland should be more receptive and responsive to the horse owners' wishes. Don't you agree that the Blue Grass should be postponed and run tomorrow?" John wasn't aggressively in agreement, but he said he thought we should think about it. Arthur and John then went to Bill May, who was chairman of the Kentucky Racing Commission. Bill listened to them intently for a while, and then he walked over and took me aside and said, "What do you think about this? We'll go along with what the track recommends."

Meteorology is not one of my fields of expertise. But I did know something about our Keeneland racing surface—then and now, it drains very quickly. I also had great faith in our track superintendent, Hobart Burton, who I knew was out there with his tractor crew between every race, kneading the surface into acceptable shape. Hobart was a magician concerning that sort of thing.

By four o'clock, the sun came out. The track was still sloppy, but the crowd, which numbered 14,977, was appreciative. They saw a splendid race, with the 6–5 favorite, Master Derby, taking a three-length lead at the eighth pole, then holding off a late charge by Honey Mark to win by three-quarters of a length. One horse did have some problems, though, and as fate seemed to decree it, he was Arthur's. Watching the race film later, after Arthur had once again expressed his unhappiness with me, it looked to me like Avatar's head was turned to the left when our starter sprang the gate open. The footnotes in the *Daily Racing Form* chart partially stated: "Avatar, away sluggishly and over the heels of Decipher (who was a 45–1 long shot in the race), continued to lag until the second turn where he launched his bid from the outside, lost additional ground while bearing out entering the stretch, then engaged in a bumping match with Ruggles Ferry (a 52–1 shot) through the drive and lacked a closing response." This is what those of us in racing call a troubled trip.

Once the race was declared official, I steadfastly adhered to tradition, which meant the winning owner had to walk across the track for the trophy presentation. I prepared to escort Mrs. Lehmann, who looked at the sea of mud in front of us, and she said slowly, "Are . . . we . . . going . . . to . . . walk . . . across . . . that?"

And I said, "Yes, Mrs. Lehmann, and I'm sorry, but we will have your shoes cleaned when we return, I assure you." I took her by the arm, and we started to go across. Halfway there, I looked down and noticed that Mrs. Lehmann was resolutely going on, but with only one shoe. I looked back, and there was the other shoe, sinking into the goo. The mud had pulled it right off her foot. I stopped and thought, What should I do? Should I go back and pick the shoe up? Or should I go on? And then I thought, Let's proceed. I looked at Mrs. Lehmann, who was standing there in the shin-deep mud, one shoe off and one shoe on, and said, "Do you think you can continue?"

She said, again very slowly, "Yes . . . I . . . can." Someone, I believe it was one of the maintenance people, retrieved her lost footwear and brought it to the winner's circle, and there's a photograph of Mrs. Lehmann being presented with both the trophy and her shoe.

Several days afterward, Mrs. Lehmann told me she had also lost her watch. I look back now and I'm embarrassed for having so stubbornly, so idiotically refused that afternoon to yield to practicality. Some years later, I was asked to present the winner's trophy to Mrs. Lehmann after one of her horses had won a stakes at Fair Grounds on a muddy track. She said to me, "At least they have a portable walkway here, Mr. Bassett." By that time, we had one at Keeneland, too, comprised of ply-boards that the maintenance and starting-gate crews would put across the track.

A couple of postscripts: Wagering on the Blue Grass Stakes alone in 1975 totaled $313,590, which in those days before simulcasting was a record for an individual Keeneland race. And in the Kentucky Derby that year, Avatar had a half-length lead at the eighth pole when a horse named Diabolo lugged in and bumped him briefly off stride. Another horse, named Foolish Pleasure, the 9–5 favorite, then swept by and won the race. Avatar finished second, and Master Derby was fourth. But two weeks later, Master Derby won the Preakness. And on the first Saturday in June, Avatar, under one of the most masterful rides of Bill Shoemaker's career, upset Foolish Pleasure by a diminishing neck in the Belmont Stakes. It took a while, but luck had finally swung Arthur Seeligson's way.

§

Honest Pleasure, owned by Bertram R. Firestone and trained by LeRoy Jolley, was such a prohibitive favorite when he ran in the 1976 Blue Grass that he caused a minus win pool of $41,876.20. I will explain what that means. Under Kentucky's racing rules back then, from each dollar wagered, the state received 4.5 percent, the track received 10.5 percent, and the remaining 85 percent was returned to the betting public. But for each winning $2 ticket on a horse, the minimum that could be returned to the bettor was $2.20. If the aforementioned 85 percent returned to the bettors turned out to be less than $2.20 for each winning $2 ticket, the difference had to be made up by track management. The amount management would have to (ahem!) contribute from its own funds to get to the $2.20 figure was referred to as the minus pool.

Seven horses were entered in the 1976 Blue Grass, but it nonetheless was expected to be a romp for Honest Pleasure, who had been champion of his division at age two, had won nine of his eleven career starts, and was undefeated at age three when he came to run in the Blue Grass. With the exception of a daily double on the first and second races each day, Keeneland did not have any exotic wagering back then—no exactas, quinellas, or trifectas, no superfectas or pick threes or pick fours, and whatever else you will find on the betting smorgasbords of today. We had win, place, and show wagering, and for Honest Pleasure's Blue Grass, we canceled the place and show pools.

Two days before the race, a fellow flew in from New York, black bag in hand. To this day, I don't know if he was a messenger or a member of a betting syndicate or someone that's referred to in the racing industry as a bridge jumper, who is willing to wager a large amount of personal funds on what he considers to be a sure thing, guaranteeing a small but quick return. The idea is not completely without merit. Even if the return is only 10 cents on the dollar, that's still 10 percent. Back then, banks were paying 5 percent annual interest on deposits, but if you put your money on a horse instead, you could get twice that return in only a few minutes. Of course, if your horse lost, you might be inspired to jump off the nearest bridge.

We found out that the fellow's black bag contained $40,000, and he intended to bet it all on Honest Pleasure to win the Blue Grass. As it turned out, he was responsible for nearly one-eighth of the $331,242 wagered on the race that year. A week earlier, a heavily favored filly named Optimistic Gal, who was also owned by the Firestones and trained by

Jolley, had won Keeneland's Ashland Stakes and caused a minus show pool of $18,730.65. So, with the minus pools from the Blue Grass and the Ashland, we were looking at losses totaling in excess of $60,000, which was a lot of money for us back then.

A complete cancellation of wagering on the Blue Grass was something we did not view as an option. Keeneland's policy concerning this sort of situation was a long-standing one, and Louis Lee Haggin had hammered it into me: The public came out to see the horses, and they wanted to wager on them, and by putting their $2 or $5 through the betting windows, they were not only spectators but also participants in the event. This is, I believe, racing's strongest lure. Later on, we petitioned the Kentucky Racing Commission to revise the rules and allow the state's tracks to lower the minimum return on a $2 wager from $2.20 to $2.10. The commission members pondered the issue for quite some time and finally agreed with us, although not unanimously.

One of the things I remember most vividly about Honest Pleasure's Blue Grass is an incident that occurred on a Tuesday, nine days before the race. It was early in the morning, a light frost was on the ground, the sun was just beginning to warm the day, and Honest Pleasure was on the backside of the racetrack, going through a one-mile workout with Jolley's assistant trainer, Johnny Nazareth, aboard him. Jolley was wearing a green hunting jacket turned inside out so that the bright orange lining showed. He often did this to allow the exercise riders to easily spot him standing at the grandstand rail. Jolley was watching Honest Pleasure intently. Nazareth had the colt under an extremely tight hold, trying to keep him from surging forward. The idea is to prevent the horse from draining his energies during a workout, but in this case, it required such an effort on Nazareth's part to restrain Honest Pleasure that he was almost standing up in the saddle. Jolley saw this, took off his jacket, and began to wave it frantically over his head, signaling Nazareth to let Honest Pleasure go. The official clocking for Honest Pleasure's workout that morning was listed in the *Daily Racing Form* as 1:39, which was surprisingly slow for a horse of that caliber. Jolley had an absolute fit, and when Nazareth dismounted I remember LeRoy chewing him out, using language that will not be printed here.

Honest Pleasure's jockey was Braulio Baeza, one of the best to ever practice his trade. He also rode Optimistic Gal, but despite winning the Ashland with her, Baeza had been criticized by Jolley for going too fast during the early portion of the race. A *Racing Form* clocker, timing the race with a stopwatch, recorded Optimistic Gal blazing through the opening half mile in 0:44⅘. Although she won by a length and a quarter, Optimistic Gal appeared to be very weary during her closing strides.

Baeza, perhaps overly determined to prevent the same thing from happening with Honest Pleasure in the Blue Grass, employed as firm a grip on his reins as I have ever seen. Joe Hirsch politely referred to this in the *Racing Form* as a "tight hold." Gerald Strine wrote less politely in the *Washington Post* that Baeza was "strangling the colt." Bill Nack, who was then reporting for *Newsday*, wrote that Baeza took "such a hold of [Honest Pleasure] that the colt was running with his mouth open on the lead" and that Baeza "was strangling the horse to slow him down."

Honest Pleasure won the Blue Grass, but Jolley was really angry now, to the degree that when he filled out the official entry slip three days before the Derby, he did not name a jockey. On the overnight sheet for Derby day, which listed the horses and riders for Churchill's entire nine-race card, there was no rider next to the name of the Derby favorite, who would ultimately exit the gate at 2–5 odds, the lowest for any horse in the race since Calumet's Citation and Coaltown entry twenty-eight years earlier.

Ultimately, Baeza did ride Honest Pleasure in the Derby. But they were outrun by a colt named Bold Forbes, who led throughout the race and beat Honest Pleasure by one length. After he finished fifth as the 9–10 favorite in the Preakness, Jolley gave Honest Pleasure a two-month hiatus from the races. And Baeza, making the situation more bewildering, took an unannounced hiatus of his own. In late May, he disappeared for two days, failing to show up for his mounts at Belmont Park, one of which was Optimistic Gal in the Acorn Stakes. Agents from the Thoroughbred Racing Protective Bureau eventually found Baeza, who was summoned to a hearing by the New York stewards. He told them he had "overslept," and the stewards said okay and fined him $500.

In August of that year, Baeza was inducted into racing's Hall of Fame. But Jolley replaced him aboard Honest Pleasure and Optimistic Gal with a jockey named Craig Perret. Under Perret, Honest Pleasure set a track record in winning the Travers Stakes at Saratoga, and the following spring, he returned to Keeneland and won the Ben Ali Handicap. And in October 1976, Perret rode Optimistic Gal to a five-length score in what back then was the featured event of Keeneland's fall meet, the Spinster Stakes.

But neither Honest Pleasure's Blue Grass win nor Optimistic Gal's achievements at Keeneland remain as vividly in my mind as Jolley waving that hunting jacket with the bright orange lining turned inside out. It's odd, sometimes, what one remembers the most.

§

As the 1978 Triple Crown approached, a terrific rivalry had developed between two colts—Alydar, bred and owned by Calumet Farm, and Affirmed, a homebred from Louis Wolfson's Harbor View Farm stable. They had raced against each other on six occasions at age two, with Alydar winning twice and Affirmed winning the other four races. At season's end, Affirmed was voted the Eclipse Award as North America's outstanding juvenile, but there were legions of people who believed Alydar was a better horse and would prove so at age three.

Neither of them raced at Keeneland (or at any track in Kentucky, for that matter) during their two-year-old seasons, and as their three-year-old campaigns began to unfold, their rivalry took on an East Coast versus West Coast connotation. Alydar was based in south Florida, where he won the Flamingo Stakes and the Florida Derby. Affirmed was based in Southern California, where he won the Santa Anita Derby and, in his final Triple Crown prep, the Hollywood Derby at Hollywood Park.

But Alydar's final Triple Crown prep was to be the Blue Grass. Calumet was then owned by Mrs. Lucille Markey, the widow of Warren Wright Sr., who had inherited Calumet in 1931. Wright died in 1950, and two years later, Lucille married Admiral Gene Markey, who had been an infantry lieutenant in the U.S. Army during World War I, served on "Bull" Halsey's staff in the Navy during World War II, and retired as a rear admiral in 1955.

Lucille and Gene Markey were as engaging a couple as I have ever met. Lucille remains one of the great grande dames in racing lore. During her years at Calumet, the farm was represented by two homebred Triple Crown winners, Whirlaway and Citation, and six additional Kentucky Derby winners—Pensive, Ponder, Hill Gail, Iron Liege, Tim Tam, and Forward Pass—all of whom were homebreds as well. And the Admiral? He was a Dartmouth graduate and a novelist, playwright, movie producer, newspaper caricaturist, and raconteur—one of the most dashing, engaging, charming men ever to live in the Bluegrass region. Much of his writing was done in a log cabin on the Calumet property. The Admiral had been married several times prior to meeting Lucille (his earlier wives had included actresses Joan Bennett and Hedy Lamarr). The late *Blood-Horse* editor in chief Kent Hollingsworth once quoted Admiral Markey on the proper way to make a mint julep:

> A mint julep is not the product of a formula. It is a ceremony, and must be performed by a gentleman possessing a true sense of the artistic, a deep reverence for the ingredients and a proper appreciation of the occasion. . . . It is a rite that cannot be entrusted to a novice or a statistician, for it is an emblem of hospitality, a vehicle with which noble minds can travel together upon the flower-strewn paths of happy and congenial thought.

I did not know then, and do not know now (and I am not inclined in inquire), what age Lucille Markey was when Alydar ran in the Blue Grass, but I do know the Admiral was eighty-two. Neither of them was in good health. And even though Lucille and the Admiral spent their winters on La Gorce Island near Miami in Florida, neither of them had ever in person seen Alydar race.

A few days before the Blue Grass, Margaret Glass, who was Calumet's business manager, phoned me to inquire if Keeneland might be able to provide some seats on the afternoon of the race for the farm's staff. I told her, "Of course, we can. But what about the Admiral and Mrs. Markey?"

Margaret told me, "Well, they don't go to the races anymore. They'll watch the Blue Grass on television."

I said, "Would they like to come? I can make special arrangements."

Margaret said she would check with them, and when she called back she told me, "Yes, they would love to be on hand, if the weather is okay."

We always hope for good weather on Blue Grass day. But I do not believe I ever prayed more fervently for it than the year Alydar ran. And I got what I asked for—a clear sky and temperatures in the middle to high sixties. We sent a Keeneland employee named Robbie McGoodwin with our Keeneland station wagon to pick the Markeys up, and Robbie chauffeured them through the iron gate that leads into the clubhouse enclosure, which was a lush green lawn adjacent to the track. There, the Markeys had easy access to the rail and would not have to walk any great distance or be impeded by the crowd, which that day would number a then-record 22,912.

ABC was doing a tape-delayed telecast of the Blue Grass, and Jim

McKay and his colleagues recorded one of Keeneland's most unforgettable vignettes. The Blue Grass field came out on the track, nine horses, and Jorge Velasquez, who rode Alydar, cut away during the post parade and guided him to Lucille Markey at the clubhouse rail. Lucille was very stylishly dressed and wearing white gloves. The Admiral was outfitted in a tweed British cap and an ascot. Velasquez said to Lucille, "Good afternoon, madam," and then he said to Alydar, "Bow for your lady." And Alydar lowered his head! I am not exaggerating. This was captured on videotape. Lucille Markey put her hand out and gently touched Alydar's nose, and the Admiral said, "God bless you, Jorge."

Then Alydar went out and won the race by thirteen lengths. As he approached the eighth pole, widening the distance between him and his competitors with every stride, Lucille Markey raised her hand in a sort of salute. The Admiral was waving and applauding, and the whole Keeneland crowd was joining him. I truly treasure the memory of that afternoon, of the joy that was reflected in the Markeys' eyes, and of the joy all of us felt at seeing them there.

Affirmed, of course, won all three Triple Crown races, with Alydar finishing a gallant second each time—I don't think I've ever seen a horse try so hard and not quite get there. The Admiral passed away in May 1980, and Lucille's death occurred in July 1982. An irreplaceable couple, I assure you.

§

I don't think we have ever had in Keeneland management a greater element of anticipation, of excitement, than we did with the approach of the 1979 Blue Grass and the participation of Spectacular Bid. The season prior, he had been North America's champion two-year-old, winning seven of nine starts, and all but the first of those victories had been achieved in stakes.

During the early months of his sophomore campaign, Spectacular Bid had swept the major stakes for three-year-olds at Gulfstream—the Hutcheson, the Fountain of Youth, and the Florida Derby—and he had been a twelve-length winner of the Flamingo Stakes at Hialeah. Racing had already had a trio of Triple Crown winners during the prior six years—Secretariat in 1973, Seattle Slew in 1977, and Affirmed in 1978. A lot of handicappers were predicting that Spectacular Bid was going to make it four Triple Crown winners in seven years.

Commencing with Sir Barton in 1919, North America has had eleven

Triple Crown winners. But the only one who had ever run at Keeneland was Whirlaway. He had been victorious in the Breeders' Futurity at our track at age two and had been defeated by Our Boots in the Blue Grass the following year. At age four, Whirlaway returned to Keeneland and finished second to his Calumet Farm stablemate Devil Diver in the Phoenix Handicap, again over a muddy track. Whirlaway also ran in a trio of lesser races at Keeneland, winning two of them. But no Triple Crown winner had gone to the post at Keeneland in the ensuing decades.

Then along came Spectacular Bid. The idea that a horse with his proven ability was running in the Blue Grass created the most media interest and public awareness that I can ever recall for the race. There are racing people who believed then, and continue to believe now, that Spectacular Bid was actually better than Secretariat. While Secretariat set three track records, equaled another, and also set a turf course record during his racing days, Spectacular Bid set seven track records and equaled an eighth. In winning the 1980 Charles H. Strub Stakes at Santa Anita, Spectacular Bid set a world record for one and a quarter miles on the dirt, 1:57⅘, that has yet to be equaled, never mind surpassed. But I'm getting ahead of myself here.

Grover Delp, who went by the nickname "Bud," was Spectacular Bid's trainer. When he brought Spectacular Bid to the Blue Grass, Delp was forty-six years old and had long been successful on the East Coast. Delp was enthusiastic and very vocal, and with Spectacular Bid, he had what he stated to be "the best horse ever to look through a bridle."

Delp had a nineteen-year-old jockey aboard Spectacular Bid, a boy named Ronnie Franklin who was from a town near the southern outskirts of Baltimore. Franklin had dropped out of high school during his junior year. He was the right size for a jockey—five feet tall, 106 pounds—and a neighbor took him to Pimlico one day to see if he might be able to get a job. Delp hired Franklin, originally as a hot walker (whose job is to cool horses out after a race or morning workout), but almost immediately realized, in the way knowledgeable horsemen sometimes do, that he had terrific potential as a jockey. In 1978, Franklin had 262 wins, and he received the Eclipse Award as champion apprentice.

Both Delp and Franklin were lifelong Marylanders. Maybe that helped explain why they had a father-and-son relationship. Franklin not only rode horses for Delp, he actually lived with Bud and his family. But despite Delp's lengthy record as a successful trainer, and despite Franklin's

Eclipse Award, many horsemen, members of the press, and racing fans questioned the decision to entrust Spectacular Bid to Franklin.

And some of the doubt had turned into outright hostility in the aftermath of the Florida Derby, which had been run seven and a half weeks before the Blue Grass. In the Florida Derby, Spectacular Bid had been the 1–20 favorite. And although he won that race by four and a half lengths, his trip could best be described as resembling an unguided missile. A group of highly accomplished and aggressive jockeys, including Hall of Famers Angel Cordero Jr. and Jorge Velasquez, also had mounts in the race, and they apparently decided to gang up on Franklin, which added to the bizarre circumstances of what unfolded. The footnotes from the *Racing Form*'s chart of the Florida Derby read partly as follows:

Spectacular Bid banged into the left side of the gate at the start, moved along the inside going into the first turn, was steadied and altered course over Sir Ivor Again's heels midway the turn, accelerated quickly along the backstretch, was forced to steady again leaving the backstretch while trying to get through on the inside, was steadied again midway the turn, was eased back to the outside, came four wide into the stretch, was hit six times right handed with the whip at the head of the stretch and into the stretch, bore in slightly, was hit twice left handed and drew well clear in the final sixteenth.

Reporters quoted Delp as saying that he wanted to plant one of his size ten-and-a-half shoes in Franklin's hind area. There were numerous urgings in print and over the media airwaves that Franklin should be replaced by a more prominent jockey. Delp said that he had discussed the possibility with Spectacular Bid's owners, Harry, Teresa, and Tom Meyerhoff, of Bill Shoemaker, Darrel McHargue (North America's Eclipse Award-winning journeyman in 1978), Jacinto Vasquez or Chris McCarron, or even Velasquez or Cordero replacing Franklin. The Meyerhoffs said no to the first four names on the list, and Delp rejected Velasquez and Cordero. "They couldn't ride a billy goat," Delp told reporters. "And I couldn't recognize Cordero if he was climbing out of a banana tree."

Two and a half weeks after the Florida Derby, Spectacular Bid, breaking from the outside post position and staying on the outside (and thus avoiding traffic obstacles all the way), easily won the Flamingo Stakes. Next stop: the Blue Grass at Keeneland, which Spectacular Bid would make his final start before the Kentucky Derby. When the time came to draw post positions two days before our race, only three other horses had entered, and we knew we would have to again (for the second time in four years) cancel place and show betting and would have a minus win pool—but it amounted to only $3,605.45.

Well, Spectacular Bid won our race easily by seven lengths. Altogether, it was the most spread-out conclusion of a Blue Grass I had ever seen—the second-place finisher, a colt named Lot O'Gold, was eight lengths clear of the third-place finisher, Bishop's Choice, who in turn finished ten lengths in front of Pianist, who came in last. The time of the race was unremarkable, 1:50, but it was a solid tune-up for a colt who many, if not most, believed was going to be the fourth Triple Crown winner of the decade, matching the number achieved during the 1940s, when Whirlaway, Count Fleet, Assault, and Citation all achieved Triple Crown sweeps.

We invited the Meyerhoffs, Delp, and Franklin up to the library for a champagne toast. This was a Keeneland tradition after a stakes race. We would also have scotch, bourbon, gin, and vodka available there, along with a television monitor and a videotape of the race, so the winning interests could watch the rerun. But we seldom had beer, and Delp's first request was for a Heineken. I got on the phone to the Turf Catering people, and they quickly brought up two or three bottles of Heineken. Delp kept asking to watch the race again, and every time he did, he drank another Heineken. So I got on the phone to the Turf Catering people again, but they said they didn't have any more of that brand of beer. I told them, "Go out to a 7–11 store or someplace like that and get a couple of six-packs! Make it quick!" (Oh yes, the duties of a Keeneland president.) When Delp finally left that afternoon, he took one of the six-packs of Heineken with him.

Spectacular Bid won the Kentucky Derby and the Preakness. But less than twenty-four hours before the Belmont Stakes, while in his stall at Belmont Park, he stepped on a safety pin that apparently had dislodged from one of his leg wraps, and the sharp edge of the pin got embedded a half inch into his left front foot. Spectacular Bid went into the Belmont sore-footed, and there's a possibility that Franklin also moved to the front too soon with him in the mile-and-a-half race, and he finished a fading third.

At age four, Spectacular Bid had one of the greatest campaigns in racing history. Ridden by Bill Shoemaker, he was undefeated in nine starts. In his final career start, the mile-and-a-quarter Woodward Stakes at Belmont Park, no other horse showed up to take him on. This resulted in one of racing's true rarities—a walkover. To earn his $73,300 in purse money, Spectacular Bid still had to gallop around the track, which he did in 2:02 ⅖, exactly the same time he had recorded when he won the Kentucky Derby the previous year.

§

A substantial argument can be made that the most competitive field we ever drew in the Blue Grass was in 1983. We had twelve horses, and those who had shipped in included representatives from California, Florida, New York, Arkansas, and Maryland—every major racing center in the United States. Nine of the horses in the field had already won stakes, and two others were stakes placed.

It was the largest Blue Grass field in nine years, and we haven't had one as large since then. Six of the jockeys who rode in that race—Jerry Bailey, Don Brumfield, Pat Day, Sandy Hawley, Chris McCarron, and Jorge Velasquez—went on to become Hall of Famers. Jean Cruguet, who had guided Seattle Slew to his 1977 Triple Crown sweep, rode in the 1983 Blue Grass. And Brumfield at that time was Keeneland's all-time leading jockey. It was truly a compelling Triple Crown prep.

The 3–2 post-time favorite, Marfa, was trained by D. Wayne Lukas. A month earlier, Marfa had won the Jim Beam Spiral Stakes at Latonia Race Course (which is now Turfway Park) in northern Kentucky. It was a controversial triumph, for multiple reasons. The Jim Beam was also limited to twelve runners, but when the time came to draw entries for the race, sixteen horses were vying for spots. Under the terms of the race, as published in Latonia's condition book, preference would be given to horses with the highest career earnings, which seemed fair and simple to comprehend. A horse named Asked to Run ranked eleventh on the list of Jim Beam candidates, with $29,005 in career earnings, and Marfa ranked thirteenth, with $28,050. On entry day, though, Latonia officials had the erroneous information from the *Daily Racing Form* that Marfa's earnings were $2,000 higher. So he became one of the horses officially entered in the Jim Beam, when that position rightfully belonged to Asked to Run. The mistake wasn't noted until Saturday morning, the day of the race, when the *Racing Form* published the past performances of the Jim Beam horses, complete with a revised career earnings total for Marfa. By that time, it was too late to right the wrong.

Marfa's jockey in the Jim Beam was Velasquez, who was riding him for the first time. Marfa won the race by eight lengths, but he had to survive a claim of foul before the race was declared official, for in the stretch run, he had twice lugged in on another horse named Noble Home, who ended up finishing second. And to make everything just a little more complicated, Latonia posted Marfa's time as a stakes record 1:42⅖ for the one-and-one-sixteenth-mile distance. But the *Racing Form* clockers had recorded his time as 1:44⅖.

On April 10, in an effort without incident, Marfa was the three-length winner of the Santa Anita Derby. But Marfa's notoriety had been established in the Jim Beam, and when he came back to Kentucky for the Blue Grass, he bore the title of Marfa the Mugger. Lukas found this amusing. "We're fully prepared," he told the gathering at the Blue Grass press dinner. "We have our veterinarian, our blacksmith, and our lawyer."

Desert Wine, a multiple stakes winner, also shipped in from California. This was quite a coup in my mind. In those days, I spent a lot of time recruiting Blue Grass horses from the West Coast. Getting two from that region, with both of them being major Kentucky Derby contenders, had never happened for the Blue Grass before. Other entrants included Copelan and Highland Park, who had won the two divisions of the Fountain of Youth Stakes at Gulfstream Park; a colt with a misspelled name, Deputed Testamony, who had won the Federico Tessio Stakes at Pimlico Race Course; and Play Fellow, who had finished a fast-closing third in the Everglades at Hialeah.

On Blue Grass day, we got hit by a pretty sizable storm—not of the magnitude of the one in 1975, but there was a sudden, quick, heavy downpour between the fourth and fifth races, which seemingly in an eye blink changed the condition of the track surface from fast to sloppy. The Blue Grass was the seventh race on the card, and it was dark and murky when the horses went out on the track, making it difficult to see from any sort of distance exactly what was going on. Don Plunkett, who was Keeneland's starter during the spring meets in those days, said later that Marfa walked into the starting gate, looked around, and then sat down—in the mud!

The race turned out to be excellent, although Marfa lived up to his nickname. Despite a concentrated effort by Velasquez to keep him on course, Marfa bore out on the second and third wagering choices, Copelan and Desert Wine, in the upper portion of the stretch, then battled it out with the 19–1 long shot, Play Fellow, to a tight photo finish. Play Fellow was ridden by Cruguet and conditioned by Harvey Vanier, a longtime popular and respected trainer who regularly stabled at Keeneland during the spring and fall meets.

It seemed to take an enormous amount of time for the official results to be determined because there was a photo, a stewards' inquiry, and two claims of foul against Marfa that had to be sorted out. I remember seeing Harvey pacing back and forth through the slop on the track, anxiously looking again and again at the tote board, which is where the results would be revealed, for Keeneland did not then have a public-address system. Harvey's wife, Nancy, was with him. She was a co-owner of Play Fellow, and they were hesitant to go across the track to the winner's circle.

Well, Play Fellow won by a nose. To this day, it remains only one of three runnings of the Blue Grass decided by so small a margin of victory. Marfa was disqualified from second to fourth position, behind Desert Wine and Copelan.

Nine days later, Sunny's Halo, who had won the Arkansas Derby at Oaklawn Park, was victorious in the Kentucky Derby too, as Desert Wine finished second, Marfa fifth, and Play Fellow sixth. But in mid-May, Deputed Testamony, who had finished an undistinguished sixth in the Blue Grass, was a two-and-three-quarter-length winner of the Preakness. And in August of that year, Play Fellow won the Travers Stakes.

§

By 1985, the Blue Grass had grown to be a $150,000-added stakes. What were referred to as Breeders' Cup Premium Awards were also put into the purse, and it had a total value of $195,900 that year. But only four horses went postward. One of the reasons for this was that Chief's Crown, who went off as the 3–10 favorite, appeared to be a formidable Triple Crown contender. He had been North America's two-year-old male champion in 1984, having accumulated five stakes victories, one of which was the inaugural running of the Breeders' Cup Juvenile. And during the winter of 1985, he was the most prominent three-year-old in Florida, winning the Swale Stakes at Gulfstream and the Flamingo at Hialeah.

But there was another point to consider, involving the growing belief among many trainers and owners that the Blue Grass was scheduled too close to the Derby. The trend was to give three-year-olds longer breaks between starts. Long gone were the days when Whirlaway won a handicap race at Keeneland, finished second in the Blue Grass, was second in the

Derby Trial at Churchill, and then won the Derby, with all four of these efforts coming during a period of only twenty-three calendar days.

Chief's Crown was trained by Roger Laurin, whose father, Lucien Laurin, had trained Secretariat. Lucien had also trained Secretariat's stablemate Riva Ridge, who won the 1972 Blue Grass. So the interesting prospect existed of a father and son both being the trainers of record of Blue Grass winners, which is something that had never happened before. The other three horses in the race that year were Floating Reserve, who had won a minor stakes at Santa Anita; Banner Bob, who had won the Hutcheson Stakes at Gulfstream and the Jim Beam at Turfway; and Under Orders, who had either won or placed in each of his five career starts, all of which had come at Fair Grounds in New Orleans.

The owner and trainer of Under Orders was Louie Roussel III, who, with his father, owned Fair Grounds. In 1985, very few people beyond New Orleans knew of Roussel, although at Keeneland he quickly became a figure of interest—and bewilderment. Roussel felt that the Keeneland barn area was too dusty, and he donned a surgeon's mask to protect himself from the particles allegedly floating through the air. He also instructed his stable personnel to do the same (I am not making this up). Roussel did not wear his surgeon's mask to the Blue Grass press dinner. But when Joe Hirsch queried him about the formidability of the task confronting his colt, Roussel paraphrased Tennyson's "Charge of the Light Brigade": "Into the Valley of Death runs Under Orders," Roussel said.

The following afternoon, before a crowd of 18,364 in wonderfully warm and sunny weather, Chief's Crown took the lead right out of the gate and was never challenged, winning by five and a half widening lengths in a time of 1:47⅗—a clocking that remains tied for the third fastest Blue Grass ever run. We allowed only win wagering on the Blue Grass that year, and the mutuel return was $2.60. Floating Reserve came in second, Banner Bob finished third, and Under Orders was fourth, beaten by sixteen and a half lengths. Pat Day rode Under Orders and assessed his performance as follows: "He just kind of loped around and jumped up and down."

Nine days later, Chief's Crown went off as the 6–5 favorite in the Derby. But that was the year of Spend a Buck, who, in one of the most electrifying performances I have ever seen, led wire to wire, clocking a time for one and a quarter miles of 2:00⅕, which remains the fourth fastest in the 134-year history of the race. Chief's Crown finished third. He went on to run second in the Preakness and third in the Belmont Stakes, and although he won the Travers at Saratoga in August and the Marlboro Cup (beating older horses) at Belmont Park in September, it was Spend a Buck who was honored as North American three-year-old champion and Horse of the Year.

And a note about Roussel's future deeds: Three years later, he won Keeneland's Lexington Stakes and the Preakness and Belmont Stakes with Risen Star, who would be named North America's three-year-old male champion. Roussel co-owned Risen Star with a New Orleans car dealer named Ron Lamarque. The Triple Crown press booklet referred to Lamarque as "a silent part-owner" of the colt, but Lamarque was far beyond silent after Risen Star won the Preakness. Dressed in a white suit and red tie, he broke into song before a national television audience, warbling, "Way down yonder in New Orleans, Risen Star is the King of Kings." I will spare you the remainder of the lyrics.

§

The 1985 Blue Grass Stakes was my last as Keeneland's president. In March of the following year, Bill Greely was elevated to that position, and I became Keeneland's chairman of the board. From that point onward, I was more of a spectator to the Blue Grass rather than a management official responsible for annually putting the race together and staging it.

In 1989, the Blue Grass Stakes' position on the calendar was moved back so that it would henceforth be run three weeks before the Kentucky Derby. Since 1996, it has been sponsored by Toyota, and its official name is now the Toyota Blue Grass Stakes. In 2008, the Blue Grass offered a purse of $750,000, which is more than twenty-three times what its value was when I came to work at Keeneland in 1968 and more than four and a half times what the Kentucky Derby purse was back then.

Most certainly, the Blue Grass has retained its status as a premier Triple Crown prep. In 1987, Alysheba became the first (and to date only) Blue Grass winner to be disqualified, having interfered with another horse during the stretch run. But Alysheba went on to win the Derby and the Preakness, and he was the Breeders' Cup Classic winner and Horse of the Year in 1988.

The 1990 Blue Grass winner, Summer Squall, also won the Preakness. The 1991 Blue Grass winner, Strike the Gold, won the Derby. The 1993 Blue Grass winner, Prairie Bayou, was a Preakness winner too. During the 1990s, three other Blue Grass participants—Unbridled, Sea Hero, and Thunder Gulch—were Derby winners. Another, Louis Quatorze, was a Preakness winner. And three others—Thunder Gulch, Editor's Note, and Lemon Drop Kid—were all Belmont Stakes winners.

A bit of a dry spell ensued to start the current decade. But in 2007, Street Sense missed winning the Blue Grass by a nose and then went on to be a two-and-a-quarter-length winner of the Derby. I was so glad to see that happen.

I must reluctantly confess, however, that I have a nostalgic longing for the Blue Grass Stakes when it was run on a Thursday afternoon, with all the nationwide media coverage and community fascination that accompanied the race. For forty-eight years (the lone exceptions being from 1943 to 1945, when it was at Churchill because of wartime restrictions), the Blue Grass was run at Keeneland just nine days ahead of the Derby. Nine continuous days filled with fun and excitement and anticipation.

The Blue Grass press dinner no longer exists. It has become a Toyota appreciation dinner, a celebration of sponsorship rather than of journalistic contributions to the sport. Modern realities have dictated the change in emphasis. For me, it is very distressing to see the decline that has occurred in racing coverage in the major newspapers. The racing columnists, whose prose once constituted a major force in fueling circulation, have nearly vanished. The newspaper turf writers, en masse, have been tendered buyouts and have not been replaced. Jennie Rees continues to have a full-time position covering racing with the Louisville *Courier-Journal,* and those of us who live and work in central Kentucky are very thankful for this. But what has happened to all those other reporters, from all sections of the country, with whom I recalled so many gaffes and embarrassments, exchanged opinions, and shared so many jokes?

There is nothing diluted, though, about the Blue Grass Stakes history. And there remains in my heart a desire to see a Blue Grass Stakes winner sweep the Triple Crown. I am in the late autumn of my life, but there is still the possibility of having my wish fulfilled.

Chapter 9

Lucy

THERE IS NO one else in my life as special as Lucy. She is my jewel. She was raised in Woodford County, amidst the beautiful environment of Lanark Farm, where she developed an innate appreciation of all things beautiful. It was also an environment that allowed her to develop a digni- fied charm and an intuitive understanding of what is appropriate for an occasion, or not appropriate at all. Decision making has never been a labo- rious process for Lucy. She simply recognizes what is right and what is wrong and always acts accordingly.

Lucy is a very private person. She inherited from her mother, Eliza- beth Simms Gay, a disdain for publicity and a strong aversion to being photographed—much to the bane of Bert Morgan, Tony Leonard, and Bill Straus, whose jobs have been to chronicle, with their cameras, the events and personalities that constitute racing's heritage. It's okay, as far as I'm concerned, to have my tired face exhibited to the masses. But having her photo taken is just not Lucy's cup of tea. She has a knack of turning her head just as the camera shutter clicks. Straus, who was an official Keeneland photographer for a quarter century, often tried to outfox her by using a long-distance lens from an obscure position. But his success, at best, was never more than limited.

Lanark is Lucy's ancestral home. Her early childhood coincided with the years of the Great Depression. But her family did not suffer the eco- nomic stresses that had to be endured by many other citizens in central Kentucky and elsewhere throughout the country. Lucy's father, A. B. "Gus" Gay, was one of the founding vice presidents of the Keeneland As- sociation. He was also a Keeneland director for forty-eight years, and when Mr. Gay died in April 1983, he was the last surviving member of the asso- ciation's original twenty-one-member board. Mr. Gay (I always called him "Mr. Gay"—that's how much I respected him) was a horseman. He bred the 1941 Santa Anita Derby winner Porter's Cap, who was owned by Charles S. Howard and trained by Tom Smith, the same duo that campaigned Seabiscuit. Mr. Gay also bred a horse named Viking Spirit, who in four racing seasons, from 1962 to 1965, won nine stakes and placed in ten others. In winning the 1964 Longacres Mile Handicap, Viking Spirit equaled the track record of 1:34⅖. Mr. Gay was a University of Kentucky alumnus and served in the Army during World War I. He served on the Kentucky Racing Commission and was a founder and the first president of the Idle Hour Country Club. And in addition to horses, he raised cattle, tobacco, and corn. He was a man of enormous practical sense, which was manifested in his business decisions, and I always respected his judgment and paid close attention to what he said.

The Lanark property, which is named for Lanarkshire County in Scotland, has been in Lucy's family for over 200 years. The farm was originally named Woodburn and was founded by Lucy's great-great-uncle Robert Alexander (who never married). In the early 1780s, when Benjamin Franklin was in France trying to garner French aid for what would become the United States of America, Alexander was one of his private secretaries. He subsequently studied at universities in Cambridge and London, then returned to America and on March 2, 1790, purchased from the heirs of General Hugh Mercer what was listed in the deed book as "2,000 acres, more or less," adjacent to Elkhorn Creek, situated in what was then the Virginia county of Kentucky.

Through the generations of Alexanders, the property evolved into Woodburn Farm, and during the second half of the nineteenth century, it became one of the most prominent Thoroughbred breeding operations in the land. It has since been divided into several parts with different owners, but we do know that the barn that housed Lexington, who is generally recognized as the greatest Thoroughbred sire in North American history, was located on what is now Lanark. The horse Preakness, for whom the Preakness Stakes is named, was a son of Lexington and was born at Woodburn and raised there until he was a yearling.

When we moved from New York back to Kentucky in 1954, Lucy and I took up residence in the "White House," which was the original Alexander house and dated back to shortly after the farm's founding. The center of the house consisted of an old log cabin—two rooms that had been constructed with massive logs, twelve to fourteen feet long and eighteen to twenty inches wide. One was the living room, the other was the dining room. Both, along with nearly every other room in the house, had fireplaces. The numerous wings and additions had been put on through the generations, but in the center portion, cracks had developed between the logs, which rendered it nice and cool in the summer but freezing cold in the winter. But we loved living in that house, and it was a wonderful place to entertain. We lived there for forty years before moving into Lanark House, which is the main house, in 1994.

§

The first time I ever saw Lucy was in the summer of 1946, at a dance that her parents held for her at the Lexington Country Club. She had just graduated from the Madeira School, which is a four-year college preparatory school for women in McLean, Virginia, twelve miles from Washington, D.C. Several of her Madeira classmates were visiting her. Coincidentally, a friend named Jeff Wiedemann and I had a conversation with Lucy's father one morning in downtown Lexington. We had recently returned from the armed services, and we must have made a good impression on Mr. Gay, because we subsequently received invitations to the dance.

I remember arriving at the Lexington Country Club and gazing across the dance floor and wondering who this young, stunning blond lady was. Lucy and I were introduced, and soon afterward we had several dates. I was age twenty-four, a fossil compared to her contemporaries, who were younger than me and had not participated in World War II. I was concerned about our age difference and was careful about where I would ask her to go to dinner. We went several times to a place called the Old Mill. It was popular, it always drew a lot of people, and there was a jukebox there, with records by Glenn Miller, Artie Shaw, and Tommy Dorsey and their orchestras. I can still see, in my mind, the jukebox spinning those records.

Lucy wanted to attend Stanford University in California. That was her dream. But the idea of her going clear across country to attend college did not appeal to her father and mother. She was accepted at both Stanford and Smith College in Northampton, Massachusetts, and after a good deal of soul-searching, she chose to attend the latter. Years later, she fell in love with Southern California and has mused that if she had gone to Stanford she probably would have married some wine tycoon instead of a struggling newsprint salesman.

Smith College was established in 1871. Its alumnae include such distinguished women as Margaret Mitchell (who authored *Gone With the*

Wind), Ann Morrow Lindbergh, and two first ladies, Nancy Reagan and Barbara Bush. Lucy lived in Capen House, which actually dates back to 1825 and is a splendid example of Greek Revival architecture, with its columned temple front.

My father had purchased a car for me when I went to work for the Great Northern Paper Company. It was a black Ford coupe, and I thought it was the greatest thing in the world. The antiquated place where I was living, Hotel Millinocket, did not have telephones in the rooms, so I would call Lucy from the company offices. I would tell her that I might be able to get next weekend off and ask, "Could I come down and see you?"

She was always very kind and very cordial, but her answer would often be, "I'm very sorry, but I'm going down to Princeton. I've been invited down there for a football weekend."

I would then say, "Well, what about the following weekend?"

Lucy would respond, "Let me look and see. I think I am going to be at Yale."

The whole situation would begin to boil up inside my brain. It was proving a very difficult chore for me, a twenty-five-year-old mill hand, to get a date with this extremely attractive gal. She was always going somewhere, every weekend—if it wasn't Princeton or Yale or Harvard, it was New York City. I was jealous of all the people she was going out with and seeing.

But occasionally there was room for me within Lucy's busy social calendar, and I would get in the Ford coupe early on Saturday and drive down to Smith. Gas was 25 cents a gallon, and I ran that coupe hard. I would rip out of Millinocket and be constantly looking in the rearview mirror, hoping not to see an automobile with a flashing red light chasing me down. It was a tortuous journey of something like 385 miles one way, through Maine towns such as Dover-Foxcroft, Skowhegan, and Rumford; across the New Hampshire border and through towns called Moultenboro, Lochmere, and Hooksett; and finally into Massachusetts. I would mark the routes on a piece of blue Hotel Millinocket paper—go so many miles, then turn right on Route 150, that sort of thing. I would arrive in time to take Lucy to a late dinner.

And on Sunday evening, I would leave Northampton at about eight o'clock, drive most of the night, and get back to Millinocket at 4:30 or 5:00 A.M. on Monday. I would then take a shower, get into my coveralls and shoes or whatever I was wearing to the mill, and try to get a little sleep.

I would lie down on the floor of my hotel room instead of the bed. I had to be at work at 8:00 A.M. on the dot, and I didn't want to sleep too soundly. I'd eat breakfast and walk to the mill, which was about three-quarters of a mile away, all the time thinking, "God, I hope I can make it." And all day long I'd be looking at my watch, waiting for my shift to end at 4:00 P.M. so I could go back to the hotel and finally get a night's sleep. We do things like this when we're young.

During her years at Smith, Lucy wasn't interested at all in getting married. She was having a marvelous time in college, and her mission was to get her degree. After she graduated, I chased her passionately. And after a four-year courtship, we were wed on December 2, 1950.

There had been a gigantic snowfall in central Kentucky and the surrounding region the week before the wedding. The University of Kentucky had played a football game at the University of Tennessee, and my father and future father-in-law had been marooned in Knoxville for a few days. Lanark was heavily laden with snow. But Gus Gay was a great friend of Guy Alexander Huguelet, who was founder and president of Southeastern Greyhound Bus Lines. Gus prevailed on Huguelet to send a Greyhound bus, with a driver but without passengers, to try to clear a driving path into the farm. Back in those days, farms didn't have bulldozers. Triangular-shaped wooden sleds towed by tractors are what farmers used for snow removal. But the path to our wedding was made possible by this big Greyhound bus moving back and forth, making tracks along the one-mile entranceway leading from Old Frankfort Pike to the main house at Lanark.

After honeymooning in Nassau, Lucy and I moved into an apartment at 277 Park Avenue in New York City. It was a nice place, but small—a living room, kitchen, bedroom, and bath. My job as southern regional manager for the Great Northern Paper Company required me to travel a lot. My territory started at Washington, D.C., and extended into the South to Virginia, North Carolina, South Carolina, Georgia, Alabama, and Tennessee and up through Kentucky and West Virginia too.

To keep herself busy, Lucy initially secured a job as a receptionist for the Texaco Company on the twenty-first floor of the Texaco Building in Manhattan. Subsequently, in line with her interest in dancing, she took a job as an instructor at an Arthur Murray Studio. This struck sheer panic in the minds of her father and mother. A dancing instructor in New York? What in the world was their daughter doing? But this is typical of Lucy. Challenges have never daunted her. And she was not being a rebel in any sense of the word. She knew intuitively the right thing to do. She immensely enjoyed teaching dancing and did it for about two years. Neither she nor I can recall the actor's name, but he was an older gentleman, and he had to learn how to waltz for a television program he was appearing in. Lucy taught him how to do it. And we got a huge kick out of watching him dance on the black-and-white television with a twelve-inch screen that we had back in those days.

§

Sporting activities have appealed to Lucy since she was a little girl. She began riding a Shetland pony when she was only three or four years old. An older friend would give her lessons, much to the dismay of Lucy's mother, who pretty much viewed pleasure horses as inventions of the devil. Being a country lady, Mrs. Gay knew more than a few people who had suffered serious injuries from either being thrown by horses or falling off of them, and she did not want this happening to her only daughter. My future mother-in-law put up every reasonable roadblock she could, but Lucy continued to ride, and as she grew more experienced, she began going over jumps. You can make suggestions to Lucy, and she will consider them, but nobody has ever really been able to tell her what to do.

Golf has also long been one of Lucy passions. During our vacations to the Homestead resort in Hot Springs, Virginia, she would go out to the driving range and hit golf balls by the hundreds. The Homestead is in the heart of the Alleghenies, and the Cascades Course there is regarded as one of the finest links in North America. Since it was designed eighty-five years ago, the Cascades has hosted seven United States Golf Association championships, including the Women's Amateur in 1928, the Women's National Open in 1967, the Men's Amateur in 1988, and the Women's Amateur again in 1994. It is a wonderfully scenic and demanding course, and Lucy loved the challenge of playing there.

Herman Peery, a famous old golf pro, lived in Hot Springs, and Lucy took lessons from him for years. Even after Peery retired, he was still willing to tutor her, and Lucy would have a lesson with him every day. Peery even managed to improve my golf game a little bit, which may have been his greatest feat. He was a master teacher who stressed golf fundamentals. His basic theory was that golf is not a complicated game—it's all about grip, swing, and stance. In a matter of minutes, Peery could have you hitting balls farther than you thought possible. But in comparison to Lucy's, my game has always been inferior. Yes, inferior! With an exclamation point. At my very best, I would be lucky to break 90 for eighteen holes. Lucy, consistently, was always much, much better.

Three times, Lucy was the Idle Hour Country Club women's champion. In 1963, she came within one hole of tying Jackie Chestnut in the Lexington Women's City Golf Tournament, which was held that year during the first week of August at Picadome Golf Club. The Women's City tournament involved match play—two golfers were paired up against each other, and the player who won the most of eighteen holes went on to the next round. (This is distinct from the more familiar medal play, where the player with the overall lowest score in the tournament wins.) In match play, if the two golfers have played sixteen holes and one is ahead by three holes at that point, the contest ends, because even if the trailing player won the remaining two holes, that wouldn't be enough to overcome the other golfer's lead.

Jackie was perennially the top amateur woman golfer in the area—even as a teenager, she was a star. Jackie had already won the Women's City tournament in 1957, 1958, and 1962, and in 1963 she was trying for an unprecedented fourth victory. Lucy had played in the tournament before but had never been a finalist. Jackie was twenty-two years old, a University of Kentucky graduate, and a schoolteacher. Lucy was thirteen years her senior. Both of them cruised through the tournament's early stages, and they both easily won their semifinal matches by identical scores of five holes with four remaining (which is "five and four" in match-play parlance).

On the morning of the match between Lucy and Jackie, which was played on a Friday, John McGill, the golf writer for the *Lexington Herald,* had a column that noted, "The finalists have clashed several times in other tournaments, with the brilliant Miss Chestnut always the victor." But it turned out to be a close, thrilling contest. Jackie went two up through the opening five holes. Lucy chipped in from twelve feet off the green to gain a hole on the sixth and then drew even on the seventh hole. Through nine holes, Jackie was up by one. Lucy drew even with her by taking the tenth hole. Jackie took the lead again on hole eleven. Both players birdied the twelfth hole, but Lucy retied the match by taking the thirteenth.

What happened on the fifteenth hole probably was the biggest factor in the match's outcome. Lucy had an eighteen-inch putt, which, if she made it, would have given her the lead for the first time. And she missed it. "To this day, I can still see that ball rolling around that cup and out," Lucy says. She and Jackie halved that hole, and then Jackie took a one-hole lead on the sixteenth. That remained the margin going into the eighteenth hole, where Lucy had a forty-foot putt that, if she made it, would have tied the match. The putt was on a perfect line—and stopped rolling three inches directly in front of the cup.

Jackie Chestnut later married and became Jackie Hacker. During the ensuing six years, she won the Women's City tournament four additional times, and in 1973 she was Kentucky's state champion. Jackie and Lucy still see each other every now and then, and I am very appreciative of the comments Mrs. Hacker recently made about my wife. "Mrs. Bassett was a beautiful person to me," Jackie said. "She was always such a gracious competitor. She had a very smooth, rhythmic swing and was very consistent with her game."

§

Lucy's career as a Thoroughbred breeder began after her father died. "We had to do something with the farm," she told a reporter during an interview. "Daddy had a couple of older mares. I kind of backed into it, really." That is her modest, almost self-effacing explanation of how she got started in the business. Lucy's breeding operation remains small, but throughout the quarter century she has had it, she has been rather successful.

The September Yearling Sale at Keeneland is where you will find Lucy's horses. Her first consignment to that vendue was in 1985, when she sold a colt by a stallion named Our Michael for $37,000 and a filly by the Belmont Stakes winner Avatar for $15,000. That was the same year a colt by Nijinsky II fetched a world-record price for a yearling, $13.1 million, at our July sale, so I'm not going to suggest that Lucy's horses stood out in any way. But I am pleased to say that both of them made more than their purchase price in purse earnings once they went to the racetrack.

At the 1991 September sale, Lucy sold two yearlings that turned into very good racehorses. One was Secrage, a Secreto filly purchased for $17,000 by Horse France, a European outfit headed by a man named Paul Nataf. At age two, Secrage won a pair of stakes in Italy. She also won a stakes at Deauville, France, called the Prix de Cabourg, in which she beat a colt named Kingmambo, who later became a splendid European miler and sire of a yearling colt that sold at Keeneland in September 2006 for $11.7 million. This remains the record for that sale.

Lucy's 1991 consignment also included a Green Dancer colt named Lindon Lime, who was purchased for $55,000 by a British bloodstock agent named Anthony Penfold. Lindon Lime was subsequently gelded and raced for two years in England and France, winning a trio of races, none of which were stakes. He was then resold at Tattersalls in England for $81,800 to American trainer Elliot Walden on behalf of a client named Frank L. Mancell, a retired Wall Street investment banker. Walden brought Mancell's new purchase back to the United States. At age four, Lindon Lime won the Sam Houston Handicap at Dueling Grounds, which is a Kentucky track just across the border from Tennessee. He also won the River City Handicap at Churchill Downs. And the following year, Walden took Lindon Lime to Woodbine, near Toronto, where he won the Niagara Handicap. He also won Churchill's Louisville Handicap and the Sycamore Stakes at Keeneland. Altogether, once he returned to his home shores, Lindon Lime earned $627,808 in purse monies.

There certainly have been others, too. Lucy's 1996 consignment included a colt by Eastern Echo named Eastern Daydream, who was purchased for $20,000 by Harry and Tom Meyerhoff, the same father and son associated with Spectacular Bid. Eastern Daydream won a trio of stakes in Maryland and earned $355,605 in purses.

Her consignment in 1999 included a Gilded Time colt that was a half brother to Secrage. The colt, who subsequently was named Crystal Castle, was purchased for $65,000 by John Hammond, a trainer based in Chantilly, France. At age two, just like Secrage, Crystal Castle won the Prix de Cabourg. At age four, he won a stakes called the Brunswick Diadem at Ascot in England and another called the Prix de Meautry at Deauville. During his career, Crystal Castle also finished either second or third in five other stakes in Europe.

And back home again, Lucy's consignment in 2000 included Buster's Daydream, a colt by Housebuster and a half brother to Eastern Daydream. Buster's Daydream was purchased for $38,000 by Steve Barbarino, who races under the name S. J. Bee Stable. At age two, Buster's Daydream won three stakes, including the Sanford at Saratoga. His career purse earnings totaled $199,625. I am not telling you these things because I'm bragging. But I do want you to know about some of the things my wife has accomplished.

Real estate has also been one of Lucy's endeavors. Her career as an agent dates back to the mid-1960s. During the 1970s and 1980s, she developed a blue-ribbon list of national and international clients who were interested in purchasing central Kentucky farmland for Thoroughbred breeding purposes.

A willingness to seize opportunities is paramount when you're dealing in real estate, and as Lucy says, "Agents have big ears." We were at a dinner party at John Y. Brown's one evening, and among the guests was Stavros Spyros Niarchos, the self-made Greek shipping magnate and one of the most prominent Thoroughbred breeders and owners in Europe. At the party, Lucy overheard Niarchos say that he might be interested in purchasing a farm in Kentucky. She told him she would be pleased to show him some available properties, and he responded, "I only want to see the best." Lucy showed him only one—Spring Oak Farm. Niarchos purchased it, and Spring Oak became the headquarters for his North American broodmare band. It was at Spring Oak (known today as Oak Tree Farm) where Niarchos bred the outstanding filly Miesque, who won the Breeders' Cup Mile for him in both 1987 and 1988 and was honored multiple times as a champion in North America and Europe.

Jack Kent Cooke, owner of the Washington Redskins, Los Angeles Lakers, and Los Angeles Kings, listed Elmendorf Farm with Lucy when he decided to sell it in 1997. Cooke passed away in April of that year, and the following November, Lucy handled the sale of Elmendorf by his heirs to Dinwiddie Hampton Jr. Lucy was also the agent for Allen E. Paulson when he purchased the original Pin Oak Farm in 1988 and for David Brillembourg when he purchased Villa Blanca Farm in 1982.

For the past eight years or so, Lucy's professional efforts have been entirely devoted to breeding Thoroughbreds. She has her own self-implied restraints. For example, Lucy will not breed any mare who is over twenty years of age, which is something that reflects unusual discipline in the commercial climate of today. She is steadfast in her beliefs, and she sticks to them. At Lanark, even the mares that have produced stakes winners are not sold; they are retired to pasture. As Lucy told a writer for the *Blood-Horse* several years ago, "I keep all my old horses. Once they're inside the gate, they stay."

Her broodmare band has never exceeded more than a dozen members. The success Lucy has had is attributable not to quantity but to her attention to detail. She has sought advice from other successful breeders and pedigree experts. When Lucy initially became a breeder, John Prather helped her plan some of the matings, and John Williams of Elmwood Farm remains one of her advisers today. But the decisions Lucy made have always been her own.

Further, she has consistently anchored her breeding activities in fiscal reality, with a sensible, practical bottom line. Lucy has never been one to borrow money—it has always been pay as you go. High-priced stud fees do not lure her. Neither do high-priced mares. And I have had almost no influence on this component of her life. My strengths are in administration—the operation, marketing, and promotion of race meetings and horse sales. I have always felt strongly, and do to this day, that the members of Keeneland's management team should not be in competition with the association's customers. Especially in regard to sales, Keeneland staff members should be motivated by what is best for the buyers and sellers, and not their own personal interests.

One of the happiest days during my thirty-eight years of involvement in the Thoroughbred industry was seeing the four-year-old filly that Lucy had bred, Adoration, win the 2003 Breeders' Cup Distaff at Santa Anita. At odds of 40–1, she was the longest shot on the board. Adoration was ridden that day by a jockey named Patrick Valenzuela, who had her in front wire to wire.

David Hofmans trained Adoration for a wonderful couple, John and Jerry Amerman. Lucy had sold Adoration when she was a yearling for $40,000 at the Keeneland September sale to Chameleon Stable, an outfit headed by Californian John O'Hara. The Amermans subsequently purchased Adoration in a private transaction. Prior to the Breeders' Cup, Lucy said she was "horrified" that Adoration had been entered. "This is going to be awful. She's going to come in last by about 100 lengths," Lucy said. But the day before the race, Lucy went to Hofmans's barn to see Adoration and thought she looked "wonderful." And when Adoration won on Breeders' Cup day, Lucy was true to her character. One did not witness an explosion of wild enthusiasm and celebratory antics. Lucy was proud. She was pleased. She was her usual dignified self, accepting the congratulations from friends and horse people and those in the crowd who came by. That's her. That's who she is.

At age five, Adoration won the Santa Margarita Invitational at Santa Anita. This made her a multiple grade 1 winner. During her three seasons of racing, Adoration also registered five other stakes wins, four of them in graded events. Her career earnings on the track totaled $2,051,160. And to top everything off, in 2007 the Amermans sold Adoration for $3.1 million at the Keeneland November Breeding Stock Sale. She was in foal to Smart Strike, who was North America's leading stallion that year, and John Magnier bought her.

Adoration's dam, Sewing Lady, is still at Lanark—her last foal was a filly by Strong Hope. On January 1, 2008, Sewing Lady turned twenty years old, and Lucy retired her.

Horses sent to public auctions frequently have "reserves," which are minimum prices that have to be attained in order for them to be sold. If the bidding on an individual horse does not go as high as the reserve price, the horse goes back to the consigning owner. This was the case with a yearling filly Lucy sent to the 2005 Keeneland September sale—Book 5, Hip Number 3088—a chestnut daughter of Out of Place out of the Mining mare Thoughtful. Lucy brought the filly home, named her Meditations, and the following spring sent her to a trainer named Ralph Ziadie at Calder Race Course in south Florida. Ziadie is not well known outside of Florida, but he has a very interesting history. He is originally from Kingston, Jamaica, and was the leading trainer at a track in his home country called Caymanas Park. Ziadie immigrated to the United States in 1977 and sold used cars and worked in his wife's restaurant before renewing his training career at Calder in 1982.

In 1985, Ziadie trained a horse named Reggae Man that won seven consecutive starts. He led the Calder trainer standings in wins from 1990 to 1992, and as the years have gone on, Ziadie has compiled an impressive record with the horses he has shipped out of state. In 1998, he won the Cigar Mile Handicap at Aqueduct with Sir Bear. The following year, he sent Sir Bear out to win the Metropolitan Handicap at Belmont Park. Both of these are major races, as is the Hopeful Stakes at Saratoga, which Ziadie won in 2003 with a colt named Silver Wagon.

Ziadie does not believe in rushing horses through the early stages of their racing careers, which blends perfectly with Lucy's philosophy. So they took it easy with Meditations. She made her career debut as a racehorse on September 9, 2006, at Calder, and she finished second, beaten by only three-quarters of a length. Her odds were 15–1 in that race. The next time Meditations answered the call to the post, on October 7 at Calder, she was the 6–5 favorite. And she won by ten and three-quarter lengths. Nearly two months went by. Then, on December 2, Meditations ran in a $100,000 race, the Three Ring Stakes at Calder. As the 7–2 second choice in a field of seven, she won again by ten and three-quarter lengths. Lucy was pleased. I was overjoyed for her. Ziadie began mapping out a schedule for Meditations' three-year-old campaign that potentially had her running in a pair of major stakes at Gulfstream Park, then perhaps the Ashland

Stakes in April at Keeneland, and, if everything went well, maybe the Kentucky Oaks at Churchill Downs the day before the Derby.

In her seasonal debut, the Davona Dale Stakes at Gulfstream on February 10, Meditations went off as the odds-on favorite. Under a fine young jockey named Rafael Bejarano, she was moving well, in good position on the rail, through the opening quarter mile. Then, suddenly, Meditations took a bad step, and Bejarano pulled her up. She was vanned off the track with a severe injury to her left foreleg. Two days later, surgery was performed on Meditations in Ocala, Florida. She will probably never race again, but if the leg heals properly, Lucy might be able to breed her. Regardless, Meditations has a permanent home at Lanark. Injuries are part of horse racing. All of us in the business know that, but it is always disquieting when they happen. When the Kentucky Derby favorite Hoist the Flag broke down in the early spring of 1971, the great sportswriter Red Smith wrote a column in which he referred to "the harrowing uncertainties of the sport." He was right.

§

Pets are not our whole life, but they help make our lives whole. Every pet we have ever had at Lanark has been a stray who either walked onto the farm or who we found abandoned elsewhere. My very special companion was Honeybear, a thirty-pound, white-haired, mixed-breed dog who was a bundle of pure joy and affection.

Lucy was the one who found her. She was driving down Third Street in Lexington one morning. Traffic was heavy, and Lucy suddenly saw what she described as "an animated dirty mop" coming toward the car. It was Honeybear. The little dog was gaunt and dehydrated, and her long white hair was matted with burrs and dirt and covered with fleas. In desperation, she had chewed through the rope that had kept her tethered to a pole or fence railing or whatever. Well, Lucy stopped the car, got out, and picked the dog up and took her directly to a veterinarian. She was tended to, bathed, and fed, and we placed an advertisement in the lost dog section of the *Lexington Herald-Leader*. A week went by and there was no response, so we gave the dog a name, Honeybear, and she became a permanent member of the Lanark menagerie.

This began an idyll for me that spanned twelve years. No matter the time of day—morning, noon, or night—Honeybear's sensitive radar always had her waiting at the front door for my arrival home. During the early evening hours, we would take a mile-and-a-half journey together through the woods. Ice, snow, rain, heat—nothing stayed us from this adventure. No matter how weary I was from the day's work, even on days filled with frustrations, we would be 500 yards into our trek, and all burdens would simply be put on hiatus. And Honeybear—she would be darting to the left and right, playfully chasing but never catching the squirrels, rabbits, raccoons, and deer that came near or crossed our path. During our evening journeys, Honeybear and I would log ten and a half miles a week. Lucy would tell people, "Ted adores that dog," and I never attempted to deny it. When Honeybear died in March 2005, I wept without shame, and the memories of her and the fun we had still bring tears.

The deer at Lanark constitute one of the farm's defining characteristics. Many of them rove throughout Woodford County and down to the Kentucky River. But those who take up permanent residency at Lanark continue to increase in number. Once again, this is largely Lucy's doing, and when she makes up her mind that animals are endangered, nothing impedes her quest.

Of the properties that border ours, most are highly developed commercial horse farms, with limited tree groves and very little cover—they do not lend themselves to the development of wildlife. But Lanark's 1,000 or so acres are heavily wooded and contain lots of thick cover, and Lucy has installed a wire fence, for the purpose of protecting the deer from hunters, that is twelve to fourteen feet high and extends for over a mile. Some of the deer do get out onto Old Frankfort Pike, which allows them to go around the fence. But I would estimate that our resident deer herd currently numbers 100 to 200—maybe more.

If you are going by automobile from Keeneland to Lanark, it is about a twenty-minute drive. But you have to allow an additional six minutes or so for the one-mile trip up our driveway to the main house, because the deer seem to be everywhere, and your top speed can only be about ten miles per hour. We have deer signs posted along the driveway. Some of the deer will just be standing in the woods or at the edge of the streams, eating or drinking, their minds acting slowly. But others will walk right up to the car. And some will go bounding along, parallel to the car, as you move along the driveway. They may get a step or two ahead of the car and then suddenly take a hard ninety-degree turn. Although I have brushed one, I have never really hit one—but I would have, many times, had I not slammed my foot on the brake pedal.

The big male deer, the bucks, have a particularly awesome presence. You will see them in the fall, winter, and spring, the racks of antlers on their heads like the branches of a tree. But we rarely see them during the summer. The bucks mark their breeding territories, using their antlers to braze the trunks of trees. Once the breeding season is over, they shed the antlers, and on occasion, I've found a pair while strolling on the farm property.

Lucy has a section of the farm, about eighteen acres, where she grows special species of grass that have been recommended by the state's wildlife department as being especially nutritional for deer. We put out blocks of salt for the deer to lick, and when there is heavy snow during the winter months, she arranges for bales of hay to be broken up and spread on top of the fields, which assures that the deer have something to eat. I have carried many of those bales out there and broken them up and spread them myself.

Hunters are a problem. The property adjacent to the south side of Lanark is owned by a hunter, and during the winter he has a cover crop, which is very attractive as a feeding place to deer—and is one of the reasons why Lucy has put up that high fence. Kentucky law allows for deer to be hunted with bows and arrows from early September through mid-January and with firearms during a two-week period in November each year, and particularly in the latter period, the traffic is often bumper to bumper on Aiken Road, which fronts the east side of Lanark. Some of the automobiles and pickup trucks are occupied only by sightseers. But many contain hunters, who use binoculars to spot the deer and high-powered rifles, equipped with telescopic sights, to shoot them. Between 500 and 600 deer are harvested annually in Woodford County alone. It is against the law to shoot from the road, and to get onto our property, hunters have cut holes in our fences and sawed off the locks on our gates. In recent years, Lucy has hired special security personnel during the hunting seasons to keep the trespassers at bay.

She also has a wonderful relationship with the game wardens, who respect Lucy as a land conservationist and animal preservationist. Hunters, though, sometimes view things differently, and much to my dismay, Lucy goes out and patrols the property herself. She gets in her Jeep and, with no one else for accompaniment, will drive back and forth on the roads that thread through Lanark and on Aiken Road, and if she sees a trespasser she will stop and politely but firmly say, "This land is posted, and no hunting is allowed."

For years, I did the same thing. But I had to stop because of my temper. Back when I had my State Police cruiser, I felt more confident while patrolling the property, but that is not the case now. Rather than Lucy's diplomatic manner, I was more inclined to say, "What the hell are you doing out here?" This frequently generated a response along the lines of, "Who the hell are you, buddy?" And something that both my Marine Corps training and my State Police experience taught me is that it's unwise to get into a heated dispute with someone carrying a loaded rifle, particularly if you are armed with nothing more than car keys and a penknife.

People eat venison, and I understand that. But still, I find it extraordinary, almost impossible to understand how someone could find enjoyment in shooting one of these beautiful, defenseless animals. Using a high-powered rifle equipped with a telescopic scope—where is the sport in that? Of course, this is part of the Kentucky culture, handed down for decades from fathers to sons, teaching the boys how to bag their first deer. It is something that dates back to the days of Daniel Boone, and probably even well before that.

§

Airplanes and Lucy do not make a good mix, for she has a deeply held fear of air travel. Not helicopters—for some reason, those don't bother her. But airplanes? They truly frighten her. During the early years of our marriage, she attempted to overcome the fear by learning how to fly. She took several lessons at Blue Grass Airport, but that's as far as she got. As Lucy once told an interviewer, "Ted has traveled more than I have. I've been a lot of places, but not as many as him." The major reason for this is her aversion to air flight.

Our departures on planes, both here and abroad, always have required substantial preparation. First, the five-day weather forecast is always carefully scrutinized for anything that might appear troublesome—frontal systems, windy conditions, storms. During our journey to the airport, she is constantly peering at the sky and the cloud formations. When entering the aircraft, Lucy always visits the cockpit to talk to the pilots. "I'm a nervous Nellie," she tells them. "I'm very concerned, and I hope I don't disturb you by asking some questions." On British Airways, when we took the Concorde to Europe, the pilots would allow her, once we got halfway across the Atlantic, to sit in a little jump seat behind them. (They would not allow her to do this when we flew on Air France.)

Upon arriving at our destination, however, Lucy is immediately within her element. While it is my responsibility to have the transportation arranged and schedule my business appointments, Lucy's role involves scheduling the remainder of each day's activities. She is a tour guide at heart, and visiting sites of historic importance is a high priority for her. Lucy always does substantial beforehand research on whatever city or area of the world we'll be visiting. Many times, if we are heading for France or some other destination where French is frequently spoken, she secures the services of a tutor from the University of Kentucky to help with the language.

The first trip Lucy and I ever took to Europe was in late November 1975: Pan American Flight 100, seats 1A and 1B, John F. Kennedy Airport in New York to Heathrow Airport in London. The Boeing 747 we were on had a spiral staircase leading up the first-class lounge, where the tables were covered with white linen cloths and the eating utensils were made of silver—so different from today, when people are squeezed into airplanes like cattle. No subsequent flights, not even on the Concorde, were as memorable as that first one on Pan American. I think the unbridled excitement I felt had something to do with it. For, regardless of how many trips one eventually takes to Europe, none of them can surpass that first adventure.

One of our reasons for going was to attend the Tattersalls Thoroughbred sale at Newmarket. But the thrill of finally visiting London, staying at Claridge's Hotel, and seeing all those famous landmarks that I had read and heard about all my life—Westminster Abbey, the Tower of London (which is actually a complex of twenty-one towers), St. Paul's Cathedral, the British Museum, Trafalgar Square, the Houses of Parliament—they all made immense and lasting impressions. In many respects, it was like I was transported back to the mind-set of my boyhood days at Kent School. I was awestruck.

Paris was our next stop, and after a bumpy trip through a low overcast on British Airways we landed at Charles de Gaulle Airport. We checked in at the Hotel Ritz—it was about four o'clock in the afternoon, and Lucy decided to take a nap. But I went rushing out across the Place Vendome, trying to get my first glimpse of the Eiffel Tower. This did not turn out to be as easy as I thought it would be. It was kind of a gloomy late afternoon, twilight was on the verge of setting on and there are lots of tall buildings in Paris. So, I'm going up and down streets, crossing blocks, not really knowing which way to look and saying to myself, "Where is it? Where is it?" I guess I could have asked a Frenchman for directions, but I did not want to appear as some sort of jerk tourist. After about twenty minutes of this, I saw the Eiffel Tower. "There it is! There it is!" (I reacted exactly the same way when I first saw Big Ben in London.)

In the subsequent days, Lucy, as is her custom, organized our daily tours—to, yes, the Eiffel Tower and to the Arc de Triomphe, the Louvre, and the Cathedral Notre Dame. But what made the biggest impression on me was Fontainebleau, which is about thirty-five miles south of Paris. The Chateau de Fontainebleau is right on the edge of the 40,000-acre forest whose name it bears. The intricate architecture, the majestic columns, the allegorical paintings in molded plasterwork with the framing rolled into detailed scrolls, along with the majestic patterned gardens that were laid out over 400 years ago—it's astonishing to realize that these things were constructed centuries before the advent of modern-day technology.

Rome was the final destination of our inaugural trip to Europe. On our drive from Leonardo da Vinci Airport to the city, I kept gazing out the car windows, expecting each moment to see the Coliseum of Rome or St. Peter's Basilica. We stayed at the Hassler Roma, which is at the top of the Spanish Steps and provides a magnificent view of Rome, the Eternal City, with its 3,000-year history and maze of historical monuments. The trip whetted my appetite to see more of Europe, and Lucy and I returned there together a dozen times in the ensuing years.

One of our most memorable trips to France involved a weeklong tour of the Loire Valley. It was set up by one of Lucy's clients, Jean-Luc Lagardere, who was chairman of the Lagardere Group, which deals in banking, technology, communications, electronics, transport equipment, and missiles. Under Lagardere's leadership, the company annually did something like $12 billion in business and employed 60,000 people. Lagardere was also president of France-Galop, the ruling body of French racing, and he owned one of France's leading breeding operations, Haras du val Henry—Lagardere bred the 2001 Breeders' Cup Mile winner Val Royal. Well, the trip he planned (Lagardere provided us with his personal automobile and driver) took Lucy and me to the Chateau de Chenonceau, which for centuries served the needs of members of the French royalty, their wives, and their mistresses. Located adjacent to the River Cher, the Chateau de Chenonceau, during World War II, was a means of escaping from the Nazi occupied zone on one side of the river to the free Vichy side on the other.

During that trip, we also went to the Renaissance gardens at the Chateau de Villandry, on whose site, late in the twelfth century, King Phillip

II of France met with King Richard I of England to discuss peace. During the early nineteenth century, the Chateau de Villandry was occupied by Napoleon's brother, Joseph Bonaparte. We went to these places and so, so many more, and Lucy and the guides she hired spoke, and I listened. Credit me for having enough wisdom to have done that.

Of all the great historic cities in Europe, Lucy's favorite is Vienna. Each journey there has always required a visit to Schönbrunn Palace, which was the home of Emperor Franz Joseph, who ruled Austria from 1848 to 1916. A tour of the palace includes seeing the sitting rooms and parlor of Empress Maria Theresa, where a six-year-old named Wolfgang Amadeus Mozart would come and give private clavier, violin, and organ recitals for her. At Schönbrunn, we would visit the Tirolean Garden and its Palm House, which has three climate zones and plants gathered from rain forests in South America, Africa, and Asia. And we would enjoy the puppet show, with its beautiful, hand-carved figures and elaborate settings.

Vienna's State Opera House is also always one of the places we visit. Home of the Wiener Staatsoper (Vienna State Opera) and the Vienna Philharmonic Orchestra, it began construction in 1861 and took eight years to complete. Its neo-Romantic style initially brought so much criticism that one of its two architects, Eduard van der Null, committed suicide, and the other, August von Siccardsburge, died shortly after of a heart attack. But what these two men created became the prototype of opera houses worldwide. There are tiers of boxes surrounding the sides of the stage and elegantly dressed and distinguished-looking people sitting in those boxes, many of whom have their little opera field glasses. It is just like you see in the movies, except this is real life. Lucy and I sat in a box by ourselves when we went there. I confess I do not remember the name of the opera we saw, and neither does Lucy, but the opera house itself is something that forever remains in my mind's eye.

At the opera, we did not have the best seats, but they were all right. In Europe, when you're staying at the five-star, classic hotels, access to events is best obtained by working through the concierges. They have their fingers on the pulses of the great cities. They are the masters of the ship—they control the tickets to performing arts activities, the reservations to the best restaurants, the cars and drivers. You must tip the concierges rather handsomely, but they open the doors. Of course, you can try to forgo the concierges and stand in line. But that's a good way of finding yourself either stuck in the caboose or missing the train altogether, which did not appeal to Lucy and did not appeal to me.

The concierge at the Hotel Imperial in Vienna obtained tickets for us to the Spanish Riding School, the Wiener Hofreitschule. Founded in 1572, it features classic dressage, practiced in its purest form. The horses there are of the Lipizzaner breed—black in their early portion of their lives, they turn white as they reach maturity. They and their riders stage their elegant and extremely complex performances in the Vienna Hofburg, also known as the Imperial Palace, which first opened in 1735 and is adorned with magnificent chandeliers. It was not until 1920 that tickets to performances were made available to the public, and I can tell you that they are very expensive but worth every dollar you spend on them.

Of all the places for tourists we have visited in London, the one that resides most prominently in my mind is Westminster Abbey. Following the death of Sir Winston Churchill in 1965, the Queen unveiled a green marble memorial stone permanently honoring him in the Abbey. We went there during our inaugural trip in 1975, the year following the 100th anniversary of Churchill's birth, and there were incredible floral arrangements, dozens and dozens, perhaps hundreds of them, at the Abbey's entrances. Also displayed was a note from Churchill's widow, Clementine, that began with the words, "To my dear husband." I believe she signed it, "Your Darling Clemie."

I have gone into a bit of detail here concerning some of these experiences because I want to emphasize how educational these trips have been for me. And I largely credit Lucy for this. She has always been so well prepared, so well informed about what we will be seeing. And she has always been insistent that we allocate the time and energy to see everything thoroughly. I'm her silent accomplice, to whom she points out things left and right. On occasion, I probably have not displayed as much enthusiasm about these sightseeing tours as I should, but that has never deterred Lucy. The true philosopher never loses the love for learning, and Lucy has seen to it that the quest for knowledge is never extinguished for either of us.

Chapter 10

Racing Personalities

THE FIRST TIME I met D. Wayne Lukas was on October 14, 1978. I recall the exact date because it was the day of the Alcibiades Stakes, which was and remains Keeneland's premier event for two-year-old fillies. Lukas had a filly in the race named Terlingua, who had generated tremendous interest among the racing press and the public because she was the first of Secretariat's daughters to run in a stakes at our track. Terlingua had been purchased for $275,000 at the Keeneland July sale as a yearling, and she had won four of her first five career starts, all of which had occurred in stakes races.

Lukas was then forty-three years old. I did not know much about him. I had been told he was based in Southern California and had been very successful as a quarter horse trainer but recently had switched full time to Thoroughbreds. The Breeders' Cup had not come into existence yet, and if Terlingua won the Alcibiades—which had a distance of seven furlongs that year and a purse of $137,875—there was a great chance that she would be North America's juvenile filly champion. This is something, of course, we always love to see with a Keeneland sales graduate, especially if the championship gets sealed in a Keeneland stakes race.

So, as the fillies were being saddled, I approached Lukas in the paddock, introduced myself, and thanked him for bringing Terlingua back to Keeneland. It was getting to be late in the afternoon, and it was dark. There were storm clouds overhead. The wind was picking up. Terlingua was the 1–2 favorite in the field of seven, and as the fillies exited the paddock and were going through the tunnel leading to the main track, a tremendous bolt of lightning flashed across the sky. A brief shower of hail immediately ensued, and then the rain really began to pour down. Terlingua, who had a jockey named Darrell McHargue aboard her, decided she had seen enough. She reared and then tried to turn around and go back into the tunnel. "She was a lot smarter than most of us," Lukas told me later.

The race started, and an 8–1 shot named Angel Island took the lead during the first few strides out of the gate and never relinquished it, drawing away to win by six lengths. Terlingua kept close to her until the eighth pole but then faded and finished a distant second. Lukas said that the sudden onslaught of lightning, hail, and rain had unsettled Terlingua, and he was probably right. She didn't run anywhere near her best that day. And a pair of fillies named Candy Éclair and It's In the Air, neither of whom raced at Keeneland, ended up being co-champions of the division.

My next contact with Lukas was in February 1980. I had flown out to Southern California to solicit nominations for the Blue Grass and Ashland Stakes (the latter is Keeneland's premier event for three-year-old fillies). I was trudging through the mud and muck on Santa Anita's backside and suddenly came upon a barn that had been transformed into a mini-oasis, with manicured grass plots bordering the front and gleaming white stall panels that bore enlarged DWL letters in green. There were leather bridles and shanks with gleaming brass displayed on a wooden rack—no tack store displayed its wares better. Peering into the stalls, I saw deep beds of clean, fresh straw, enticing enough for human rest. And there was deep green alfalfa hay, enclosed in woven rope sacks, attached to the stall doors. I thought, "Who is the master magician that transformed a drab horse barn into a mini-showcase?" And there was no question in my mind about the message that was being delivered—it was obvious. We do things differently. We are better.

I found Lukas sitting astride his pony outside his tack room. He was immaculately attired and turned out, wearing a wide-brimmed western hat and sitting on a big silver-buckled saddle. He was sitting up stone straight and looked imposing. Although we had met once before, Lukas didn't seem to remember who I was. But he was courteous. I told him I was hoping our Blue Grass Stakes interested him, and his first question was, "What's the purse?" I told him it was $100,000. He did not seem very impressed. He said, "You expect me to ship all the way across country for $100,000?" And I replied (or perhaps stammered a reply is more like it) that running in the Blue Grass provided a great opportunity for a horse to acclimate for the Kentucky Derby. Lukas asked me about the deadline for nominations. I told him they closed on February 15, and he suggested that I come back just before that date.

That was the year Lukas had Codex, a colt for whom he initially did not have high regard but that was showing some promise. Codex had won in maiden company and had registered a couple of allowance wins, but he had been unplaced and unimpressive in his only stakes try. When I returned to Lukas's barn on February 15, I pleaded with his son, Jeff, to nominate a horse for the Blue Grass. And Jeff said, "Okay, put Codex in."

A few minutes later, I saw a Pimlico Race Course representative who was soliciting nominations for the Preakness (in those days, horses were nominated separately for each of the Triple Crown races). I told him, "I just picked up a new one for the Blue Grass. Codex. You may get him for the Preakness." The Pimlico representative followed up on the suggestion and got the nomination.

In late March, Codex suddenly found his best stride and won the Santa Anita Derby. He did it at odds of 25–1. Two weeks later, he won the Hollywood Derby. He had unexpectedly emerged as the best three-year-old on the West Coast. But Lukas had not nominated him for the Kentucky Derby. Codex didn't go to the Blue Grass either (which that year was won by Rockhill Native, from the barn of the Keeneland-based trainer Herb Stevens). But Codex did go to the Preakness, where, ridden by Angel Cordero Jr., probably the most aggressive jockey I've ever seen, he crowded the Kentucky Derby–winning filly Genuine Risk at the head of the stretch and then went on to win by four and three-quarter lengths.

During subsequent years, I don't believe there has ever been another example of Lukas failing to nominate a qualified horse for a major race. And look at the results he has gained: four Kentucky Derby victories; a career total of five in the Preakness and four in the Belmont Stakes. Commencing with the 1994 Preakness and culminating with the 1996 Kentucky Derby, Lukas won six consecutive Triple Crown races, a feat that may go unmatched for as long as record books are kept.

Look at his record in the Breeders' Cup—from 1984 to 2005, Lukas horses made 145 starts in Breeders' Cup events and won 18 of them. That worked out to a win ratio of 12.4 percent competing against the top stables from North America and Europe. The Breeders' Cup purse earnings of his horses totaled $19.65 million, nearly twice the figure achieved by any other trainer. Here's another statistic: Excluding the steeplechase, in all the Breeders' Cup races run during that twenty-two-year period, Lukas had at least one starter in 50.9 percent of them.

As the 1980s progressed, Lukas became acutely aware that central

Kentucky was a Mecca of racing and that he could expand his network of prominent owners by becoming a powerful force at Churchill Downs and at Keeneland. He is second to only his fellow Hall of Famer Bill Mott in career wins and stakes wins by a trainer at Churchill. And at Keeneland, Lukas is peerless in the overall trainer rankings. Through the fall of 2008, he was the all-time leader here in wins, with 272. He is the all-time leader at Keeneland in stakes wins, too, with 50.

The media gravitate in huge numbers toward Lukas. Part of this is because of his success, but part of it is also because no matter what question he's asked, he always provides a direct response. The phrase "No comment" has long eluded the Lukas vernacular. In regard to television, he understands what ten-second sound bites are and has an unending supply of them. He is gracious in both victory and defeat. Losing a major race is a wrenching, disappointing thing for him. There have been times when Lukas has been extremely critical of the way a jockey rode one of his horses, but I've never seen him flare up in public at a rider.

He's exceptionally organized. When I was Keeneland's president, I always liked to spend a lot of time in the barn area during the race meets, to go there and greet the trainers, to express appreciation for shipping in with their stables. Their horses fuel the meet's engine, and we were in competition with other tracks to get them, so I saw this as an important part of my job. I'd say things to each trainer like, "How are you doing? Glad to have you back. Did you have a good winter (or summer)?" Small talk, sure, but it made a difference to prominent, established trainers and to the younger ones just coming along. It's also critical, I think, to the successful operation of a racetrack to have direct lines of communication with people in the barn areas. A great place to do this is in the track kitchen—although that's a place where Lukas rarely goes. In fact, Lukas told me that, despite all his years in racing, he doubts he's been in more than three or four track kitchens for any reason.

I don't know when he eats breakfast, but he rises at 3:30 A.M. each day, seven days a week, with never a miss. I'd see Lukas arrive at the start of a race meet or sale at Keeneland and ask him if he needed assistance with hotel room reservations for his clients.

"Nope."

"Well, could we help you with rental cars?"

"No, they're already taken care of."

"Well, is there anything . . ?"

"Nope, thank you very much."

I think one of the lesser-known facts about Lukas, and probably about Keeneland as well, is that of the two dozen North American champions he has trained over the years, ten of them were purchased at Keeneland yearling sales. In chronological order of their champion seasons for Lukas, the horses are as follows:

Horse	Keeneland Sale	Sale Price	Champion Season
Life's Magic	September	$310,000	1984 (three-year-old filly) 1985 (older filly or mare)
Family Style	September	$60,000	1985 (two-year-old filly)
Capote	July	$800,000	1986 (two-year-old colt)
Sacahuista	July	$670,000	1987 (three-year-old filly)
Winning Colors	July	$575,000	1988 (three-year-old filly)
Timber Country	July	$500,000	1994 (two-year-old colt)
Thunder Gulch	July	$40,000	1995 (three-year-old colt)
Serena's Song	July	$150,000	1995 (three-year-old filly)
Orientate	September	$250,000	2002 (sprinter)
Azeri	September	$110,000	2004 (older filly or mare)

But Lukas has, at times, been unhesitant about voicing displeasure with various aspects of Keeneland and its fiscal policies. Regarding the drainage system on our racetrack surface, Lukas would say to me, "Ted, I want you to come out some morning when it rains and show me how the water can drift down to the rail and then jump four inches into that drainage hole." And he'd say, "Ted, is there some sort of trapping device in the Keeneland vault? Is there some sort of triggering method that engages it when you fight your way through those cobwebs and get to those old, moldy certificates of deposit that have been laying there for all those years and years? If the idea somehow gets into your head that Keeneland needs to spend some money on something, does the trapping device slam down on your hand when you reach into the vault to get one of those certificates? Just how does that all work?"

There was one morning during one of the race meets when Lukas was standing at the rail in front of the grandstand in the presence of two reporters, one from the *Daily Racing Form* and the other from the *Lexington Herald-Leader.* He was upset about the condition of the track surface and made some pretty strong comments about it. The reporters said, "Are you kidding? Do you really believe that?"

Lukas replied, "Damn right!"

The reporters said, "Can we print that?"

Lukas said, "Absolutely you can print it."

Well, the next day, there are these headlines, "LUKAS CRITICIZES KEENELAND SURFACE." Big letters. Bill Greely and I see them, and we're hot. So we went looking for Lukas and found him upstairs in the corporate box area, in the hallway outside of William T. Young's corporate box. I think the first race of the afternoon had just been run. Greely and I have Lukas in our sights, and he sees us. We're marching toward him, and he's got this look on his face that reads, "Oh hell, I'm going to have to deal with this, I might as well take it head-on now."

I reached out with my right hand, clutched Lukas's forearm, and said to him in a tight voice, "Wayne, your comments strained our relationship." Yes, I was angry.

Lukas looked at me and said, "Oh, come on, Ted, the first time I bid a million dollars on a yearling at Keeneland's next sale, our relationship will be immediately back in order." Lukas grinned, and I started to laugh. And he started to laugh. And Greely was laughing too. The mini-crisis was over.

§

Don Brumfield's persona fits Kentucky in the same manner he fitted the horses he rode. Calm. Taciturn. Sometimes droll. But Brumfield was always professional when it came to being a jockey. Originally from Nicholasville, Kentucky, he is one of our state's native sons who made good. Admired and respected by both the racing public and his peers, Don attained the status of a folk hero at Keeneland. Before retiring from the saddle in 1989, he had accumulated sixteen Keeneland riding titles, seven in the spring and nine in the fall.

All told at Keeneland, Don had registered 716 wins, 32 of which had been accomplished in stakes. At the time, he was not only the track's all-time leader in both categories, he had accumulated more than twice as many wins and stakes victories here than anybody else. And his Keeneland stakes triumphs spanned a twenty-five-year period. His first came in the 1964 Ben Ali Handicap with a horse named Copy Chief. And his final one came in the 1989 Beaumont with a filly named Exquisite Mistress.

One of my fondest memories of Don involved the 1974 Ashland Stakes. The race was divided into two divisions that year, and he won both of them—the first division with a filly named Winged Wishes, and the second division with a filly named Maud Muller. Don had actually bred Winged Wishes, and she was owned by his mother, Viola Brumfield. The *Daily Racing Form* chart stated that Winged Wishes was "sharply roused in the upper stretch," and from there she went on to win by a length and a half. And Winged Wishes was trained by Don's close friend David Kassen. Never in all my years have I witnessed a more exuberant meeting in the Keeneland winner's circle of owner, jockey, and trainer. To make the story complete, the filly returned $14.20 to win, and Mrs. Brumfield's pocket-book was bulging with cash afterward.

But Don's greatest season was in 1966, when he won the Kentucky Derby on Kauai King. In the winner's circle, Don said, "I'm the happiest hillbilly hardboot alive." From that quote, he got the nickname "Boot." The boots Don wore in that year's Derby are now fashioned into lamp stands that adorn his den. Also in 1966, Don rode Native Street to victory in the Kentucky Oaks, and he remains just one of six jockeys to score a Derby-Oaks double in the same year.

The final race Don rode was at Turfway Park on September 16, 1989, when he guided a horse named Batim to a fourth-place finish in the Aly-sheba Stakes. It was his 33,222nd career race. He had won 4,572 of them, and his mounts had accumulated $43.56 million in purses. Don was fifty-one at the time, and when it was suggested to him that his advancing years had effected his retirement, he said, "Age doesn't say when a rider is over the hill. Some guys can't ride in a boxcar with both doors shut." That fall, Don went to work as a patrol judge at Keeneland, a position he held for several years. He also worked in Florida as a steward.

It really does strike me as unfortunate that Brumfield never won the Blue Grass Stakes. His Blue Grass record was 0 for 13, the best he ever did in the race being a second-place finish with Our Native in 1973. Still, Don will always be regarded among central Kentuckians as the homegrown legend, possessed with a brilliant ability to get the best efforts from young horses. He won the Ashland Stakes three times, the Alcibiades Stakes three times. And he won the Breeders' Futurity five times, a record that remains unmatched by any jockey to this day. Don Brumfield was a rider who needed no assist when he donned his racing silks.

§

Woody Stephens was also one of Kentucky's native sons. He was originally from Stanton, a small town that borders the Daniel Boone National Forest. Boone became a legend in his own time, and the same was true of Woody.

His full name was Woodford Cefis Stephens. When he was ten years old, his family moved to Midway, which is only a dozen miles or so northwest of Lexington. At age thirteen, Woody was breaking young Thoroughbreds at Parrish Hill Farm. He ultimately became one of the most successful trainers in racing history.

In 1974, Woody won the 100th running of the Kentucky Derby with Cannonade. And he won the 1984 Derby with Swale. But Woody's greatest accomplishment was winning five consecutive runnings of the Belmont Stakes, from 1982 to 1986. In his later years, during just about any conversation you had with him, he would eventually say, "You know, I win five straight Belmonts." He always said "I win," not "I won." His statement was ungrammatical, but everyone knew what Woody was talking about.

Whenever Woody came into Keeneland's backside kitchen, it was like a presidential entrance. His memory was extraordinary—he had phenomenal recall. You could ask him about the colt he ran in the 1957 Blue Grass Stakes, and Woody would immediately respond, "Well, I had two in that Blue Grass—Lucky Dip and One-Eyed King. I train both of them for Harry Guggenheim. That was Round Table's year. Lucky Dip gave Round Table a run down the backside, and One-Eyed King challenged him in the stretch, but at the eighth pole . . ." You half expected Woody to call off the time fractions.

He did win the Blue Grass three times, and among trainers, only Ben Jones, LeRoy Jolley, and Nick Zito have matched that standard. Woody won a grand total of nineteen stakes at Keeneland, including the Ashland four times (a standard that to date has remained unmatched by anybody) and the Breeders' Futurity four times. He trained eleven North American champions. He was a great friend of the Nuckols brothers, Alfred and Charles, who also grew up in the Midway area. Woody had an uncanny ability of maximizing a horse's talents. The media loved him. Unfortunately, the Breeders' Cup did not come into being until late in Woody's life, when he was seventy-one, and he never had a winner in a Breeders' Cup event. He was always very complimentary about Keeneland. But those five consecutive Belmont wins will always be what stands out about him the most. An unbelievable feat.

§

The 1980 Blue Grass Stakes was won by Rockhill Native. He was conditioned by Herbert K. Stevens, who was the unofficial dean of the trainers who stabled year-round at Keeneland and the walking definition of a *hard-boot,* a term applied to Kentucky horsemen of the old school. At age thirteen, Herb had galloped horses for his father, James D. Stevens, at the Kentucky Association track. After getting out of the U.S. Army following World War II, Herb established a stable at Keeneland and had been conditioning horses here ever since.

When Keeneland was not running, Herb would ship to River Downs near Cincinnati, where he won at least five training titles; to Latonia, which is now called Turfway Park; and to Miles Park, which was located in the southern part of Louisville. These were minor-league tracks. Herb did win one training title at Churchill in the fall of 1970, when a horse from his barn, named Princess Ericann, scored at 53–1 odds on the final day of the meet.

But Barn 39 at Keeneland, high upon a hill on a distant sector of the grounds, had been Herb's base of operations for thirty-five years. During that time, he had dealt almost entirely with claiming stock. Herb and his brother, Tommy, were joined to multiple generations of Stevens family members involved in Thoroughbred racing and breeding. Well back into the nineteenth century, the Stevens men were active in the Bluegrass region, raising and training horses and mules.

A story Herb would tell involved his great-grandfather, John, and his grandfather, Tom, driving through the rural areas of Kentucky in a buggy with a horse hitched to the front and another to the back. The area was full of small towns, and a half mile or so before entering one, they would switch the positions of the horses. Many of these towns had fairs where horse racing would take place, and there was always a local merchant or farmer who reputedly had the fastest horse in those parts. The locals would start bragging and take John and Tom to see the horse. At that point, John would say, "Hey, he doesn't look like much. The horse pulling my buggy could beat him." The locals would then make some hefty wagers. They figured John's horse had been pulling the buggy and was tired. Besides, he was only a buggy horse! What they did not know was that both of the Stevens's horses were speedy, seasoned racing stock and that the one pulling the buggy was fresh. Tom would climb aboard the horse, the race would be run, and the Stevens men would collect their winnings. "My grandfather told me they never lost," said Herb.

Back in 1887, Tom Stevens campaigned a pair of fillies named Florimore and Wary, who finished first and second, respectively, in the Kentucky Oaks. James D. Stevens trained horses in Kentucky for over half a century. Herb himself had twice won training titles at the Keeneland fall meets. But he had never before had a horse bearing anything close to the ability of Rockhill Native.

Harry A. Oak, a former vice president for United Parcel Service, had bought Rockhill Native for $26,000 as a yearling at Keeneland in September 1978. He was only the second horse that Oak had ever owned. Gelded before he ever raced, Rockhill Native had won stakes at Churchill, Monmouth Park, and Belmont Park at age two and had received the Eclipse Award as North America's two-year-old champion. At age three, he had won the Everglades at Hialeah and was expected to be one of the favorites in the Kentucky Derby.

But talk about local angles! Rockhill Native had been bred at a Lexington-area farm. He had been purchased at Keeneland, which remained his home base. He was conditioned by Stevens, a native of Lexington, whose family heritage in racing dated back more than 100 years. And Rockhill Native was ridden by John Oldham, who was born in Hamilton County, Ohio, had registered his first career win on a horse trained by Herb at Keeneland in the fall of 1973, and was a regular member of our jockey colony.

Nine days before the Blue Grass, Rockhill Native won a one-and-one-sixteenth-mile allowance race at Keeneland in wire-to-wire fashion by a widening six and three-quarter lengths. By that time, Rockhill Native had a nickname, "Rocky," which I am sure does not surprise you, and he had an enormous following in central Kentucky. A crowd of 18,480 came to watch Rockhill Native run in the Blue Grass. He went off as the 1–2 favorite and won by two lengths. I remember Herb in the winner's circle, wearing a wide, cream-colored Stetson, with his wife, Lady Louise (her baptized name), at his side. When Governor John Y. Brown Jr. presented him with the trophy, Herb said, "This one's for the local people." As Rockhill Native was being led back to the barn, people continued to line the rail, applauding him. It was all part of a great story. But Rockhill Native, Herb Stevens, Harry Oak, and John Oldham turned out to be only minor players in the grand conclusion.

That was the year Genuine Risk won the Kentucky Derby. She remains only one of three fillies to have done so. Rockhill Native, the favorite at 2–1, finished fifth in the Derby. He skipped the Preakness and then finished third in the Belmont Stakes. And after that, he never raced again.

Herb Stevens retired in 1996. Now in his nineties, he continues to attend Keeneland's annual Blue Grass dinner. To me, Herb is one of the last representatives of a vanishing era. John Oldham works at Keeneland as a supervisor for the United Tote Company. Rockhill Native is pensioned at Sycamore Farm, which is owned by Louis Haggin III. He turned thirty-two this year and is now the oldest living horse who's a Blue Grass winner.

§

October 13, 2005, will always be a date I'll remember. It was Pat Day's fifty-second birthday, and we were having a celebration at Keeneland to honor his retirement from riding. Pat chose the occasion to pay us a tremendous tribute. He said, "Riding at Keeneland was like a working vacation. It was always more like a sporting event than a betting one." These were kind words from a kind man, who emerged at an early age from his native Colorado to become one of the nation's most admired and respected jockeys.

Pat's quarter century of competition at Keeneland resulted in 22 riding titles and 918 overall victories, including 95 in stakes. He is the all-time record holder in all three of these categories and might remain so forever. Pat is a jockey who dealt in multiples. He won the Blue Grass Stakes four times, with Taylor's Special (1984), Summer Squall (1990), Menifee (1999), and High Yield (2000). He won the Breeders' Futurity four times, the Spinster Stakes five times, the Bewitch Stakes six times, and the Ben Ali Stakes thrice.

My earliest memory of Pat involves his ride aboard Try Something New in the 1983 Spinster. Try Something New won the race by a neck. She was owned by John A. Bell III, a proper, popular horseman who was a longtime Keeneland director. And it was the first grade 1 victory at Keeneland for Try Something New's trainer Claude "Shug" McGaughey III, who was born and raised in Lexington and is now a member of racing's Hall of Fame. McGaughey's wife at the time, Mary Jane, was one of his top assistants, but she had broken her right leg several days before and had a full cast on the leg that stretched to well above her knee. Back then, the Spinster was run on the closing day of the fall meet, and a crowd of 20,516 was on hand. As Try Something New was being led to the winner's circle, it seemed to me like nearly half the crowd crossed the track to join her there—John Bell and his wife, Jessica, had many friends and relatives. But as they all were posing for the winner's circle photo, Pat, who was still astride Try Something New, held up his hand, as if asking for a pause, and then pointed toward the track. And there, making progress the best she could with a pair of crutches, dragging her wounded leg, came Mary Jane McGaughey. She was determined to be in the winner's circle photo too. Seeing this, the people in the grandstand let out a tremendous roar. It's a scene I'll never forget, that young woman struggling, with tears flowing down her eyes. We held up the winner's circle presentation until Mary Jane was able to get there. Pat, with his raised view—he was perched on Try Something New, which allowed him to see over the winner's circle gathering—he was the person who had seen Mary Jane and had made the moment possible.

In 1992, Pat won the Kentucky Derby with Lil E. Tee. He won the Preakness five times, the Belmont Stakes three times, and was victorious in twelve Breeders' Cup races. He was a four-time Eclipse Award winner as North America's leading jockey and was elected to the Hall of Fame the first year he met eligibility requirements. But he will long be revered even more for being a special person. Pat is known as racing's Good Samaritan, reaching out to the forgotten and those all too often overlooked, those in need on the backside, consoling, counseling, spreading the faith—in accordance with the life-changing religious experience he had in 1982.

As is the case for many others who know Pat, my most vivid memories of him do not involve his on-track victories but rather how he conducted himself aside from his riding. His friendly smile, his openness with the public, his willingness, again and again, to endure endless questions from the press and unending requests for autographs from the racing public. Whenever Keeneland had an impending problem with riders, whether it was related to the condition of the track surface or the usage of safety vests and helmets or the practices of the outriders or the policies of the Jockeys' Guild, Pat Day was always the first person we contacted, to see what this fair-minded and logical man's approach would be. And Keeneland always listened.

Another indication of how gentlemanly Pat has conducted himself involves the post-race press conference after he rode Easy Goer to an eight-length victory in the 1989 Belmont Stakes, upsetting Sunday Silence's quest for a Triple Crown sweep. Sunday Silence had been a two-and-a-half-length winner of the Kentucky Derby, which had been run over a muddy surface, upon which Easy Goer had a hard time getting his footing. Two weeks later, in arguably the most scorching stretch duel ever witnessed in the Preakness, Sunday Silence had prevailed by a nose. However, the Belmont had turned out to be Easy Goer's showcase and a crushing disappointment for Arthur Hancock III, Dr. Ernest Gaillard, and Charlie Whittingham, who co-owned Sunday Silence. Pat, ever sensitive to the feelings of others, shared the disappointment of Sunday Silence being unable to win the Triple Crown's third jewel. He did not exult publicly in Easy Goer's victory, even though the colt had provided him with his first career win in the Belmont, and years later, he called Easy Goer the very best horse he had ever ridden.

Today, true to his faith, Pat is embarking on a new career but continues to fulfill an old commitment—he is a national spokesman for the Racetrack Chaplaincy of America.

§

The Keeneland Library has a winner's circle photograph dated October 20, 1966, of a filly named Summer Scandal. She had just won the sixth race on that day's Keeneland card, and she's standing for the photo in front of the grandstand with her jockey, Kenny Knapp. Summer Scandal's trainer of record was J. Woods Garth, but she had been saddled that day by a skinny eighteen-year-old assistant who can also be seen in the photo, named Nicholas P. Zito. I was still director of the Kentucky State Police at the time, so you can say that Zito accomplished something at Keeneland years before I ever did.

Nick Zito, originally from New York City, is a New Yorker's New Yorker—he's a textbook example of what hard work, commitment, and dedication can achieve. And while today, more than forty years later, he still speaks like a guy who was raised an arm's length from Long Island (or, as Nick would say, "Lawn Guy-Land"), Kentuckians have adopted him to the point where he might as well be a native son of the Bluegrass. He is a master strategist, be it with horses or with people. Please tell me, who other than Zito could persuade, orchestrate, and manage such a high-profile stable of owners as George Steinbrenner III, Marylou Whitney, and Rick Pitino and publicly keep them all reasonably content? Zito always calls me "General," even though I've informed him many times that the highest rank I ever achieved was colonel, conferred upon me by the Kentucky State Police.

In 1991, Zito shipped from Keeneland to Florida with a stable that included a pair of very nice colts, Strike the Gold and Thirty Six Red. Strike the Gold was a three-year-old. Six months earlier, he had finished ninth, beaten by twenty-one and a quarter lengths, in the first start of his career, but in his most recent effort, he had finished a strong second in the Florida Derby. Thirty Six Red was a year older. In 1990, he had won the Wood Memorial and finished third in the Breeders' Cup Classic, and Zito had him prepared to make his four-year-old debut in a seven-furlong allowance race at Keeneland on April 10.

Thirty Six Red went off at 2–5 odds, and under Jerry Bailey, he finished first by three-quarters of a length. But the stewards immediately lit the inquiry sign on the tote board, and a jockey named Ricardo Lopez, who had ridden the fourth-place finisher, Momsfurrari, lodged a claim of foul against Thirty Six Red. The taped replays of the race showed Thirty Six Red drifting in on Momsfurrari at the eighth pole. It was Zito's opinion afterward that "when Lopez checked his mount, he made it look pretty good." The stewards disqualified Thirty Six Red to second. Zito was dumbfounded. To him, it was a terrible call. But when interviewed on the radio afterward, he said the stewards were only doing their jobs and that one had to believe in their integrity. I was proud of Nick for doing that, and when I saw him the following morning, I simply said a single word—"integrity." Zito replied, "Yeah, General, but you've still got three blind mice up in that stewards' box."

Three days later, Strike the Gold was a three-length winner of the Blue Grass Stakes. And three weeks following that effort, he won the Kentucky Derby. Strike the Gold then went through one of the most unusual droughts I've ever seen for a racehorse. He made twelve starts, eleven of them in stakes races, and finished second four times and third three times but did not record a single win. Four different jockeys rode Strike the Gold during that drought, but none of them could get him home in front. It was baffling.

The drought was finally relieved in early May 1992 when Strike the Gold won the Pimlico Special. He was ridden by Craig Perret that day, his fifth jockey in twelve months. I phoned Nick to congratulate him, and Nick, although born and raised a Roman Catholic, told me my call was more important to him than if he had gotten one from Pope John Paul II. I appreciated the sentiment. But, as I told Nick later, I really don't think popes make phone calls, and if they on rare occasions do, I doubt if the calls are to trainers of racehorses.

In 1998, Zito won the Blue Grass for a second time with Hallory Hunter, a colt partly owned by Pitino, who had won a national championship as the University of Kentucky's basketball coach in 1996 and at the time coached the Boston Celtics. And in 2004, Zito won the Blue Grass a third time, with The Cliff's Edge, a colt named for the Equibase chart caller and Nick's longtime friend Cliff Guilliams. (Cliff later told me that handling the chart-calling responsibilities for the victory by The Cliff's Edge was his greatest thrill during his three decades covering racing. I wish there was a happier ending to this part of the tale. On a Sunday midway through the 2008 Keeneland spring meet, Cliff did not show up for work. The Keeneland publicity staff became alarmed and phoned the hotel where he was staying. Cliff was found in his bed, dead of a heart attack at the age of fifty-two. Nick looked upon him as one of his favorite Kentuckians.)

Further on in the 2004 season, we witnessed another instance of the persuasive effect of Zito's personality, this time in the aftermath of his victory with Birdstone in the Belmont Stakes. With all the hoopla, hype, and pent-up anticipation of Smarty Jones finally breaking the jinx and becoming the first Triple Crown winner in twenty-six years, his upset by Birdstone created a silence of disbelief. I cannot help but believe that the presence in the winner's circle of New York's favorite trainer and Birdstone's gracious owner, Marylou Whitney, prevented the usually raucous New York crowd from breaking into a roar of rejection.

In 2008, Zito won his second Belmont, this time with a colt named Da' Tara. It was Nick's fifth career triumph in a Triple Crown event, which makes him one of the most accomplished Thoroughbred conditioners in modern times—indeed, of any time.

Articulate, engaging personalities and proven winners such as Lukas and Zito constitute the tonic that our racing industry needs to revitalize the public awareness, interest, and support it must have in order for the sport to survive and prosper.

§

My introduction to Joe Hirsch, the executive columnist for the *Daily Racing Form,* occurred thirty-nine years ago. I had received a phone call from a staff member in the press box at Hialeah, inviting me to join Joe for lunch in the Turf Club. It was the week of the Flamingo Stakes, and the invitation was like a papal summons from the Vatican. Can you imagine the leading turf columnist in North America inviting this neophyte, this greenhorn—the most inexperienced member of the Keeneland staff—to have lunch with him during what was then the most important time of year for south Florida racing?

But this was one of Joe's beguiling characteristics—his willingness to reach out to novices, whether they were horse owners, trainers, journalists, or someone simply in need of encouragement and direction. There was a subtle logic to his approach, for he felt that whenever he helped someone, he was also helping the racing game. From the elite to the depressed, he never ignored anybody. And this allowed him access and privy to every participant in racing, from the most prominent owner-breeder to the obscure jockey who suddenly booted home a 100–1 shot in a stakes. A phone call from Joe was a polite summons to respond to a query or offer a comment. Few people, if any, ever complained that Joe misquoted them.

His annual arrival at the spring meet at Keeneland was akin to the appearance of a major public personality. Joe would always call me from the press box to say hello and to let me know he was there. He usually had several requests. The *Racing Form* room in the press box was shared by the publication's chart-calling crew and another writer, and Joe was never comfortable with this arrangement. During the meet, Joe would start his daily columns of "Derby Doings," and he was constantly on the phone, calling owners and trainers across the country. One year during the early 1970s, we put in a new phone for him, but Joe wanted a speaker phone, which was kind of an oddity back then.

He often wasn't pleased with the height of his work desk. One year, we provided him with an adjustable office chair, and Joe would say to me it's too high. We had it adjusted, and then he told me it was too low. I remember sending one of the maintenance carpenters up to the press box with a ruler to set the exact height he wanted of the chair, as Joe sat there with his typewriter. He was always polite, always courteous, but rather direct, and sometimes he could nearly send our publicity director, Jim Williams, into orbit.

Joe considered himself somewhat of a gourmet. If you ever had dinner with him, you knew how knowledgeable he was about food and wines. During my early days at Keeneland, we didn't have the ability or the will, or the interest, in stocking the press box with sandwiches and libations. Joe would usually call Turf Catering and ask for a sandwich, and they'd have a waitress bring it up to him. One day, the sandwich arrived without any mustard or mayonnaise or dressing. Joe didn't think it was very palatable as such, so he called me and said, "Ted, in the far reaches of Turf Catering, is there any Grey Poupon?" It was a request I will always remember—here I am, the president of Keeneland, being charged with the responsibility of locating a jar of Grey Poupon. I called Turf Catering and said, "If you haven't got it, send out for it."

But Joe's presence was a joy. What a privilege it was for Keeneland during those spring meets to have him based in our press box, writing his pre-Derby week columns and race reports, and at the same time covering the Blue Grass and other stakes. He would walk into the Keeneland barn area, always clutching a small notebook in his left hand, making cryptic notations that only he understood. No matter how busy a trainer was, even if he was in the process of saddling a horse for a morning workout, he would always stop what he was doing and talk with Joe. The trust that horsemen had in him was his hallmark. And it provided Joe with the opportunity to provide the public with a wide range of not what I would call inside information, but pertinent information regarding the trainer's plans and the well-being of his horse. Joe was always out there by himself, walking slowly, deliberately, never in a rush. And he never missed a day.

Joe would usually leave us briefly, flying out to cover the Wood Memorial in New York or the Santa Anita Derby in Southern California. Then he'd fly back to Lexington in time to be the master of ceremonies at our Blue Grass press party in the Keeneland clubhouse. This is something he did for more than thirty years, conducting—or maybe I should say orchestrating—the interviews at the press party and displaying the ability and self-assurance to take a prickly moment or a dreary gaffe and, in a flash, turn it into something hilarious.

Harvey Vanier was one of Joe's favorite trainers to interview. Harvey is a friendly, communicative person one on one, but in front of a crowd, he would become monosyllabic. I remember one year, microphone in hand, Joe began the interview by asking, "How's your horse training for the Blue Grass, Harvey?"

Vanier replied, "Okay."

Joe said, "His last work was impressive. Were you pleased?"

Vanier replied, "Yeah."

"Have you named a rider yet?"

"No."

"Have you got anyone in mind?"

"Yes."

"Would you be willing to tell the CIA who the rider is?"

"No."

With that, Joe passed the microphone to Vanier and said, "Maybe we'd be better informed if you asked *me* the questions, Harvey."

Vanier replied, "Why?" The exchange brought down the house with laughter.

The 2005 Breeders' Cup was held at Belmont Park. A week before the event, I called Joe to ask him if we could have lunch while I was in New York. He told me to meet him at his apartment on East Fifty-sixth Street in New York City, and we would go to P. J. Clark's. While Joe has been suffering from Parkinson's disease for over twenty years, inhibiting his mobility, there has been no impairment of his mind and his uncanny memory for names and places. Although P. J. Clark's is only a block or two away from Joe's apartment, we took a taxi, for he had great difficulty walking. When we entered the restaurant, it was jam-packed with people, and there was a waiting line to be seated. I became deeply concerned because, with Joe's frail physical condition, there was no way we could cope with a long delay. Suddenly, the crowd parted, a narrow path opened, and I followed Joe to the back room. There, a table awaited us. No word had been spoken, no arm had been twisted. It was that simple matter of calm command, that Mr. Joe Hirsch had arrived.

We had a great time at lunch, recalling many faces and happy moments. We discussed at length his library of racing books and photo albums, and he advised me that in his will he is leaving them to the Keeneland Library—the librarians Cathy Schenk and Phyllis Rogers have had a close bond with Joe for many years, and they frequently assisted him with the research for his columns and the books he authored. Joe and I also discussed the problems of the New York Racing Association. We talked about what a difficult job D. G. Van Clief had, heading both the Breeders' Cup and the National Thoroughbred Racing Association. Our lunch took up most of the afternoon. As we were leaving P. J. Clark's, I said to Joe, "Why don't you wait here while I go out to find a taxi to take us back?"

He said, "No. Let's walk. It's only two blocks."

We did, and it was a mistake. It was the longest two blocks of my life. Joe manfully struggled with every step, every painful step, suffering from the lack of breath, but never complaining.

There is no question that the racing world has been made better by Joe Hirsch's presence. He will be fondly remembered as the gentleman with the regal bearing, always outfitted in the traditional suit, tie, and dark glasses, with the notebook grasped in his left hand, documenting irrefutable quotes from racing's elite and rank and file.

§

Now, a few paragraphs about Thomas H. Meeker, who in 2006 retired as president and chief executive officer of Churchill Downs Inc. Tom has been my racetrack colleague and Breeders' Cup confidant for nearly a quarter of a century. He is very well educated, with degrees from Northwestern University and the University of Louisville School of Law. He is also a fellow former member of the U.S. Marine Corps.

As is the case with politicians, racetrack executives are often maligned by the media, horsemen, and patrons. They are frequently flayed at the public whipping post for their inabilities to completely satisfy everybody at once. But rarely have I ever heard a disparaging word about Tom from a Churchill Downs Inc. stockholder. When Tom initially came to work for Churchill as its president in 1984, the company owned its namesake track in Louisville—and nothing beyond that. But today, Churchill also owns Arlington Park near Chicago, Calder Race Course in Florida, and Fair Grounds in New Orleans. With the exception of a one-month period that extends from late March to late April, a Churchill-owned track is conducting live racing somewhere in the United States every week of the year. And the races are simulcast throughout North America and to countries on other continents, too.

Churchill Downs Inc. has become a mega-conglomerate. Its stock trades on the NASDAQ Exchange (the symbol is CHDN). Churchill continues to stage one of North America's premier annual sporting events, the Kentucky Derby. Its Kentucky Derby Museum (which, in my mind, is the best of its kind within our industry) is open to the public year-round. The track in Louisville is the site of corporate conventions, wedding receptions, high school proms, and numerous other business and social events. Much of this has come about because of Tom's competence and aggressiveness.

At times, Tom can be tactless and insensitive. But who among us is flawless? The bottom line is he has long had what I believe to be one of the toughest jobs in racing. Tom never shirked a challenge; he always did his best to deliver. He has a brilliant intellect and a head for business that has brought many dividends for Churchill's stockholders. So, from one old Marine to another, I say to Tom, may you always keep up the fight. And "Hold High the Torch!"

§

Joe Hirsch and I are devoted fans of Charles Cella, whom we often refer to as "Le Grande Charlie." My first contact with Charles occurred nearly forty years ago at a dinner party hosted by Spencer Drayton, who served the duel roles of executive vice president of Thoroughbred Racing Associations and president of its investigative agency, the Thoroughbred Racing Protective Bureau. The dinner party was held at Lutece, a restaurant on East Fiftieth Street in New York City. Spencer had suggested to his guests several appetizers for consideration, emphasizing the Lutece specialty, mint steak tartare. Charles and I were both greenhorns. He had just inherited Oaklawn Park in Hot Springs, Arkansas, from his late father, John Cella, and I was the novice of the Keeneland staff, and we were anxious to please our host. But two bites into the mint steak tartare, our eyes filled with tears, our noses twitched, and we were gasping for breath. Our mouths were so much on fire we could have activated the overhead sprinkler system. We both reached for our vodkas and gulped them down, with the hope they would quell the flames. For Charles and me, this marked the beginning of an admittedly intriguing friendship that has endured and survived countless bashes and soirées, both within and beyond America's shores.

Charles's grandfather and great-uncle founded Oaklawn in 1905, and the Cella family has owned and operated that racetrack ever since. When I think of Charles, a myriad of descriptive adjectives come to mind, for he can be many things to many people, often depending upon the hour of day or night. Indomitable. Indestructible. Unpredictable. Certainly unconventional. And, lest I overlook the most obvious, unforgettable. Charles listens to his own drumbeat and revels in making his way against what sometimes is a tide, and sometimes a tidal wave, of industry opinion.

In accordance with this, I have for decades served as the racing industry's designated diplomatic envoy, beseeching Charles to change his obstinate stances on a variety of initiatives. The Breeders' Cup? "Run by idiots!" Equibase? "Absolutely unnecessary!" The graded stakes system? "Preposterous and wholly unfair!" Prior to dealing with Charles concerning industry issues, I always prepare a volley of reasons why he needs to alter his thinking. I meet with him, fire an opening salvo for effect, and then become dismayed as he, the target, stands stubbornly and defiantly implacable.

While Charles has historically been resistant to ideas and suggestions from his peers, he has also been abnormally gullible, susceptible to the most illogical scams from seemingly absolute strangers who want to disrupt his modus operandi. Through the years, my mounting failures of persuasion have led me to retribution measures, which, coupled with a mischievous and thoroughly misguided sense of humor, have led to a series of fabricated phone calls. My personal favorite, and the one that inflicted the greatest Cella angst, involved a racehorse Charles had purchased in Argentina. I phoned Charles and, disguising my voice as an Argentina customs official, told him there were 68,284 pesos due "on zee export tax on zee 'orse."

Charles exploded. His trainer, Ron McAnally, had paid the bill in full, he angrily said.

"Well, Senor," said the bogus customs official in painfully fractured English, "no pay zee fee, no water for zee 'orse. He no look good today."

"Well, you call my trainer!" yelled Charles into the phone.

"Oh, Senor McAnally?" said the voice on the other end.

"Yes!"

"No can find."

"Well, you're going to have to find him! I'm not going to pay!"

"Okay, Senor. But no money, no water for zee 'orse."

I later learned that Charles subsequently called Ron and was furious with him. Ron, of course, had no idea what he was talking about.

There was another time when I called Charles's long-suffering valet and man Friday, Alonzo, and told him I was the "Lock Doc," which is the name of a local locksmith in Hot Springs. Adjacent to the eighth pole at Oaklawn, Charles has a large log cabin where he and his guests often stay. I said to Alonzo, "Marylou Whitney is visiting, and Mr. Cella has a habit of sleepwalking at night and going into her bedroom. Mr. Cella has instructed me to come over and change all the locks."

Alonzo then called Charles in the Oaklawn VIP room and told him, "Okay, boss, we've got it all set up to have the locks changed." A flabbergasted Charles asked him why. "Because you've been sleepwalking into Mrs. Whitney's room," Alonzo said.

"What! What! WHAT?!" said Charles. It took him a while to figure out that it was me who had actually called. I thought it was hilarious, although I cannot say that Charles immediately shared my merriment. It took him a while.

Charles is one of the world's great hosts. He loves to throw a party. One I particularly recall occurred in October 1985 at Hotel Le Bristol in Paris, France. Originally constructed in 1758 by the supervisor for King Louis IV, Hotel Le Bristol is furnished with eighteenth-century antiques and adorned with master paintings that once hung in the Louvre, and it is reputed to have the largest bathrooms in the city. The party was staged the night following the Prix de l'Arc de Triomphe at Longchamp, which that year had been won via disqualification by a horse named Rainbow Tree. It remains the only disqualification in the Arc's eighty-eight-year history.

I was president of Thoroughbred Racing Associations (TRA) back then, and I had taken the presidents of fifteen TRA racetracks to the race. We were all invited to Charles's party, which was a black-tie affair. For entertainment, he had brought in a famous female piano player from the Philippines. She was only about three and a half feet tall and had to sit on a stool to reach the piano keys. But she could play any type of music, and she entertained Charles's guests all the way through dinner. There were also magicians performing, and jugglers. There was a fellow on a unicycle who kept weaving his way around and between the dinner tables. The French guests who were there expressed shock and disbelief at such a varied series of entertainers.

Many times over the years, I have conspired with Pierre Belloq, the great caricature artist for the *Racing Form,* to recapture some of Charlie's most volcanic and interpretive moments. "Peb," as Belloq is known, did one particularly masterful cartoon several years ago that related to an article that was published in the *Racing Form* and mentioned that the "rites of spring" had truly come to Oaklawn, for a couple had been observed in the track's infield in a state of undress, making supreme efforts to please each other. The cartoon hangs on a wall in Charlie's Oaklawn den. It depicts him in a French presidential outfit (similar to the one Charles de Gaulle wore), jumping up and down on the grandstand roof, pointing with his binoculars toward the passionate couple (who are discreetly covered by a flapping blanket) and shouting, "Are they members of the turf club?"

Another Peb cartoon I treasure depicts a rickety old sloop called the *Astral* sailing up the Mississippi River toward the Archway to the West in St. Louis. The real *Astral* had been charted by Charles some years earlier to sail across the Atlantic Ocean with him at the helm and a group of close friends as passengers. The ship got blown off course and missed its destination by 364 miles, which is equivalent to the distance between Boston, Massachusetts, and Atlantic City, New Jersey. It was a voyage that challenged human sanity. In the cartoon, Charles is depicted standing defiantly at the *Astral*'s helm, splendidly attired in an admiral's uniform and being served a martini by Alonzo. The ship's cargo consisted of many of Charles's bêtes noires, both individuals and organizations. Each was shackled by chains or tied by rope, ready to be tossed overboard. On the far shore is a pitiful, ragged, barefoot urchin whose strained face bears a likeness to one James E. Bassett III. Huffing and tugging on a line attached to the *Astral*, the urchin is agonizingly trying to pull Charles against the tide. Meanwhile, Charles is pounding on the ship's rail, and the caption has him bellowing, "Damn the torpedoes! Full speed ahead!"

I will also mention, however, two moments that involved Charles that rank among the most special in my life. One occurred in the winner's circle at Belmont Park on October 28, 1995, after Charles's colt Northern Spur won the Breeders' Cup Turf. I was there to present the trophy to him. The other occurred in the ballroom of the Beverly Wilshire in Beverly Hills, California, on January 24, 2005, when I presented Charles with the Eclipse Award of Merit for a century's worth of contributions that Oaklawn and the Cella family have made to racing.

There is no question one could write a book about Le Grande Charlie. But only one person in the history of letters could have really done justice to the subject, and that is Robert Ripley, who created the series *Ripley's Believe It or Not*. And if I could muster one last wish from my old convivial host, it would be for just one more Cella bash before the white coats come for both of us.

Chapter 11

The Breeders' Cup

ON A MORNING in mid-April 1988, Will Farish came into my office at Keeneland and asked me if I would be willing to become president of Breeders' Cup Ltd., the organizational body in charge of staging the Breeders' Cup championship day of races each year. Two years earlier, I had retired as the Keeneland Association's president and was now serving as Keeneland's nonsalaried chairman of the board. Farish, among his many other responsibilities, was chairman of the Breeders' Cup executive committee. His question to me that morning came completely out of the blue. The presidency of the Breeders' Cup was something I had never considered. I told Farish I would think it over and then get back to him. And oh, was there a deadline for my decision? Farish said yes, that there was a Breeders' Cup board meeting scheduled for April 28, and at the meeting he would like to give the board members the opportunity to either confirm or reject my appointment.

Allow me to provide just a little bit of background here. The Breeders' Cup was the brainchild of John Ryan Gaines, who envisioned a single year-end program of major championship stakes, bringing together the finest Thoroughbreds on the North American continent for a single afternoon of competition. Horses from other continents, most notably Europe, would participate too. The purses would be record setting, the races would be televised live on a major network, and the results would have major impacts as to which horses would be crowned champions of their various divisions. Gaines was a breeder, an owner, and a major consignor to sales —and a Renaissance man, an inquisitive intellectual whose bent was analyzing industry problems and coming up with out-of-the-box solutions. He was a free thinker who preferred to go from *A* to *Z* without pausing for *G, M, Q, R,* or *S* in between, and he was impatient with those reluctant to immediately embrace his theories.

Hollywood Park was the site of the inaugural running of the Breeders' Cup. This occurred on November 10, 1984. There were seven Breeders' Cup races, with purses totaling $10 million. The featured race was the $3 million Breeders' Cup Classic, which at the time was the richest race in the world. Attendance at Hollywood that day was 64,254. The winners of five of the seven races—Chief's Crown, Outstandingly, Eillo, Royal Heroine, and Princess Rooney—were named divisional champions. On-track wagering for the full card totaled $11,466,941. The races were simulcast to sixteen North American hubs, and wagering from all sources (on-track and simulcast combined) totaled $19,476,050.

To give you an idea how much the Breeders' Cup has grown in the ensuing years, wagering from all sources for the 2008 Cup at Santa Anita totaled $155.47 million. The Breeders' Cup nowadays is simulcast to thousands of sites throughout the world. The only continent where you cannot today wager, at least somewhere, on the Breeders' Cup is Antarctica.

But the early days of the Breeders' Cup were rocky and controversial, rife with dissension and, at times, open hostility. The plan was (and remains) for the event to rotate among major racetracks, but only a few have the necessary facilities to stage it. Early on, many of the medium-sized and small tracks, and some of bigger ones, too, were fearful that the status of their own premier stakes would be eroded by the Breeders' Cup. And even the potential host tracks, along with the members of the Horsemen's Benevolent and Protective Association, had strong reservations about Breeders' Cup's proposed requirement that it would keep all proceeds from the on-track pari-mutuel wagering on Breeders' Cup races. There were countless meetings among the three parties and veiled threats of boycotts by the horsemen.

Many breeders and stallion managers, both nationally and internationally, were hesitant and in some cases downright resistant in regards to Breeders' Cup eligibility fees. First, they had to annually pay an amount equal to an individual stallion's advertised stud fee in order for his offspring to be Breeders' Cup eligible—this could range anywhere from the low four figures to (in the case of Northern Dancer) $750,000 a year. Second, they had to pay a one-time $500 fee for each of the stallion's nominated foals. Doing so would render a foal eligible for not only Breeders' Cup Championship day but also Breeders' Cup supplementary purses in races that were annually held at major and minor racetracks throughout North America.

After intensive negotiations, a consensus was finally reached that on

Breeders' Cup day, in order to defray the costs of purses, television, promotion, and marketing, the host tracks had to make financial sacrifices for the purpose of promoting racing. The host tracks agreed to give their share from the pari-mutuel takeout on Breeders' Cup races to Breeders' Cup Ltd., if the organization was willing to guarantee that the tracks would receive the same revenues that they would normally receive on that day—which was a Saturday, normally their best day of the week. A corresponding guarantee would also be provided to local horsemen regarding purses of other races that were offered at the host tracks on Breeders' Cup day—they would remain the same as well.

During the first five years of its existence, the president of Breeders' Cup Ltd. was C. Gibson Downing, a central Kentucky attorney and Thoroughbred breeder. Downing held the position on a voluntary basis, but during the early months of 1988, the Breeders' Cup board of directors decided the organization needed a full-time president and chief executive officer. That's when Farish approached me, and he gave me about a week to decide. But it wasn't a difficult decision. I discussed it with the Keeneland trustees Louis Lee Haggin III, Charles Nuckols Jr., and William C. "Buddy" Smith, to see if they would consider this a conflict (which they didn't). Seven of Keeneland's directors—Farish, Downing, Brownell Combs II, G. Watts Humphrey Jr., Warner L. Jones Jr., Alfred H. Nuckols, and Charles Taylor—also served on the Breeders' Cup board at the time, and they realized that there were organizational problems over there that needed to be addressed.

Of course, I also talked it over with Lucy, and she agreed that the Breeders' Cup opportunity was something that would be interesting and challenging. So I met again with Farish a day or two before the April 28 meeting and told him I would accept the position, with a pair of caveats. One, there would be no contract. Two, I would receive no salary. I felt that I would not be at the Breeders' Cup for long, that I would go over and assess the administrative situation and have them refocus it. Within ten to twelve months, everything would be properly redirected and reorganized, and there would be no further need at the Breeders' Cup for me.

The Breeders' Cup board met as scheduled and announced my appointment as president the same day. Then, about one and a half weeks later, Farish came to see me again. This time, he told me that the board members didn't want me to be just an unpaid consultant; they wanted me to be an active, hands-on CEO. The board felt that my commitment would have more structure if I would accept a salary. I told him, all right, I would. Thus began a tenure as president and CEO of the Breeders' Cup that would last for eight years and eight months.

§

When I went to work for the Breeders' Cup, the only staff member I really was familiar with was D. G. Van Clief, who had been the organization's executive director from the days when it was founded in 1982. He had an outstanding reputation in the industry at large and was greatly admired by the Breeders' Cup staff. I had known D. G. for years, and there was a feeling of mutually held respect between the two of us, but also an acknowledged competitiveness. I was still the chairman of the board of Keeneland, and he had retained the position of chairman of the board of the Fasig-Tipton Sales Company, our primary rival regarding public auctions of Thoroughbreds.

That first day, I was finding my way around the Breeders' Cup headquarters when I came upon D. G.'s office. He was there, behind his desk, which was piled high with files, books, stacks of paper, and mementos. I said to D. G., "What are you doing?" I was so astonished, I asked the same question a second time, with a somewhat dramatic, somewhat incredulous pause between each word. "What . . . are . . . you . . . doing?"

D. G. looked at me and replied, "Will Farish called and told me that you were coming over here to serve as president. He told me to make room for you in my office and find another place for myself."

My reaction was initially one of shock. And then anger. I said to D. G. rather bluntly, "Put those goddamned things back in your desk and sit in that chair. I'll find a place to go. You've earned the right to be here, and I need you more than you need me."

And I did need him, dearly, for little did I know how difficult a job I was taking on—one that involved wonderfully challenging and energizing tasks, new faces, new names, and new ideas. The staff at the Breeders' Cup was young—when I became president, D. G. himself was only thirty-nine. But one of the aspects of the friendship and working relationship we developed is that neither of us took ourselves seriously. We could always laugh at each other's gaffes, and, believe me, there were more than a few of them.

One of the first problems I had to face at the Breeders' Cup stemmed from the simple fact that I was too much of an establishmentarian and traditionalist. To put it another way, I wasn't hip. At Keeneland, I had fo-cused on the horse sales and on the three-week race meets each April and October. We had a policy back then at Keeneland that corporate sponsors would not be allowed to attach their names to our stakes races. We thought we had done something really clever, we were so pleased, when in 1986 we contracted with the Ashland Oil Company to sponsor the Ashland Stakes. That race has a history that dates back to the old Kentucky Association track, where it was first run as the Ashland Oaks in 1879. It was named for the homestead and breeding farm of nineteenth-century Kentucky states-man Henry Clay. The first running of the Ashland at Keeneland occurred during the inaugural meeting in the fall of 1936. Therefore, at the time when Ashland Oil became the race's sponsor, its heritage as the Ashland Stakes had been established for over a hundred years.

But I was dealing with something entirely different when I became Breeders' Cup president. Marketing, promotion, corporate sponsorships, and corporate hospitality—all of these were major factors crucial to the event's success. Thus, we had the Consort Hair Spray Breeders' Cup Sprint, the Paradise Island Resort & Casino Breeders' Cup Mile, and the Bud-weiser Breeders' Cup Turf. And we worked very closely with a New York City–based firm, Sports Marketing Television International Inc. (SMTI), which was headed by Michael Letis and Michael Trager.

SMTI was the conduit between the Breeders' Cup, its sponsors, and NBC, and Letis and Trager guarded their channels of communication aggressively. They were two highly professional Madison Avenue people who were clued in to the workings of sponsorships and television and had some very strict guidelines they insisted we follow. In regard to sponsor-ship representatives, their seats had to be in absolutely premier positions, and the signage, banners, and logos pertaining to their products had to be displayed in prominent locations. And NBC, as I recall, wanted 500 pre-ferred seats, the majority of which went to clients of commercial enter-prises that sponsored television shows completely unrelated to the Breeders' Cup—situation comedies and the like. If we wanted to talk to NBC about the content of the telecasts, especially in regard to any objections or reser-vations we had, the means of doing so was through SMTI.

I learned that when you're heading a fledgling organization, which the Breeders' Cup was, concessions such as these constituted the means to successfully conduct business. And it wasn't a one-way street. When NBC televised the Olympics, certain VIP clients would be invited to travel to and attend the games as guests of the network. I was invited by NBC to the 1988 Summer Olympics in Seoul, South Korea, and to the 1992 Summer Olympics in Barcelona, Spain. Regrettably, both times I was unable to attend. However, I recall that Tom Meeker and other Triple Crown executives attended those events and had wonderful experiences.

My first Breeders' Cup as president of the organization was in 1988. It was also the first one held at Churchill Downs, which had some sort of sponsorship arrangement of its own with the Miller Brewing Company. But the Breeders' Cup had a major sponsorship deal with Budweiser. Churchill had set up a hospitality tent, and early on race day, Letis walked in there with several Budweiser VIPs, who were served drinks in cups adorned with the Miller High Life logo. Letis blew a gasket. Threw a tantrum. He went to the caterer and told him to immediately remove the Miller containers and reissue all the drinks in cups bearing the Budweiser logo. Which was promptly done. Letis had guaranteed the Budweiser people that public awareness would be centered on their brand, and he was not about to have his integrity compromised.

We knew Letis was right. But we were also concerned about creating a rupture with Churchill management. A lot is demanded by the Breeders' Cup from a host track. The Breeders' Cup receives the share of the parimutuel handle that the track would normally retain; the Breeders' Cup takes control of 9,000 VIP seats; it takes control of the winner's circle presentation—and those are just the items at the top of a very long list. And it requires the track to accede to the demands of television in regard to camera angles and where the cameras will be set up around the track. Everything is a continuous exercise in firm-handed diplomacy.

But it's easy to goof. When we decided to award the 1996 Breeders' Cup to Woodbine in Toronto, Canada, our two major sponsors were Budweiser and Mobil Oil. What we did not take into consideration was that Budweiser did not sell beer in Canada and that Mobil Oil did not sell gasoline or other petroleum products there either. Neither the Budweiser nor the Mobil people were particularly enthralled by this venue. They said, "Why are you taking this event to a place where we don't have a presence commercially?" We learned another lesson, and from there on, the Breeders' Cup has never been awarded to a track in a region that has restrictions or prohibitions on the sale of its sponsors' products.

§

Individual performances in races provided many highlights during my tenure as Breeders' Cup president. But some, of course, truly stand out.

Personal Ensign came into the 1988 Breeders' Cup Distaff at Churchill with a perfect record of twelve wins in twelve career starts. This would be her final race before going to the breeding shed, which meant she had the opportunity to be the first Thoroughbred of major stature to retire undefeated since Colin in 1908. Rain had fallen during the morning. A heavy mist continued throughout the afternoon, and the main oval at Churchill was muddy. Ogden Mills Phipps, known to his friends as "Dinny," had bred Personal Ensign, and the filly raced under the name of Dinny's father, Ogden Phipps, who was then seventy-nine years old. Just before Dinny went into the paddock to see the horses being saddled, he handed his field glasses to me, and I remember searching through the crowd trying to find him afterward. I kept thinking, "Dinny will need these to see the race."

Winning Colors, who six months earlier had become only the third filly to win the Kentucky Derby, was also entered in the Distaff, as was a filly named Goodbye Halo, who had won that year's Kentucky Oaks. You had, therefore, the two best three-year-old fillies on the continent, who had already accounted for the two oldest and most prominent races annually run at Churchill, challenging a four-year-old filly whose résumé contained not a single blemish.

The Distaff is run at a distance of one and one-eighth miles, and Winning Colors sprinted to the lead immediately, with Goodbye Halo to her outside just a few lengths back. But through the opening three-quarters of a mile, Personal Ensign was in fifth position, eight lengths behind Winning Colors. That's a formidable margin to overcome when mud is being kicked back into a horse's face, and there were only three-eighths of a mile remaining. At the eighth pole, Winning Colors was drawing away from a tiring Goodbye Halo, and Personal Ensign still trailed the Derby winner by four lengths. At that point, I thought it was impossible for Personal Ensign to win. And the countless times I've seen the replay of the race in the ensuing years, it still appears impossible. But somehow, by no more than the tip of her nose, Personal Ensign got to the front in the very last stride. Tom Durkin was calling the race for the NBC television audience, the simulcast network, and the on-site crowd at Churchill, and millions heard him say: "Here comes Personal Ensign! Unleashing a furious run on the outside! But, it is still Winning Colors! Goodbye Halo! Personal Ensign! A sixteenth of a mile from the wire. Winning Colors is there.

Personal Ensign! A dramatic finish! And here is the wire! And it is Personal Ensign!"

A jockey named Randy Romero rode Personal Ensign. He was thirty years old, a native of Erath, Louisiana, which is a small town near the central Gulf coast. Four and a half years earlier, Romero had been terribly burned when he had rubbed himself down with alcohol and climbed into the hot box at Oaklawn Park, and his skin had actually ignited. Romero was a tough little guy, and he would later be a key player in another Breeders' Cup drama involving a brilliant filly named Go For Wand, who I will talk about a little bit later.

§

In 1989, the Breeders' Cup was run at Gulfstream Park for the first time. The finale on the card, the mile-and-a quarter Breeders' Cup Classic, was also the culminating event in the rivalry between a pair of superb three-year-old colts, Sunday Silence and Easy Goer.

It was one of those East-West duels for supremacy, filled with dramatic twists. Easy Goer was a Phipps family horse who at age two had been a multiple grade 1 winner at Belmont Park and had received the Eclipse Award as champion of his division. He began his three-year-old campaign in Florida and New York and had won the Wood Memorial at Aqueduct. Sunday Silence was based in Southern California. At age two, he had run in nothing higher than allowance company. But at age three, he had won the Santa Anita Derby by eleven lengths. The two horses met for the first time in the Kentucky Derby. Sunday Silence won by a margin of two and a half lengths over a muddy surface that appeared to give favored Easy Goer difficulty with his footing.

Their first rematch was to occur in the Preakness, although a persistent foot problem threatened to keep Sunday Silence out of the race altogether. I do not know what sort of wizardry Sunday Silence's trainer, Charlie Whittingham, and a veterinarian, Alex Harthill, performed on the foot. But Sunday Silence ran in the Preakness, and he beat the again-favored Easy Goer by a nose at the culmination of an incredible stretch-long battle.

In the Belmont Stakes, Sunday Silence was the favorite as he sought to become the first Triple Crown winner in eleven years. But Easy Goer made a powerful move to draw away from Sunday Silence in the stretch and won by eight lengths. It was one of those situations where he suddenly went whoosh! And he was gone.

During the ensuing months, Sunday Silence won the Super Derby at Louisiana Downs. Easy Goer won the Travers Stakes at Saratoga and the Whitney and Woodward Handicaps and Jockey Gold Cup Stakes against older horses—with the Belmont included, this gave him five consecutive grade 1 wins. But Sunday Silence had still accounted for two out of the three Triple Crown events.

When they met for one final showdown in the Breeders' Cup Classic, the Horse of the Year title was on the line. Easy Goer was the 1–2 favorite in the wagering. Sunday Silence was the second choice at 2–1. It did not, however, turn out to be merely a two-horse race. A 21–1 shot named Blushing John was in front with a quarter mile remaining. Inside the eighth pole, Sunday Silence rolled by him to take the lead. Easy Goer was still behind by four lengths but going with all engines on full. He wore down Sunday Silence's lead to three lengths, two lengths, and then a diminishing length as they neared the finish line. "Easy Goer, with one final acceleration!" shouted Durkin into his microphone. But there was Sunday Silence, driving across the finish line, still in front. "And Sunday Silence holds on! And he wins by a desperate neck! Easy Goer was too late, not enough to win it! And it was Sunday Silence, in a racing epic!" proclaimed Durkin.

And he was right. Later, I obtained a photograph that had been culled from an NBC videotape that showed Arthur Hancock III, one of the co-owners of Sunday Silence, down on his knees with his hands up in prayer—imploring the heavens for his colt to win. And in the photo was Arthur's wife, Staci, and she was screaming. A remarkable set of images, forever captured.

§

In 1991, the Breeders' Cup returned to Churchill Downs. The weather was sunny but unusually cold for Kentucky in the first week of November—the temperature at the time of the first race was only forty-three degrees.

This was the year that Allen E. Paulson's colt Arazi shipped over from France with trainer Francois Boutin to run in the one-and-one-sixteenth-mile Breeders' Cup Juvenile. Even though he was sent off as the 2–1 favorite, I don't think most people were prepared for what they saw. There were fourteen horses in the field, and through the opening quarter mile, Arazi was next to last, already trailing the front-running Bertrando by nearly ten lengths. Bertrando was considered the most prominent of the twelve North American–based competitors in that year's Juvenile. His odds at post time were 5–2, making him the second choice in the wagering, and he continued to hold the lead approaching the head of the stretch run. At that point, Arazi, who had been steadily threading his way between horses, rushed up on the outside of Bertrando and ran right by him. It was electrifying. There were 66,204 people at Churchill that day, and their reaction was not so much a roar as it was a collective gasp. Arazi drew off to win by five lengths.

Thus, there came upon us a superstar—or, more accurately, a horse that many media members, racing fans, and others attempted to elevate to superstardom. Four days after the Breeders' Cup, Arazi underwent arthroscopic surgery to have small bone chips removed from both of his knees. He resumed training during the ensuing winter months, and on April 7, 1992, he made the first start of his three-year-old campaign, wining a one-mile turf race at St. Cloud in France by five lengths.

From there, he went straight to the Kentucky Derby. More than a few members of the media were proclaiming him to be "the world's greatest horse." During his morning exercises at Churchill during Derby week, people stood in crowds seven deep on the backside, watching him go down the track. Allen Paulson got as caught up in the fervor as anybody. An ESPN reporter asked him, "Have you ever owned a horse like this before?" Allen replied, "Nobody's ever owned a horse like this before." In the Derby, Arazi went off as the 9–10 favorite. In the early stages of the race, he was next to last in the eighteen-horse field and then made a sudden move going down the backstretch to reach contention. But with an eighth of a mile remaining, Arazi appeared dearly in need of fuel. He finished eighth, the worst performance in history by an odds-on Derby favorite.

Paulson sent him back to Europe, where Arazi made three more starts, registering (in chronological order) a fifth-place finish, a third-place finish, and a win. He subsequently returned to the United States and, on October 31, went off as the 3–2 favorite in the Breeders' Cup Mile. The Breeders' Cup was run that year at Gulfstream Park. Arazi showed a little bit of early speed, then faded badly and finished eleventh of fourteen.

Arazi was a good horse, good enough to win the Breeders' Cup Juvenile in impressive fashion. But greatness eluded him.

§

The longest shot to ever win a Breeders' Cup race was a horse named Arcangues (pronounced *Are-Kong,* with emphasis placed on the second syllable), who went off at the extraordinary odds of 133–1 in the Classic at

Santa Anita in 1993. Arcangues had never before raced at a North American track. Although he had been bred in Kentucky by the art dealer who also campaigned him, Daniel Leopold Wildenstein, Arcangues had done all of his prior competing in France and England. Prior to shipping to Santa Anita, he had been victorious only once in 1993, in a group 1 race called the Prix d'Ispahan at Longchamp in May.

To make his chances of winning the Classic even more remote, Arcangues came into the race with fourteen career starts, all of them on the grass—he had never before raced on a dirt surface. He was to be ridden in the Classic by Jerry Bailey, who later said the first time he ever saw Arcangues was in the Santa Anita paddock, fifteen minutes before the race. "The trainer [France's André Fabre] gave me instructions, but I couldn't understand anything he was telling me," Bailey said.

Well, Arcangues was tenth through the opening half mile; moved into seventh position through three-quarters of a mile; threaded his way between horses on the far turn; came on the outside to challenge the pace-setting favorite, Bertrando, at the eighth pole; took the lead; and drew off to win by two lengths. It's not an exaggeration, I think, to state that at least 99 percent of the crowd of 55,130 at Santa Anita was dumbfounded. I was dumbfounded. Bailey thought the whole thing was hilarious.

Arcangues, the longest shot on the board, returned win-place-show mutuels of $269.20, $54.20, and $18.20. His winner's share of the purse was $1,560,000. The following year, Arcangues was victorious just once, in the John Henry Handicap on the turf at Hollywood. He subsequently was sent to stud at the Stallion Nakamura farm in Japan, and the last time I looked, Arcangues's annual stud fee was 500,000 yen.

§

Cigar twice ran in the Breeders' Cup Classic. The first time was on a muddy track at Belmont Park in 1995, and he won by two and a half lengths. His final time, 1:59⅖, was up to that point the fastest clocking ever recorded in the race. It was Cigar's twelfth consecutive victory in a streak that would ultimately extend through sixteen races.

Approaching the finish line, Cigar seemed the epitome of explosive power, and, once again, Durkin provided a brilliant race call. As Bailey drove Cigar through the final yards, Durkin, with ever-so-brief dramatic pauses, said, "And, here he is! . . . The incomparable! . . . Invincible! . . . Unbeatable! . . . Cigar!"

The following year's Breeders' Cup was at Woodbine in Toronto,

Canada, the only instance to date where the event has been hosted at a track outside of the United States. At this point, Cigar's winning streak was behind him. Two and a half months earlier, he had been defeated by a horse named Dare and Go in the Pacific Classic at Del Mar. He rebounded in his next start to win the Woodward Stakes at Belmont Park but subsequently was beaten in a photo finish by the three-year-old, Skip Away, in Belmont's Jockey Club Gold Cup.

Still, at Woodbine, Cigar was trying for a repeat victory in the Classic, a feat that up to that time had never been accomplished by any horse. And it was also known that his Woodbine effort would be Cigar's final career start. He was sent off as the odds-on 3–5 favorite but in a photo finished third—the winner, by a nose, was a 19–1 shot named Alphabet Soup, and in second position, by a head, was an 18–1 shot, Louis Quatorze.

Earlier that year, Louis Quatorze had been a wire-to-wire winner of the Preakness, which in most stakes races would be an enormous credential for a horse to have on his résumé. But the bettors apparently considered it a modest accomplishment when compared to what Cigar had achieved.

§

One cannot recall some of the most memorable highlights of the Breeders' Cup without making note of the low points as well. For me, the absolute nadir occurred in the 1990 Breeders' Cup Distaff at Belmont Park when the gallant three-year-old filly Go for Wand matched up in an incredible stretch duel with the equally gallant six-year-old mare Bayakoa. For both horses, it was the race of their lives. And for Go for Wand, the race ended up costing her life.

Go for Wand was bred and owned by Mrs. Jane du Pont Lunger, who raced under the name of Christiana Stables, which she had founded with her late husband, Harry Lunger, in 1937. Mrs. Lunger was a most gracious lady and a splendid horsewoman. I had more than a passing acquaintance with her. Mrs. Lunger's homebred Linkage had won the 1982 Blue Grass Stakes, and I also had the pleasure of presenting the trophy to her when Go for Wand won the 1989 Breeders' Cup Juvenile Fillies at Gulfstream. And earlier in 1990, Go for Wand had won the Beaumont and Ashland Stakes during Keeneland's spring meet.

Bayakoa campaigned for Frank and Jan Whitham, both of whom were fourth-generation descendants of pioneer families that had moved to the far western region of Kansas from Indiana and Iowa. The Whithams' holdings included banks; a beef cattle finishing plant; 8,000 acres of land where they grew corn, wheat, and alfalfa; and 240,000 acres of pastureland. Wonderful people. At the time, they had been in the Thoroughbred business for about a decade and had attained extraordinary success with Bayakoa, who had received the Eclipse Award as North America's champion older mare in 1989.

But Go for Wand had been an Eclipse recipient in 1989 too, for she had been champion of the two-year-old filly division. Heading into the Distaff, she had won seven of her eight starts at age three, and six of those victories had come in grade 1 events. Bayakoa, on the other hand, was going for her second consecutive Distaff victory. She had won six of her prior nine starts that year, and trainer Ron McAnally had her primed for a top effort.

Ron and I were sharing a clubhouse box at Belmont when the race went off. There were just the two of us in the box, and no one else. Go for Wand was favored in the wagering at odds of 7–10, and Bayakoa was second choice at 11–10. Almost immediately, the two horses separated themselves from the remainder of the field. Go for Wand, on the inside, was a head in front of Bayakoa through the opening quarter. And by a half length through the opening half mile. But then Bayakoa closed to within a head of Go for Wand through three-quarters of a mile. With an eighth of a mile remaining, Go for Wand was again half a length in front. But with a sixteenth of a mile to go, it seemed that Bayakoa had pushed her nose in front. Both of them were straining, striving with everything they had for victory. When suddenly, Go for Wand tumbled over in a horrific summersault, unseating her jockey, Randy Romero, like he was a rag doll and thrashing in immense distress on the ground as the other horses thundered by. The image of all this will be locked in my mind forever.

Go for Wand had suffered a major breakdown of her right front ankle. In full view of the crowd of 51,236 at Belmont and millions more watching on national and international television, she partially rose to her feet and, in a stumbling, lurching effort, with her injured leg dangling, tried to walk in the direction of the clubhouse apron. A team of veterinarians ran to her side, but so great was Go for Wand's distress that she had to be immediately euthanized on the track.

Meanwhile, Bayakoa, who was ridden by Laffit Pincay Jr., won the Distaff by six and three-quarter lengths. But no notions of celebration entered Ron McAnally's mind. At first, he was not sure which horse had gone down—he closed his eyes for a few moments, and when he reopened them, he realized it was Go for Wand. Ron had never trained for Mrs. Lunger, but he knew and admired her. He was stunned and perplexed, confronted with the terrible task of having to cope with the mixture of tragedy and triumph.

The whole thing occurred right in front of the box we were sitting in. I remember seeing Ritchie Jones, who was Mrs. Lunger's son-in-law, jump over the outside rail and run across the track to where Go for Wand was flailing in agony. Grooms were running to her as well, and veterinarians. The crowd was in a state of hysteria. Martha Gerry, a very prominent Thoroughbred breeder and owner, came up to Ron and angrily shouted in his face (as though it were somehow his fault), "I'll never attend the races again!"

Ron began to shake, and I told him, "Take it easy," and then I escorted him to the winner's circle. By the time we got there, Ron was in tears. He was besieged by a hoard of media members firing questions at him, against a backdrop of shrieks of hysteria from the crowd. Ron tried desperately to be cooperative and correct. When asked repeatedly by reporters why the accident had happened, he responded, "Go for Wand was doing what she was bred to do, racing with the heart of the champion she is." And Ron further said, "I love horses too much to handle seeing something like this. These animals give their lives for our enjoyment."

After an awkward trophy presentation ceremony, I told Ron, "Come on, we've got to get out of here." Some VIP tents had been set up in back of the Belmont paddock, and we went to the bar in one of them and ordered a scotch tranquilizer. Ron inquired about Romero (who seemed okay at the time but later was discovered to have suffered eight fractured ribs and a fractured right shoulder). Otherwise, we just sat at that bar in the tent amidst a numbing silence, for neither of us could make a meaningful comment. The expression on Ron's face remained glazed, puzzled. While relieved for one owner, he was distraught for another. And he was equally distraught for Go for Wand's trainer, his friend Billy Badgett Jr. Ron later told me those conflicting emotions were waging a war within him and that they remained in conflict for weeks, even months.

§

There were actually two accidents during the Breeders' Cup program in 1990. The first occurred in the Breeders' Cup Sprint when a horse named

Mr. Nickerson suffered a fatal heart attack nearing the far turn. Another horse, Shaker Knit, fell over Mr. Nickerson and suffered severe spinal cord damage, which necessitated his being euthanized later in the day. Then there was the situation with Go for Wand in the Distaff.

We lost a total of three horses that afternoon, and the circumstances involving their deaths were shown again and again on television replays. But any sort of expert commentary concerning these situations was absent—a circumstance that invariably leads to speculation, much of it undisciplined.

In the aftermath of this, there arose a public demand for the racing industry to provide coherent professional information regarding the condition of a horse that becomes injured in a race. People wanted to know exactly what the injuries involve and what steps could and were being taken to provide for the injured animal's care, comfort, and well-being. In response, a group comprised of the Breeders' Cup, The Jockey Club, Keeneland, Churchill Downs, the NBC and ABC television networks, and the American Association of Equine Practitioners (AAEP) developed a program that we named Veterinarian On Call. Henceforth, at major races, experienced equine veterinarians would be on hand to provide medical expertise to the media. This would include calm, professional explanations of the injuries and of the treatments being rendered.

The Veterinarian On Call program was in place for the 1991 Triple Crown races. It received a major test the following November at Churchill Downs when the favorite, Housebuster, had to be pulled up during the Breeders Cup Sprint and another horse, Filago, was pulled up in the Breeders' Cup Turf. Both horses suffered suspensory injuries. In each case, an AAEP representative explained to the media what a suspensory injury is (a damaging of the ligaments in the fetlock area of a horse's leg). The representative further explained that braces and support bandages had been immediately applied and that the injured horses were being transported back to their barns, where further examinations by veterinarians would take place.

We also contracted with a Chicago public relations firm, Pederson/McGrath Associates Ltd., to conduct a series of training sessions for jockeys, trainers, and owners on how to conduct themselves in media interviews in a professional and intelligent fashion. The firm was run by Myrna Pederson and Joan McGrath. Both were Northwestern University graduates and seasoned broadcast journalists. They were well known and respected for their tough, insightful training of people who appeared on television, preparing them to calmly and articulately handle any eventuality, including crisis situations.

§

In December 1992, officials of the Ontario Jockey Club (OJC) came down to Lexington and made a compelling presentation in their quest to host either the 1994 or 1996 Breeders' Cup at Woodbine. The OJC contingent was accompanied by federal, provincial, and local government officials. Among them was Thomas Hockin, the Canadian minister of small business. They all were convincing in their support of Toronto as a host city.

Among other inducements, the province of Ontario pledged $1.5 million to help pay for capital improvements to Woodbine's facility, along with other costs associated with the event. A new press box would be constructed at the track, and the turf course would be reconstructed so that it would extend for one and a half miles completely around the outside perimeter of Woodbine's one-mile dirt oval. (At every other Thoroughbred racetrack in North America, the turf course is inside the dirt oval or the all-weather oval, which we now have at Keeneland.)

Late the following February, we announced that the 1996 running of the Breeders' Cup would be at Woodbine. The Breeders' Cup board had also agreed to hold the event a week earlier than its original date and had scheduled it for October 26, which also happened to be my seventy-fifth birthday.

Having Woodbine as a host site for racing's championship day was a dream fulfilled for Charles Taylor, who was the vice president of the OJC's board of trustees and a founding director of the Breeders' Cup. Go back further into Charles's life, however, and one realizes he was a member of one of the most remarkable families in the history of Canadian racing. There have been two racetracks named Woodbine that have operated in the Toronto area. The first one opened in 1860. The second, the modern-day Woodbine, opened in 1956, and Charles's father, Edward Plunkett (E. P.) Taylor, was the man primarily responsible for building it. The elder Taylor was a brewing magnate and master of Windfields Farm, which had divisions in Ontario and Maryland. During a period that commenced in 1960 and extended through 1985, E. P. Taylor led all North American breeders in races won in nineteen of those twenty-six years.

Charles was an alumnus of Queen's University in Kingston, Ontario, and became a foreign correspondent for the *Toronto Globe and Mail,* for which he filed articles and dispatches from fifty countries during his career as a newsman. At one point, he was the only North American journalist stationed in Peking (now known as Beijing), where the communist authorities suspected that he was a spy. The Chinese cryptographers would examine the communications sent to and by him very carefully, and one of Charles's favorite stories involved the telegram he received from his father on May 17, 1964: "NORTHERN DANCER FIRST. THE SCOUNDREL SECOND. HILL RISE THIRD. LOVE DAD." Well, if you didn't know anything about North American Thoroughbred racing in general or the Triple Crown in particular, you might have thought this was some sort of secret message. But E. P. Taylor was actually informing his son that the family's homebred colt, Northern Dancer, had won the Preakness Stakes the day before. (The Scoundrel and Hill Rise were the second- and third-place finishers in the race.) Charles would relate this tale, inhale on his pipe (he always smoked a pipe), grin broadly, and say, "Can't you imagine a whole room of Chinese cryptographers trying to break down this ingenious occidental code?"

Northern Dancer subsequently became one of the greatest sires of the twentieth century. From 1974 through 1988, the sons and daughters of Northern Dancer fetched the highest average prices of all sires represented at the Keeneland July Yearling Sales twelve times, and that constitutes a record that may last forever.

During the autumn of E. P. Taylor's years, Charles ended his globetrotting journalistic exploits and took over responsibilities for Windfields. Charles subsequently became one of the great advocates for Canadian racing and for the Breeders' Cup. Commemorate, carrying the turquoise and gold silks of Windfields, finished second in the inaugural running of the Breeders' Cup Sprint in 1984.

Other major breeders from north of the border—Sam-Son Farms, Kinghaven Farms, and the Ontario division of Stronach Stables among them—followed Charles's example. The result was that Ontario became one of the top five regions in North America in regard to the nomination of foals to the Breeders' Cup. And a continuing result of this is that numerous Canadian champions have competed in the Breeders' Cup—including Imperial Choice, Ruling Angel, Afleet, Play the King, With Approval, Isvestia, Dance Smartly, Peaks and Valleys, Mt. Sassafras, Chief Bearhart, Thornfield, Quiet Resolve, Wake at Noon, and Soaring Free, all of whom were recipients of Sovereign Awards as Canada's Horse of the Year. Of this group, Dance Smartly won the 1991 Breeders' Cup Distaff, and Chief Bearhart won the 1997 Breeders' Cup Turf. Considering all this, I think you can understand why there was a strong feeling of obligation among many Breeders' Cup board members, and even more so among our staff, that the OJC deserved an opportunity to host the event.

§

We did have concerns, but most of them revolved around the weather. In late October, it can be quite cold and even snowy in Ontario. But there is never a guarantee, anywhere, as to what kind of day it's going to be weather-wise. The 1991 Breeders' Cup was run during the first week of November at Churchill, with temperatures throughout the day in the low forties. And the 1994 Breeders' Cup was also run in early November at Churchill, with temperatures throughout the day in the mid-seventies.

But weather wasn't the only potential obstacle. During the winter of 1996, I was aware that the OJC had not been able to reach a new agreement with Woodbine's pari-mutuel clerks, who numbered approximately 700 and were unionized. There was an issue over hourly wages, and other issues concerning longevity of the workweek and job security. When Woodbine opened its eight-and-a-half-month live racing season on March 23, the union clerks had been locked out, and nonunionized replacement workers were manning the mutuel machines. Picket lines were formed, and accusations flew between OJC officials and union representatives, many of which were picked up and reported by the press. These things happen with management-labor disputes at racetracks, and resolutions almost invariably follow. At the Breeders' Cup, we took notice of what was happening at Woodbine but were not particularly concerned, for we felt a resolution would soon be forthcoming.

The first signal we received that serious storm clouds were brewing came in early April, when the OJC announced that the Queen's Plate was being moved from July 13 to July 6. The Queen's Plate, which dates back to 1860, is Canada's most important and historic horse race. For nearly a century and a half, it has anchored the annual Woodbine stakes schedule, and members of Great Britain's Royal Family (including kings and queens) have frequently been on hand to present the trophy to the winning owner. In accordance with this tradition, Princess Margaret had planned to attend the 1996 Queen's Plate as the Royal Family's representative. But, in conjunction with announcing the change of the date of the race, the OJC recommended to Princess Margaret that she probably should not come. The Royal Family is disinclined to attend any sporting event where a major labor dispute is involved. And OJC officials were making it known they did not expect the dispute with the pari-mutuel clerks to be resolved in short order.

A second storm flag was raised in late May when Gordon Wilson, who headed the Ontario Federation of Labor (which represents all unions in the province), announced that his organization was planning a pair of major protests against the OJC on Breeders' Cup weekend. One of the protests was going to be in downtown Toronto, and the other protest was going to be at Woodbine.

And the day following Wilson's announcement, I received a letter from Andrew Stern, president of the Service Employees International Union, whose membership included the pari-mutuel clerks as well as Toronto's restaurant and hotel workers. Stern's letter stated that although he really didn't want to involve the Breeders' Cup in the labor dispute, he was obligated to use every vehicle available to his union to get the clerks back to work with a reasonable contract signed and in force.

Already, D. G. and I were pretty much convinced that the labor dispute could not be resolved by Breeders' Cup time. But Stern's letter represented the first threat we had received regarding disruptions of public services at restaurants and hotels. It had not, beforehand, entered the minds of either D. G. or me that "Unwelcome" signs would effectively be hung out at establishments where people would eat and spend the night. Now we were fully grasping what might happen, and we were not going to subject the visitors who were coming to the Breeders' Cup to these sorts of situations.

I notified David Willmot, president and CEO of the OJC, that because of the threat by the Federation of Labor, if the situation with the pari-mutuel clerks wasn't straightened out, the Breeders' Cup would be pulled from Woodbine and run somewhere else. I said to Willmot, "Don't let any grass grow under your feet. Don't let this dispute drag on indefinitely. We are looking very seriously at alternative options."

We also put out a press release alerting the racing industry, the media, and the public that a problem existed. In the release, we said our primary responsibility was to ensure that the Breeders' Cup is run under the most advantageous circumstances. The event occurs once a year, the release said; it is Thoroughbred racing's championship day, the Breeders' Cup is of international prominence, and we would be acting irresponsibly if we exposed it to any unnecessary or unreasonable risk.

Immediately after the release was sent out, the OJC canceled a lottery it had planned for distribution of 3,500 reserve seats at Woodbine on Breeders' Cup day. OJC officials also staged a press conference at which they distributed their own press release. It quoted Willmot as saying that while it was important to them for Woodbine to host the Breeders' Cup, they were not going to bend over and effectively buy the event by giving in to the demands of the pari-mutuel clerks.

Wilson responded by publicly reaffirming the Federation of Labor's hard-line position. In doing so, he called OJC officials "a bunch of arrogant, snotty bluebloods." He further stated, "We'll take those bluebloods and turn their blue noses red. And no one will want to come anywhere near Toronto on Breeders' Cup day."

From that rather unpromising set of circumstances, the situation moved into the first week of June. Lucy and I went to New York to attend the Belmont Stakes. The OJC had made an offer in regard to working hours and salary to the Woodbine pari-mutuel clerks. But on June 6, which was a Thursday, two days before the Belmont, the clerks met in Teamsters' Hall in Toronto and voted overwhelmingly to reject the offer.

That same day, D. G. and I consulted with our staff and with Will Farish, who remained chairman of the executive committee of the Breeders' Cup, and we made a definitive decision. We issued a press release stating that the event had effectively been canceled at Woodbine and that a new, alternate site for the Breeders' Cup would be announced within a month. During the following one and one-half days, officials of nine U.S. racetracks expressed their interest in hosting the event. But we gave consideration to only two of the tracks, Churchill Downs and Santa Anita, both of which had successfully hosted the Breeders' Cup multiple times before. Some of the other tracks had also been Breeders' Cup host sites, and some had never served in that capacity. We didn't feel we could go to an entirely new location. Seating would have to be totally revamped, as would advertising and promotions and facilities for horsemen. There would be a quarantine situation that had to be resolved for horses that shipped in from overseas and regulatory obstacles that would have to be resolved with the racing commission with jurisdiction over the new host site. All these things would take time, and our window of opportunity was narrowing.

Most people assumed Churchill would be our choice. I later admitted that, logistically, going to Louisville would have been our most efficient move because of Churchill's vast experience in hosting major events—the Breeders' Cup had already been run there three times and had produced the three largest crowds in the event's history, including what was then a record 71,621 in 1994. And of course, Churchill at that time had also conducted 122 editions of the Kentucky Derby, which annually draws the largest crowds for any horse race on the North American continent.

We immediately directed our Breeders' Cup staff to begin booking hotels in Louisville. Tom Meeker, the president and CEO at Churchill, had come to New York for the Belmont, and on Friday we had a preliminary discussion with him and explained the difficulties we were having with Woodbine. Tom then got on a plane and flew back to Louisville to get his staff together and to begin preliminary preparations for discussing and drawing up a contract with us to host the Breeders' Cup.

That same day, I went to see Ken Schanzer, the executive vice president of NBC Sports, to advise him of the likelihood that we would be moving the Breeders' Cup from Toronto to an alternative site and that it probably would be Churchill. He told me that NBC Sports president Dick Ebersol was in Chicago at the National Basketball Association finals. Schanzer said that he would talk to Ebersol that afternoon and relay the details of the situation to him and then would get back to me. But Schanzer also said that if the Breeders' Cup had to be moved, NBC Sports would be cooperative.

Throughout this period, the media had been very aggressive in following and reporting the story. When I returned to the Pierre Hotel in Manhattan, where Lucy and I were staying for the weekend, I asked her that if there were any telephone calls, would she be kind enough to say I was not in, for I had nothing new to add to the story. We were taking Stephen Keller, the president, board chairman, and CEO of Santa Anita Operating Company, and Jack Robbins, the vice president and founding director of the Oak Tree Racing Association, and their wives to dinner at 21 that night, and I needed some personal time to clear my head.

I was in the middle of taking a shower when Lucy knocked on the bathroom door and said, "There is a telephone call for you."

I said to her over the noise of the shower, "Please, I've asked you . . ."

Lucy then said, much more emphatically, "I think you had better take this call!"

So I got out of the shower, put on a bathrobe, and went to the phone.

The voice on the other end was that of Michael Deane Harris, the premier of the province of Ontario. He asked me to tell him exactly where we were in regard to moving the Breeders' Cup from Woodbine. I told him what was transpiring, and he said, "Is the decision final?" I said it was if the issues of labor protests and the disruption of services at Woodbine and Toronto were not resolved. Premier Harris said to me, "Mr. Bassett, neither you nor I wish to embarrass Canada, do we? I'm prepared to convene the provincial legislature for a day to try to work out an agreement, if that's necessary. But I've been informed that progress is being made. What do we need to do to delay your decision?"

Never before had I been in the position where I was negotiating with a governmental official—the premier of Ontario, no less—while dressed in only a bathrobe. My hair was wet, and the water continued to drip from my shoulders down to my feet as I outlined four requirements to Premier Harris: (1) We would need a letter from Gordon Wilson, giving his assurance that there would be no labor action or work stoppage in Toronto from October 25 to 27. (2) We would need a letter from you, Mr. Premier, with your assurance that the Breeders' Cup would proceed without any impediments or disruptions. (3) We requested a letter from Fred Sykes, the president of the pari-mutuel clerks, assuring his support. (4) And we wanted a letter from the OJC, indicating that organization's continued commitment and enthusiasm to host the Breeders' Cup.

Premier Harris told me he would attempt to get these letters. The following morning, which was Belmont Stakes day, I received a phone call from Ernie Eves, who was Ontario's deputy prime minister. He wanted to reiterate to me, he said, the determination of both the provincial government and the office of the premier that the Breeders' Cup would take place as scheduled at Woodbine, unimpeded and uninterrupted. I told the deputy premier that the assurances by him and by Premier Harris were encouraging, but we would still require the letters as outlined.

But steps were being taken to resolve the impasse. Carmen DiPaola, president of the Ontario division of the Horsemen's Benevolent and Protective Association, played an essential role in bringing the two factions together and negotiating a settlement. What DiPaola did was masterful. He enlisted the support of his counterpart in the Ontario harness racing industry, Malcolm McPhail, which meant that the horsemen representing the two breeds that raced at Woodbine, Thoroughbreds and Standardbreds, would speak with a single voice concerning the matter. DiPaola then met with Brian Henderson, the union's chief negotiator, and got him to agree to a proposal that included a pay cut for the clerks but more assurances for job security. The proposal was presented to the union's negotiating committee, underwent some revisions, and then DiPaola called Willmot and arranged for a meeting between the adversaries that began at midnight and extended until 3:00 A.M. on Belmont day. By the time the meeting was over, a tentative three-year deal had been reached. Further maneuverings and refinements concerning the deal occurred on Saturday. On Sunday, a meeting of clerks was held, during which the union's bargaining committee recommended that the package be accepted. The clerks voted overwhelmingly to do so and left the meeting chanting, "We saved the Cup!"

On Sunday afternoon, I got back to Lexington and learned from a message Willmot left on my recording machine that the union had voted to accept the OJC's offer. DiPaola called to advise me of the same and expressed the Ontario HBPA's strong commitment to support the Breeders' Cup. DiPaola further urged me to have Breeders' Cup management reconsider our decision to move the event. But we couldn't do that until we had received all four letters that I had requested.

The following day was Monday, June 10. At my Breeders' Cup office, via fax, I received the letters I had asked for from Wilson, Premier Harris, and the OJC. Willmot subsequently called—he was anxious, he said, to find out if we were rescinding our decision. "Not until we receive the letter from Sykes," I told him. And about noon, again via fax, it arrived.

I informed the members of the Breeders' Cup executive committee that all the letters were in hand, that they would receive copies of them by fax, and asked that if they had any questions, would they respond within two hours? If I hadn't heard from them by that time, I would call Willmot and tell him that the Breeders' Cup would remain at Woodbine, and that's what happened.

And, weather-wise, it turned out to be a great day. The sky was sunny, the temperature was sixty degrees at the time of the first post. The attendance, 42,243, was an all-time record for Woodbine. Despite a forty-one-minute malfunction of its pari-mutuel system, Woodbine also recorded a record wagering handle: $8,706,002. And wagering from all sources totaled $70,519,423, which at the time was the fourth highest in Breeders' Cup history.

A truly sad memory I have of that Breeders' Cup, though, is that

Charles Taylor was unable to attend. He was terminally ill with cancer, a disease he battled for the final ten years of his life. D. G. and I had dinner with Charles and his wife, Noreen, at their home during Breeders' Cup week. It was an emotional evening, with Charles sitting there, suffering from the ravages of chemotherapy. But he remained excited about the Breeders' Cup coming to Canada. Charles had done so much to bring the event to Woodbine, but at the end, his illness prevented him from being there on Breeders' Cup day. He nevertheless reveled in the records that had been set, and the following week we had a wonderful telephone conversation about it. Charles Taylor—Charles Plunket Bourchier Taylor was his full name—died on July 7, 1997. At the time of his death, he was only sixty-two.

§

I would have to say the oddest equine tale I encountered during my Breeders' Cup tenure also occurred the year we went to Woodbine—the saga of Ricks Natural Star. He was a gelding whose career record included twenty-five starts, two wins, five second-place finishes, a pair of thirds, and purse earnings of $6,093—which constitute something less than championship credentials. Yet his owner-trainer, Dr. William H. Livingston, entered Ricks Natural Star in the $2 million Breeders' Cup Turf at Woodbine. Livingston's gelding had never before raced at a distance beyond one mile, had never raced on the grass, and had not competed anywhere during the prior fourteen months—his last start had been on August 25, 1995, when he finished ninth in $3,500 claiming company at Ruidoso Downs in New Mexico.

The idea of having a horse of such limited caliber in the same race as the winners of the Turf Classic Invitational at Belmont Park, the Coronation Cup at Epsom, the St. Leger Stakes at Doncaster, the Grosser Preis von Baden at Baden-Baden, and the Prix Saint-Alary at Longchamp—all of them events of major stature on the international calendar—seemed preposterous. But Dr. Livingston believed otherwise. He was a sixty-six-year-old veterinarian from Artesia, New Mexico, whose practice, he said, "ranged from parakeets to elephants." Livingston had developed an equine vaccine that he said had cured Ricks Natural Star of a bacterial infection that had compromised his soundness. Livingston concluded that the Breeders' Cup would be a great venue to showcase the miraculous effects this vaccine could induce. He had taken out a $40,000 mortgage on his house to pay the preentry and entry fees for the Breeders' Cup Turf and had recently obtained his first trainer's license from the New Mexico Racing Commission.

We first got wind of Livingston's plans when Pamela Blatz-Murff, who was director of nominations for the Breeders' Cup, received a cryptic phone call from a commission employee. The employee informed Pam that a horse might be coming up from New Mexico but wouldn't tell her either the horse's name or the name of the man who owned and was training him. We found out the answers to both questions when Livingston officially preentered Ricks Natural Star on October 15. Pam was dumbfounded. She never believed that anyone would even think of doing something like this. Livingston told her, well, he felt that Ricks Natural Star was doing exceptionally well, that the vaccine had helped him "overcome all sorts of complications," and that "I want to put my money where my mouth is." The preentry check for $20,000 cleared, and Livingston put Ricks Natural Star in his one-horse van and left New Mexico, headed northeast.

Breeders' Cup rules stated that any horse that had not raced during the past thirty days had to have a least one published workout within thirty days of entry to be eligible. But there was nothing in the rule book stating it had to be a competitive or aggressive workout. Livingston fulfilled the criterion by stopping at Remington Park in Oklahoma City, where on October 18, Ricks Natural Star worked six furlongs in a time of 1:21.46. Going by the rule of thumb in racing that one second is equivalent to five lengths, this would have put Ricks Natural Star approximately sixty-seven lengths behind the Remington track record for the distance. There's a saying that if you are going to race in the Indianapolis 500 and all you have is an old Volkswagen Beetle, you better know a hell of a shortcut. But Livingston was not dissuaded. "I'm going to win," he told a *Daily Racing Form* reporter who had contacted him on the phone.

Livingston's itinerary was to cross over into Canada from Detroit. But at the border, he was stopped by Canadian officials. The prior year there had been an outbreak in the New Mexico equine industry of vesicular stomatitis, a contagious disease that can cause painful ulcers in the mouth. Livingston did not have the necessary health clearance papers with him and was detained until he could receive them by fax. So Livingston spent the night in a Detroit-area Budget Inn. He put up a makeshift rope corral on the lawn in back of the motel for Ricks Natural Star. The papers arrived, and Livingston and Ricks Natural Star went across the border to

Windsor, Ontario, and from there up Route 401 to Toronto, completing a trip of 1,900 miles. They arrived at Woodbine late on the evening of October 21.

By this time, other horsemen with Breeders' Cup Turf contenders were voicing alarm. Their stock was worth multimillions of dollars—and the possibility was growing, by the hour, that smack in the middle of the field was going to be a horse that had proved to be a dud in $3,500 claiming company. Inarguably, Ricks Natural Star was the most unqualified horse in Breeders' Cup history. But by the morning of October 23, when entries were scheduled to be taken, reality had outdistanced apprehension. If Livingston wanted to run his horse, there wasn't anything we could do to stop him. Ricks Natural Star had a recent published workout. He had been schooled from the starting gate at Woodbine. Dr. George Mundy, a veterinary consultant for the Breeders' Cup, had examined Ricks Natural Star. "There's nothing wrong with him," Mundy concluded. Livingston was in no violation of Breeders' Cup rules. He was in no violation of Ontario Jockey Club rules. Sixteen horses had preentered the Breeders' Cup Turf. Two of them had withdrawn, which meant we could not deny the participation of Ricks Natural Star on the grounds that his earnings were too low. The race allowed for a fourteen-horse field. And because he was one of exactly fourteen horses officially entered for the post position draw, he was in.

The draw itself flirted with calamity. The long-held process in racing had involved shaking numbered pills out of a bottle and matching each one with a horse's entry sheet that had been randomly pulled from a shuffled stack. This was fair but rather boring. I concluded that this year, for the Breeders' Cup, we needed to introduce some life into the procedure. The lottery was a pretty big deal in Canada, and during my prior visits there, I had seen some televised lottery drawings where numbered ping-pong balls were blown around by an air jet in a glass enclosure. The balls that emerged from the enclosure constituted the pick three, pick four, and whatnot lottery numbers for the day. I thought it would be great if we could adapt this concept for the post position draw for the Breeders' Cup races.

The lottery company set the machine up for us, and on draw day, we were set to go with all these horse owners, trainers, and media members in attendance to watch. Well, when we turned the air machine on, it hadn't been set properly. The air jet blew all the ping-pong balls to the top of the container, and they kept bouncing around up there. And we stood and watched. After about a minute, one of the balls came down. After two more minutes, another came down. Two additional minutes went by. Nothing happened. Then another minute. Another ball came down. Three more minutes passed. The remaining balls continued to gaily dance at the top of the container, but none of them would descend. Mike Letis of SMTI was steaming. He said to me, "Bassett, was this another one of your crackpot ideas?" Finally, Letis went over to the technician who had brought the machine and said, "For God's sake, get this thing straightened out!" The technician proceeded to make a slight adjustment, reducing the velocity of the air jet, and suddenly everything worked properly. The balls fell at random, and we completed the draw. I felt like someone who had almost received the gong on the *Amateur Hour.*

Meanwhile, the press attention Ricks Natural Star was receiving was enormous. Three days before the Breeders' Cup, the front page of the *Daily Racing Form* featured two stories. One was about the condition of Woodbine's main oval, and the other was about Ricks Natural Star. Two days before the Breeders' Cup, the front page of the *Daily Racing Form* again featured two stories. One was about D. Wayne Lukas, and the other was about Ricks Natural Star. And the day before the Breeders' Cup, the *Daily Racing Form*'s front page once again featured two stories. One was about Cigar, and the other was about Ricks Natural Star. In the Woodbine stable area, Livingston had been inviting members of the media to climb aboard the horse. Several did, and with shank in hand, Livingston took them on short rides around the shed row.

At post time on Breeders' Cup day, the odds on Ricks Natural Star were 56–1. Which, of course, rendered him a long shot, the longest shot in the field. They were considerably lower, however, than the 99–1 he had been accorded in the morning line. And here are a couple of additional informational tidbits you might find interesting. There were seven horses competing in Breeders' Cup races that day that actually went off at longer odds than Ricks Natural Star. One of them, Mt. Sassafras, finished fourth in the Classic and came within three-quarters of a length of winning it. Another, Critical Factor, finished third in the Breeders' Cup Juvenile Fillies. To take the bewilderment a step further, over the years there have been more than two dozen horses that competed in the Breeders' Cup Turf at longer odds than Ricks Natural Star. And to take it even further, in all the Breeders' Cup races combined, there have been more than 200 horses that went off at longer odds—which is enough world-class equine stock to fill the entirety of two Breeders' Cup cards.

With Ricks Natural Star, we knew no miracle was forthcoming. I went to George M. Hendrie, the OJC's board chairman, and asked him to get the track stewards to have a frank talk with Lisa McFarland, the thirty-three-year-old jockey to whom Livingston had offered the mount. Lisa wasn't a name rider. She had won only seven races the year before, and in 1996, she was tied for twenty-eighth position in the Woodbine standings with eleven wins. Nobody was faulting Lisa for accepting Livingston's offer. She had an opportunity to ride in the Breeders' Cup, and she took it. The stewards told Lisa to keep Ricks Natural Star on a straight path until he ran out of gas and then take him to the far outside. Which she did.

If you look at the video of the race, you see him break cleanly from the number-four post and subsequently weave so far across the track that he was closer to the outer rail than the inner one. The opening half mile was run in a slow fifty seconds, at which point Ricks Natural Star was in second position, just a length and a half from the lead. But from that point onward, Ricks Natural Star appeared to be going backward as the field flooded by him in one huge rush. Within a quarter of a mile, he went from second all the way to last. The length of the Woodbine stretch was 975 feet, and as the horse in the thirteenth position crossed the finish line, Ricks Natural Star had yet to reach the turn for home. Lisa McFarland kept him going, though, and the Woodbine crowd let out a pretty substantial cheer as Ricks Natural Star finally came loping toward the wire—a good three-quarters of a minute behind everybody else.

He raced two more times after that. Twenty days after the Breeders' Cup, Livingston accepted a $5,000 appearance fee to run Ricks Natural Star in an 870-yard race that included both Thoroughbreds and quarter horses at Los Alamitos, which is a small track in Southern California. He finished next to last. Seven weeks later, on January 12, 1997, Ricks Natural Star came in seventh in a claiming race at Turf Paradise in Phoenix, Arizona. In the latter event, he was claimed for $7,500 by a horseman named Larry Weber from Scottsdale. Weber promptly announced he was retiring Ricks Natural Star and shipped him up to Sunnyside Farm, which is near Paris, Kentucky, and is co-owned by Dr. Robert W. Copelan, a very respected veterinarian, and the farm manager, Jeff Thornbury. Rick's Natural Star remains at Sunnyside today, living the relaxed life of a happy pensioner.

§

My retirement from the Breeders' Cup took effect on December 31, 1996. I had turned seventy-five years of age in October, and I felt it was time to gracefully exit. I also felt it was time for D. G. to become president and CEO of the organization, to take the foremost position on the stage. He and I had a wonderful working relationship—we were a formidable team, and to this day, we remain immensely proud of our association and our accomplishments. D. G. was age forty-eight, and there was no question in my mind that he was ready, capable, and fully qualified to assume the reins.

To give you an idea of how much the Breeders' Cup had grown, when it was inaugurated at Hollywood in 1984, it generated a wagering handle from all sources of $19.48 million. My first year there, the handle totaled $44.71 million. My last year there, it was $70.52 million. And for its 2006 running at Churchill, the final Breeders' Cup organized during D. G.'s stewardship, the handle from all sources was a record $140.33 million.

Back in 1984, the ratio of Breeders' Cup wagering that occurred off-site was 41.1 percent. Twenty-two years later, that ratio had more than doubled to 87 percent. Yet the on-track handle in 2006 at Churchill, $18.26 million, was a Breeders' Cup record too. In 2007, the Breeders' Cup added three new races; was held at a new venue, Monmouth Park on the New Jersey shore; and was expanded into a two-day championship. Purses totaled $23 million, well more than twice the amount offered in 1984. And in 2008, with the Breeders' Cup now involving fourteen races, purses rose to $26.4 million.

This is all rather impressive for an event that has only been around for a quarter century.

Chapter 12

Trips as an Ambassador for Racing

IN EARLY 1986, Lucy and I were members of a group invited by Sheikh Maktoum bin Rashid al Maktoum, the ruler of Dubai, to visit his country. The invitees, all from central Kentucky, further included Governor Martha Layne Collins; Otis Singletary, president of the University of Kentucky; Charles Shearer, president of Transylvania University; Gordon Duke, the state's finance secretary; and several of the region's business leaders and prominent horse breeders.

The weeklong journey began on February 9. A trio of Lear jets took us from Lexington to Dulles International Airport in Washington, D.C. A fourth Lear jet was used to carry our luggage. At Dulles, we all got on a British Airways Concorde, a plane capable of speeds of 1,330 miles per hour and which most of us had never been on before. Cruising at 60,000 feet, we avoided all weather and turbulence and could look down and see the 747s and DC-10s and other jumbo jets flying at what seemed a tortoise's pace four miles below us. The curvature of the earth was in full view. It was an extraordinary start to what all of us came to refer to as the "Magic Carpet Trip."

The Concorde took us directly to Heathrow Airport in London. There, a fleet of Rolls-Royces ferried us to the hotel where we were staying at the culmination of the first leg of our trip, the Jumeirah Carlton Tower, which is owned by the Maktoum family. A lavish dinner awaited us in the Carlton Tower penthouse that night, and the Dubai ambassador to Great Britain was the principal speaker.

Sheikh Maktoum and his brothers had several stallion farms in the Newmarket area, and we were allowed the opportunity the following day to visit them. The Rolls-Royces took us down to a heliport adjacent to the Thames River, where three helicopters awaited us. Snow flurries were in the air, and we flew through them over St. Paul's Cathedral and the houses of Parliament. Hovering in the air at a low altitude, we could really see and appreciate the historic beauty of old London. We landed at Dalham Hall Stud, just outside of Newmarket, which headquartered the Darley Stud operation of Sheikh Mohammed bin Rashid al Maktoum. It was snowing more heavily there, two or three inches were on the ground, and I remember Governor Collins was wearing open-toed shoes. We toured the barns and on-site veterinary clinics, had a lavish lunch, and flew back to London, where another lavish dinner awaited us. These are the ways Sheikh Maktoum entertained his guests, and the trip had just started.

On the following morning, the Rolls-Royces took us to London's Gatwick Airport, where we boarded the sheikh's private 727. Remember, the year was 1986, and it was the first time I had ever seen a television monitor with a map and a miniature airplane on it, allowing you to trace the route of the trip right at your seat. We flew over Czechoslovakia, over the island of Crete, over Saudi Arabia. It was an eight-and-a-half-hour nonstop flight. After we arrived at Dubai International Airport, another fleet of Rolls-Royces and Mercedes took us to the Sheraton (which, over there, is pronounced *Sher-rotten*) Dubai Creek Hotel & Towers, which rates five stars by any means of assessment.

Omar Assis, the personal representative of Sheikh Maktoum, was really the major planner and organizer of our trip. After checking in at the Sheraton and receiving the keys to our suites, he told us he did not want anyone to take a lot of time changing clothes, for we were all to meet in the hotel lobby in exactly one hour, and from there we would go to the penthouse. In each of our suites, there was a sea of gifts, wines, liquors, dates, nuts, and cheeses. The suites looked out on what is called Dubai Creek but is, in essence, a large estuary that leads into the Persian Gulf. The view was spectacular.

Promptly at 8:00 P.M., we all met in the lobby and got on the elevators together and rode up in unison to the penthouse. As we strolled down the hallway to the dining area, we saw displayed a huge commonwealth of Kentucky flag that had been imported for the occasion, and we all oohed and aahed. As we entered the dining area, we could hear "My Old Kentucky Home" being played on a piano. And the pianist was Mike Allen, a renowned black musician from Lexington! Omar, during one of his own visits to Kentucky, had attended a number of parties where Mike had played. Omar liked what he heard and had arranged for Mike to be flown across the Atlantic the previous day. We were astonished, we couldn't get over it. Here he was. It was really him!

Subsequent days were equally extraordinary, and educational too. In the mid-1960s, oil was discovered 75 miles off the coast of Dubai. The British protectorate was lifted from the Persian Gulf in 1971, and in December of that year, Dubai joined with six other entities to become the United Arab Emirates. From that point onward, Dubai has maintained control of its own destiny. Its entire area encompasses only about 1,500 square miles—it is smaller than the state of Rhode Island. But the Maktoum family, whose rule in Dubai dates back to 1833, has, during the past thirty-five years, developed an economy that is exceptionally diverse.

Today, only about 6 percent of Dubai's gross national product relates to oil production. Tourism is a huge industry. Dubai annually hosts the world's richest horse race, the $6 million Dubai World Cup. Other annual sporting events include the Dubai Desert Classic Golf Tournament and the Dubai Tennis Open. A resort has been built among the sand dunes where one can ski indoors, down man-made mountains, on real snow. Powerboat racing, a rugby festival, an international film festival, and an international jazz festival are held in Dubai each year. A project is now under way to double the country's number of hotel rooms from 29,000 to 58,000.

There is a wonderful tax-free incentive in Dubai for companies from foreign countries to come in and set up operations. Over 12 million air passengers annually go through Dubai International Airport. Dubai has terrific road systems, hospitals, and schools. The volume of construction projects is immense. There are plans for there to eventually be 500 skyscrapers in Dubai, and it has been estimated that upward of 25 percent of the world's cranes are in use there. True, Dubai remains a monarchy—there is no broad representation of the people in Dubai's government. But the Maktoums are highly sensitive to the needs and welfare of the overall citizenry.

During our trip, we toured some extraordinary facilities. We went to visit a desalinization plant, which involves a tremendous cavern that stretches a half mile out into the Persian Gulf. The water flows down through a great tunnel to a hydraulic plant, where electricity is generated and salt water is converted into fresh water.

Dubai has an extensive history as a major link in the Africa-to-India trade route—decades, even centuries ago, African merchants selling items made of gold and ivory would use it as a starting point for their journeys through the Strait of Hormuz. Today, Dubai's Jebel Ali is the largest man-made port in the world—it has sixty-seven berths and is the foreign port most often frequented by U.S. Navy vessels.

We spent a day at the camel races, which have a huge following in Dubai (although they are not as popular as its number-one sport, soccer). Then we were all moved from the Sheraton to the Jebel Ali Hotel and Golf Resort, which is between the coast and the desert, about ten miles from the center of Dubai. We were told we were going to spend the evening at a party in the desert and that Sheikh Maktoum had provided dishdashas, the traditional Arab robes, for all the men. And he wanted us to wear them. I felt as uncomfortable as when I was in Claridge's, getting outfitted in a morning coat and top hat prior to being the Queen's guest. But I dutifully donned the white dishdasha, which reminded me of a nightgown (although it only came down to my thighs), along with the matching headdress. I became Bassett of Arabia. Lucy and I apprehensively left our room and took the elevator down to the lobby. There, all the male guests looked at one another and started laughing. We had all obeyed the sheikh's dictum for appropriate attire.

It was now about 7:00 P.M. and dark outside, and we all boarded a bus, which already had Omar and a guide aboard. The bus began its journey through the desert. We were served drinks and kept wondering exactly where we were going. The guide kept pointing out landmarks. The trip lasted for about forty minutes, and then the bus pulled through a grove of trees, and we suddenly saw a great festoon of tenting. We got out of the bus and walked up a palm-laden walkway through a canopy of silks and into a room that contained seemingly acres of couches and food and wine. And a magnificent orchestra. All in the middle of the desert. Then we realized we were actually back at the hotel and had been escorted in through a different entrance, one that bordered the desert. The sheikh had taken over the hotel's main ballroom and transformed it into the setting of an enormous Bedouin tent. We were astonished.

Our visit to Dubai lasted four days. On day five, we were flown on Sheikh Maktoum's private jet back to London, where we again spent a night at the Carlton Tower. The next day, we boarded the Concorde for the flight back to the United States.

The Magic Carpet Trip was a fascinating experience, an opportunity to tour what was once a feudal country that has so transformed itself. The nomadic culture and way of life that pervaded for centuries in Dubai have, within a period of less than four decades, been replaced by thriving financial and business enterprises and a booming tourist industry. The purpose of our visit was to discover and help spread the excitement about this "new" Dubai. And to gain an appreciation of the unlimited potential of an international zone that has no personal or corporate income taxes. Images of the ever-changing present and visions of an extraordinary future are in evidence everywhere.

Some scientists predict that by the decade of the 2030s, oil reserves will have been depleted in the Middle East. But by that time, Dubai will likely be the trade Mecca in that portion of the world. Oil helped give modern Dubai its foundation. And what is rising on top of that foundation appears boundless.

§

This section would not be complete if I failed to provide testimony to the economic impact the Maktoum family has had on central Kentucky. During the past quarter century, they have acquired thousands of acres, much of which primarily was tobacco and cattle farming land. And they have transformed those properties into Thoroughbred stallion stations and breeding farms—true showplaces within the worldwide scope of the industry. Darley Stud, which was formerly Jonabell Farm, on Bowman Mill Road in Lexington, is owned by Sheikh Mohammed. He also now owns Gainsborough Farm in nearby Versailles, Kentucky. (Gainsborough was founded by his late brother and our former Dubai host, Sheikh Maktoum, who died in 2006.) And Shadwell Farm on Fort Springs Road in Lexington is owned by another brother, Sheikh Hamdan bin Rashid al Maktoum.

The Maktoums' importance to the Bluegrass region has at the very least been equivalent to that of a midsize manufacturing plant. And as economic generators, think of the ripple effects their farms have had in regard to local building and construction firms, farm equipment and supply businesses, legal and accounting firms, and, of course, the auctions at Keeneland.

Special tax incentives from the state have not been utilized to bring the Maktoums here. But they have provided the region with a broad taxable base in regard to property, sales, and jobs. Staff members at their farms, almost all of whom are Americans, love working for them. The Maktoums pay fair wages and provide excellent family benefits, and you

In the Keeneland paddock with Kentucky governor John Y. Brown Jr. and his wife, Phyllis George.

Alydar, just prior to the 1978 Blue Grass Stakes, was brought to the Keeneland clubhouse rail, where Lucille Markey awaited him.

Lucy, playfully responding to a photographer who was taking her picture.

Adoration, bred by Lucy G. Bassett, wins the 2003 Breeders' Cup Distaff under jockey Pat Valenzuela.

D. Wayne Lukas and me, perhaps in the midst of a friendly disagreement, in the Keeneland clubhouse.

In the Keeneland paddock with Nick Zito.

With Joe Hirsch, executive columnist for the *Daily Racing Form*—for over thirty years he served as master of ceremonies at our Blue Grass press dinner.

Enjoying a victorious moment with Charles Cella, "Le Grande Charlie," of Oaklawn Park.

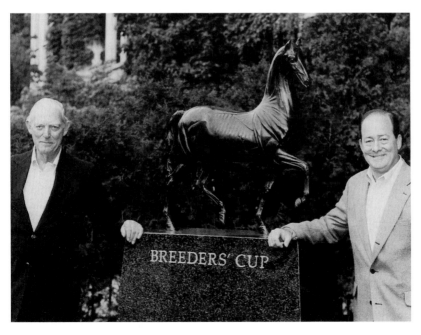

D. G. Van Clief and me, flanking the Breeders' Cup Ecorche statue at Belmont Park.

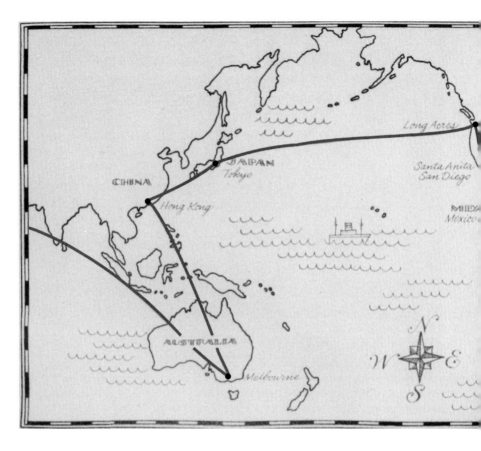

(Above and facing page) This map displays my trips to and within six continents as an ambassador for racing.

(Facing page) Sheikh Mohammed bin Rashid al Maktoum, the ruler of Dubai—always a most gracious host.

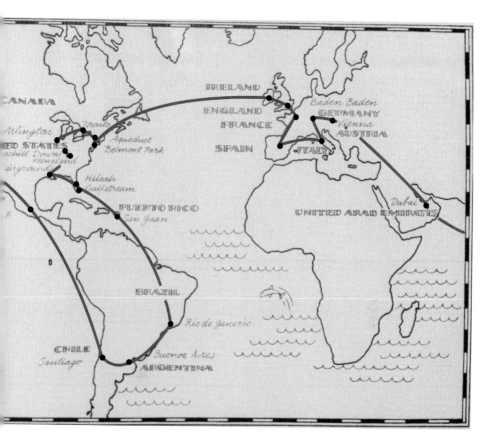

Bill Greely and me, dressed in traditional Arab clothing during our trip to Dubai.

Presenting the Melbourne Cup Trophy in 1986—to date, the only American ever allowed the honor of doing this.

At a Halloween party with my dear friend Ron McAnally, who attended dressed as his wife.

The late William T. "Bill" Young, whom I always relied upon when I needed help.

At southern Africa's Victoria Falls during a photo safari in 2003.

Receiving an honorary doctorate from Eastern Kentucky University in 1987.

The U. S. Marine Corps presented me with the Superior Public Service Award in 2007.

Lucy—my wife and partner in life for fifty-eight years.

If I had but one wish, it would be to live my life again.

rarely hear about one of their employees being fired or otherwise terminated, unless some gross malfeasance is involved.

Additionally, the Maktoums are concerned and responsible neighbors. They are always on the contact list of every major fund-raising drive in the Lexington area. Their generosity toward the Maxwell H. Gluck Equine Research Center at the University of Kentucky has been magnificent. Dr. Peter Timoney, who spent nearly two decades as Gluck's director, told me that a $5 million gift from the Maktoums (essentially an endowment) was the "fulcrum" for the center's growth. It has led to major gifts and endowments from other individuals. The resulting quality and scope of the Gluck research program have benefited horsemen not only in central Kentucky but around the world.

Back in 2006, the turf writer Andy Beyer wrote a column for the *Washington Post* (it was also reprinted in the *Daily Racing Form*) in which he referred to the Maktoums as "remote figures" and to their racing operation as "joyless." Beyer also said, "Most wealthy people in the sport won't spend money in a fashion that makes them appear foolish or vulgar. The Maktoums are unfettered by such constraints." I take exception to what Beyer said. When they win a major race, the Maktoums are not as gregarious, they are not as openly enthusiastic as Americans tend to be when they do the same. But the Maktoums are serious competitors. They race their horses at major tracks around the world, and you never see them dodge a challenge because somebody else has entered a horse that is an overwhelming favorite.

There have been a lot of people who have come into the racing business and have spent multimillions of dollars in an attempt to gain success and have not come close to succeeding the way the Maktoums have. They have won the preeminent races throughout Europe and in Australia, Japan, and Hong Kong, including the Epsom Derby, Prix de l'Arc de Triomphe, Melbourne Cup, Japan Cup, and Hong Kong Cup. Maktoum horses have won eight Breeders' Cup races. In 2006, Sheikh Mohammed sent out Bernardini to win the Preakness, and Sheikh Hamdan sent out Jazil to win the Belmont Stakes. The Kentucky Derby is just about the only race of international renown the Maktoums have yet to win.

The Maktoums are very patient with their horses and with their trainers. And while the Maktoums are loyal to each other, they do not engage in conflicts of interest on the racetrack. In the 2006 Breeders' Cup Classic, Invasor, owned by Sheikh Hamdan, and Bernardini, owned by Sheikh

Mohammed, fought it out foot by foot, stride by stride, through the stretch run. Invasor won by a length, and Bernardini finished well clear of the remainder of the field for second. The battle between those two colts was hugely exciting.

Throughout the existence of the Breeders' Cup, the Maktoums have been tremendously supportive, not only with the horses they have entered in the races but also with the stallions and foals they've nominated to the program. When fees have been increased, or whenever there has been a modification of the nominating procedures, the Maktoums have gone along without questions. And, yes, they have become a huge success on these shores. In 2008, the Breeders' Cup Juvenile was won by Midshipman, owned by Sheikh Maktoum. And the Breeders' Cup Classic was won by Raven's Pass, owned by Sheikh Maktoum's wife, Princess Haya of Jordan.

In our sport, whenever participants rise to a level above the crowd, there are always others who complain they took shortcuts to success. We see this happen with D. Wayne Lukas and some of his owners, such as Eugene V. Klein. We see this happen with the trainers Bobby Frankel and Todd Pletcher. And we see this happen with the Maktoums. There is always that issue of, "How do they do it?" And it stems from envy more than any other factor.

§

In the spring of 1986, Graham Campbell, a very distinguished and well-known Thoroughbred breeder in Australia, informed me that I was going to receive an invitation from Peter Armytage, chairman of the Victoria Racing Club (VRC), to be their guest at that year's Melbourne Cup at Flemington Racecourse. Campbell was a former professional golfer and had been involved with Thoroughbreds for about three decades. In 1980, with his son Phillip, Campbell had founded Blue Gun Farm in Victoria, and the following year, he sold the first yearling that had ever fetched a six-figure price in Australia's history. He had been coming to Keeneland's November Breeding Stock Sale for a period of years, and we had become very good friends.

Several times in the past, Campbell had suggested that I should go to Australia and call on the leading breeders there, some of whom I had met at Keeneland and during visits to England and France. But it would require such a long trip that I never seriously contemplated the idea. Then, at

Keeneland's 1986 July Yearling Sale, a formal invitation was extended from Armytage and the VRC, which is Melbourne's equivalent to The Jockey Club. And in late October, I departed on a trip that took me from Lexington to Chicago, from there to San Francisco to Honolulu, Sydney, and ultimately Melbourne.

As the plane was landing in Sydney, the air pressure filled my eardrums, and I tried to clear them by blowing my nose. In doing so, I ruptured a blood vessel in my right eye. The eye immediately became all clouded up, creating the impression that I was either was a cyclops or had gotten involved in a barroom fight. I had a pair of dark glasses in my suitcase and decided that, well, I'll wear these. But then I realized I didn't want to get off the plane appearing like a George Raft character. So I spurned the glasses, and when the VRC people met me in the air terminal, one of the first things I said was, "I'm sorry for looking like a cyclops. I hope it doesn't disenchant you."

Thankfully, it didn't. Despite the bloodshot eye, they could not have been nicer to me throughout my visit. Peter Armytage had said to me before I had embarked on the trip, "We would appreciate it if you would speak at the Carbine Club Derby Eve luncheon and also at Australia's Champion Racehorse dinner. But please, make sure that you give two different speeches."

I laughed, and asked Peter, "What's that about?"

He said, "Well, the gentleman whom we had as guest speaker last year was the senior steward of the British Jockey Club, and he gave the same speech at both gatherings. A good 75 percent of the people in attendance at the Carbine Club luncheon also attend the Champion Racehorse dinner."

So, in my Keeneland office, I had worked very hard on both speeches. Particularly the Carbine Club speech. It would be held in conjunction with the Hong Kong Bank Derby, which is run at Flemington the Saturday prior to the Melbourne Cup. The year I was there, perhaps as some sort of a portent, the luncheon was scheduled on Halloween.

There is also a Carbine Club Stakes, where the winning owner receives, among other things, a twelve-inch ceramic statuette of the horse for whom the club was named. A month prior to my trip, I had a phone conversation with the head of the club and asked him, "How many of your members know the history of Carbine?"

He replied, "Not many."

With the research assistance of the Keeneland librarians, I wove together a speech that in essence was a profile of Carbine's career. He was bred in New Zealand and, after a brief career campaigning in his home country, became one of the most legendary athletes, equine or human, to ever compete in Australia. Foaled in 1885, Carbine raced forty-three times and recorded thirty-three wins, a half dozen second-place finishes, and a trio of third-place finishes. His victories included the 1890 running of the Melbourne Cup, a race that involved an incredibly large field of thirty-nine horses. Carbine carried an impost of 10 stone, 5 pounds (that's 145 pounds American), which remains the all-time record for a Melbourne Cup winner. At stud, Carbine sired Spearmint, who won the 1906 Epsom Derby. Carbine was also a great-great-grandfather of Phar Lap. Discussions regarding who is the greatest horse in the history of Australia racing have long revolved around the two (although the outstanding racemare Makybe Diva added her name to the debate with three consecutive Melbourne Cup triumphs in 2003–2005).

My delving into Carbine's career became rather extensive. I figured that the people who run Australian racing really worshipped him. (If they didn't, they would not have named the Carbine Club after him.) At the luncheon, I was seated at the head table, along with the club's chairman and a number of other dignitaries, one of whom was Neil Trezise, the minister of sport and recreation for New South Wales. The protocol, as I understood it, was for Minister Trezise to make a toast, during which he would comment of the status of Australian racing and also on the purpose for the gathering. I would then be introduced and would deliver my speech. Our remarks did not necessarily have to coincide. It was more a matter of two speakers getting up and saying a few things that had some degree of meaningfulness.

Well, Minister Trezise got up and said, "You know, for years I have been coming to this club. And I have often wondered how many of you are aware of the historical significance of Carbine. And the marvelous race record that this horse accumulated throughout his career. For Carbine's accomplishments included. . . ."

I started sinking into my chair. I thought, "What am I going to do. My whole, entire speech is . . . he's giving my speech! He's eclipsing what I had in my mind! He's smashing my whole presentation! He's demolishing it! Obliterating it!" And I sank deeper into the chair. And I'm thinking, "What am I going to do? I came all this way! Over 15,000 miles! I'm supposed to be the principal speaker! And the minister is giving out all these statistics and facts and other things about what Carbine had accomplished! God, Almighty, what will I do?"

Anyway, Minister Trezise went on for about ten minutes. Ten excruciating, traumatic minutes, from my viewpoint. Then I was introduced. I had taken a rather stiff swallow of white wine, trying to regain my senses and restore some degree of self-confidence. And I started out by thanking the minister for bringing up the subject of Carbine and for detailing, indeed, what a marvelous horse he was. And I said, "Mr. Minister, were you aware that Carbine was not the original name of this horse? That he initially raced as Mauser? And did you know that his country of breeding, New Zealand, is where he first started racing, and . . . ?" What I was trying to do was fill in any gaps he had left with the research I had done. It was an impromptu, desperate plan, but utilizing a combination of significant facts and trivia, I was able to get through the speech, and I concluded it by saying: "Now, let us raise our glasses and join in a toast to that immortal champion of the Australian turf—Carbine."

Afterward, Rex Butterworth, who was Keeneland's Australian representative, a very distinguished veterinarian who taught at the University of Sydney, came up to me and said, "Boy, Ted, that was some talk you gave."

I told him, "You have no idea how close to a disaster it was."

Rex said, "Where did you get all those facts?"

I said, "From the speech I was supposed to give that never got given."

§

On the evening before the Carbine Club luncheon, I had been the principal speaker at the Champion Racehorse dinner. It was a black-tie, all-male event, and about 400 attended. Robert Sangster was given an award. I had asked the organizers of the dinner which subjects they wished for me to address during my speech, and they said they would like to hear about American racing, about the Breeders' Cup, and about the Keeneland sales. I mixed in a few other things too, including the stories I had heard from fellow Marines during World War II about the wonderful hospitality Australians had extended to them. I mentioned the exploits of the golfer Greg Norman, Australia's "Great White Shark," and Greg Shipley, a shortstop for the Los Angeles Dodgers who was the first Australian to play major league baseball.

Well, I was delivering my speech, and I thought I was doing fairly well and moving along. Then, as I was about halfway through, there was suddenly a big commotion in the right-hand rear of the ballroom. The people up front could not see it, but I could, and what I saw was people getting up and standing. My first thought was that the speech was so bad and boring that they were getting up to leave. What I saw next, though, was a lot of rushing around and people leaning over. What I later found out was that a gentleman named Monty Millson, who had visited Keeneland on several occasions, had collapsed from a heart attack during the speech and had died right on the spot. It was, of course, a terrible thing. But at the very moment, I didn't know what was happening—the thought crossed my mind that my speech was so boring it caused somebody to pass out. And I didn't know whether to stop or continue. Should I interrupt myself and say, "Can we help? Is there a problem?" But two-thirds of the audience was unaware anything tragic had occurred. So I decided to tough it out and went on, trying to wrap up the speech as quickly as I could. Afterward, I felt terribly when I found out about Millson.

The day of the Melbourne Cup was November 4. The VRC people had provided me with accommodations in the new Hyatt On Collins Hotel in downtown Melbourne and told me to be ready promptly at 10:00 A.M. I had gone to Chesters Men's Wear, which is Melbourne's equivalent to the Moss Brothers in London, where I was outfitted with a morning suit and top hat. The morning suit, while well tailored, must have been designed for someone going to a wedding in Antarctica, because it was made from the heaviest flannel I have ever worn. But it was the only one they had that fit my frame, so I went with it. Keep in mind that early November is mid-spring in Australia.

Well, the car from the VRC came and picked me up and took me, properly attired, to Flemington. The crowd was flowing in from all directions. The Melbourne Cup is a very big thing in Australia, in many respects, even bigger than the Kentucky Derby is here. It is run on the first Tuesday in November. Australia's Parliament recesses. Airline and railroad schedules are interrupted for the running of the race. The media coverage, from television, radio, newspapers, and magazines, is enormous. A two-mile event with a field that may involve dozens of horses. Spellbinding, breathtaking, majestically orchestrated. The Melbourne Cup is truly a national spectacle.

At Flemington, I was met by Armytage and the VRC's vice chairman, Ian Bayles. They took me to a room in the club's headquarters and said,

"We want to talk to you. We have an unfortunate situation that has developed, and we would like to ask you for your assistance."

I was their invited guest and, appropriately, I told them, "Of course. What may I do for you?" In the background, I could hear the growing excitement of the crowd outside. Attendance at Flemington that day would number 86,041.

Peter Armytage said, "We would like for you to present the Melbourne Cup."

My immediate reaction was total shock and awe, and I began to sweat inside the heavy flannel morning suit. I stammered, "Good heavens, do you really mean that? What has happened?"

They were very discreet. Bayles said, "The Prime Minister has a problem. We have some difficulty in being able to accommodate him in this matter today, and he will not be able to present the trophy."

I replied, "Well, certainly you must have somebody else who would be more appropriate than me."

Armytage said, "We would like very much for you to do it. But we have to make the decision now and get the proper information to the media."

I said, "Well, yes, of course, I would be honored. Is there anything I have to do other than the presenting?"

Peter said, "Yes, you have to make an appropriate comment, you have to address his Excellency, the Prime Minister, and you have to address the public."

Bob Hawke was Australia's prime minister. He was head of the country's Labour Party, and I later found out that, in keeping with his image as a champion of labor, Hawke refused to don the requisite top hat and cutaway, which had been worn by the presenters of the Melbourne Cup for over 100 years. It all represented a classic impasse between smart politics and unyielding tradition. The dilemma required an immediate substitute, which, in a very odd twist of irony, turned out to be me, a visitor from Woodford County, Kentucky.

Gwendolyn Armytage, Peter's wife, subsequently took me aside and instructed me about the appropriate protocol. I wrote her instructions down on the back of my race program. During the trophy presentation, I was to address the Prime Minister first. I was to say, "Your Excellency, Mr. Premier (pronounced *prem-ee-yea* in Australia). Then I was to address Peter as "Mr. Chairman." Next, I was to address John Dorman Elliott, the president of Carlton United Breweries, whose Foster's Lager brand sponsored the Melbourne Cup. Then I was to address the winning owner. I was to do all this in that exact order, and not divert as much as fraction of a centimeter from the protocol.

The winner of that year's Melbourne Cup, by a neck in a three-horse photo finish, was At Talaq, a 10–1 shot who had been bred in Kentucky and was owned by Sheikh Hamdan bin Rashid al Maktoum. Just three days before the Melbourne Cup, At Talaq had won the one-and-a-quarter-mile L. K. S. Mackinnon Stakes at Flemington. Add the Melbourne Cup's two miles to that, and there is nothing more you need to be told about At Talaq's stamina. The horse had been purchased for the sheikh by an agent named H. Thompson Jones for $800,000 as a yearling. It would have been rewarding for me if the transaction had occurred at Keeneland, but alas, it took place at the Fasig-Tipton August sale in Saratoga.

Elliott had the responsibility of introducing me. In the process of doing so, he told the multitudes that he was delighted, because he had "bought the horse in the Calcutta Sweep last night." Elliott further said, "The good Lord has put on wonderful weather, and for all our foreign visitors, they can see what a real race meeting is run like. And for the first time an American horse has won the Cup, so we have a [trophy] to be presented by an American to an American horse. I hope you all had a great day, and it's a great day to be drinking the product."

Then it was my turn, and I did exactly as Gwen Armytage had instructed. Sheikh Hamdan was not on hand to receive the trophy. So I presented it to Francesca de Burgh, the wife of Hubie de Burgh, who managed the sheikh's Derrinstown Stud in Ireland. But I knew the sheikh had watched the race via satellite—the Maktoums never fail to watch the performances of their horses in major international stakes. I had met Sheikh Hamdan, of course, and he must have been shocked to see me as the trophy presenter. When I returned to the hotel, there were several messages awaiting me from Australian friends who had watched the Melbourne Cup on television, and they were shocked, too.

A couple of postscripts. Jack Elliott, who was the Joe Hirsch of Australian turf columnists, wrote a flattering opinion piece about me that was published in the *Melbourne Herald* the day after the Melbourne Cup. Elliott mentioned that I had been made a life member of the VRC, which was a rare and humbling distinction, and that I was the first "outsider" to present the Melbourne Cup trophy, which was rare to the point of being unprecedented, and even more humbling. Elliott concluded his piece by saying, "Move over Paul Hogan, Ted Bassett is our man." Hogan, you may recall, was the star of the Crocodile Dundee movies. He had also been a spokesman for Foster's, proclaiming that it tasted "like an angel crying on your tongue." I appreciated Elliott's kind words, but I really don't believe Hogan needed to worry about being replaced by me, in cinematic features or otherwise.

And around the time of the 2003 Kentucky Derby, I received a visit at the Keeneland Cottage from Andrew Sharp Peacock, an Australian friend of many years standing. He had long been a prominent figure in the hierarchy of Australian politics, had served as the country's foreign minister and ambassador to the United States, and had become chairman of Boeing Australia Ltd., a company with 45,000 employees. We were sitting in the cottage, talking about the Derby and about Will Farish (who is also one of Andrew's close friends) and the Breeders' Cup. Eventually, the conversation got around to Australian racing. I said, "You know, when I went out to Australia in '86, I was the person who presented the Melbourne Cup."

Andrew said, "Don't give me that baloney, Bassett. You could not present the Melbourne Cup. No one but the prime minister or a member of the Royal Family ever gets to present it." I told him I was telling the truth, and Andrew said, "Oh, ho, ho, no, no, have another drink or take another puff on whatever you've been smoking."

I took him to the back sitting room in the cottage and showed him a photograph of me presenting the trophy. Outfitted in a morning suit. Standing in the winner's enclosure at Flemington. Andrew could hardly believe it.

Which leads to another ironic twist. In the mid-1980s, Andrew was the leader of the Liberal Party in Australia. Had his party, instead of Bob Hawke's Labour Party, prevailed in the 1984 election, Andrew would have become the country's prime minister. And had he been Australia's prime minister in 1986 instead of Hawke, there is no doubt in my mind that Andrew would have been willing to comply with the VRC's protocol at the Melbourne Cup. The honor of presenting the trophy would have gone to him, not to some unknown American.

§

I have made two trips to Hong Kong. The first was in December 1988, a little more than seven months after I had become president of the Breeders'

Cup. I went there at the specific invitation of Sir Oswald Cheung, who was chairman of what was then known as the Royal Hong Kong Jockey Club. I was asked to give a speech at the annual dinner of the Hong Kong Racehorse Owners Association, and one of the things I said was: "On behalf of the United States Breeders' Cup, we would like to officially extend you an invitation to receive our satellite television signal of the seven championship races and to offer pari-mutuel wagering to Hong Kong's very knowledgeable and enthusiastic racing patrons. If we can enter into a cooperative venture, we can assure you that it will make racing history and make us both, the United States and Hong Kong, the envy of the racing world."

Then I introduced a five-minute videotape showing highlights of a few Breeders' Cup races, including the three-horse battle down the stretch by Ferdinand, Alysheba, and Judge Angelucci in the 1987 Classic at Hollywood Park, and the victory in the last jump by Personal Ensign over Winning Colors in the 1988 Distaff at Churchill Downs. It was important to me for these races to make an impression. And I think they did, although my invitation to simulcast the Breeders' Cup actually drew a round of laughter from the audience. The Hong Kong–based publication *Racing World* subsequently opined, "It is not believed . . . the proposal even left the starting gates. A nice try, nevertheless, Mr. James Bassett."

Well, Hong Kong, long a British colony, had a local horse racing tradition that dated well back into the nineteenth century. But the people in charge of the Royal Hong Kong Jockey Club were beginning to think in terms of becoming internationally involved in the sport. Hong Kong is a city of 6.9 million people, and my understanding is that nearly 10 percent of them have telephone wagering accounts. The city also has well over 100 off-track betting (OTB) parlors, complementing the two racetracks—Happy Valley, which is in the downtown region of the city, and Sha Tin, which is farther to the north and was constructed on a parcel of land reclaimed from the sea.

During the 155 years when it was a Crown colony and a British protectorate, Hong Kong developed a tremendous capitalistic energy and became (and remains) one of the world's greatest trading and banking centers. Hong Kong's sovereignty was transferred to the People's Republic of China in 1997, and you would think there would be an enormous clash between the capitalist and communist philosophies. But that has not happened, and the influence the Hong Kong Jockey Club retains over the province is incredible. From the wagering on horse races and on English soccer games (which the club also controls), the Hong Kong Jockey Club annually contributes about 12 percent of the annual operating budget of the city. Integrity is one of the club's great hallmarks. There's a four-story laboratory in Hong Kong where they do their own drug testing. Hong Kong's the only place in the world that I know of where the horses' feed is tested before they go and race.

The Chinese have an extraordinary zeal for racing, and in 1990 the Hong Kong Jockey Club staged the inaugural running of the Hong Kong Cup. It eventually became the culminating event in the World Series Racing Championship, involving fourteen major races, each with a purse of $1 million or higher, around the globe. In 2008, the Hong Kong Cup's purse had grown to $2.58 million (in U.S. currency), and it now annually anchors an international turf festival at Sha Tin that features four major races.

I regret that I have not been able to make trips to Hong Kong more frequently. I went there a second time in 1991 to address the Twenty-second Asian Racing Conference, an annual event that draws racing leaders from some thirty countries. Hong Kong Jockey Club officials have an affinity for great ceremonial flourishes, and one of the highlights of the conference involved the Royal Hong Kong Drum and Bugle Corps high-stepping into the room and playing an original march that had been written for the occasion. In the wake of the Drum and Bugle Corps' performance came the Royal Regiment of Wales. And in their wake came a great Chinese dragon—it must have been forty or fifty yards long, with God knows how many people underneath providing propulsion. The dragon weaved its serpentine course around and past the people at the conference tables, its purpose being to bless them with good luck. A rather impressive display of fanfare, I must admit.

From 1999 to 2004, I served as the World Series Racing Championship chairman. During that period, a race that is run each April at Sha Tin, the Queen Elizabeth II Cup, also became part of the series. Larry Wong, Ron Arculli, and Alan Li, all of whom served tenures as chairman of the Hong Kong Jockey Club, offered invitations to me each year I was with the World Series Racing Championship to come to Hong Kong as their guest. But I was never able to do it. The international races are run in December, right before Christmas, and I could not go in the midst of the holiday season. When the Queen Elizabeth II Cup is run, Keeneland is conducting its spring meet. I could not be gone during that time either.

§

I have long held a strong belief that, from a U.S. racing viewpoint, South America is a great untapped market. I see this as true not only in regard to commercial breeding and the sale of Thoroughbreds but also in regard to simulcasting our races. Pertaining to international markets, the racetracks in our country (and the Breeders' Cup as well) have primarily concentrated on sending our simulcast signals to Europe and, on a more limited basis, to major population centers in the Far East. There are major time differences involved. When the horses in the 2008 Kentucky Derby exited the starting gate, it was 6:15 P.M. in Louisville. But it was 11:15 P.M. in London and 12:15 A.M. in Paris. When the horses in the 2008 Breeders' Cup Classic exited the gate at Santa Anita, it was 3:52 P.M. in California, 6:52 A.M. in Hong Kong, and 7:52 A.M. in Tokyo. Conversely, the time zones in the eastern and central portions of the United States are much more similar to those in South America. When the Derby goes off here, it is the same time in Santiago, Chile, and only an hour earlier in both Buenos Aires in Argentina and Rio de Janeiro in Brazil. And with this being the case, think of the potential that exists for sending our simulcast signals directly south of the equator.

Over the years, more than a few horses from South America have shipped up here and performed marvelously. Canonero II was bred in Kentucky—he was actually sold for $1,200 as a yearling at Keeneland in 1969. The buyer, however, was Venezuelan, and Canonero II made ten of his first twelve career starts at the Rinconada track in Caracas, where he won seven times. In the spring of 1971, Canonero II journeyed northward and won the Kentucky Derby and Preakness. If those races had been simulcast to Venezuela, they would have generated enormous wagering handles.

Bayakoa, who won back-to-back runnings of the Breeders' Cup Distaff in 1989 and 1990, was bred in Argentina and was a grade 1 winner in her homeland before she came to North America. Paseana was bred in Argentina too, and she was a grade 1 winner there before she came north to win the 1992 Breeders' Cup Distaff. Both Bayakoa and Paseana became multiple Eclipse Award winners.

There have been others. Riboletta, bred in Brazil, was a grade 1 winner in her homeland prior to becoming North America's champion handicap mare in 2000. Pompeyo was bred in Chile, became a grade 1 winner there, and then was shipped to the United States, where she became the champion steeplechase horse in 2001.

Whenever the Winter and Summer Olympic Games occur, regardless of where they are held, people throughout the world take rapt interest in the performances of the athletes from their own countries. The same is true in the World Cup soccer tournament. I think it could be the same for South Americans when horses from their homelands race in major events in North America. And, via simulcasting, they could participate in the thrill.

I had all of this in mind when I was invited by Mauricio Serrano Palma, president of the Latin American Association of Jockey Clubs and the Hipodromo racetrack in Chile, to make a two-week visit to South America in 1995. Our itinerary took us to Chile, Argentina, and Brazil, and the purpose was to start a dialogue, specifically in regard to nominating South American stallions and foals to the Breeders' Cup. Mauricio was the leading proponent in South America of international racing, and what he revealed to us in the three countries we visited was an enormous infrastructure—strong breeding industries and racetracks that are as modern and beautiful as any in the world. Throughout the trip, I had no problems at all communicating, because almost everyone I met spoke English.

I must admit, though, that my lack of knowledge of the local social mores did bring about a series of embarrassments. In Rio de Janeiro, I stayed at the Copacabana Palace—it is probably the most famous hotel in South America. My first evening there, I was looking forward to having dinner in the Copacabana's renowned Cipriani restaurant. Well, I called the concierge and requested a reservation for one person at 8:00 P.M. However, upon arrival, I was surprised to find that the dining room was totally empty. The maitre d' came over to the dining room entrance, and I asked him if the dining room was closed. He looked me up and down, head to toe, and replied in a voice filled with aloof disdain, "Senor, our guests do not normally arrive for dinner until 9:30 or 10:00 at night. But you may come in, and we'll have a table for you if you wish." Sitting in there in solitary splendor, eating alone, did not appeal to me. I had this image in my mind of the waiters glaring at me with contempt. So, duly rebuked, I retreated to my room and ordered dinner from room service.

After finishing dinner and several vodkas, I was gazing out the window at Corcovado Mountain, which is a stately peak that overlooks the city. It had been raining that day, and there was a shroud of fog and mist that encircled the peak. Suddenly, it appeared that an enormous fire had broken out on the mountaintop, and the swirling flames were magnified by the fog and the mist. I was so startled that I took several steps backward from the hotel window and then stood fascinated by the brightness of the fire as it seemed to engulf the entire mountaintop. Then my fascination gave way to alarm. I called the hotel concierge and advised him of the danger of the spreading fire. The concierge calmly told me that the "fire" was actually the illumination of the 130-foot statue of Christ the Redeemer that stands atop Corcovado—it is considered to be one of the New Seven Wonders of the World. The illusion of a great fire, the concierge said, always happens during the rainy season with the fog and the mist on the mountain.

As it turned out, the Copacabana Palace was deserving of its reputation. A wonderful place to stay. But I still have an image in my mind of those waiters (and the maitre d') glaring at me, had I sat alone in the dining room. Muttering with disdain, "Americano. Who is this gringo tourist, so gauche in manner to demand to have dinner so early in the evening in our magnificent restaurant? Gauche gringo!" I can imagine them saying to each other as I ate alone.

§

In Chile, I also met with Roberto Allende, who was president of the Club Hipico de Santiago, and with Juan Unzurrunzaga of the Breeders' Association. In Argentina, I met with Hernan Ceriani of the Argentine Equine Foundation and with Alfredo Lalor of the Argentine Jockey Club. And in Brazil, I met with Hernani Silva of the Brazilian Breeders' Association, Jose Bonifacio Nogueira of the Sao Paulo Jockey Club, and Jose Fragoso Pires and Bertrand Kauffmann of the Brazilian Jockey Club.

The facilities they showed me were immensely impressive. The stud farms were lovely and encompassed thousands of acres. The racetracks in Chile are not huge, in the way that Churchill Downs and Belmont Park and Santa Anita are, but they possess a wonderful Old World charm, with beautiful architecture and magnificent dining rooms and offices. Much of the racing occurs on the grass, and the turf courses are breathtaking in their size and with their sweeping turns.

In Buenos Aires, the Argentino de Palermo racetrack is seven stories tall. It is the home of the Gran Premio Nacional, which is Argentina's equivalent of the Kentucky Derby. Argentina has a population of 40.5

million people, of whom about 11.8 million live in Buenos Aires. The leading citizens of the country and the city comprise the hierarchy of the Argentine Jockey Club.

Throughout the entire trip to those countries we had an enthusiastic and productive exchange of ideas about how we could be of benefit to each other. Also, I obtained the first nomination of a South American stallion whose foals would be eligible for Breeders' Cup competition. The stallion's name was Roy, and he stood at Luigi D'Allessanori's Haras Figuron farm in Chile. Roy had been the country's leading sire in 1994. Among his sons and daughters were five champions, including Barrio Chino and Gran Ducato, both of whom had been Chile's Horse of the Year.

I returned home with a strong feeling that there was the potential for some real collaboration. And I was not alone in that belief. The magazine *Latin American Thoroughbred* stated in an editorial, "[This trip] should be the beginning of a more direct form of communication, with a definite view to sporting and commercial collaboration into the 21st century."

That fall, a delegation of thirty South American racing officials led by Mauricio journeyed to New York. They were to be our guests at the Breeders' Cup at Belmont Park, which was a huge treat for them—that was the year Cigar won the Breeders' Cup Classic. First, though, there was a business meeting with the South American officials at the Plaza Hotel. Representatives of our Jockey Club were also in attendance, and we outlined areas of mutual interest regarding pedigrees, catalog standards, and racing statistics. Toward the conclusion of the meeting, I was elected an honorary member of the LAAJC, which in Spanish is known as La Asociacion Latinoamericana de Jockey Clubes. Mauricio presented me with a badge and certificate, the latter of which stated, "en reconocimiento a sus meritos en favor de la hipica mundial." I have forgotten exactly what that means in English, but it was quite flattering. I do know that.

However, the ten-year period that followed was largely disappointing, as the initiatives faltered and there were no persistent efforts on either side to further the dialogue. Technological breakthroughs were being made regarding catalog statistics and the health and welfare of horses, but they were not being utilized in an effort to strengthen the link with South American racing and breeding interests. But in 2005, a dynamic new initiative was developed, largely because of the expanding numbers of Thoroughbred mares and the overproduction of foals in Kentucky. Additional markets had to be found for them, and representatives from Keeneland

and the Kentucky Thoroughbred Association began to establish strong links with the South American countries.

Tom Thornbury and Chauncey Morris of the Keeneland sales department have developed a business model by which breeding and racing standards in Central and South American countries can be improved. The program specifically involves the Thoroughbred industries in Mexico, Chile, Argentina, Brazil, Peru, and Venezuela. A former bloodstock and equine insurance agent, Tom is the associate director of sales at Keeneland. Chauncey, a former employee of the Kentucky Department of Agriculture, has a fluent command of Spanish. They arrange seminars that are now annually held in each of these Central and South American countries for breeders, owners, and trainers. The speakers include experts from the fields of veterinary science, pedigrees and bloodlines, sales, statistical standards, and conditioning.

One of the results has been a dramatic upturn in the participation of buyers from Central and South American countries at the Keeneland sales. In 2006, representatives from the six countries Tom and Chauncey targeted purchased 248 horses at Keeneland and spent an aggregate $6.82 million. In 2007, they purchased 436 horses for an aggregate $15.13 million. The latter figures represent increases of 75.8 and 121.8 percent, respectively, in just one year.

The dialogue and direct contact have to be continued and expanded. I am talking about a persistency of effort, a willingness to extend a hand of cooperation and mutual interest. Keeneland realizes the need to make the South Americans feel like equal partners in the international scope of racing and not second-class citizens. E-mails and faxes can be exchanged, but they don't come anywhere near to achieving the same results as direct physical contact—face-to-face dealings. Doing so takes time and effort and a certain amount of money, too.

One of the premier races in South America is the Gran Premio Latino Americano, a mile-and-a-quarter event that lures top horses from Argentina, Brazil, Chile, Panama, Peru, and Uruguay. It is a race that rotates among the countries—in 2007, it was held at the Hipodromo de La Plata near Buenos Aires, Argentina, and in 2008, it was at the Hipodromo de Monterrico in Lima, Peru. Keeneland has an annual sponsorship arrangement with the Gran Premio Latino Americano and conducts a seminar in conjunction with the event. In 2007, Tom and Chauncey also conducted a seminar in conjunction with the Handicap de las Americas, a one-and-three-sixteenth-mile race held at the Hipodromo de las Americas in Mexico City.

In 2000, Keeneland sold $300,000 worth of horses to buyers from Mexico. In 2007, the figure was over $3.5 million. Central Kentucky breeders want new markets for the Thoroughbreds they produce, and Keeneland is finding them.

I would love to learn more about the history and lore of South American horse racing. I know that the sport dates well back into the nineteenth century there, and that there's a jockey in Argentina named Jorge Ricardo who has won more than 10,000 races. Ricardo and a still active North American jockey named Russell Baze vie back and forth as the all-time world leader in victories. In early August 2008, Ricardo and Baze rode against each other for the first time on the Shergar Cup card at Ascot. Neither of them won a race that day, although Baze finished second twice. But wouldn't it be interesting if it could somehow be arranged for some head-to-head competition between the two jockeys in the countries where they normally race, with Ricardo spending a few weeks in the United States and Baze doing the same in Argentina?

Many of the top-tier jockeys competing in the United States in recent decades have South American roots. Edgar Prado and Rafael Bejarano are from Peru. Jose Santos is from Chile. Ramon Dominguez, Eibar Coa, and Javier Castellano are from Venezuela. The names and talents of all these riders are familiar to almost any North American racing fan. And I have to believe that in their homelands, at least some of these jockeys have attained legendary status. Wouldn't their fellow countrymen be interested in wagering on the major races they ride in via simulcasting?

Consider some additional editorial commentary from *Latin American Thoroughbred:* "For the Breeders' Cup to develop a following amongst [South American] punters, it is imperative that a small but necessary quota of nationalism be incorporated. An Argentinian will want an Argentine horse to represent him; a Chilean will give preference in betting on a Chilean horse, and so on. Identifying ourselves with our idols and home-bred champions is a weakness and especially attractive."

Be assured, there are wonderful opportunities for cooperative efforts between the North American and South American breeding and racing industries, and these should be explored. There's an expanding market in South America for U.S. mares. And there are a lot of mares in South America that would produce first-class foals if they were brought here and bred to prominent U.S. stallions. In countries such as Chile, Argentina, and Brazil, our North American racing industry would do well to establish full-time offices. We need to sustain this initiative and keep it growing.

Chapter 13

The Ever-Evolving Economics of Racing

FROM A BUSINESS standpoint, one of the most important dates in North American racing history is March 15, 1990. On that day, a decision was made to go ahead full steam with the formation of the Equibase Company. From that point onward, the Thoroughbred racing industry itself was going to take control of the past-performance data from races, which is so vital to pari-mutuel wagering. In doing so, the sport was challenging a monopoly that had existed for almost 100 years—the *Daily Racing Form.* Since its first issue, which was published on November 17, 1894, the *Racing Form* had been the primary chronicler of all sanctioned Thoroughbred races on the North American continent. The *Form* employed its own legion of race callers, call takers, and computer operators, whose work resulted in the official race charts.

The decision came in the immediate aftermath of a meeting in the board room at the Aqueduct racetrack in New York. Those in attendance included Dinny Phipps, Alan Marzelli, Hans Stahl, David Haydon, and George "Nick" Nicholson, representing The Jockey Club; Alan Dragone, Gerry McKeon, Tom Meeker, and Cliff Goodrich, representing the Thoroughbred Racing Associations (TRA) tracks; Fred Grossman and Bill Williams, representing the *Racing Form;* and Marty Singerman, representing Rupert Murdoch's News Corporation, which had recently purchased the *Form.*

I was not at the meeting—at the time, I had no reason to be there. Lucy and I were vacationing at Lyford Cay in the Bahamas. But within twenty-four hours of the Aqueduct meeting, I received a phone call from Dinny. Would I be willing, he asked me, to be chairman of the newly formed, wholly owned Jockey Club subsidiary called Equibase? For months, Dinny told me, The Jockey Club and TRA had been engaged in discussions and negotiations with the *Racing Form* regarding the need to put more information in the daily programs of racetracks for the benefit of fans. But they essentially had never progressed beyond the impasse from which they had started.

Historically, racetrack programs had contained the names of the horses in each race; their saddlecloth and post position numbers; the weight each horse was assigned; their gender and color; the names of their jockeys, owners, sires, and dams; and their morning line odds. And that was pretty much it. The standard size of a program was about four by nine inches, and it could easily fit into a shirt or pants pocket.

But the *Racing Form* contained much more information, most notably the past-performance lines of each horse's most recent efforts. One could see what position a horse had been in through each point of call during those efforts—at the start, through the opening half mile, through three-quarters of a mile, with an eighth of a mile remaining, and at the finish. One could also see by what margins the horse had led or trailed at key points of the races. The track conditions (fast, sloppy, muddy, and so forth) were noted or, if it was a grass race, the turf conditions (firm, good, yielding) were noted. The *Form* also provided fractional and final times for each race, statistics pertaining to each horse both for that year and its overall career (starts, wins, second- and third-place finishes, and purse earnings), the name of the horse's breeder, the amount of weight a horse carried, and the horse's post-time odds in recent efforts. The *Form* compiled and published the charts of each race, along with footnotes pertaining to the action of the race and the performances of individual horses.

Further, the *Form* carried handicappers' comments and selections and articles and columns by its writers pertaining to racing around the country and on foreign shores. It was published in various editions. The eastern edition was a broadsheet, measuring approximately 14½ by 22¼ inches. The other editions (including the one for Keeneland) were tabloids, measuring approximately 11 by 15¾ inches. For nearly a century, the *Form* had served as a repository of primary source material. It was regarded as Thoroughbred racing's Bible.

But as the years went on, producing the scripture had become prohibitively expensive. The cost of newsprint had increased dramatically. The cost of maintaining chart-calling crews at every track had risen steadily, as had the printing and delivery costs of the product. TRA officials had become increasingly concerned that past-performance information, the underlying staple of their pari-mutuel business, might soon come into jeopardy in regard to supply on a day-to-day basis.

Meanwhile, the *Racing Form* was passing on those higher costs to racetrack bettors. When I began working at Keeneland in 1968, the price of our program was 25 cents. By 1990, the price had doubled to 50 cents. But during that same time period, the price of a *Racing Form* had more than quadrupled, from 60 cents to $2.50. Also, the simulcasting of race cards, with off-track betting parlors and one track offering betting on races from multiple tracks, was undergoing explosive growth throughout the country. Multiple editions of the *Form* usually had to be purchased if a racetrack patron wanted to wager on races from multiple locales.

Veteran *Racing Form* officials, though—the old guard, so to speak— had convinced Murdoch and his News Corporation that they retained complete control of the situation and that they could continue to dictate what was to be and what wouldn't be. They believed history revealed that racetrack executives had never been able to agree among themselves on a single issue. Proclamations of industry unity, they said, invariably turned out to be false. Besides, efforts had been made to challenge the *Form*'s monopoly before. A daily called *Sports Eye* had made a couple of attempts to be a competing publication. The first attempt was reasonably serious and ended with the *Racing Form* paying *Sports Eye* a seven-figure settlement to terminate its efforts. The second time, all that *Sports Eye*'s people really did was put together a mocked-up business plan, present it to TRA officials, and then leak what was going on to the *Form*. The *Form*, in turn, paid another settlement fee and got *Sports Eye*'s owners to sign a five-year standstill agreement.

When this happened, TRA officials contacted The Jockey Club and asked for help. And after the Aqueduct meeting, Dinny called and requested my involvement. I agreed to do it, thinking that my participation might last twelve to eighteen months. It ultimately spanned nearly seven years.

Simply stated, the purpose of Equibase was to create an industry-owned database. The business plan had four principal architects—Marzelli, who was the chief financial officer of The Jockey Club; Stahl, who was The Jockey Club's executive director; Haydon, who ran the commercial subsidiary Jockey Club Information Systems Inc.; and Nicholson, who was a recent addition to The Jockey Club staff. This group had been working on the plan for about a year when I got involved

Marzelli has since told me that early on in the project, he, Stahl, Nicholson, and Haydon would sometimes sit in a restaurant at night and ponder how they ever got into this situation. "Let's see," they would say to one another, "some 40 million *Racing Forms* are sold per year. The *Form* annually brings in $120 million in gross revenues. We bring in none. The *Form* has 700 employees. We have 15. The *Form* has been in business for nearly a century. Equibase is a start-up company. And we're somehow supposed to get this done, right?"

And yes, indeed, it is not easy to prevail against a long-established monopoly. The primary reason why Dinny wanted me involved is I was a past president of the TRA and remained on its board of directors. I had professional working associations with racetrack executives throughout North America. But believe me, this did not automatically translate into ready acceptance of my Equibase efforts. Many if not most of the racetrack executives had problems with the *Racing Form's* "our way or the highway" attitude. But trying to get those same executives to accept a change in long-established practices was daunting. Better to have the devil one sees and knows than the mysterious one that may lurk in the bush.

The *Racing Form's* executives were not entirely uncooperative. They were willing to make some data available for use in programs. But not nearly enough, from our point of view. Both sides had agreed that the program should contain a minimum of six past-performance lines for each horse. But the *Form* was willing to provide the margins at each point of call and all the fractional times only for a horse's most recent race.

We did have one final meeting on the issue. It occurred at Saratoga on August 19. I had been aboard the Equibase project for about four and a half months and was aware of the smoldering anger that existed on both sides. Once again, no accord was reached, or even approached. The *Form* would not budge. We would not budge. It is very hard to be diplomatic under such circumstances, but I briefly tried. I had a lot of very good friends in *Racing Form* management. One of them was Grossman, the publication's editor. "We'll keep the door open," I told Grossman and Singerman before they got up to leave the room at Saratoga.

Singerman extended an index finger and cocked thumb, put them to his temple, and said, "You're asking me to take a gun and put it to my own head." (I later learned he had made the same dramatic gesture at the Aqueduct meeting in March.)

There was silence. And then I pointed a finger at Singerman and sternly said, "Marty, don't make us do this to the *Form.*" And the meeting ended.

A little less than a year and a half later, on January 1, 1992, Beulah Park in Grove City, Ohio, became the first track to put out a program with Equibase past performances. A pair of tracks owned by the Edward J. DeBartolo Corporation—Remington Park in Oklahoma City and Thistledown near Cleveland—became the second and third tracks to do so. The New York Racing Association tracks, Aqueduct, Belmont Park, and Saratoga, followed; as did Keeneland (of course); the Maryland Jockey Club tracks, Laurel and Pimlico Race Course; and some smaller tracks in the Northeast, such as Philadelphia Park and Penn National Racecourse.

Not surprisingly, the *Racing Form* played hardball, using threats for the purpose of dividing and conquering. Cooperate with Equibase, and we won't deliver our newspapers to your racetrack. If you use the Equibase past performances, we won't give you anymore coverage. There were also a few cases where tracks used the leverage they had gained through Equibase for their own self-interests, and they cut deals with the *Racing Form*—getting financial kickbacks based on the number of *Forms* they sold on-site each day—which was something I was not too happy about. Further, members of the *Racing Form*'s chart-calling crews received a stream of phone calls, memos, and letters from the publication's headquarters, instructing them not to cooperate in any way with Equibase personnel. If you do, they were told, your job with the *Form* would be immediately terminated. And go ahead, go to work for Equibase if you want, but they're going to fail!

Start-up costs were provided by The Jockey Club, by way of a $4.8 million loan to Equibase. Methods had to be devised to get the entries from racetracks into the Equibase computer system and then get them back to the tracks with the past performances attached. Software had to be developed, along with the system that would collect, house, and disseminate the information. These were the pre-Internet days, and nearly everything had to be done manually and by fax machine.

The company charged tracks 25 cents for each program that contained the Equibase information. There was some complaining about this. And to allow room for the past-performance lines, the program's size had to be expanded to eight by eleven inches, and there were a lot of protests from racetrack executives about that, too. In racing, revolutions are not easy things to stage.

Please be mindful that throughout all this, I continued to wear multiple hats. I remained chairman of the board of Keeneland, trying to extend a voice of goodwill throughout the Thoroughbred racing and breeding industries. At the same time, as Breeders' Cup president, I was trying to coax the tracks into relinquishing some of their autonomy in supporting Breeders' Cup day and the Breeders' Cup stakes programs. And as Equibase chairman, I was trying to pressure and persuade the tracks to utilize Equibase data and follow its guidelines when putting together their programs. I felt like I was standing on a bushel of eels. One day I was up, and the next day I was down.

In November 1992, the Breeders' Cup was being held at Gulfstream Park. Prior to the event, a terse conversation had taken place between me and Douglas Donn, who was Gulfstream's president and CEO (his family had owned and operated Gulfstream since the mid-1940s). Doug was skeptical of the value of Equibase, and he did not like the idea of revamping the size and format of his race programs. I told Doug that on Breeders' Cup day, Gulfstream must—repeat, must—have programs with Equibase data in them. This was nonnegotiable, I said to him, and if he did not agree, the Breeders' Cup was going to print and distribute its own program for the event. Definitely, I was overstepping my boundaries. But Doug relented, and on Breeders' Cup day that year, we debuted a beautiful forty-eight-page program with up to seven Equibase past-performance lines for each horse. The program sold for $2 at Gulfstream. And, of course, that day's *Racing Form* was sold at Gulfstream as well—it was never our intention to replace one monopoly with another.

This was the first "event program," so to speak, that racing ever had. It has now become the standard not only for the Breeders' Cup and Triple Crown races but also for most major tracks on an everyday basis. The one sold at Keeneland during the 2008 fall meeting carried up to ten past-performance lines per horse, contained articles by respected industry writers along with a great deal of other information, and sold for $2 per copy. An individual copy of the *Racing Form* cost $5.50.

One thing I want to make very clear about this is it never was our intention at Equibase, or my intention personally, to put the *Racing Form* out of business. I know there have been accusations to that effect over the years, and they constitute nonsense. What other sport can or, indeed, has been able to boast of a daily publication the size and scope of the *Racing Form*? The answer is none. Not baseball. Not football. Not professional basketball. Nobody. This has now been the case for 115 years, and I am fully cognizant of the benefits it brings to racing. But I am also just as cognizant of the need to properly serve racing's customers, the fans, young and old, who don't feel they have the financial wherewithal to purchase a *Racing Form* every time they want to wager on a race. Customers appreciate the opportunity to make choices, to purchase one or the other or both. And if a degree of competition exists, I view that as healthy. Racing has two weekly trade publications, the *Blood-Horse* and *Thoroughbred Times*. The existence of one continually inspires the other to try harder.

In December 1997, I retired from my position as Equibase chairman. This came in conjunction with the company's announcement that it had fully paid back its start-up loan from The Jockey Club, which was tremendously gratifying to me. I was even more gratified when, three months later, on March 12, 1998, Equibase and the *Racing Form* made a joint announcement that they had agreed to end their eight-year war. During that period, each had employed its own chart callers and compiled its own charts and past-performance lines. But at the March. 1998 news conference, which took place on the first floor of the Keeneland clubhouse, Marzelli, who had become the president and CEO of Equibase, and Bill Dow, who held identical positions with the *Racing Form,* announced that hostilities were over. The *Form* was granting equal right, title, and ownership to Equibase for historical records gathered prior to 1991. And Equibase would henceforth provide racing data to the *Form* by terms of a nonexclusive license under which both companies could package and market the data without restriction.

Today, Equibase employs eighty people, including fifty-five who are chart callers. In 2007, the company had $15 million in gross revenues, of which $3.3 million was paid in dividends to its partners, the TRA tracks and The Jockey Club. Since 1998, the cumulative dividends to the partners of Equibase have totaled $21 million, two-thirds of which has gone to the tracks and one-third of which has gone to The Jockey Club. Equibase has become one of racing's most successful enterprises.

The *Racing Form* has continued its recent history of multiple ownership changes. Triangle Publications (which also owned *TV Guide* magazine) had sold it to Murdoch, who in turn sold the *Form* to K-III Communications in 1992. In August 1998, K-III, which had changed its corporate name to Primedia, sold the *Form* to a group headed by Steven Crist, a former *Harvard Lampoon* editor, *New York Times* turf writer, and

New York Racing Association vice president. Crist had also been the editor of the *Racing Times,* a daily publication that had used Equibase data during its ten-month existence from April 1992 to February 1993. The *Racing Times* was intended to be a competitor to the *Racing Form,* and its editorial staff was arguably the best ever assembled by a racing industry publication. But the *Racing Times* lacked a business plan and a viable distribution system. After its founder, Robert Maxwell, fell (or perhaps jumped) from his yacht in the waters surrounding the Canary Islands, it was discovered that he had bankrolled the *Racing Times* by looting the employee pension plans from some of his other ventures.

During his *Racing Times* tenure, Crist had referred to the *Racing Form* in print as "Monopoly Downs." One of the lessons he apparently learned is that, sometimes, there is merit in the saying, "If you cannot lick them, join them." Crist's primary partner in the purchase of the *Racing Form* was Alpine Capital Group. When announcing the completion of the purchase, Crist said, "*Daily Racing Form* still makes money. It has never lost money. This isn't an issue of survival, but of big turnaround with the product itself."

In May 2004, the *Racing Form* was sold to the Wicks Group, an equity firm that deals in media and communications. And in August 2007, Wicks announced that it was selling the *Form* to a Washington, D.C.–based equity group called Arlington Capital Partners. Throughout these recent changes, Crist has remained the *Racing Form*'s publisher. One can make an argument that the *Form*'s future is cloudy, because companies keep unloading it. On the other hand, one can argue that the *Form*'s future is filled with promise, because companies keep buying it.

The *Racing Form* now sells much of its data electronically, via the Internet, as does Equibase. I have no idea what the *Form*'s bottom line looks like. But my fervent hope is, long live the *Form.* It continues to be a publication filled with pertinent editorial content and past-performance data each day, every day, with the exception of Christmas. That is the only day during the year when every North American Thoroughbred racetrack is closed.

§

During the early days of the Breeders' Cup, an agreement was hammered out with representatives of the European Breeders' Fund regarding the payment of an annual financial supplement. The Breeders' Cup organization was willing to pay this fee to gain the support of European breeders and owners and to get them to run their horses in the Breeders' Cup championship races, thereby making them truly international events. At the time, European buyers had gained a major presence at the prominent North American Thoroughbred sales, including the ones at Keeneland. And as a result of their economic impact, the European breeders were able to leverage a deal that grew to be highly lucrative for them, while at the same time becoming a growing fiscal strain on the Breeders' Cup budget.

Here is the way it worked. Because of the enormity of the North American stallion colony and the foal crops they annually sired, compared to those in the European countries, it was agreed that the Breeders' Cup would annually pay a 5 percent fee to the European Breeders' Fund, derived from the difference between the total sum of the North American stallion nomination fees and the total European stallion fees. For example, if the North American stallion fees totaled $1 million and the European stallion fees totaled $500,000, the European Breeders' Fund would receive 5 percent of the $500,000 difference, which was $25,000. The money was used to supplement races in Europe for two-year-olds. This was done, in theory, to assure the Europeans a level playing field.

Well, the best-laid schemes of mice and men oft go astray, and from the Breeders' Cup viewpoint, this one certainly did. By the time I became Breeders' Cup president, the annual supplement to the European Breeders' Fund had climbed to around $800,000. The board of directors of the Breeders' Cup charged me with the responsibility of going to Europe, engaging the European Breeders' Fund representatives in a meaningful dialogue concerning the situation, and, above all, developing a means of exiting from the original agreement. In other words, my instructions were—do something, Bassett! Reduce the annual supplement! Or, better still, get rid of it entirely!

Charles Taylor went with me to Europe. I have already talked about him earlier—he was master of Windfields Farm and the owner of Northern Dancer, the most prominent stallion in the world. Northern Dancer's sons and daughters were in great demand throughout Europe. And Charles was also a Breeders' Cup director. I knew I would be perceived by the European breeders as the guy wearing the black hat, the villain who was trying to take money away from them. Charles, who they truly respected, would be perceived as the hero wearing the white hat.

The meeting took place on October 4, 1989, in the Queensbury

House in Newmarket. It was chaired by Michael Wates, who was also chairman of the board of both the European Breeders' Fund and the British Bloodstock Agency. Europeans in attendance also included Robert McCreery, representing the English breeders; Jonathan Irwin for the Irish breeders; Alec Head for the French breeders; Herr H. von Loeper, head of the Directorium of Germany, which is the German Jockey Club; Dr. Franco Castelfranchi, head of the Italian Jockey Club; and Sam Sheppard, executive director of the European Breeders' Fund.

Wates opened proceedings in a very formal manner, diplomatically saying that the meeting had been called at the request of the Breeders' Cup and that the European Breeders' Fund representatives were there to hear what we had to say. I gave my presentation, explaining the financial dilemma the Breeders' Cup perceived it was facing, and at the finish, I was met not with stony silence but with deathly silence. This was followed by thirty to forty minutes of discussion that ranged from futile to near confrontational. I finally, in a fit of angry frustration, slammed my file folder on the table, then jammed it into my briefcase and said, "Charles, it appears we are not welcome. Let's go to the airport."

In a very icy tone, Wates told us that the European Breeders' Fund representatives wanted to go into executive session. And would we please leave the room? There was a large glass door that opened into a lovely garden, and Charles and I walked out (marched out might actually be a more accurate description) and went to the end of the yard. But through the glass door, we remained in full view of Wates and his group. We stood there for a couple of minutes, and then I said to Charles, "Why don't we try the bad guy–good guy approach?"

"Charles," I said, "I want you to start shaking your finger at me. Shake it hard, right in my face, and I want you to appear angry as you do it. Make it look like you and I have had a big falling out over this." So Charles walked up to me, stuck his index finger only a couple of inches from my face, and started shaking it. Aggressively. And pointedly. I told him, "Good, good, now shake it harder." Which Charles did. And then I told him, "Charles, now start pointing back toward the glass door, as though you're indicating to me that I'm being unfair to the European breeders." And Charles promptly did that, too. Meanwhile, I gave Charles a dismissive wave, negatively shook my head, kicked the grass, stamped my feet, and put a few yards of separation between us. All the time, we were jawing at each other, too. "You might have stubbornly stuck your feet in concrete,

Bassett!" is what Charles appeared to be saying. "But not me! These people deserve a fair deal!" Now, what Charles was actually saying was, "Where do you want to have dinner tonight, Ted?" And I was replying, "Oh, I don't know, I think I'd like to have some nice baked salmon. And maybe a glass or two of vodka." But the European breeders did not know we were saying this. They thought Charles and I were engaged in a real brouhaha, just short of fisticuffs, with him taking their side and telling me off. I was the bad guy, the target of their resentment. Charles, however, well, Charles was championing their cause. He was their ally. The good guy.

Wates eventually summoned us back to the room. He said, "We have discussed this matter, and there is no way in good faith we can accept your proposal to do away with the supplement. Is there anything further you wish to say."

Feigning aggravation, I turned my head and said, "Charles?"

And Charles started out in his gentle, tactful, diplomatic way of saying how important it was for the Breeders' Cup and the European Breeders' Fund to be working together, setting an example of goodwill for the international breeding and racing community. "Is there not room for compromise, where both sides could save face and move forward?" asked Charles. "Certainly there must be some means by which we can compromise. What might you need from us to ensure you can keep operating your organization at the same level as in the past?"

And from that point, the negotiations really started. We devised a formula by which the supplement from the Breeders' Cup would be reduced to $500,000 in 1990 and continue to be reduced by $100,000 increments each year until it was eliminated entirely. What we had done, in a sense, was employ a tactic I had learned during my days with the Kentucky State Police—the "bad cop–good cop" approach. It is a classic law enforcement technique during interrogations. The bad cop acts really hard-nosed and is almost a threatening presence, and then the good cop comes in with a demeanor filled with compassion. Of course, the one thing I did not want to do under any circumstances was to go back to the Breeders' Cup board and say, "We really didn't get anything done." My job had been to get the supplement off the books, entirely if possible, and the mission was accomplished. With the help of Charles, I had staged a bluff, which is something that has been in my repertoire at times. And if the Breeders' Cup gave out Academy Awards, Charles Taylor would have received one for the best performance by an actor in a supporting role.

§

Simulcasting involves televising races from a track and conducting wagering on them at other facilities. To be perfectly frank, when the possibility of doing this arose in the late 1980s, we at Keeneland had no real understanding of where it could lead.

The first time we were approached about simulcasts, our response was, who in the world would want to come out here to a darkened grandstand in the middle of winter and bet on races from Turfway Park? Not us, that's for sure. There would be substantial costs involved in regard to heating, lighting, security personnel, and the pari-mutuel operation. And for what purpose?

I told Bill Greely to go over to the Red Mile, which is the harness track in Lexington, and see if they would be interested in doing this. Greely met with John Cashman, who was president of the Red Mile, and members of his management team. They told Bill, no, they thought simulcasting could not be profitable, and too much of a financial gamble was involved for them to do it. Bill came back and relayed their response to me. I said, "Look, Bill, the idea that people would come out here in January, February, and March—braving the cold and the ice and the snow—to wager on races from anywhere is a nonwinner if I ever heard of one. But go back to the Red Mile and tell them we would be willing to split the red ink with them." Regardless, the Red Mile again said no, which provoked us. So we decided to spend some $700,000 winterizing the Keeneland grandstand and very reluctantly got into the simulcasting business. For us, it represented a severe break with tradition.

Now, two decades later, simulcasting occurs at Keeneland year-round. We do it five to six days a week during the midwinter months, when Gulfstream Park and Fair Grounds are running. We also do it six days a week during the midsummer months, when Saratoga is running. The remainder of the year, we simulcast races five days per week. We carry the races from all the Kentucky Thoroughbred tracks; from out-of-state tracks to the north, east, south, and west; and from tracks in countries such as England, Japan, and Dubai. We even simulcast races into Keeneland during our live race meets. And at the same time, we simulcast Keeneland's races out—in 2007, our signal was sent to tracks and OTB sites in sixteen countries on three continents.

What this has done for our purses has been enormous. In 1987, which was the year before Keeneland entered the simulcast market, our daily purse distribution averaged $164,810. In 1993, which was the year before we began simulcasting full cards from out-of-state tracks, Keeneland's daily purse distribution averaged $266,475. In 2007, Keeneland's average daily purse distribution was $645,000. Only Saratoga distributed more money on a daily basis. A major reason for this increase was our year-round simulcasts of races from other tracks, which generated a handle of $85.6 million. The simulcasts of our own races, to both in-state and out-of-state locales, generated an additional handle of $256.4 million—which was more than six times the $41.7 million we did on-track. Simulcasting, which started in most places as not much more than an afterthought, has become the economic lifeline for many tracks—the engine that drives the bottom line.

Simulcasting provides racing patrons with multiple opportunities to wager on such events as the Triple Crown, the Breeders' Cup, the Prix de l'Arc de Triomphe, and the Japan Cup. Curlin was North America's Horse of the Year in 2007. He was a very popular champion, and when Curlin ran in (and won) the 2008 Dubai World Cup, people could both watch and bet on the race at Keeneland. If there is a substantial pool for the pick six at a New York or California track, racing fans in Lexington can wager on it. And if Keeneland has a sizable pick-six carryover, you can wager on it as far away as Austria.

Almost every Saturday, when I'm not off on a trip someplace, I eat lunch on the third floor of the Keeneland grandstand. Afterward, I take a walk through the simulcast area. It is often jam-packed with people. On a Saturday in March, we might do a handle of $800,000.

Recitations of numbers might bore some people. But if you are in the racetrack business, you have to pay close attention to them. In 2008, a crowd of 22,387 came to Keeneland on Kentucky Derby Day, and they wagered nearly $1.97 million on the Derby alone. Such figures would have absolutely astonished Arnold Hanger and Louis Lee Haggin, whose eras involved wagering on-site on the live product and nothing else.

§

The founders of Keeneland selected two of the most wonderful months of the year in central Kentucky, April and October, to conduct our live race meets. Over the years, there has been pressure, some of it subtle and some of it not, to increase our live offerings. Pressure to conduct a race meet in July. Or one in August. Either of which would be folly—we would be going against Saratoga and Monmouth Park, for God's sake, competing with those tracks for horses!

There has been pressure, too, about lengthening our existing meets, so they would each span four weeks or longer. Advocates of this do not seem to comprehend the economics of what we would face. At Keeneland, we race five days per week. If we wanted to add a week in the fall and still maintain our $645,000 per-day purse distribution, we would have to come up with an extra $3.23 million. If we added a week in both the spring and the fall, it would be an additional $6.46 million. From where would the bulk of such money be generated? Right now, from a combination of our live handle, the simulcast signal we send out, sponsorships, and our year-round in-house simulcasting, the Keeneland racing program is paying for itself. But just barely. While we are a not-for-profit institution, we do pay taxes. And we continue to maintain Keeneland's lovely parklike setting. When we do race, our offerings are first class. It is a formula I would not be inclined to tamper with.

§

In the concluding months of 1993, there was a movement in Kentucky to allow for alternative gaming at the state's racetracks—specifically, slot machines. The idea, championed by an organization called Kentucky to the Front, had not been received with a great deal of interest within the State Senate or the General Assembly during prior legislative sessions. No enabling bill had been drawn up. No senator or assembly representative had come forth as a sponsor.

At the time, riverboat casinos had been operating for several years in Illinois. Legislation had been enacted in Indiana that would allow for riverboat casinos. And legislation was pending in Missouri and West Virginia that would allow for land-based casinos. All four states, of course, border Kentucky.

Churchill Downs was a member of Kentucky to the Front. So was Turfway Park, which at the time was owned by a partnership headed by Jerry Carroll. Other members included Ellis Park, Dueling Grounds, Paducah Downs, and the Red Mile—indeed, every pari-mutuel racetrack that operated within the state's boundaries, with the lone exception of Keeneland.

Kentucky to the Front was seeking a constitutional amendment to be put on the November ballot that year, leaving it up to the state's voters as to whether or not they wanted casinos. But at Keeneland, we were opposed to the idea, and we were not alone among racing interests in feeling that way. The Kentucky Thoroughbred Association (KTA), whose membership was comprised of 700 breeders, owners, and trainers, voiced its disapproval through its executive director David L. Switzer. "The presence of casino/riverboat gambling in Kentucky would signal the death knell of horse racing as we know it today," Switzer told the *Lexington Herald-Leader*. "Like it or not, horse racing and casinos/riverboats have never found a mutual area for coexistence." A seconding of the KTA's thumbs-down position had come from the national Thoroughbred Owners and Breeders Association (TOBA), which, among other things, owned *Blood-Horse* magazine.

But the Kentucky tracks advocating casino approval had industry allies too, including the Horsemen's Benevolent and Protective Association (HBPA) and the Kentucky Harness Horsemen's Association Inc. (KHHA). Studies had been commissioned by Kentucky for the Front from Richard Thalheimer, an associate professor in the College of Business and Public Administration at the University of Louisville, and by Governor Brereton Jones from the Kentucky Development Corporation. Figures were tossed around concerning potential job losses and job gains, potential revenue losses and revenue gains, the draining of Kentucky's economy, the boosting of Kentucky's economy.

The whole thing was evolving into a bedlam of rhetoric, with dire predictions of fiscal shortcomings, shouts involving imminent dangers of moral ruin, promises of instantaneous poverty and overnight wealth (all depending upon which side of the issue you were on). To get a better handle on the situation, in the early weeks of 1994, the General Assembly's Tourism, Development, and Energy Committee staged a series of public hearings on the casino issue.

Two of the Kentucky to the Front tracks had enlisted the lobbying services of former Kentucky governor Julian Carroll. While Carroll was an evangelical Christian, this did not prevent him from championing the casino cause. In the manner of a revivalist preacher, Carroll told committee members on February 8 that without casinos in Kentucky, racetracks would die, thousands of jobs would be lost, and the state would lose hundreds of millions of dollars in revenues when people went elsewhere to gamble. This was not a compromise of morals, Carroll told the committee. "I know the devil," he said. "I face him every day." In fact, Carroll said, the legalization of casinos was all about guaranteeing a better Kentucky for our children and grandchildren. And at the beginning of the following week, Carroll further expressed the depth of his convictions by stating, "We're going to make the governor and the General Assembly an offer they can't refuse."

Meanwhile, the Temperance League, the Kentucky Council of Churches, the Kentucky Baptist Convention, and the Kentucky Charitable Gaming Association (which represented bingo operators) were all adding their voices opposing casinos to the growing din. It was all brewing into a rather remarkable ruckus.

At Keeneland, we took the position that we would defer comment until the other Kentucky tracks had made their arguments. On Wednesday, February 16, at the invitation of chairman Rex Smith, I presented Keeneland's views before the House Tourism, Development, and Energy Committee. What I said that day became known as "Bassett's Mythical Armada Speech," for reasons that I think you will understand.

Bill Greely drove me over to the state capital that day. We hardly exchanged a word with each other during the trip to Frankfort. I had put together an outline of what I was going to say but had not prepared the text of a formal speech. I wanted my presentation to be professional and compelling.

I was aware that Governor Carroll was preceding me, which was advantageous to my position. Judy Taylor, Keeneland's lobbyist, had masterfully orchestrated the situation so that my presentation would come near the culmination of the hearings. This put Keeneland in a position to finalize the discussion. I told the committee, in part:

> Thoroughbred racing and breeding is more than just gaming and gambling. It is part of the historical and traditional fabric of Kentucky—part of our history and legacy.
>
> Domino theory is a typical ploy. . . . If Kentucky does not follow the herd, then Indiana will enact casino gambling and divert dollars from Kentucky's economy.
>
> We have conducted five focus groups in an attempt to determine Keeneland's course of action regarding the issue of casino gambling.
>
> Our primary purpose was to determine not only what was best for Keeneland and the Thoroughbred racing and breeding industry, which is our reason for being—but to also ascertain what is in the best interests of the community and the state.

We invited individual groups representing (1) industry and corporate leaders; (2) legislative leadership and representatives; (3) Thoroughbred industry leaders—representing large and small breeders and owners; (4) the media—print, television, and trade publications; and (5) representatives of the general public—selected at random by a professional research firm, to discuss a variety of issues.

Now, how can racetracks combat casino gaming if passed [in neighboring states]?

(1) We need to be more responsive to our customers' needs and efforts.

(2) We need to be more receptive to suggestions for improvement of operations.

(3) We need telephone betting joined with interactive television.

(4) We need modern intertrack wagering facilities.

Our findings lead us to conclude that introducing casino gambling as an alternative source of gaming to pari-mutuel wagering will be injudicious, incompatible, injurious, and inimical to the best interests of Thoroughbred racing and breeding in Kentucky.

We are not going to cave in to the hypothetical threat of a mythical armada cruising down the Ohio [River] from Ashland to Paducah, under the disguise of a legislative act that has yet to be passed in most of our neighboring states.

In a subsequent *Sports Illustrated* article, Bill Nack wrote that my presentation marked "the moment that 'Kentucky to the Front' became 'Casinos to the Rear.'" I do not know if I would ever credit myself with such powers of persuasion, although the Louisville *Courier-Journal* also opined in an editorial:

[Bassett's] message couldn't have been more of a contrast to Mr. Carroll's. While Mr. Carroll has ranted and raved like a revivalist preacher urging legislators to stand up and declare their belief in casino gambling, Mr. Bassett was the voice of calm and reason. . . . The moment he stopped, legislators rushed to distance themselves from the issue, and wisely so.

But in the same editorial, the *Courier-Journal* further stated:

Of course, although legislators left on Wednesday talking about "the last nail in the coffin for casino gambling," the story may not really be over. . . . Casino gambling may look pretty good in a few years. The racing industry may not be in crisis today, but tomorrow may be different. Certainly the armada may be mythical now, but that doesn't mean it always will be.

I don't remember how I came up with the "mythical armada" phrase. I am somewhat a student of history and knew about the Spanish Armada, but there was nothing mythical about that. (As it turned out, the *Courier-Journal* was borderline prophetic—the riverboats on the Ohio River weren't a myth, either.)

What I told the committee is what I believed. And I strongly believed it back then, as did the majority of Keeneland's twenty-four-member board of directors. But I will readily concede that what seemed appropriate for me to say fifteen years ago to a legislative committee would not be in touch with the gaming climate of today. The casino armada is now permanently moored along the Indiana side of the Ohio. From a fiscal standpoint, throughout this country, casinos have fired one broadside after another at pari-mutuel tracks that do not have alternative gaming. But they have also invigorated tracks where alternative gaming has been allowed to be brought in.

In some states, Delaware, West Virginia, and Iowa among them, on-site slot machines have kept racetracks in business. In other states, such as Louisiana, New Mexico, and Pennsylvania, along with the Canadian province of Ontario, on-site slots have allowed tracks to offer supplemented purse structures that have greatly improved racing's entertainment value. Breeding programs have been tremendously enhanced. Leading stables have shipped their horses in to compete. Existing jobs within the racing and breeding industries have been made more secure, and new jobs have been created.

Among the major racing states, Florida has alternative gaming at some of its tracks. New York does at some of its tracks. California does not. Neither does New Jersey, and the future of racing in that state is densely clouded. Adjacent to the Atlantic City boardwalk exists the second highest concentration of casinos in the United States. But slot machines, or any forms of alternative gaming, are forbidden at the Meadowlands and Monmouth Park. Maryland is bordered by three states where racetracks have alternative gaming. In November 2008, Maryland's electorate voted to allow slots, but without any guarantee they will be at Laurel Park and Pimlico Race Course, whose bottom lines are looking bleaker each year.

I am not suggesting that the bottom lines of Churchill Downs and Keeneland are, at this moment, similarly bleak. And I am not suggesting that casinos have become my cup of tea. I'm a racing person. What I am saying is that present-day realities are radically different from those of fifteen years ago. Today, if I made the statement that alternative gaming at Kentucky's racetracks would be "injudicious, incompatible, injurious, and inimical" to the best interests of the sport, I would be out of touch with reality.

Contrary to what many people believe, Keeneland, back in 1994, did not arbitrarily oppose alternative gaming. We had hired a reputable public relations firm to conduct an in-depth public opinion poll on alternative gaming. The poll was not restricted to the citizenry of central Kentucky—it encompassed a wide expanse of the state's population. These are the numbers the public relations firm gave us: 46 percent of the respondents were in favor of slot machines at Kentucky's racetracks, 47.5 percent were opposed, and the remaining 6.5 percent were undecided. This convinced us that we should stick with the status quo. Had the results been different, had they indicated that Kentuckians overwhelmingly wanted slot machines at the tracks, Keeneland would have joined the movement to legalize them.

In recent years, one poll after another has indicated that Kentuckians want to put the matter to a vote by means of saying "yes" or "no" to a constitutional amendment. For this to happen, the enabling constitutional amendment would first have to receive 60 percent approval by both chambers of the Kentucky legislature. And for such passage to occur, all beneficiaries of the state's racing industry would have to be pulling in the same direction. I'm talking about horse owners, horse breeders, racetracks, and the municipalities where they are located.

But you need to have a sizable majority of legislators favoring the idea, too. I have done a great deal of work in the state capital over the decades, going back to my tenures with the Department of Public Safety and the State Police. One lesson I learned very early is that in most cases it's much easier to stop a bill than it is to get it passed. This is not only true in Kentucky; it is true in any state. All sorts of circumstances can be roadblocks to a bill's enactment into law—the influence of special-interest groups, disputes between political parties, disputes within political parties (especially when they involve which faction of the party will be in control).

And, of course, a governor's veto. If a measure is by any means controversial, its opponents always have an advantage over its proponents, because it is almost invariably easier to convey the downside to the public rather than the upside. The downside resonates more in the public's collective mind.

I have immense respect for legislators. Theirs is an extraordinarily difficult responsibility, and I have found most of them to be honest and hardworking people, dedicated to the task of reconciling what their constituents want with what they perceive as the greater good for the greater public. At least 75 percent of Kentucky legislators have constituencies that are strongly religious. And in this state, we have always had—and likely always will have—disparities in philosophy between the mind-sets of the urban and rural regions. These disparities help provide balance to the political decision-making process, and that is not a bad thing.

In 2008, a proposed constitutional amendment to allow casino gaming in Kentucky never gained firm footing within the General Assembly. The amendment was not even introduced in the Kentucky Senate. A lot of work by the horse industry pretty much went for naught, and this inspired substantial amounts of resentment and public finger-pointing as the legislative session came to a conclusion. Such reactions are understandable, but they are also nonproductive. The high road is a better avenue to future success than the low road.

For the good of our state and for the good of our racing industry, the sourness of 2008 needs to be put aside and replaced by an attitude that this can be achieved. Considering that 60 percent of Kentucky's electorate approved the lottery amendment in 1988 and that Governor Steven Beshear, while endorsing casino gambling, received 59 percent of the statewide vote when he was elected in November 2007, is it unrealistic to conclude that the majority of the public would support the amendment? However, an enabling amendment can only be achieved by way of a clearly defined message and support from the legislative leadership. Thirty other racing states have faced the very same obstacles that exist in Kentucky and have legalized casino gaming (at least in some form) at their tracks. Why cannot, or should not, that happen here?

Undeniably, the idea of in-state casinos, or "racinos," as racetracks with casino gaming are often called, remains controversial among Kentucky's electorate. But I must reiterate that the results of poll after poll show that Kentuckians want the opportunity to vote statewide on this issue. It boils down to two things, really: the state budget and Kentucky's signature industry. With a properly designed constitutional amendment written in terse, plain English, every voter in this state could exercise his or her right to help make the decision. To wit: "Should Kentucky legalize casino gaming to address shortfalls in the state budget and to assist the horse racing and breeding industry?" Yes or no?

These are my beliefs on the subject. And, in regard to the comments I made fifteen years ago about caving in to a mythical armada cruising down the Ohio, well . . . I fear I shall always be branded by them, as long as the issue of slot machines remains on the Kentucky political table.

§

In January 1999, Keeneland finalized an agreement with GTECH Holdings and Harrah's Entertainment Inc. to purchase Turfway Park, a northern Kentucky racetrack located about ten miles from Cincinnati, Ohio. Turfway's primary owner, Jerry Carroll, wanted to get into the NASCAR business (he subsequently headed the group that built Kentucky Speedway in Sparta). Turfway had been on the market for six to eight months, but from what we could gather at Keeneland, there seemed to be no interest from anyone in the horse racing business to purchase it.

During this period, we received an invitation from William O'Connor, the chairman and CEO of GTECH, to fly to Rhode Island in the company's corporate jet, tour their corporate headquarters in West Greenwich, and meet with his executive staff. The purpose was to discuss the possibility of forming a partnership between Keeneland and GTECH involving one or possibly two off-track betting facilities in Kentucky. Of particular interest to us was the Ashland area in the northeastern sector of the state, just across the Ohio River from Huntington, West Virginia. There wasn't a single OTB parlor that operated anywhere in that area, and we saw it as fertile ground.

GTECH had been the online games vendor for the Kentucky lottery since its inception in 1989, and it wanted to cement its relationship with the state by becoming a partner in another business endeavor. The company had a wide customer base that included racetracks in the mid-Atlantic area, and O'Connor advised us that he had heard rumors that one or more of them did have an interest in acquiring Turfway. To be frank, Keeneland was not at all enthused about the possibility of track operators from out of state setting up a base in Kentucky. If that happened, it could present a serious challenge to the status quo, particularly in regard to the division of live racing dates on the annual calendar.

So our discussion with GTECH shifted from an Ashland OTB parlor to the potential of forming a partnership to purchase Turfway. Carroll and his partners had a debt of $13 million they owed to Harrah's, from a loan the latter had made to them when they were trying to get slot machine legislation passed some five years earlier. Harrah's is one of the most prominent casino operators in North America, and GTECH had a good business relationship with them. GTECH agreed to make a confidential inquiry to Harrah's, to see if they would be interested in being involved in a partnership that would own and operate Turfway. Keeneland's interest in participating was not initially disclosed by GTECH to Harrah's. But Harrah's expressed immediate enthusiasm, and GTECH began to pressure us to be more definitive about Keeneland's commitment, both administratively and in regard to financial involvement. The pace of negotiations quickened, for we thought Turfway would be a good fit for us.

Turfway annually conducted more live race dates than any other track in Kentucky, spanning January through early April, early September into early October, and late November through December. Almost all of Turfway's live racing occurred at night, which made it very attractive for the simulcasting markets east of the Mississippi River.

Equally important to us was Harrah's reputation and expertise within the casino gambling field. Should slot machines be legalized in Kentucky, owning Turfway would eliminate the responsibility of having to install them at Keeneland. We could protect Keeneland's traditional revenue base, while at the same time install them at Turfway and benefit from a new source of revenues.

GTECH, Harrah's, and Keeneland became equal partners in the venture—each owning one-third of Turfway. The price was $37 million, divided three ways. Truth be known, there have been many days since then when I've had serious second thoughts about pushing and persuading my colleagues at Keeneland to agree to do so. There have been nonending financial pressures, the need for additional infusions of capital, and managerial problems. The proximity of Indiana's riverboat casinos and the ever-present threats (and realities) of canceling racing during the winter because of bad weather have caused numerous headaches.

In August 2005, GTECH pulled out of the venture. While the track no longer fit into GTECH's long-term plans, both Harrah's and Keeneland believed that Turfway's long-range future looked very favorable. That same summer, a synthetic racing surface called Polytrack had been installed at Turfway. Polytrack had the potential of greatly reducing injuries to horses' legs. It also had great potential to reduce the interruptions of winter racing because of weather. And that could inspire the willingness of more owners and trainers of prominent stables to winter in Kentucky, making for larger fields and a more attractive simulcast product.

Thus, Keeneland joined with Harrah's to buy out GTECH's share, and we became 50 percent partners in Turfway. There was another element about this, too. The Turfway property is adjacent to Interstate 75 on the east and the Greater Cincinnati Airport on the west. The area is known as the "Golden Triangle of Northern Kentucky," with lucrative and forever escalating land values and great potential for industrial development. If Turfway did turn out to be a losing proposition, we could always sell a portion or all of the land and more than recoup our original investment.

What happens in the future with Turfway will likely be directly tied with what the Kentucky legislature does or does not do. The racing and breeding industry is a very important component of the state's economy— but it needs the competitive relief that would be provided by the passage of legislation allowing for alternative gaming at the tracks. We live in a new era. I have made the philosophical adjustment to understanding this. I trust and hope that our legislators are willing to do the same.

§

In recent times, discussions have taken place about Keeneland becoming a part owner of the Red Mile. The two tracks are only a twelve-minute automobile ride from each other. Fayette is the only county in Kentucky with two separately owned pari-mutuel facilities within its boundaries. As this is written, the Red Mile has four owners, each with a 25 percent interest in the track. Nick Nicholson has met with them, and the subject of Keeneland purchasing an interest in the Red Mile has been discussed at several lengthy meetings among the Keeneland trustees.

I have serious reservations about the idea. At Keeneland, we know very little about the harness racing industry. We do not have anyone on our staff with extensive experience in the sport. And we have heard that the Red Mile is losing in the range of $2 million to $3 million a year. And again, the Red Mile issue is predicated on slot machines and what the legislators in Frankfort may or may not do. The theory exists that if casino wagering were legalized in Kentucky, and if Keeneland were a partner in the ownership of the Red Mile, the largess would be all the greater.

But I do not believe that our city is big enough for two casino operations. And, just as importantly, there remains the undeniable fact that Keeneland is the dominant racing entity in Lexington. This has been the case for nearly three-quarters of a century, and it will always be the case. Keeneland has a well-established revenue flow. It has a sound, ongoing business plan. It has plenty of property upon which to expand its facilities. And I want Keeneland to continue to be in a position where it can stand alone. The idea of becoming a partner in an industry we know little about makes little sense. The impetus behind such a move would be greed, and greed has never been a motivating factor at Keeneland.

Chapter 14

Special People and Special Projects

DURING A TRIP to Santa Anita in the winter of 1980, Lucy and I were invited to a Valentine's Day party at the home of Muriel and Maxwell Gluck in Beverly Hills. It was a costume party, Muriel said. Guests were to come in the guises of the people they most admired. We were very reluctant to accept—neither Lucy nor I was comfortable with the costume idea. But Muriel was insistent, to the point where she mandated our attendance. "Come dressed as you are," she told us. Which is what we did.

Upon arriving, we found the main room in the Gluck house filled with people outfitted in all sorts of outlandish costumes. We did not recognize anybody. Being the only man there who was wearing a conventional suit and tie, I felt like the proverbial sore thumb personified. I armed myself with a glass of vodka and kept wishing I was somewhere else. Eventually, I began looking around the room, and amidst all these jolly people I saw a lovely blonde woman with a long cigarette holder. She was staring intently, right at me. My first reaction was that her gaze was one of disapproval, that she was holding me in contempt because of my lack of imaginative attire. I began, self-consciously, to move around the room. And as I did, the blonde kept her gaze fixated on me. Minutes passed, and whenever and wherever I moved, she kept staring at me. It suddenly occurred to me that maybe she had been introduced to me at a prior function. Since nobody else seemed interested in my company, I cautiously went over to the couch where she was sitting and said, "I'm Ted Bassett. Have we met before?"

The blonde woman took a long drag on the cigarette in her holder, batted her eyes, and in a low, husky voice said, "Hello, Ted." Suddenly, the voice was familiar, and with an uproarious laugh the woman morphed into the trainer Ron McAnally. I was so convulsed with disbelief that I collapsed onto the couch. Ron had come to the party masquerading as his wife, Debbie, and she came dressed as him!

Ron McAnally. I have the greatest respect and admiration for him. He is one of racing's special people, forever blessed with a twinkle in his face. A native of northern Kentucky, Ron lost his mother to tuberculosis when he was a little boy. When Ron was five years old, he and his two brothers and two sisters were placed by their father in an orphanage. Ron lived in that orphanage for nine years.

He got involved in racing through his uncle, the trainer Reggie Cornell. This was shortly after World War II concluded. Ron went to California to join Cornell. By rail, in a freight car, accompanied by a string of horses. Cornell's subsequent claim to fame was training Silky Sullivan, who had an astonishing closing kick. Ron had a lot to do with helping to develop him. In 1958, Silky Sullivan came from forty-one lengths behind to win an allowance race at Santa Anita and from twenty-six lengths behind to win the Santa Anita Derby. He became something of a folk hero among racing fans, but that status ended when Silky Sullivan finished twelfth in the Kentucky Derby.

It was sometime in the early 1970s when I first met Ron. By that time, he was well established with his own stable and was headquartered in Barn 99 on the Santa Anita backside. The barn was on a hill, adjacent to Baldwin Avenue, and years earlier it had been occupied by Calumet Farm. It required quite a trudge to get up there, and I would be carrying Blue Grass and Ashland Stakes nomination forms or hauling an armful of July sale catalogs. Ron and I would talk, and as time passed, we began meeting over a few drinks and eventually, we and our wives began having dinner together.

As the years went on, Ron won three Eclipse Awards as North America's outstanding trainer. He conditioned John Henry, who was Horse of the Year in both 1981 and 1984. All told, Ron has trained five divisional champions and over 150 stakes winners. He has won more races at Del Mar than any other trainer, surpassing such conditioners as Farrell Jones and Charlie Whittingham for the top position. And Ron has done exceptionally well at Keeneland—he has won the Spinster Stakes four times, which is also a record among trainers.

Here's another story that involves Ron. On February 8, 1985, ceremonies were held at the Century Plaza Hotel for the Eclipse Award winners of the previous year. The Horse of the Year competition was very close between John Henry, who, despite his advanced age of nine years, was male turf champion, and Slew o' Gold, who at age four was the champion older male on dirt surfaces. As it turned out, a tiebreaker was needed. The *Daily Racing Form* staff had voted 42–24 for John Henry as Horse of the Year. The National Turf Writers Association members had voted 47–46 for Slew o' Gold. The racing secretaries at the Thoroughbred Racing Associations (TRA) had split their votes 10–10. This resulted in a deadlock among the three voting blocks, triggering a tiebreaking system in which all individual votes were tallied to determine the winner.

I was TRA president that year, and one of the perks—actually, the only perk—of being in that position was that I got to present the Horse of the Year award. The auditors of the voting were required to keep the name of the winner secret from everybody (including me) until the presentation. I was up on the stage, appropriately dressed in a tuxedo, and was handed a sealed envelope containing the result. The orchestra played a drum roll. I took the envelope and tried to break the seal. And it would not break. A second drum roll. I still could not wedge the envelope open. I was fumbling like a hapless, helpless waif. I thought, "An iron welder must have sealed this damn thing!" A third drum roll. The orchestra leader was looking at me with an expression of both pain and scorn. And by the grace of God, the seal finally broke. I looked and saw John Henry's name, turned to the assembled multitude, and without thinking said, "Like old wine . . ." Kent Hollingsworth later wrote in the *Blood-Horse,* the "1,364 in attendance rose with applause, for no other horse ever improved so much with age." Well, it may have seemed like a semibrilliant line from me, but it was actually something I just blurted out—after the exasperating chore of getting that envelope open.

Sam and Dorothy Rubin, the owners of John Henry, came up on the stage. But it took what seemed like a long time for Ron to get up there. When he finally did, I impatiently asked him, "What took you so long?"

Ron replied, "I was trying to find a letter opener for you." (Note: After my performance, J. B. Faulconer, who was then the executive director of the TRA, sent a written memo to the staff and the auditors, telling them that in the future, the flaps on the Eclipse Award envelopes would be inserted rather than sealed.)

In 1985, I was also chairman of the board of the Kentucky Horse Park, which is a 1,200-acre recreational facility on Iron Works Pike on the northeastern outskirts of Lexington. The Horse Park is devoted to the celebration of all equine breeds, and in 1985, we were seeking a major attraction to stimulate public interest in what was going on there.

John Henry had been retired from racing at the culmination of the 1984 season, but in the spring of 1985, he was briefly returned to training. That change in plans, however, was short-lived. After John Henry injured a tendon in July, the Rubins announced that he was being retired again, this time permanently. My reaction was immediate. Although locales on both the East and West Coasts had expressed strong interest in serving as John Henry's retirement home, I thought the Kentucky Horse Park would be perfect for him. He would be cared for very well, and hundreds of thousands of tourists could visit him each year. Ron agreed with me, and after some effort, he convinced the Rubins to allow John Henry to be brought to the Horse Park. This was during Martha Layne Collins's tenure as governor of Kentucky, and she made the formal announcement at an August 1 press conference held at the Horse Park's Hall of Champions barn.

Governor Collins designated Saturday, August 31, as "John Henry Day." There would be free admission to the Horse Park. Mimes, musicians, cloggers, and jugglers would be on hand for the festivities, and the inaugural John Henry Polo Tournament would be held. The evening prior to all this there would be a black-tie dinner at the Horse Park's Big Barn. The master of ceremonies would be Joe Hirsch, and the guests of honor would be John Henry and Ron McAnally.

On the afternoon of the gala, the governor and the media were frantically trying to locate Ron. But they could not find him. After hours of searching (this was before the era of cell phones), of calling his barn and his home in Southern California, with no results, I finally got a hold of him and demanded to know, "Where are you? Where have you been?" In typical Ron McAnally fashion, he told me he had been at the Covington Protestant Children's Home, which was the orphanage where he and his siblings had been raised. Ron had been participating in the dedication of a new wing at the orphanage, for which he had helped pay the construction costs. There had been no publicity about this. No fanfare. Just a quiet act of generosity by Ron—of his money and of his time.

Five years later, in the summer of 1990, Ron was inducted into the National Museum of Racing's Hall of Fame in Saratoga Springs, New York. He and Debbie wept in gratitude that day. So did I.

§

In December 1996, I received an urgent phone call from Nina Bonnie, who was one of my successors chairing the board of the Kentucky Horse Park. Nina was highly admired and respected and not a person to be easily shaken. This day, though, she was dealing with a matter deeply troubling her. The Calumet Farm Trophy Collection had been on loan to the Horse Park since 1982. But Nina had been notified that the collection was going to be put up for auction, to satisfy a court decision regarding the bankruptcy status into which the historic farm had descended.

The history involved in all this is somewhat complex, but I will try to provide you with a sketch of some major details. Calumet was established in Lexington in 1924 by the baking powder magnate William Monroe Wright. Initially, it was a Standardbred operation—Wright won the 1931 Hambletonian with a trotter named Calumet Butler. In 1932, following Wright's death, Calumet was converted by his son, Warren Wright Sr., into a Thoroughbred breeding and racing farm. From that point until the death of Warren's widow, Lucille Wright Markey, Calumet recorded 2,401 victories, of which over 20 percent occurred in stakes races. Stakes winners bred and owned by Calumet totaled 148, and among them were a pair of Triple Crown winners, Whirlaway in 1941 and Citation in 1948.

Eleven Calumet horses—Alydar, Armed, Bewitch, Citation, Coaltown, Davona Dale, Real Delight, Tim Tam, Twilight Tear, Two Lea, and Whirlaway—along with the farm's legendary father-and-son training team Ben and Jimmy Jones, have been inducted into the National Museum of Racing's Hall of Fame in Saratoga Springs, New York. Ben Jones's face was on the cover of the May 30, 1949, issue of *Time* magazine, which gives you an idea of the import horse racing in general and Calumet in particular had back then. Calumet horses won the Kentucky Derby eight times and the Preakness Stakes seven times, both of which remain records. From 1934 to 1982, a grand total of eighteen Calumet horses won North American divisional championships.

Following the death of Warren Wright Sr. in 1950, Lucille married Admiral Gene Markey (I discuss Lucille and the Admiral in more detail in chapter 8). There was a large sitting area, called the Pine Room, on the first floor of the Markeys' home at Calumet. As the years went on, they would display the farm's trophies in that room during the month of May. But during the remainder of the year, the trophies would be stored in a basement vault. I'm talking about magnificent gold and silver cups, trays, urns, bowls, plates, and so on—well over 500 individual trophies in all, along with three dozen oil paintings of famous Calumet horses.

The Markeys usually spent the month of August in Saratoga Springs. They owned a house there, and the Admiral developed a very close friendship with Whitney Tower, who had formerly been the racing writer for *Sports Illustrated* and had become the vice president of the National Museum of Racing and chairman of its Hall of Fame committee. Throughout the 1970s, Whitney had tried to convince the Admiral to donate the Calumet trophies to the museum. In the spring of 1979, the Admiral told Margaret Glass, who served for over four decades as Calumet Farm's secretary, to pack the trophies in boxes and send them up there. Margaret was horrified—she felt that since Calumet Farm was located in central Kentucky, that was the region of the country where the trophies belonged, now and forever. Period. Margaret wrote a two-page letter to Lucille Markey in which she made an impassioned plea for Lucille to reconsider the decision. Margaret must have been very convincing, because Lucille promptly put a hold on the shipment.

The Admiral died in 1980, and Lucille Markey passed away two years later. But several weeks before her death, she agreed to allow the trophy collection and the oil paintings to be loaned to the Kentucky Horse Park for an annual lease fee of $1. John Y. Brown Jr., who was then Kentucky's governor, and I were very active in the negotiations to do this. At the time, I was also a member of the board of trustees of the Racing Museum, and the situation created a cool estrangement between Whitney Tower and me. Whitney felt Kentuckians had engineered a coup to keep the trophies for themselves.

During the years following Lucille's death, the Wright family heirs became entangled in a web of debt, and in 1991, Calumet filed for bankruptcy. The Calumet property, encompassing 762 acres, was saved from liquidation the following year when it was purchased by Henryk de Kwiatkowski. However, there were still many creditors to be assuaged, and the farm's other assets, including the trophies, remained subject to the rulings of the bankruptcy courts.

A New York auction house, Sotheby's, had appraised the value of the collection at between $800,000 and $1.2 million. An Owensboro, Kentucky, real estate developer named Robert H. Steele indicated he was willing to pay the latter figure. But Steele was vague as to exactly what he would do with the collection, and belief was growing that a judge might rule that the collection could be sold or auctioned off piece by piece. That is why I received the phone call from Nina, during which she asked for Keeneland's assistance and advice.

Initially, I was both thoughtless and speechless. So I turned to Margaret Glass, my old friend and ally. We were an unlikely duo of amateur fund-raisers. But we nonetheless took it upon ourselves, with a staff of none and a budget of zero, to attempt to work out some sort of plan to organize community and industry support to raise the necessary money to comply with the wishes of the court. Together, along with Nina Bonnie and the Horse Park's museum director, Bill Cooke, we formed the Committee to Save the Calumet Trophies.

We started off by hosting a media luncheon at the Horse Park on January 7, 1997. Our invitation list included reporters from the *Lexington Herald-Leader* and Louisville *Courier-Journal* and television and radio broadcast personnel from both cities. The luncheon was essentially a plea on our part for help. What a travesty and embarrassment it would be, for both the Thoroughbred industry and the greater central Kentucky community, if the Calumet trophies left our area without us putting up a gallant fight to keep them!

So began the tumultuous, two year and nine month struggle of trying to spread our net, to garner the necessary financial support from the public. We sent letters. We made speeches. We went to social gatherings, civic meetings, schools—to wherever there would be listening ears. Margaret and I called on corporation and bank executives, appeared on local television and radio shows separately and together. We did interviews, almost all of which were conducted at the Horse Park, with Calumet's two Triple Crown trophies carefully placed in the background.

At first, we did not receive unilateral support, for there was a widespread belief that the heirs to the Markey estate had squandered a rather large inheritance. A lot of people felt that if Calumet had all these creditors and the trophies had so much value, why shouldn't they be auctioned off? Don Edwards, a columnist for the *Herald-Leader,* wrote what I consider to be a superb response to the negativity. This is part of what Edwards said:

> The crown jewels of the [Horse Park] have been the Calumet trophies. They are the gilded metaphor for a golden age, a time before simulcasting, OTB and casino gambling trying to muscle in on horse tracks.

The trophies are unique and irreplaceable. They have transcended their private origin and have become a Commonwealth cultural heritage.

Contributions began coming in on January 14—the first one we received was a check for $1,000 from Alice Chandler. A lady from Montgomery, Alabama, sent $15, and another lady from Pullman, Washington, sent $20. Before the month was over, Mace Siegel, who had won the 1995 running of Keeneland's Ashland Stakes with a filly named Urbane, had sent $1,000. A man from Omaha, Nebraska, sent $5; a man from Providence, Rhode Island, sent $25; and a clergyman who declined to reveal his address donated $20.

Momentum was slowly developing, and by mid-February, we had raised a little over $66,000. We needed something to give us a big push forward, something that would really pique the public's interest, and we received it when Margaret was asked to speak to the fourth- and fifth-grade classes at Cassidy Elementary School on Tates Creek Road in Lexington. In her incomparable fashion, Margaret told the schoolchildren about the glory days at Calumet and about the trophies. The children were entranced by what she said and decided they wanted to participate in the fund-raising effort. They took Coca-Cola cans, wrapped them in the traditional devil's red and blue colors of Calumet, and went door-to-door in their neighborhoods, collecting quarters, dimes, nickels, pennies, whatever people were willing to contribute. On February 21, the Cassidy schoolchildren were bused to the Horse Park, where I was there to greet them, and a little girl walked up and presented me with a check for $501.13—the result of their efforts to save the Calumet trophies. The news media gave it a great deal of coverage, and the widespread effect was electrifying. By May 3 (Kentucky Derby day) of the following year, contributions received had reached $836,000. Further, the Lexington Visitors and Convention Bureau pledged $160,000. The *Herald-Leader* pledged $25,000. A donor who preferred to remain anonymous pledged $100,000.

To our frustration, though, obstacles seemed to be forever materializing. Originally, we thought we had to raise $1.2 million—which we did. By the time it was all over, we actually raised about $1.62 million. Contributions came in from forty-four states and three foreign countries. However, in August 1997, another New York auction house, Guernsey's, assessed the value of the collection at $5.23 million. You can imagine the impact this had on Calumet's creditors. We had no hope of coming up with such a sum. But I kept on reminding our volunteers that probably no one else could, either. An assessed value is one thing. What somebody is actually willing to pay can be another thing completely.

In the 1998 legislative session, Kentucky lawmakers earmarked upward of $1.5 million in taxpayer money to assist in purchasing the collection. I lobbied hard for this to happen, speaking before committees and privately to individual lawmakers, carefully detailing what a magnet for tourism the Horse Park had become—and how hundreds of thousands of visitors per year were drawn to the Calumet collection. I further arranged for one of the children from the Cassidy school project, a young lady named Betsy May, to provide testimony before the lawmakers too. Betsy told them, "I want to be able to bring my grandchildren to the Horse Park and tell them that I helped save the Calumet trophies."

A bankruptcy court judge set a deadline of 5:00 P.M., August 31, to submit bids on the collection. Our offer was $2.7 million. Nine other parties indicated that they might enter the bidding. My nerves were on fire as the deadline date and hour approached. And then, suddenly, the deadline passed, and nothing happened. By God, we won! The Calumet trophies would henceforth be in Kentucky forever.

We had a big party at the Horse Park on September 23 of that year. Paul Patton, then the governor of Kentucky, symbolically presented an oversized check to Horse Park officials. The children from Cassidy School were on hand, clapping and laughing with joy—some had grown about six inches since I had last seen them. On November 18, we had a dinner celebrating our achievement. I was asked to make some short remarks, and I am including the bulk of them here:

This evening is not just a tribute to the efforts of a few who comprise the Calumet Committee, but it is a tribute to the community, the state, the industry at large, for it was the efforts of many which achieved the possible and what at times seemed frustratingly impossible.

It would have been a tragedy, a travesty, an embarrassment to the community if we all stood idly by and permitted the dissolution of this incomparable historic collection.

I have struggled and agonized whether to take the monumental risk of thanking each of you personally for your generosity. My heart says yes, my Alzheimer's blemished mind says no, for fear of omitting or overlooking someone who played a major role.

But I must say this to you—this effort to save the Calumet trophies was one of the truest, purest examples of community pro bono one can imagine, when we all work together towards a common goal.

You all may be interested to know that not the first dollar was ever expended to defray expenses. There were no media costs of advertising or promotion. All radio, television, and newspaper advertising were donated free. There were no legal fees, despite the countless hours donated by Joe Scott and Bill Bagby sifting through the complexities and greed of the bankruptcy process.

It was a wonderful example of private enterprise for the public good and public enterprise for the private good.

Over a full decade has now gone by since all this took place. I won't be around by the time Betsy May brings her grandchildren to see the collection, but I have no doubts that she will someday do it. Every now and then, especially on a summer morning, I drive over to the Horse Park and stroll through the area where the trophies are displayed. They are dazzling as a whole, and fascinating with their individually distinctive designs: the massive silver urn, made in London, England, a century and a half ago, that was awarded to celebrate Whirlaway's win in the 1942 Louisiana Handicap—it was his final career victory; the fourteen-carat gold urn, with diamond-encrusted horseshoe, celebrating Ponder's victory in the seventy-fifth running of the Kentucky Derby; the silver urn adorned with deer antlers, awarded for Bardstown's victory in the 1956 Buckeye Handicap.

There is a sign at the entrance to the collection. It says, "James E. Bassett III Gallery." I have often suspected that my name is up there in Velcro, a material that's used to close gaps in clothing. You can easily lift Velcro off with your fingers. I have this feeling that when I come through the Horse Park gate, an attendant calls in and says, "Bassett is present. Put his name up there." And as soon as I leave, they take it down. No, they wouldn't do that. Or would they?

§

As is the case with the people upon whom they are bestowed, trophies have unique histories. I am going to tell you about the one attached to the

Lexington Bowl, which Keeneland awarded to the owners of the horses who won the Blue Grass Stakes from 1937 to 1952.

The Lexington Bowl was commissioned in 1854 by the citizens of the city whose name it bears. It was presented as a token of their esteem to Dr. Elisha Warfield, who bred the great nineteenth-century racehorse and sire Lexington. The bowl was manufactured by a local silversmith firm, Garner & Winchester. Fifteen inches in height, it bears the image of a full-scale race—complete with horses, jockeys, a packed grandstand, and people on the rail cheering the horses on—that extends around the bowl's entire circumference. The top of the bowl is adorned with flowers and scrolls. It was, and remains, a remarkable piece of art.

When Dr. Warfield died, the bowl became the property of his daughter, Mary Jane, the wife of Cassius Marcellus Clay, who was the U.S. minister to Russia during the Abraham Lincoln administration. When Mrs. Clay died in 1900, the bowl was inherited by her only living son, Brutus J. Clay, who at the time was the national commissioner to the Paris Exposition, and five years later, he was appointed by Theodore Roosevelt as U.S. minister. Brutus Clay took the bowl to Europe with him and utilized it to serve punch, eggnog, and other libations to guests. When he died in 1932, the bowl was inherited by his daughter, Mrs. Edward D. Johnson of Huntsville, Alabama. During the winter of 1937, Brutus Clay's second wife (and widow) purchased the bowl from her stepdaughter. And in April of that year, it was announced in the *Thoroughbred Record* that the Lexington Bowl had been purchased by "three nationally known sportsmen, who asked their names to be withheld," to be presented every year to the winning owner in the Blue Grass Stakes.

The three sportsmen, I'm pretty sure, were Arnold Hanger, Jock Whitney, and Louis Lee Haggin II. I do not know how much money they paid for the bowl, but it must have been a substantial sum. The idea was that each year the name of the winning horse would be engraved on the bowl. The bowl would then be retained by the winning owner until the following year's running of the Blue Grass, when it would be presented anew. This was the practice through 1952, at which point there was no more space on the bowl to add the names of future winners. It was then that Keeneland began the practice that continues today of awarding a gold mint julep cup to the winning owner. It never occurred to Keeneland officials to have a duplicate made of the Lexington Bowl for further presentations. But apparently, it did occur to some very prominent horse people.

In 1971, Louis Haggin and I were attending a meeting of the Kentucky State Racing Commission in Louisville. It was being held in the corporate offices of George Eggar, who owned a local television station and had been an owner and director of a number of corporations, including a distillery, a bakery, and a frozen food manufacturing company. Eggar was also a Republican and had served as Governor Louie B. Nunn's campaign chairman. Nunn had subsequently appointed Eggar chairman of the racing commission.

Racing commission meetings were held only two to four times a year in those days, but they could be very contentious, especially over the issues of which track, Churchill Downs or Keeneland, would host racing on the final Saturdays of April and October. We accepted the idea of culminating Keeneland's spring meet on a Friday because the following day had become the traditional place on the calendar for Churchill's Derby Trial Stakes, which in the early 1970s still bore some importance as a Kentucky Derby prep race. But we were against forfeiting the final Saturday in October to Churchill. It was a college football Saturday, with the University of Kentucky team often playing a night game at home, and this helped generate a very large crowd at Keeneland during the afternoon.

Louis was often in a testy mood when these racing commission meetings ended. This particular day, we were just about to leave when the vice chairman of the commission, Laban P. Jackson, came up to us. Laban was a longtime Thoroughbred breeder from Shelby County and also owned a fertilizer company. He was carrying a box wrapped in brown paper. Laban said to us, "I've got something here I would like to show you and see if you would be interested in acquiring it." He unwrapped the package, and there was the Lexington Bowl.

I am not sure how to describe the color that Louis's face turned. Somewhere between deep blue and purple. He said, or half-shouted might be a better way of describing it, "Where did you get that?"

Laban replied, "I purchased it from Wakefield-Scearce [which is a noted antiques dealer in Shelbyville, Kentucky]. I thought that Keeneland might be interested, so I brought it here. Are you interested?"

"No! Not at this time!" Louis said. "Come on, Ted! We're going back!" We got into Louis's gray Thunderbird, and he proceeded to drive at a rate of ninety-five miles per hour from Louisville to Lexington. We hardly spoke a word to each other en route. I kept looking in the side mirror, expecting the flashing blue light of a State Police patrol car to come into sight at any time. But I did not tell that to Louis. He thought the Lexington Bowl, a trophy he had helped purchase, had been stolen, and nothing was going to deter his dash back to Keeneland.

Louis drove us through the Keeneland entrance to the clubhouse gate, and for a few seconds, I thought he was actually going to drive into the clubhouse itself. We got out of his car and ran up the steps of the administration building to the Keeneland Library, which was the repository for most of the association's traditional old trophies. Louis, by this time pretty much out of breath, stormed through the door, stood there huffing and puffing for a moment, and then said to a rather startled Amelia King Buckley, our head librarian, "Where is the Lexington Bowl?"

Amelia looked at him, turned around, led us to a bookcase, pointed, and said, "There it is."

Louis said, "Amelia, is that the one? Is that the real one?"

Amelia replied, "Why, yes, Mr. Haggin."

Well, at that point, Louis began to calm down. And Amelia, who herself was a great reservoir of historical information relating to Keeneland, said, "I recall that Elizabeth Arden, who had owned Maine Chance Farm and won the Blue Grass Stakes with Lord Boswell in 1946, was so taken with the Lexington Bowl that she had a duplicate made by Tiffany & Company."

And Louis and I went, "Ah-ha!" That explained it.

After Elizabeth Arden's death, during the period when her estate was being settled, a number of her trophies were auctioned off. Apparently, Wakefield-Scearce had acquired her duplicate of the Lexington Bowl. Louis said, "Well, thank God the real one's here, where it belongs." And that was the end of it.

Or so I thought. Fast-forward to April 2007. In conjunction with the start of Keeneland's spring race meet, the *Lexington Herald-Leader* published a special supplement that included a brief write-up of the Lexington Bowl story. I promptly received a phone call from the Kentucky Horse Park's Bill Cooke "You mean to tell me," he said, "that the Lexington Bowl we have in the Calumet Trophy Collection isn't the real thing?"

I suggested that he take the trophy out of the case, examine it, and call me back. Which he did. "The trophy appears to be authentic. But it has Keeneland's name on it," Bill said. Yes, but "Keeneland" was never engraved on the Lexington Bowl. "It contains the initials L. P. W.," Bill said. Okay, L. P. W. stands for Lucille Parker Wright (Markey), the grande dame of Calumet. "On the bottom, it says 'Tiffany,'" Bill told me. "And the list of Blue Grass winners on it contains only two names, one of which is Bull Lea [the Calumet homebred who won the Blue Grass in 1938]."

Here is my speculation. Lucille Wright and Elizabeth Arden were great rivals on the racetrack, but they were social friends. After Elizabeth won the Blue Grass with Lord Boswell, she incredulously said to Lucille, "Can you imagine? Keeneland presented me with the winner's trophy but isn't allowing me to keep it! They want it back before the next running of the Blue Grass! How distressful."

To which Lucille replied, "Oh, darling, yes, I know. I had the same situation with Bull Lea. And I had a duplicate made for my own collection. I'll give you the name of the people who made it, so you can do the same."

So the Lexington Bowl is not precisely one of a kind. Or even two of a kind. A mystery remains—we know where Lucille's duplicate is but have no idea what happened to Elizabeth Arden's duplicate. But Keeneland retains the original in a locked, glass-enclosed case in the directors' room. In 2008, the Lexington Bowl was appraised by Wakefield-Scearce Galleries to have a value of $25,000.

§

Fund-raising is not easy. But neither is it as complicated as sending a rocket to Mars. It requires a strong belief in the mission, coupled with effort and persistence. A working committee is essential to the start of any fund-raising campaign. But generally, after a period of time, if the goal has not yet been achieved, the interest and the effort it inspires begin to wane. At that point, responsibility falls upon the campaign's chairman, and he must be willing to carry the major portion of the load and set an example for solicitation.

Personal calls, direct contacts, and networking are a hundred times more effective than form letters requesting support. I have learned that there are two key ingredients for success in fund-raising. The first is having a portion of the money raised before going public with the campaign. The second involves having a prominent donor step forward with a sizable gift shortly after the campaign is announced. The latter ingredient is what establishes momentum—it ignites the public's interest and inspires further response. You can rely on sheer luck for this to happen, but it's much better if arrangements are made privately with the major donor beforehand.

There must be a common denominator between the donor's interest and his or her pocketbook, between the appeal of the mission and his or her ability to pay. And one has to be careful about not going to the same well too often. Over-rattling the tin cup can render you persona non grata.

In 1998, I was asked to chair a project to raise funds to build two new YMCA facilities in Lexington. One would be in the Beaumont Centre complex, and another in the northern sector of the city. An additional goal of the project was to renovate the existing YMCA facility on East High Street. One of the first people I turned to was my old friend William T. Young, master of Overbrook Farm. I remember Bill's initial words when I went to see him: "Well, Ted, what are you working on now?" I began to give him a short speech about the YMCA's significance, but I was less than halfway through it when he cut me off. "Listen, I don't want to be told about the Y," Bill said. "I wasn't a child of privilege. My parents couldn't afford to join a country club. It was at the Y where I first participated in sports, where I learned how to swim. When I was a child, the Y was a second home for me. Tell me what you need me to do."

I said to Bill, "I need your 'good housekeeping' stamp of approval on the merits of the campaign to build the two new facilities and to upgrade the one on High Street." Bill immediately granted that wish. And he made a pledge of $100,000 to give me the impetus to move forward.

We had T-shirts printed up for the volunteers working on the YMCA campaign. The T-shirts bore the image of a stork devouring a frog. However, the frog was not going gently into that good night. Although his upper torso was already halfway down the stork's mouth, the frog's hands were still free, and he had a stranglehold on the stork's throat. The image was captioned:

Don't EVER give up!
YMCA Capital Campaign

I developed my own mantra: "Remember the frog!" When spirits would ebb, which is inevitable among the people involved with the fundraising, I would give them a stern look and say, "Remember the frog!" Sometimes I would state this in a voice cracked with anger, accompanied by my right fist pounding on the nearest table. You might look upon this as ridiculous. And in a way, it was—it probably did not have as dramatic an impact as "Remember the Alamo!" did to the Texans who fought at the

Battle of San Jacinto. But it had an effect. It helped keep the volunteer team amused. And the more the volunteers enjoyed what they were doing, the more charged up they became. And yes, I believe that the chairman's role in a fund-raising project is partially that of a cheerleader. You need to continually tell the people involved, "You can do it!"

It is important, as well, to let them know they are special. Jan Brucato, the president and CEO of the YMCA, would sometimes phone and say, "I'd like to bounce something off you that has nothing to do with the campaign. Can I come over to see you at Keeneland?"

My response always was, "Of course. When do you want to come?" Sometimes she would come to see me in the Keeneland track kitchen, and as soon as I would see Jan come through the door, I would bounce right up to greet her. Treating a person this way costs nothing. But it made Jan feel special, and she was special. She had a difficult job, and she did it well.

As time went on, Saint Joseph HealthCare made a substantial donation to the YMCA project. As did Lexmark International Inc. As did the John S. and James L. Knight Foundation. Everyone kept plugging away. And at the end of four years, we had raised the $14.2 million that was needed.

§

In 2004, I agreed to be the chairman of a fund-raising campaign to construct a new headquarters for the Central Kentucky Blood Center. The proposed building would contain 40,000 square feet of floor space, twice the amount of the facility the Blood Center was operating out of at the time.

The Blood Center had been in existence since 1968, when it was founded by a group of local physicians. Prior to then, each hospital in the Lexington area had its own blood-collecting division. It was a circumstance that was costly, and it was risky too, for in an emergency situation, a hospital might not have a blood type in storage (B negative and AB negative are particularly rare) that matched that of an individual patient.

During the Blood Center's early years of operation, it was located in the basement of a Lexington restaurant, the Perkins Pancake House, on Limestone Avenue. The restaurant was across the street from the University of Kentucky Chandler Medical Center. Students would be among those who came to donate blood, and as an incentive, the Blood Center people would sometimes take them upstairs and buy them a pancake breakfast.

A decade later, the Blood Center relocated to a 21,000-square-foot facility on Waller Avenue, where it had remained ever since. Subsidiary blood donation branches were established in Somerset, Prestonburg, and Pikeville.

The Blood Center grew to the point where it was serving the needs of fifty-nine counties in central and eastern Kentucky. Blood was collected from donors, tested for infectious diseases, separated into components (red blood cells, liquid plasma, and platelets), stored in refrigerators, and distributed to sixty-seven hospitals and clinics as needed. I am talking about 78,000 pints (or 39,000 quarts, 9,750 gallons) annually to a region containing 2 million (fully half) of Kentucky's residents. If you know anyone who has ever had major cancer or heart surgery, received a transplanted organ, or had a premature birth, at least one blood transfusion was almost certainly required for a return to health.

For nearly thirty years, the Blood Center operated out of the Waller Avenue facility. To fulfill its ever-expanding responsibilities, the Blood Center itself needed to expand. It was employing 200 full-time workers. New diseases were constantly emerging—the West Nile virus, for example—and the size of the Blood Center's testing laboratory needed to be doubled. Further, its refrigerator and freezer capacities needed to be increased by at least two-thirds.

Susan Berry-Buckley was the Blood Center's CEO, and Jack Hillard was (and remains) the director of development. Including purchase of the land, architectural design fees, construction, laboratory and storage equipment, and so forth, they were looking at a cost of $8.2 million for the new headquarters. The Blood Center was capable of covering $5.3 million of the bill. But the remaining $2.9 million needed to be obtained by way of community support.

Two consulting firms were engaged: Jerold Panas, Linzy & Partners of Chicago and Johnson, Grossnickle and Associates of Indianapolis. Both concluded that there was not sufficient financial support within the central Kentucky community to do a capital campaign of such magnitude at that time. Well, this is exactly the sort of thing that gets my dander up—that brings out the old Marine Corps veteran residing within me. Jerold Panas, Linzy et al. and Johnson, Grossnickle et al. deservedly hold fine reputations for the work they do. But once again, they're located in Chicago and Indianapolis. I'm located in central Kentucky and have been for the vast majority of my life. I know this community. And I knew the necessary fund-raising could be accomplished.

Here is a brief anecdote I am sure you will appreciate. The morning after the September 11, 2001, terrorist attacks occurred, hundreds of people were lined up outside the Blood Center. Many had been there all night, so anxious were they to be donors. The city of Lexington had to dispatch several policemen to direct traffic on Waller Avenue—that's how jammed up everything became. This tells you a lot about the citizenry of central Kentucky.

When we analyzed the list of potential contributors to the Blood Center's capital campaign, we looked at central Kentucky's major corporations, especially those whose employees annually donated blood. The greatest participation, for two decades, had come from Toyota Motor Manufacturing in Georgetown. The people who worked there had given the Blood Center more than 50,000 units of blood. We also looked at the Blood Center's most prominent users, which, not surprisingly, were the three largest hospitals in Lexington—the University of Kentucky Medical Center, Saint Joseph HealthCare, and Central Baptist.

Of course, I already had a business relationship with Toyota, which had been sponsoring the Blue Grass Stakes at Keeneland since 1996. We went to Kim Menke and Nila Wells, who headed Toyota's community relations department, and Dan May, who headed the blood drives there. Once again, this was a quest to get a stamp of approval from a bellwether figure or organization. And right off the bat, Toyota stepped up and pledged $100,000.

This gave us momentum to delve further into the corporate community. Central Baptist was the first hospital to get involved. I went to Bill Sisson, the president and CEO there, and told him, "Bill, we need someone from the Lexington hospitals to step forward. You're in the best position to be that person. I want you to be that person." Bill enthusiastically pledged $250,000 from Central Baptist. The UK Medical Center and Saint Joseph were slower to come aboard, but they eventually pledged $250,000 and $150,000, respectively. And Pikeville Medical Center pledged $250,000, which made the participation of the region's four major hospitals complete.

The Keeneland Foundation came through as well, with a $60,000 pledge. For decades, Keeneland's employees have willingly met the challenge to be blood donors, and I cannot express to you enough how proud I am about that. I always like to set a good example, so I decided I would roll up my sleeve and be a blood donor too. But the Blood Center people would not let me do it, a circumstance that briefly released the legendary

Bassett temper. "Well, why the hell not!?" I demanded to know. So they told me. Taking blood from me would be a violation of FDA regulations. I was disqualified as a donor because of my chronic high blood pressure and because of the melanoma I had developed a year earlier on my big toe. One of my mantras is, "Do not take no for an answer!" But this time, I did not have a choice.

Potential capital campaign contributors were not saying no, however. Central Bank & Trust and Fifth Third Bank each pledged $50,000. The Honorable Order of Kentucky Colonels pledged $25,000. My close friend Alex Campbell pledged $10,000.

Ground was broken for the new Blood Center headquarters, which would be located at Beaumont Centre, on September 23, 2005. As the steel columns were put up, donations kept coming in. One year, five months, and twelve days later, on March 5, 2007, the ribbon-cutting ceremony took place. What two highly reputable consulting firms concluded could not be done, had been done.

It is my belief that this story has yet to reach its final chapter. Here is what I am thinking: The Lexington–Fayette County area now ranks sixty-sixth among population centers in the United States. And it is the largest in Kentucky, larger even than Louisville. I want our Blood Center to be more than a place for Kentuckians. I think it can serve a large portion of the Midwest and be a regional hub—a primary reservoir of blood and blood components—for the U.S. Department of Defense. To achieve this, blood donations would need to increase. But anybody aged seventeen or older and in good physical health has the capacity of being a donor. Forty percent of the population meets these standards, but only 5 percent are blood donors. This is true nationally. And, according to statistical analyses done by Central Kentucky Blood Bank personnel, that is true here as well.

We live in an age of threats from international terrorists, and while their attacks on this country have to date been restricted to the East Coast, you never know when a midwestern metropolitan area could be a target. What a jewel it would be for central Kentucky if our Blood Center grew to the point where it served as a midwestern hub in case of emergency—be that emergency caused by terrorists, an earthquake, an outbreak of tornados or other catastrophic occurrences. And don't you dare try to tell me that central Kentuckians are not capable of creating such a hub. Do so, and you will get an immediate argument from me.

§

If you are a general manager or CEO, one of the things you must understand is that there's a very thin line between familiarity and authority. It's important to be approachable. But at the same time, you must be careful about being too accessible. It is the supervisor's role to create a degree of space. I learned the importance of these fundamental management practices during my days in the Marine Corps, and I relied on them during my tenures with the State Police, at Keeneland, and at the Breeders' Cup. On one side of the thin line is a sense of austerity and detachment. On the other side is a sincere concern for an employee's personal welfare, both on and off the job.

In the Marine Corps, a good officer listens to his men. And in the business world, it is absolutely essential for a manager to be a good listener too, in establishing productive lines of communication with your employees. In the process of availing yourself of the expertise, managerial skills, and experience the employees have, you formulate the perception that everyone is operating as a member of a team, and not in their personal cocoons of isolationism.

You also have to try your best to have a connection with each individual, to develop the ability to put a name to a face. During my tenure as Keeneland president, I could walk past a member of our maintenance crew and say, "Hello, how are you today?" and the response would be routinely appreciative. But if I was willing to stop for a minute or two and say to the same man, "Hello, Johnny. I understand your father had surgery recently. How is he feeling?" I would be showing that employee that I have consideration for him beyond the daily routine. I just might make his day a bit better. And he would return the favor with a greater appreciation of Keeneland and a greater dedication to his job. Name recognition and properly putting a name with a face are key components of this philosophy. If you walk up to someone and say, "Hello, Bob, how's your daughter doing at Dartmouth?" but it's actually Bill you're talking to, and he has no daughter and his two sons are in Iraq, that sets you back with him for about two centuries.

The way you carry yourself is important. Back during World War II when I was in officer training school at Quantico, the first time we had liberty, an old drill sergeant told us, "Now, listen dumbheads, you're going out in public in the Marine Corps uniform. And when you walk down the street, do it like you have a destination, like you know where you're going, with purpose and direction." I have a tendency to do that today.

Still, I have always wanted my employees to feel I am accessible to them. I am concerned about whatever problems they have—especially the ones pertaining directly to their professional lives. In turn, employees become more devoted to lessening each other's concerns. Whenever we have a heavy snowfall in central Kentucky, there's something our entire Keeneland staff knows—that while they may have difficulty navigating the streets in their cul-de-sacs and their neighborhood side roads, once they get to Keeneland, they will find the roads and parking areas on the property have been cleared and salted. This is because of the dedication of our maintenance people to serve their fellow employees.

It is necessary, of course, to be discerning about employees' needs, and I will admit that complaints about their parking places not being close enough to the main building have never particularly moved me. But the employees who demonstrate they are thinkers, who are truly concerned about how the operation could improve and move forward—those people, regardless of their positions on the totem pole, receive my full attention. There are, invariably, employees who steadfastly resist any change to the status quo. They may complain constantly to their fellow workers about the way things are, but if change is in the wind, they will object, sometimes passively, sometimes aggressively. They may want circumstances to change, but they themselves don't want to change at all. You cannot allow this attitude to prevail, and dealing with it sometimes requires ingenuity.

Here's an example: The Kentucky State Police have a merit system, defined in the administrative code by KRS Chapter 16, which, among other things, states that your job is protected as long as you perform in accordance with the rules and regulations and that political or outside influences cannot play a part in your staying employed. When I became State Police director, Governor Breathitt told me to reorganize the organization's command hierarchy—specifically, to redefine the duties of James Hughes, Charles Crutchfield, and David Espie, all of whom held the rank of captain and were part of the "old boys' club." Breathitt's directive created a lot of unease. Had I transferred Hughes, Crutchfield, and Espie to other posts, say in Mayfield or Morehead, this would have forced their families to relocate too. I handled this by reappointing Hughes to the Bureau of Investigations. Crutchfield went to the Bureau of Supply. And Espie went to the Bureau of Records. They all stayed in Frankfort, but they no longer had any authority over the State Police's command and field operations. A few years later at Keeneland, I did a similar thing with William T. Bishop, moving him from general manager of racing operations to the position of director of finance.

Believe me, I have never been a maverick or a rebel. I am an establishment person—this is a trait that is reflected in the way I talk, in my manner, in my dress, in just about every way I comport myself. But at the same time, I have never been fearful of buying into an environment of change. More than anything, what makes employees receptive to change is leadership. Employees must believe in what the leader is doing. And their belief, in turn, is inspired by the enthusiasm the leader conveys. But the leader has to be willing to make the decision that institutes change. You can conduct the interviews with your workers. You can solicit and absorb their intellectual input. If you leave them, however, to wait, wait, wait and nothing happens, your credibility takes a hit, and deservedly so. When I have found resistance to be uncompromising, my philosophy has been not to ignore it but to attack it. That's the old Marine Corps philosophy, and it's a sound one.

§

The phone calls from him always began the same way—"Hello, Ted, this is Bill Young." Actually, Bill's voice needed no introduction. I recognized it immediately. He was one of the great entrepreneurs, philanthropists, and horsemen ever to grace the central Kentucky area. Bill made fortunes in the food manufacturing, trucking, warehouse, and health care industries. He donated millions of dollars to Transylvania University and the University of Kentucky. And as master of Overbrook Farm, he won five Triple Crown races, including the 1996 Kentucky Derby with Grindstone.

Phone calls from Bill never led to casual or trivial conversations. He always had a purpose. Well, one day following the 2002 fall race meeting at Keeneland, he called me and said, "Why don't we do something for those wonderful waitresses in the Keeneland clubhouse who make our life so pleasant?" I told Bill it was a wonderful idea. And what would you like to do? Give them a luncheon? Treat them to dinner? Bill responded, "Oh no, nothing like that. I'm suggesting something really special. Maybe taking a trip in my jet."

"That sounds great," I said, thinking that maybe he meant flying to Louisville or Cincinnati or perhaps someplace else in the Midwest.

But Bill then asked me, "The people you would invite—how many of them do you think have been to New York? How many have been to a Broadway musical?"

After that, my enthusiasm reached high gear. I knew Bill was primarily thinking about the wonderful Turf Catering employees who always waited on him in the clubhouse and in the Overbrook corporate box. Particularly Angel Stivers, his all-time favorite waitress, and Rhonda Booth, Turf Catering's chargé d'affaires. But I also wondered if there might be others included. I asked Bill how many people he was thinking of taking. He replied, "Oh, about seven or so. And Ted, you make the selections. Pick those who don't have the opportunity to travel to New York and have been loyal, dedicated employees at Keeneland."

Finding people who had not been to New York, at least for a long time, was easy. Finding those who had never flown in a private jet was even easier. And finding those who had never attended a Broadway musical was easiest of all. The selection process was unscientific, but I tried to be impartial. Bill and I agreed that there should be invitees from each of the departments at Keeneland, with preference given to those who had the longest records of service. Upon being notified, the invitees were told that the departure time from Keeneland would be 8:00 A.M. on January 22, 2003. And that they should wear warm clothing. Because of family pressures from husbands and children, we finally had to reveal beforehand that we were taking them to New York. But we didn't tell them anything beyond that.

On the day of the trip, we all met at the Keeneland Cottage and rode the association's bus across the street to the private hangar that housed Bill's 604 Challenger jet at Blue Grass Airport. The invitees included Angel and Rhonda; Beth Daugherty, my former secretary, who was now in charge of customer service at Keeneland; Jan Landers, who was in charge of human resources; Lori Lilly, the little cleaning lady who took care of the cottage; Phyllis Rogers, the assistant librarian; and Freida Shuffett, a longtime employee in the horse sales department.

Upon getting aboard Bill's jet, we presented each of our guests with a rose. We took off promptly at 8:30 A.M.—destination, LaGuardia Airport. En route, Bill pointed out to the group the features and safety factors of the plane and identified geographic points of interest as we flew over them. Sandwiches and soft drinks were served on white linen tablecloths. We arrived at LaGuardia at 10:00 A.M. and were met by the longest stretch limousine I have ever seen. We all got in, and from that point onward, Bill was a masterful tour director.

We crossed the Brooklyn Bridge to Battery Park (where we got a splendid view of the Statue of Liberty), spent an hour at Ground Zero, went past the United Nations, through Times Square, and up Fifth Avenue to Bill's penthouse, which overlooked Central Park. Then the limo took us to the Broadway theater where *42nd Street* was being performed. Our seats were in the center of the orchestra section, row seven. One of the great moments to always remember occurred when I looked upon the mesmerized faces of our traveling group, which were so alive with the extreme joy, amazement, and excitement of seeing a Broadway musical.

From there, the limo took us to Rockefeller Center, where we ate dinner on the sixty-fifth floor at the Rainbow Grill. We had a window table, with a spectacular view of the Empire State Building, the island of Manhattan, and the Hudson River as the sun was setting. Afterward, we went to St. Patrick's Cathedral, where we lit a candle and said a prayer for Rhonda (who had cancer). There was one last trip in the limo down Broadway, with all of its bright lights gleaming. And then to the airport for the journey home.

We arrived back in Lexington at 11:00 P.M., and a light, gentle snow was falling—a perfect ending for a mystery fairy-tale trip. A few days later, Bill sent each of the ladies who went on the trip a CD of the *42nd Street* music. He also sent me a note in which he said, "I almost get teary thinking about the seven 'wide-eyed' girls."

Bill passed away almost exactly a year later. Rhonda died just a few weeks after him. And Freida died in October 2007. I dearly miss all of them.

Chapter 15

Retirement—
I Don't Have Time for That

WHILE YOUTH MIGHT be largely a frame of mind, one cannot hold back the clock or the calendar. As time passes and the twilight years approach, we develop a kinship with the metallic man—as we gain silver in the hair, gold in the mouth, and an increasing amount of lead in the posterior.

Back in 1986, the expected age of retirement within our society was still pretty much thought of as sixty-five. And at sixty-five, I had made up my mind to retire as Keeneland's president. My decision was made during a long, solitary walk on a beach in Hawaii, halfway through the trip home from the Melbourne Cup. Making the decision was difficult, to a degree. And to a degree it was not. I have always believed that there is a time to arrive and a time to leave. One's arrival is often determined—and this has definitely been true in my case—by fortuitous circumstances, by luck. But one has to rely more on his own logic and intelligence when it is time to leave.

Leaving one position, though, did not mean that I would refrain from taking on another. I was hoping that Keeneland's directors would name me chairman of the board, which they did, and I served in that position for sixteen years. And it was also during that sixteen-year period when my tenure as president of the Breeders' Cup occurred. It was during that period that I served as chairman of Equibase. It was during that period that I served as president of the World Series Racing Championship and when the Calumet Trophy collection was saved for permanent display at the Kentucky Horse Park.

Throughout my professional life, I have always harbored a deep fear of overstaying my time. But on the other hand, I am equally fearful of the idea of settling into a rocking chair on the back porch. I prefer to be involved in something productive. As I write this, I am eighty-six years old, soon to turn eighty-seven. But even nowadays, when I walk through the Keeneland grounds, members of the maintenance crew ask me, "Where are you going in such a hurry?" Often my response is, "Well, I really don't know." It may be I'm in pursuit of the next challenge.

I still have recurring dreams about being back in the Marine Corps. Not in a combat situation—I certainly had my fill of that as a young man. But in boot camp. There's this one dream I keep experiencing where this salty old sergeant looks at me and says, "Bassett, what the hell are you doing here?" And I tell him, "Well, I've come back to prove that I can go through basic training again." The sergeant then says to me, "Let me see your birth certificate, you old fart!" And I stammer and stumble around, but I don't want to dare tell him that I'm an octogenarian, hoping to somehow muddle through. And then I wake up in a cold sweat from the fear of being rejected.

As I have said before, my career path has never been defined. Throughout my adult life, I have more or less gone with the flow as opportunities have arisen. I am not trying to be modest when I say this. I'm simply being truthful. However, there has always been, and there remains, one factor that's very clear. Total retirement has never, ever been an option for me. If I retired completely, I would be in my grave soon afterward.

§

Africa is a rainbow of landscapes
Endless and diverse
A crucible of emotions
Both ruthless and serene
Africa is a visitor's fantasy
A photographer's paradise
A hunter's Valhalla
It's boundless and hypnotic
Compelling one to return.

I would not say the above lines qualify as poetry, but I wrote them after going on a photographic safari in South Africa in the summer of 2002. If you ever have the opportunity to do the same, it is something you should unhesitatingly do, for you will never regret the experience. Africa is gripping. It is a magical, mystical experience to travel through the bush and see what God and nature have created.

The safari was a gift from Keeneland, presented to me upon my departure as chairman of the board. I was to remain (and would remain for five years) as a Keeneland trustee. But Keeneland was generously providing me with an opportunity to visit a corner of the globe I had never gone to before. And something I have never grown weary of is seeing the wonders of the world. My companions on the safari were D. G. Van Clief and his wife, Trish, and Dr. Jim Holloway and his wife, Kay. D. G. and I, as previously noted, worked together at the Breeders' Cup. Jim and I grew up together and were colleagues at Yale. What we saw and photographed was unforgettable—beautiful, extensive landscapes, free of the erosions of civilization, populated by the most varied species of animals imaginable.

The initial leg of the two-week trip took us to Cape Town. We spent a day at the Cape of Good Hope Nature Reserve, from where we ventured to several wine estates, sampling the local fare. The following day, we began our journeys into the bush. We visited Thornybush, a private game reserve adjacent to the 7,332-square-mile Kruger National Park in the northern portion of South Africa. It was there that we commenced our search for Africa's famed "Big Five," which are lions, leopards, rhinoceroses, buffalo, and elephants. We then were transported by a light airplane to the Sangita Private Game Reserve, which is also adjacent to Kruger.

The camps we stayed at had names such as Sussi and Chuma and Royal Malewane. They were luxurious—there were lavatories, showers, tubs, air-conditioning, heat, excellent food, and impeccable service by the native South Africans. But the camps were also constructed so that they blended in beautifully with the landscape. Each morning, we got up at six o'clock and went to the main lodge for coffee, tea, and rolls. Then we would load up, the five of us, in a Land Rover, accompanied by the guide (or "ranger," as he was properly called) and tracker, who would stay with us the entire time at a particular camp. The mornings were brisk, and we would be bundled up in sweaters and gloves, and there were blankets in the Land Rover we could also use. By midmorning, though, the temperature would be in the mid-seventies, perfect weather in which to shoot photographs.

I cannot understand what sort of thrill might be involved in using a high-powered rifle and telescopic sight and killing an animal that is 1,500 yards away. But the challenge and thrill of using a telescopic or, better yet, a close lens to photograph an animal, be it walking or loping, grazing or charging, is to me a thrill almost beyond description. And with a camera, you have the satisfaction of being able to capture the moment and share it with others forever.

Throughout the bush there are little sand roads, and they led us across country. We would periodically hear on the Land Rover's intercom that there was a herd of zebras or elephants ahead, or a pride of lions, or antelopes or rhinoceroses, four or five miles away.

The tracker was a fascinating person. Those involved in his profession go to school and receive training, but knowledge of the subtleties that trackers look for is passed down from one generation to another. And in Africa, tracking tends not to be done by part-timers. Trackers are devoted to what they do and make lifetime commitments to be in that field. There was a seat on the left front fender of our vehicle. Our tracker would sit there, and by subtle arm and hand signals, just a slight indication of his wrist or fingers, signal the driver to go right or left. Befitting his occupational title, the tracker was looking for tracks, and it was remarkable how he was able to identify them by species. Of course, just about anybody can identify an elephant track. But he could immediately sort out the footprints of a giraffe from those of an antelope, or a zebra's footprints from a water buffalo's. He would see the impressions in the sand and direct the driver accordingly. And suddenly, 300 or 400 yards out, or perhaps as far as a half mile away, we would see a group of fifty or sixty animals, or maybe hundreds of them. We saw and photographed hippopotamuses, cheetahs, giraffes, and crocodiles (the guide told me I got too close when I was taking photographs of those).

At about 10:30 A.M., after being out in the bush for four hours, we would return to the camp for breakfast—eggs, omelettes, bacon, waffles, cakes, toast, and lots of very good fruit. Following that meal, we would go to our lodges (we each had one) to shower, shave, rest, and read, whatever we wanted to do. There would be a light lunch at 1:00 P.M., and at 2:30 P.M. we would get in the Land Rover and go to a different area of the bush. We would stay out for another four hours, seeing more animals, taking more photos, and then our driver, guide, and tracker would stop and set up tables for an "African Sundowner." Sandwiches, scotch, bourbon, vodka, and white wine would be brought out, and we talked and gazed over the land and watched the sun go down. When darkness came, we would start off in the pitch black for the one-and-a-half-hour journey back to the camp, where we'd have dinner and drinks and then retire—half exhausted, but immensely thrilled by the activities of the day.

§

Toward the end of the trip, we went to Zimbabwe and stayed at the Royal Livingstone, which is right at Victoria Falls and is one of the grand hotels in the world. Photos simply cannot reflect the mammoth majesty of Victoria Falls—you have to be there, viewing the scene with your own eyes, the falls themselves and miles of mist that they create.

There is a ledge that goes along opposite to the falls and takes you across several canyons. The ledge extends for about a mile or so. We were outfitted in slickers and took the walk, with the tremendous roar of the cascading water accompanying us every step. It's breathtaking to see it and to hear it. And all the time we were being drenched by the overpowering, engulfing mist.

Four of us chartered a boat and guide and embarked on a half-day trip that took us about twenty miles up the Zambezi River. It's the fourth longest river in Africa and the largest that flows from that continent into the Indian Ocean. The portion we went on was three-quarters of a mile wide and had islands on it. We were passing one of them when the guide pointed toward the vast expanse of the river and said, "Look!" We thought at first that we were looking at a big snake, perhaps a python. Then we realized it was the trunk of an elephant swimming across the river. His trunk was above the water, allowing him to breathe. The islands have pastures deep with grass, and the elephant was going from one island to another.

It was extraordinary, being able to see so many species of African wildlife in their native habitats. But we saw images relating to humanitarian concerns that we could not ignore either. The small airplanes we traveled in would fly into these little airports with grass landing strips. The airports were about eight to ten miles from the camps, and we would be driven through villages populated by hundreds and hundreds of people, most of them barefoot and barely clothed. A major means by which these people support themselves is the gathering of wood. We saw them, wearing little headbands, pulling carts laden with the wood for miles. They used the wood for fuel for cooking and heating in their grass huts, but also to sell. I have read about the problems with diseases in this part of the world, particularly with HIV, but to actually see this stream of humanity struggling to support themselves leaves an impression one never forgets. I am not going to suggest that I know what to do about this, that I am privy to the location of a gigantic magic wand that, if waved properly, will make the poverty and suffering all go away. During the 1990s, South Africa rid itself of its apartheid statutes, but many millions of the country's citizens still live in poverty. Zimbabwe, which borders South Africa, has even more problems, and one cannot venture to that part of the world without becoming aware of them. Just a few decades ago, Zimbabwe was referred to as the "Breadbasket of Central Africa." But the regime of the dictator Robert Mugabe evicted the British and Dutch farmers whose plantations had provided the agricultural exports that constituted the staples of Zimbabwe's trade. Their properties have been redistributed to the native population, a few acres per family, who have the ability to produce only what they can consume or utilize or sell to one another. Meanwhile, the modern technology the Europeans used—the farm equipment, fertilizer, and sophisticated methods of harvesting—was abandoned, and the ability to mass-produce agricultural goods in Zimbabwe vanished in the wind. The millions and millions of pounds of wheat and cattle products the country used to export disappeared with it. The same is true for about 60 percent of Zimbabwe's wildlife. The country once had the largest concentration of black rhinoceros in the world, but the herd has declined dramatically (this is something I found out during the trip). Deforestation, land erosion, toxic waste, and heavy metal pollution caused by archaic mining practices and water and air pollution—all are slowly strangling Zimbabwe. The country has freed itself from its colonial yoke and at the same time has imprisoned itself in a chaos of economic and social ruin.

I do not know what to suggest should be done about all this. Who does? But neither do I want people to get the impression that my travels through these parts of the world have occurred with a "blinkers on" view, basking in the scenic rewards of the trips while being totally oblivious to what else is going on.

Of course, the greatest benefit such travel has provided for me is experiencing the different cultures and the environments in which they exist. Our human universe is vast, and there are infinite options out there to see more and learn more, regardless of our ages and past experiences. If one's mental geography spans no more than Kentucky or the South, the abilities to compare and contrast are handicapped and forever will be. For the only thing one will really know is his or her native region. Maybe it is trite to say so, but I will always relish and cherish the memories of my trip to Africa. And I have the photographs to remind me how wonderful an experience it was.

§

Now I am going to tell you about two of my dearest friends, one separated from me by the Atlantic Ocean and the other by the Pacific. I refer to them as the "Duke" and the "Ambassador." They are Peregrine Andrew Morney Cavendish, the twelfth Duke of Devonshire, and Andrew Sharp Peacock, who among other deeds was twice elected leader of Australia's Liberal Party and subsequently served as his country's ambassador to the United States from 1996 to 1999.

I first met the Duke at Belmont Park in late October 1990. He was then formally known as the Marquess of Hartington and was in a group of Europeans who were wildly celebrating the victories by Royal Academy in the Breeders' Cup Mile and In the Wings in the Breeders' Cup Turf. The Duke, who also goes by the nickname "Stoker," quickly revealed himself to be a man of quick wit and a quicker mind. For 500 years, the Cavendish family has ranked among the richest and most influential in England, but Stoker wears his mantle of aristocracy like an old hat—it fits him perfectly and he is completely comfortable with it. His stature among English horsemen is immense. Stoker bears the title of Her Majesty's Representative at Ascot. He is also chairman of the Ascot course, which is one of the oldest (founded 1711) and most heralded in the world—Queen Elizabeth II actually owns it. Stoker became senior steward of the British Jockey Club in 1989, and four years later he helped create and became the first chairman of the British Horseracing Board, which is now the governing authority for racing in his home country.

For those who refuse to budge from traditional viewpoints or practices, beware of Stoker, because with him, change is inevitable. Commencing in 2004, major portions of venerable, august, hallowed Ascot—including the Royal Box and grandstand—were demolished. Their places were taken by a new, $347 million facility that opened in 2006. The British turf writer Richard Griffiths described it as "a devastatingly ambitious project" and "an absolute cracker."

During my tenure as chairman of the World Series Racing Championship (WSRC), Stoker was the vice chairman. Initially, the series involved nine grade 1 and group 1 million-dollar events run classic distances at tracks in eight countries: the Dubai World Cup at Nad Al Sheba in the United Arab Emirates, the King George VI and Queen Elizabeth Diamond Stakes at Ascot, the Irish Champion Stakes at Leopardstown, the

Canadian International Stakes at Woodbine near Toronto, the W. S. Cox Plate at Moonee Valley in Australia, the Breeders' Cup Turf and Breeders' Cup Classic, the Japan Cup at Tokyo Race Course, and the Hong Kong Cup at Sha Tin. The idea was to take major Thoroughbred races from around the globe and link them together by means of a point system similar to formula 1 Grand Prix. By year's end, the horse that accumulated the greatest number of points would be honored as the World Series champion. The series eventually would include the Arlington Million at Arlington Park near Chicago; the Grosser Preis von Baden at Baden-Baden in Germany, the Prix de l'Arc de Triomphe at Longchamp near Paris, the Queen Elizabeth II Cup at Sha Tin, and the Singapore International Cup. This brought the totals to fourteen stakes in eleven countries (on five continents).

Coordinating the series was a monumental task. There were cultural differences we had to deal with, differences in languages, political differences. There also were fairly intense rivalries between the racing authorities in England and France, Tokyo and Hong Kong, and so forth. The Japan Cup and Hong Kong Cup were separated by only three weeks on the calendar, and the Japan Racing Association and the Hong Kong Jockey Club annually vied for the same horses to compete in their events.

Thanks be to God we had Stoker—throughout our tenure with the WSRC, he was a source of creative ideas and business logic. Stoker was resolute when controversy arose, yet he was always open to reasonable compromise. He never missed a crucial meeting, be it in New York or Hong Kong or wherever. Stoker roamed through the backsides of racetracks on four different continents with the same ease that he moved through realms of royalty.

You could never predict, be it in Stoker's professional or personal dealings, what he might do at a given moment. One Stoker incident I will always recall occurred on October 27, 2001. The Breeders' Cup had been held that day, again at Belmont Park, and it was also the day following my eightieth birthday. A group of us had returned to the Plaza Hotel on Fifth Avenue and were socializing in the Persian Room, which had been set up as a hospitality center for VIP owners, breeders, and other guests from overseas. I was determined that my birthday would go unnoticed—what man wants to advertise the fact that he's eighty? On one side of the room there was an array of racing items and memorabilia, along with products from the sponsors of the Breeders' Cup races. They were being used for a silent auction to help raise funds for the victims of 9/11, which had occurred one and a half months earlier. Stoker, sharing the conviviality of the evening, was examining a John Deere tractor-mower. My former Breeders' Cup secretary, Deborah Lynch, was in charge of the hospitality room and silent auction, and she noticed Stoker's interest in the tractor-mower. She walked up to him and asked, "Would you be interested in submitting a bid?"

"Thank you, but no," said Stoker. "It would be rather impractical for you to ship the machine to England."

But Deborah persisted. "Did you know," she asked Stoker, "that yesterday was Mr. Bassett's birthday? Why don't you enter a bid on his behalf?"

"Does Ted have a lawn?" Stoker asked.

"Why yes, of course he does," responded Deborah.

So Stoker submitted a bid that was a trifle higher than the previous one. And several minutes later, his bid was proclaimed the winner. At that point, Stoker strolled across the crowded room and in a voice unusually loud for him said, "Ted, I hear it's your birthday today. Is it true that you're really eighty years old?"

I was seriously provoked. Well, okay, I was outraged! My secret was finally out! All those years of covering up my age had gone for naught! I let Stoker know of my displeasure. "How inconsiderate can you be? How dare you do that?" But I repented several weeks later when the spanking new John Deere tractor-mower he had purchased was delivered to Lanark Farm, where Lucy and I immediately put it to good use.

§

The first time I met Andrew Peacock was at a luncheon at Keeneland hosted by Will Farish. Andrew had recently been appointed as Australia's ambassador to the United States. (Farish himself would later serve a three-year tenure as U.S. ambassador to Great Britain and Northern Ireland.) At the time, Andrew was visiting Kentucky as the guest of Will and his wife, Sarah, attending the races and touring the horse farms.

Andrew is one of those people who have never met a stranger. And he certainly was no stranger to Australian politics. Elected to his country's parliament when he was only twenty-seven years old, he became known within Melbourne political circles as the "Colt from Kooyong." All told, he has held six Australian cabinet positions. At age thirty-six, he became Australia's minister for foreign affairs. Twice, Andrew was his party's choice for prime minister, but he lost those elections to the Labour Party candidate, Bob Hawke. Andrew was also something of an international playboy—for a time, he was the beau of the actress Shirley MacLaine.

Our friendship began when Andrew renewed his real passion, which is horse racing. While ambassador to the United States, he was named to serve as a director of Moonee Valley, which as I mentioned before is the site of the Cox Plate. Andrew was a strong supporter and promoter of international racing, and he provided a solid bridge between the authorities that governed the sport in the Southern and Northern Hemispheres.

If there was a category in the *Guinness Book of World Records* regarding "the most congenial traveling companions," Andrew would be listed among them. We have shared many hilarious, ear-splitting times together across the United States, Europe, and Dubai. No one loves a single malt scotch, a piano, and collegial song more than Andrew. Together, we have managed to drown out more talented songsters and have fumbled for more lost lyrics than either of us could ever count. One evening at the Ritz Carlton bar in Dubai, Andrew and I were with Omar Assi, singing chorus after chorus of "Volare":

> Volare! Oh, Oh!
> Cantare! Oh, Oh, Oh, Oh!
> Nel blu! dipinto di blu . . .

This went on and on until the exhausted pianist, gasping for release, pleaded with security personnel to escort the three of us from the hotel. Which they forcibly did, much to the chagrin of us and the relief of the remaining revelers.

The WSRC board met in late January of each year in New York, and it was the custom of the chairman to host a cocktail reception and dinner. After cocktails at the Plaza, we would motor up to 21 for dinner. The evening would include lots of good wine, lots of good food, and good company. The party tended to extend into the early hours of the following morning. One year, we exited 21 to find New York engulfed in a blizzard. Anyone who has ever visited New York during those conditions knows how difficult it is to find a taxi. All the other members of the board crowded into a waiting limousine. But there wasn't enough room for Andrew and me, and we found ourselves alone and forlorn, standing on the curb. After a frantic and futile search for a taxi, we decided to brave it out and walk the ten blocks to the Plaza. One week later, I was in Saint Joseph Hospital in Lexington, recuperating from pneumonia. At the same time, Andrew was confined to the Australian embassy in Washington, D.C., recovering from the flu. It was a painful lesson for both of us, and another example where Bacchus has drowned more men than Neptune.

In the spring of 2002, both Andrew and Stoker came to the Kentucky Derby. Lucy and I invited them to join us at Lanark for a post-race dinner party. At Lanark, another impromptu songfest ensued, and this time there was a nobler exit from the premises than we experienced in Dubai.

Six years ago, Andrew married Penne Percy Korth, a former Texas beauty queen who also served as U.S. ambassador to Mauritius, a small island nation off the coast of Africa in the southwest sector of the Indian Ocean. Andrew retired as president of Australia Boeing in 2007, and he is now pretty much a man of leisure. On occasion, he still ventures across the oceans wide to Keeneland. And to this day, Andrew steadfastly believes that if he had won the election for prime minister over Hawke, there would have been no need for an unknown Kentuckian to have presented the Melbourne Cup in 1986. For Andrew would have attended the event, indeed, dressed in top hat and cutaway.

Stoker became the Duke of Devonshire when his father passed away in May 2004. Among his other duties, he is guardian of Chatsworth House, which is the centerpiece of a 35,000-acre estate that includes castles, hotels, magnificent gardens, and centuries of other heirlooms—something like 600,000 people visit Chatsworth annually.

These are two gentlemen, two colleagues, whose paths likely would have never crossed with mine were it not for the allure of horse racing, that magnet that crisscrosses the globe and energizes friendships.

§

Delivering a speech is not a task I handle easily. I am sure there are people who would say, "Oh, come on, Bassett, you've done a thousand of them." Well, yes, but my response to that is I have yet to do a speech with which I have been 100 percent satisfied.

I am a strong believer in careful preparation. My Kent School training has got a lot to do with this. As does my Yale training and my Marine Corps training. I do research. I ask others (particularly the Keeneland librarians, Cathy Schenk and Phyllis Rogers) to assist me with additional facts. I write my early drafts of the speech in longhand. Only the final draft gets typed up. Even then, I am constantly trying to improve it—to the point where I bring a tape recorder with me in the car, and as I'm driving to wherever the speech is going to be given, I'm still refining a phrase here, a sentence there.

You see, I can recall the one time when I did not prepare, and although it was more than forty years ago, it still bothers me. It was during my directorship of the State Police, and the speech was in northern Kentucky to a Rotary Club audience. It had been a busy day, and I had been rushing around. I remember thinking, "Hey, I've spoken publicly about this subject many times before. I don't need to brush up." I have never considered myself to be a very smart person, but I do have a strong sense of recall. I have the ability to read a page several times and then visualize what is on it. At the Rotary Club meeting, we ate dinner. I was introduced. And I stood up and started to speak, and I was awful. My message wandered. I failed to emphasize, or even mention, several key points pertaining to the subject. People applauded when I was finished, but I sat down knowing I had made a mess of it. That time. But never again.

There are self-imposed rules I follow. Be articulate, and keep the momentum going. A speaker who simply reads from a text is apt to lose half the audience by the time he has finished the third paragraph. A speech should be delivered in a conversational tone. The impression should be that you are speaking off the cuff (even though you're not). Never, ever, start off a speech with a half-baked joke. If humor is going to be included, keep it self-deprecating. I tell the audience about the mistakes I've made and avoid making mention of anyone else's transgressions.

I'll tell you about a speech I gave recently of which I am particularly proud. It occurred at a meeting of the board of trustees of Transylvania University in May 2008. Dr. Charles Livingston Shearer was completing his twenty-fifth year as Transylvania's president. The speech had a dual purpose: to honor Dr. Shearer and to provide a moment that a hardworking mother would cherish for the remainder of her life. Here is how this blended together. Josephine Shelton is the assistant manager in the Keeneland track kitchen. She gets up at 3:30 A.M. six days a week to be at the kitchen by 5:00 A.M. Josephine is a single mom. She has a son named Charles Matthew Wilmore. About five years ago, Josephine approached me one morning and asked if I could provide advice about her son applying for college. She believed that a college education would provide Matthew with a better lifestyle and a better life experience than she has had. I asked her, "Where does Matthew go to high school?"

She replied, "Lafayette."

I said, "What kind of student is he."

She replied, "Very good."

I said, "Well, more than that, what was his ACT score?"

Josephine, with a great deal of pride in her voice, replied, "A 29."

I said, "Well, maybe we should think about Transylvania."

Josephine said, "That's a private university, isn't it? And the tuition is expensive, much higher than at a state university?"

I said, "That's true, but there are opportunities for scholarships and financial aid. Let's look into it."

I set up an appointment for Josephine and Matthew with Dr. Shearer, and he was cordial and enthusiastic. He is a president with an open-door policy, which is among the many reasons why he is so valuable to Transylvania. Dr. Shearer outlined a financial plan that involved a combination of scholarships, grants, and loans. Matthew sent his application to Transylvania, it was accepted, and he began pursuing a degree with dual majors in anthropology and sociology. At the same time, Matthew took on full-time jobs. He initially worked the night shift at Toyota. During his sophomore year, he had two jobs, one at Transylvania and another at Target. During his junior and senior years, Matthew worked at the University of Kentucky Hospital and Markey Cancer Center. And throughout this period, he continued his degree program.

All went well until midway through Matthew's senior year. At that point, he lacked two necessary courses, and the only times they were offered during the spring term conflicted with his work schedule at UK. Matthew could take the courses the following fall. But the situation prohibited him from graduating with his class in May. This was extremely disappointing to Matthew. And Josephine was crushed—she had long held the dream of seeing her son walk across the Transylvania stage, wearing cap and gown, and receiving his diploma. But there would be no commencement ceremony following the culmination of the fall term. Diplomas are simply sent out by mail.

Rules are rules, and mandates for graduation are clear, precise, and documented. But room existed to be creative. Matthew had worked so hard, had been so studious and diligent. I thought, "What might the possibility be of allowing him to wear the cap and gown, walk across the stage, and receive a blank diploma?" After all, Matthew was going to complete the two courses he needed during the fall term. His real diploma would then be secured. The facts of the situation were presented to Dr. Shearer. He conferred with faculty members. The decision was made to allow Matthew to participate in the spring commencement and receive what in essence was a blank diploma. But there was a final touch I hoped would be added, and I made my plea for it during my speech at the board of trustees meeting.

I spoke about Dr. Shearer's quarter century of service as Transylvania president, about what a perfect fit he was for the university. I talked about how he had reengaged, revitalized, and unified the faculty; about how he had increased Transylvania's endowment sevenfold to more than $140 million and how during his tenure the size of the student body had nearly doubled to 1,153. Beyond all that, I spoke about Dr. Shearer's greatest legacy being his sense of purpose, about his ability to understand Transylvania through the eyes of its students, as he catered to their needs and nurtured their ambitions. I then related the story of Charles Matthew Wilmore. And I concluded the speech by saying: "When Matthew Wilmore trails across that graduation stage, Mr. President, I hope that when you shake his hand, you will also pause for a moment and look out on the audience, so that lady from the Keeneland kitchen, that proud mom, can have the photo opportunity of her lifetime!"

On May 24, Matthew Wilmore walked across the Transylvania stage, received the blank diploma, and shook Dr. Shearer's hand. They paused for a moment, gazed at the audience, and Josephine Shelton took the photo she had long dreamed of taking. The following week, Josephine brought the photo over to the Keeneland Cottage and, with her face beaming, showed it to me. If that's not a happy ending to a wonderful story, I don't know what is.

§

The Charles Matthew Wilmore situation was one where my instincts were correct. I will now tell you about one of the most colossal errors in judgment I ever made—one that fortunately did not have lasting effects.

Back in 1958, I served as Yale's alumni representative and chairman of its enrollment and scholarship committee for the eastern half of Kentucky. One of my responsibilities was to interview high school students

351

who had applied for admission to Yale and were in need of financial assistance. The usual procedure was for Yale to forward a list of the applicants to me, and then I would conduct a personal interview with each of them. In the winter of 1958, one of the half dozen applicants I interviewed was Lance Liebman. He was from a local high school in Frankfort. I instructed Lance to meet me in my at office at the Kentucky State Police headquarters. It didn't occur to me that the environment where the interview was to be conducted might be somewhat intimidating to a teenager. During the interview, Lance's demeanor was shy, retiring, and unassuming He did not impress me as having a burning desire to attend Yale. I asked him the usual mundane questions about his involvement in high school extracurricular activities and student government and what his views were of local and national affairs.

After Lance left my office, I wrote on the Yale recommendation form that in my opinion this applicant from a rather small high school might experience difficulty in adjusting to the larger scene of undergraduate university life and the stress of Yale's academic demands. In essence, I gave Lance a thumb's down. Apparently, the officials at Yale saw something in Lance's record that I didn't, and they admitted him. He subsequently became the first student and youngest ever to be appointed to the Yale Corporation Board. In 1962, he graduated summa cum laude. Two years later, Lance received a master's degree in history from Cambridge University in England. He then entered Harvard Law School, where he became president of the *Harvard Law Review* and graduated magna cum laude in 1967.

And oh, it gets even better (or worse, depending upon your point of view). After serving as a law clerk for U.S. Supreme Court Justice Byron White, Lance became an assistant to Mayor John V. Lindsay of New York City. In 1970, Lance returned to Harvard Law School and became a full professor and associate dean. And in 1991, he became dean of the Columbia University Law School, and eight years later he was named director of the American Law Institute.

Fortunately, Yale's officials had the wisdom, experience, and foresight to recognize that Lance Liebman was a prospective student jewel who could go on to be an exemplary alumnus. As for my evaluation of his prospects—what witless and baseless words they were! How wholly wrong can one person be?

Today, when I review Lance's career, I am not merely respectful of what he has accomplished in the fields of academics and jurisprudence. I am in awe. And I will always feel the sting of embarrassment for my doltish comments of fifty-one years ago and my failure to recognize a young man's zeal to learn and will to achieve.

§

The Marine Corps will always be tied to my heart. A project I was involved with in recent years is the construction of the National Museum of the Marine Corps in Quantico, Virginia, near Interstate 95, just thirty miles from the White House. It is truly a marvelous facility, situated on a 135-acre plot, with a main structure that encompasses 118,000 square feet of floor space. The museum was dedicated on November 10, 2006, by President George W. Bush. I was there, and I will always remember what he said: "These walls remind all who visit here that honor, courage, and commitment are not just words. They are core values for a way of life that puts service above self. And these walls will keep the history of the Marine Corps alive for generations of Americans to come."

One of the more striking components of the facility is its 210-foot spire, which is made of stainless steel and rises well over the lines of surrounding trees. The spire is visible from miles away, during the day and throughout the night. Admission to the museum is free. Inside, one can take a walk through more than two centuries of Marine Corps history. Among the items displayed are a replica of the crow's nest on the USS *Constitution*, the original flag raised on Mount Suribachi in 1945, and a tank from the Persian Gulf War.

The exhibit galleries, which utilize multimedia technology, transport visitors to such locales as the Marine Corps boot camp on Parris Island, a landing beach on Iwo Jima, and a nighttime watch post on the mountainous line that separates South Korea from North Korea. There are recorded voices of Marines telling their stories firsthand and the three-acre Semper Fidelis Memorial Park, with monuments to Marine Corps organizations and the men and women who served in them. The walkways of the park are lined with commemorative bricks donated by families and friends of Marine Corps veterans.

Lieutenant General Ron Christmas was in charge of the $50 million fund-raising campaign to help build the museum. I remember saying to him at the beginning of the campaign, "General, 85 to 90 percent of us who served in the Marine Corps had a life-changing experience. I know we want to reach out to those with deep pockets, those who can write a check for six or maybe even seven figures. But we need to reach out to all those others too. The ones who will send $100 or just $10, and perhaps just a single dollar. And it doesn't just have to be Marines who saw combat. We need to have a computer file listing everybody who has ever been honorably discharged from the Corps and make contact with all of them. Maybe 50 percent won't contribute, but the other 50 percent will."

I did not have any statistical data to back me up—but sometimes, you don't need it. Your intuition is enough. Every former Marine went through the crucible of boot camp, and it is rare to find one who does not appreciate the immense pride, purpose, and sense of mission that were instilled during the Marine Corps experience. And not surprisingly, thousands and thousands of former Marines sent donations. The money was raised, the museum was built, and it will now be open to visitors from all future generations. And I'm proud that in my very small way, I helped make this happen. If it involves the Marine Corps, I am always looking to do more.

§

Revolutionary concepts, especially ones pertaining to the welfare of Thoroughbreds and the people who handle them, always gain my attention. During the past seventeen years, I have shared a special friendship and working relationship with Dr. Philip E. Shrimpton and his wife, Catherine Davis. They are an intriguing couple, blessed with an intellectual curiosity and an extraordinary work ethic. Their goal is to make horse racing a much safer sport, and they have done so by inventing a new form of weight pads for jockeys and vastly improved padding for starting gates.

I first met them following a speech I had given upon receiving the John H. Galbreath Award from the University of Louisville's Equine Industry Program in 1992. During the question-and-answer session with students that followed the award ceremony, I conveyed the message that Keeneland was always seeking to explore new products and techniques. Phil and Cathy subsequently read a transcript of my remarks and made an appointment to meet with me. Phil has a veterinary degree from Ohio State University and had spent three years as state veterinarian for the Kentucky Racing Commission. "During that time, I examined over 10,000 horses on race days at various Kentucky tracks," he told me. "I was at the starting gate for every race. I saw what went on."

Back then, Phil and his wife were in the early process of designing cushioned weight pads for jockeys. The pads would provide an alternative to the lead-carrying pouches riders had been required to carry for well over a century to comply with the weight assignments given to horses in a given race. The idea was to create pads that would fit comfortably over a horse's back and distribute weight evenly. It didn't take me long to grasp the merit of what Phil and Cathy were trying to do, and I told them that henceforth they could count on me to be in their corner.

In the ensuing years, Keeneland became a laboratory for their work. There has been a lot of trial and error, modification, and revision. But the result is the development of Best Pad Race Weight Pads, made of felt, vulcanized rubber, and high-density polymer, that sit under the jockey's saddle and completely replace the need for pouches containing lead bars. The pads range in weight from one to twenty-five pounds. Major American racetracks, including Keeneland, Churchill Downs, Del Mar, and Santa Anita, have purchased sets of them, and Hall of Fame jockeys such as Pat Day and Jerry Bailey purchased sets for their private use before they retired. And the race pads are now used in eleven foreign countries too, including Dubai, Hong Kong, and South Korea.

Phil and Cathy are self-taught in the discipline of polymer chemistry (which involves condensing small molecules into a compound of higher molecular weight) and have used that knowledge in developing their padding for starting gates. Among other ingredients, this padding uses "memory foam," which was initially developed by the National Aeronautics and Space Administration (NASA) for space shuttle seats. Eight tracks, including Keeneland, currently utilize the padding, and it has reduced injuries (among horses, jockeys, and assistant starters) at the gate. And it has correspondingly reduced the number of "gate scratches," which can decimate wagering pools, especially when a favorite is involved.

I will confess that Phil is not always easy to understand—his mind is forever at work, always thinking, assessing, analyzing. I recall having breakfast with him one morning in the Keeneland track kitchen, and Nick Zito sat down to join us. I introduced Phil to Nick and asked Phil to explain what he was doing. Phil started talking about polymers. And polyurethane, which is used with oil-drilling bits to reduce friction and is also used by Phil and Cathy to reinforce the skin of their starting gate padding. And memory foam. And the necessity of uniform weight distribution. The more Phil went on, the more technical he became. All the while, Nick sat there nodding his head. And I was nodding my head. And we both continued to nod our heads. Well, Phil eventually got up and left, and Nick then said to me, "General, I'm not sure how to tell you this—but what that guy was saying was all Chinese to me." And both Nick and I broke out in hysterical laughter. I'm not always sure what Phil is saying either. But I never question the immense value of what he and Cathy have done and continue to do. They are an unpretentious pair, dedicated to making racing a better and safer sport.

§

When thinking about my more than forty years of involvement with Thoroughbred racing, I often find myself concentrating more on the problems that were not solved rather than the ones that were. In the United States, the sport has made only minor strides toward implementing uniform medication rules and uniform fines and suspensions and installing uniform racing surfaces. We don't even have uniform pari-mutuel operations.

After working within the industry for four decades, I still cannot identify with certainty what its priorities are. It's my belief that the general public is equally perplexed and has expressed its displeasure in a very telling manner—by attending the races in steadily declining numbers and with steadily declining frequency. There are exceptions to these trends. The meets at Saratoga and, yes, at Keeneland continue to draw large crowds. The 2008 Keeneland spring meet recorded an average daily attendance of 15,225, the third highest in its history. Daily attendance for the 2008 fall meet averaged 14,065, the second highest in its history. But at the same time, Keeneland's daily wagering handle from all sources declined by $1.1 million during the 2008 spring meet and by $1.4 million during the fall meet. These figures represented drops of 10.9 percent and 17.8 percent, respectively, from the previous year. I know the economy is in enormous flux. But the declines in wagering on Keeneland races really discomfort me.

Many theories are being offered as to the reasons for the downturn in racing's popularity. One of the most valid, in my mind, is the intensified scrutiny and increasing public reaction to the debilitating injuries to horses, especially the ones that occur in our major, nationally televised events. The tragedies involving Barbaro in the 2006 Preakness and Eight Belles in the 2008 Kentucky Derby have effected widespread beliefs that racing has an image problem, a drug problem, an accountability problem. And the problems have all merged into a darkening cloud that has settled over the sport—a cloud filled with doubts concerning the humanitarian-ism within racing and the ethical treatment of horses.

I am not in any position to state why Barbaro and Eight Belles broke down. Veterinarians of global stature still puzzle over the reasons. But I am in a position to make a statement on a subject such as anabolic steroids—their use should be ruled illegal and eliminated in all racing jurisdictions. And this should not require any soul-searching. Pari-mutuel horse racing is currently conducted in thirty-eight states, and as of this writing, well less than half of them have banned the use of anabolic steroids.

In recent years, the media have often criticized racing for its lack of a national commissioner or "czar." Such a position would be endowed with the authority to make decisions and implement programs enhancing the integrity of racing and improving the health and welfare of horses. Under the regulatory systems currently in place, I don't think this will ever happen. The thirty-eight states with pari-mutuel racing within their boundaries are all subject to their own authorities. They are established by individual legislatures, their top officials are appointed by individual governors, and they are autonomous within their areas of jurisdiction. Almost always, where horse racing is involved, the state's self-interest has dominion over the industry's national interest. This curtails any meaningful authority a potential czar might have.

There have been two unsuccessful attempts to establish a national racing commissioner: when Thoroughbred Racing Associations (TRA) appointed J. Brian McGrath to the position in 1994 and when the National Thoroughbred Racing Association (NTRA) appointed Tim Smith to the position in 1998. McGrath was the former president of ISI Marketing, an international firm that had raised $170 million for the 1992 Winter and Summer Olympics. Smith had been a White House aide during the Jimmy Carter administration and was a former deputy commissioner and CEO of the Professional Golf Association (PGA) Tour. Both attempts failed, partially because McGrath and Smith were never accorded the clout to implement national policies. But while racing has been barely treading water, other professional sports have experienced enormous fan growth and economic success. Professional baseball, football, and basketball all have commissioners possessed of defined authority. They oversee structured franchises bound by corporate law. In contrast, horse racing has fragile, fragmented, and overlapping organizations, each of which is consumed by its own agenda, and each of which is pursuing the entertainment dollar by way of its own rudderless ship.

Every now and then, a small forward step is taken. The Association of Racing Commissioners International (RCI) has developed a uniform licensing application. But it needs to gain wider acceptance. And what about steps by individual state commissions, aggressively as a group, to achieve uniformity regarding medication rules and standards for racing officials? Will the realization ever take hold that there needs to be a common ground allowing for these steps to be taken? I heard these same questions being asked four decades ago. And they were greeted with the same muted, muddled responses as they are today. Oh yes, blue-ribbon committees have been appointed (I've certainly participated on my share of them). Recommendations have been written, amended, rewritten, bound together, perused, and then placed on shelves, where they have gathered lots of dust. But are there any solutions to the public's declining enthusiasm for horse racing? Or does only one solution remain—betting the farm on the fragile theory that converting tracks to semi-casinos and installing slot machines can ensure survival?

Even avowed traditionalists must admit that the lure of gambling is the magnet that attracts racing's fan base. By making a pari-mutuel wager, large or small, one becomes an active participant in a sporting event. But tell me, was it gambling alone that inspired all three of the major national radio networks to provide live coverage of the Alsab-Whirlaway match race at Narragansett Park in September 1942? Was it just the gambling aspect that lured a crowd of 51,122 to Aqueduct on the last day of October 1965 to watch Kelso win The Jockey Club Gold Cup for the fifth consecutive time? And was it merely racing's connection to gambling, its parimutuel payoffs, that put Secretariat on the covers of *Time, Newsweek,* and *Sports Illustrated* within a single week during the spring of 1973? Is it gambling alone that continues, today, to bring in those enormous crowds for our Triple Crown races? For the Travers Stakes at Saratoga? For the Blue Grass Stakes at Keeneland? Or does it really mean that racing, with its wonderful history, heritage, and traditions, is still capable of combining the spectacle of an event, the thrill of competition, and the excitement of a winning wager into something unique, enjoyable, and truly memorable?

The Thoroughbred racing industry needs to convene a national summit of six major organizations. It should include representation from the Horsemen's Benevolent and Protective Association (HBPA), because its members, by virtue of the Interstate Horse Racing Act of 1978, have authority over the simulcast signal. It should further include representation from the American Association of Equine Practitioners (AAEP), because its members have the greatest understanding of the effects of medication. Further, the summit should include representation from the TRA, because, even though this organization isn't nearly as prominent as it once was, its member tracks conduct the vast majority of racing in the United States. It should include representation from the Association of Racing Commissioners International, because their members have the responsibility of formulating the rules and determining the penalties for violating those rules in the individual states. I would like to see the summit include representation from the North American Graded Stakes Committee, because its members would have the authority to alter the status of major races. The Graded Stakes Committee has already made one important decision. In early August of 2008, it announced that if a racetrack or the state that it is in does not adopt the RCI's international model rule regarding anabolic steroids (which severely restricts their usage for horses in training), the stakes races at the track will be stripped of whatever graded status they have. A hypothetical example: if Keeneland was unwilling to mandate that participating horses in the Blue Grass Stakes must be free of anabolic steroids, the committee would void its grade 1 ranking.

And I would like to see the summit brought together by The Jockey Club, because it is the registrar for Thoroughbred racehorses in North America. The Jockey Club does not like working with the HBPA, but in this case, it would have to. The HBPA has the power to shut down simulcasting—and will do it, if for no other reason than it's not included in the determination of the resolutions.

I am specifying these organizations because they are in the best positions to make lasting impacts. I do not see the National Thoroughbred Racing Association being involved. I do not see the Thoroughbred Owners and Breeders Association (TOBA) being involved. And I do not see a consortium of racing fans in the mix. I want participation in the summit to be comprised of people who have enforcement powers.

There are four topics that would be on the table at the summit: (1) the medication issue; (2) the issue of safe racetrack surfaces; (3) national uniformity pertaining to licensing, fines, and suspensions; and (4) uniformity on commissions from simulcasting. Put anything on the table beyond that, and it will become hard to get anything resolved. But if the participants in the summit demonstrate the strength to institute changes within a narrow focus, as time goes on, they can make changes within a wider focus.

But you cannot have every single organization within the scope of the racing world involved. And you cannot try to resolve every issue confronting the sport in one huge swoop. Let's finally do something.

§

The Keeneland you see today is the result of nearly three-quarters of a century of nurtured tradition. But at the same time, Keeneland is a place that has flexed to the pressures of change, for it is a mistake to be uncompromisingly wedded to the ways of the past.

Keeneland's primary and basic keys to success can be traced directly to its original prospectus, which was written by the association's founding directors and is dated April 17, 1935. In part, the prospectus states:

What is here set forth is the shadow of a dream in that it envisions a creation the like of which has not been seen in America. But hard mathematics, solid common sense, substantial facts and the integrity of a community give substance and form to the dream. Here are set forth the mathematics and the facts for the consideration of those who would have the dream come true.

It is our desire that lovers of the Thoroughbred throughout the country will recognize in this a serious effort to establish a model race track, to perpetuate racing in the proper manner and to promote a course which will stand for many years as a symbol of the fine tradition of the sort.

In order to accomplish these ends we shall first ask the aid of sportsmen in building the track. Later we shall ask them to race their horses and to lend their own presence at the meetings. We shall ask the good will and active cooperation of many, for this is an enterprise which, if it proves successful, will be an everlasting credit to the sport of racing, not only in Kentucky, but throughout America.

As you can see, the prospectus had vision. It had validity. And it had unselfish purpose. These attributes remain as meaningful today as they did when the Keeneland Association was founded seventy-four years ago.

Keeneland's future will be assured and its mission will continue to be fulfilled as long as its management team continues to adhere to the basic principles of the prospectus. These include an emphasis on taste in lieu of crass commercialism. There must also remain a commitment to service above self. And I am not only talking about the Thoroughbred racing and breeding industry. Keeneland must also be devoted to dealing with the needs of the central Kentucky community. Those 1,024 acres adjacent to Versailles Road do not constitute an isolated island. They are vitally important to the Bluegrass region and to the people who live here. Keeneland's true mission is to be an industry and community catalyst, seeking and effecting solutions to problems. This is what its founders wanted, and this is what Keeneland should always be.

How do those of us who have served at Keeneland wish to be remembered? Well, I hope I am viewed as someone who helped nurture Keeneland's growth and expansion while at the same time guarding against any and all erosive threats to Keeneland's hallmarks—its intimate charm and ambience. It will always be important to remember that much, if not most, of Keeneland's success stems from the fact it is different from other racetracks. And it remains critically important to maintain that difference.

My days as assistant to Louis Haggin, as president, chairman of the board, and trustee of Keeneland, are now part of the past. I still hold the title of trustee emeritus, which is something of which I am immensely proud. My life has been a fascinating blur, and if I had one wish granted, it would be to do it all over again.

A Final Personal Note

ONE OF THE rewards of writing a personal narrative is that it provides an opportunity to thank those whose wise counsel and loyalty have helped me navigate those diverse twists and turns of my career. I have often pondered how to appropriately recognize this long list of exceptional and talented people who have contributed so much to whatever success I may have achieved. To list them all, in the fear of omitting some, would seem unwise. Following is a short list of those who were primarily responsible for helping to craft the major policy decisions that shaped my career and helped mask my shortcomings.

In the Kentucky State Police, I am deeply indebted to Colonels William O. Newman and Leslie C. Pyles, my two stalwart deputies, who ultimately became commissioners of the department themselves. To Governor Edward T. Breathitt, who had the courage and the fortitude to appoint an unknown, inexperienced person to such a sensitive, high-profile position.

My years at Keeneland would have been unnoted without the wise counsel of Louis Lee Haggin II and the loyal, ever-present support of Bill Greely, Stan Jones, Jim Williams, and Howard Battle.

It is impossible to recall those happy years at the Breeders' Cup without mentioning the friendship and guidance of D. G. Van Clief, Pam Blatz-Murff, and Ferguson Taylor.

An enthusiastic endorsement and congratulations to the present Keeneland staff, led by the very competent and personable Nick Nicholson, for their dedication and professionalism in managing the ever-changing challenges of the industry. My heartfelt wish to them for continued success, with a reminder to always "Hold High the Torch!"

Over the past half century, I have been truly blessed to have three extraordinarily talented, patient, and tolerant secretaries who through the years have never failed to put service above self: Mildred Salchli, Kentucky State Police, 1956–1967; Deborah Lynch, Breeders' Cup, 1988–1996; and my ever loyal, long-suffering, irreplaceable Beth Daugherty, Keeneland, 1977–2006.

To the University Press of Kentucky and its splendid staff headed by director Steven M. Wrinn, I extend my most sincere appreciation for the confidence you have had in this project since its inception and your willingness to accept the challenge of doing it.

Finally, to Keeneland—the matchless jewel of the Thoroughbred industry. Thanks for the privilege of serving. And thanks even more for the awesome memories, which will be treasured forever.

Chapter Notes
Sources, Afterthoughts, and Observations

This book was never intended to be an academic treatise, and we have not approached it as such. It is mostly made up of my personal reminiscences, complemented by other material that is utilized to add flesh to the many subjects we deal with, in order to give the reader a more complete understanding of the topics that are addressed.

When we first began working on the book in July 2005, it was agreed that, before starting the actual writing of any chapters, we had to accumulate at least 130,000 words in transcripts. This would be achieved by interviewing me and other people and then transcribing the interviews from tape recordings onto pages. I cannot tell you exactly how many hours, days, weeks, indeed, months, were devoted to this task. What I do know is that by the time the project was finished, our transcripts totaled nearly 220,000 words. The transcripts provided a rough outline for the material that would be included in the book. I say "rough outline" because the final product required much more than simply honing the interviews down to a 162,000-word manuscript.

In normal conversation, most people do not always speak in complete sentences, and the ideas they express are not always formulated in well-designed paragraphs. I am no different than anyone else in this regard. When speaking informally, I tend to jump from idea to idea, from subject to subject, in the same manner that other people do. And in many respects, this whole book is pretty much an informal conversation with the reader. It is as though we are all sitting at the table, with a bottle of wine in front of us, and I'm relating some stories to some friends who, I hope, are finding those tales interesting.

It is my further hope that many of my experiences are ones to which readers can relate. When I tell you in the opening chapter, for example, about Mr. Rosso throwing his handful of certified checks at me, and how I got down on my hands and knees to pick them up off the floor, I think many people can identify with that—for we all suffer embarrassments during our pursuits in the professional world. And in the chapter about Queen Elizabeth II, when the

Aga Khan and I fumbled the trophy exchange—had that embarrassing situation not occurred, I would have probably never given any thought to having a doctor examine my foot, and the melanoma on my toe might not have been diagnosed until it was too late. From difficult circumstances, good things often emerge.

But we did not intend this to be just a book of stories. I have done a lot of things in my life, and I've been able to see and in certain cases meet some historic figures and witness the history that surrounded them. Further, when you're in charge of running organizations such as the Kentucky State Police, the Keeneland Association Inc. or Breeders' Cup Ltd., there are laws, rules, and regulations that must be adhered to and business decisions that have to be made. It has been our goal, as well, to provide the reader with insight in regard to these responsibilities, which is why we devote space to such things as the Civil Rights Act of 1964 (State Police chapter), minus pools (Blue Grass Stakes chapter), and what is required of a racetrack to host the Breeders' Cup (Growth of Keeneland chapter). To date, I am the only person to have run both a racetrack and the Breeders' Cup, which allows me, I believe, a broader perspective than most people have on the subject.

The bulk of the actual writing of this book occurred in the Keeneland Library, where a vast array of source and source-checking material was available: the archives of the *Daily Racing Form;* the yearly editions of the *American Racing Manual;* media guides from Keeneland, Churchill Downs, the New York Racing Association, and many other tracks; and a variety of other publications, including complete collections of the *Blood-Horse,* the *Thoroughbred Record,* and the *Thoroughbred Times.* We made use of varied encyclopedias and the Internet. The one thing we did not rely upon, at any time, was guesswork. What we have presented to the reader within these pages is as accurate as we could make it.

What follows are some brief notes pertaining to each chapter.

1. Early Years at Keeneland

Billy Francis Jackson Bower, a wonderful friend who passed away at the age of eighty-six on May 30, 2006, spent portions of her final years working in the Keeneland Library. During that period, Billy completed a seven-volume collection of scrapbooks filled with James E. Bassett III memorabilia—newspaper and magazine articles, professional and personal correspondence, photographs, programs and entry badges from major racing events on these shores and overseas, and so on—which we used both as sources of information and as tools for framing timelines in the development of this book.

The late Kent Hollingsworth, who served as editor of the *Blood-Horse* magazine from 1963 to 1986 and had a law degree from the University of Kentucky, did a marvelous job covering the Keeneland horse sales for that publication. Not surprisingly, he provided detailed notice of the participation of Wendell P. Rosso in 1968. Kent's reportorial coverage of the litigation involving Dr. Arnold Pessin, Rex Ellsworth, the Keeneland Association et al. from 1967 to 1969 was equally superb and, four decades after the fact, was of immense assistance in reconstructing how the legal case developed and ultimately played out.

Stanley H. Jones retired from Keeneland in September 2000, but he continues to have an office next to mine in the cottage. Stan was one of more than forty people we interviewed. He retains great insights—on subjects ranging from Keeneland's proposed attempt to purchase majority stock in Churchill Downs in 1972 to the day when I was pulled over by Trooper H. C. Shipp on suspicion of stealing my own automobile.

2. Family Background and Kent School

Something I did not see us doing when we first embarked on the project was consulting Shelby Foote's three-volume series *The Civil War* (Random House, 1974) Granted, I'm old—but not that old! From Foote's marvelous research, we culled some information about the military career of my great-great-grandfather General William Temple Withers.

Kent, One Hundred Years, written and edited by Joan M. Beattie (Kent School, 2007), provided us with a great deal of historical background pertaining to that institution. Much of it, of course, was material I already knew, but we have strived to be as accurate as possible throughout this book, and Ms. Beattie's devotion to detail is greatly appreciated.

My own memories of the Reverend Frederick Herbert Sill, founder and headmaster of Kent School, remain very vivid. Father Sill tended to have that impact upon everyone with whom he came into contact. I wish I could say that I was one of his favorite students, but truthfully, I do not believe I was. A major reason for this is that I vacated the eight-oar shell after my second-form year at Kent to play on the school's baseball team. One of Father Sill's great passions was the varsity crew team, and in this regard, I probably disappointed him.

As emotionally difficult as it was to do, we read the local newspaper accounts of the automobile accident that took the lives of my brother and three others in 1941. We also read the police report of the accident and Brooker's death certificate. A pair of trips were made to the scene of the accident on Route 62 in Anderson County. Despite the passage of sixty-eight years, the roadway pretty much looks the same and remains one of the most dangerous stretches of highway in central Kentucky.

3. Yale and the U.S. Marine Corps

Alexander "Zandy" Harvey was consulted on several subjects in this chapter, particularly our high jinks during our Yale University days. But I did not need to consult anyone in regard to Parris Island—anyone who ever went through boot camp there will never forget the details of the experience.

Hold High the Torch: A History of the Fourth Marines, coauthored by Kenneth W. Condit and Edwin T. Turnbull (Battery Press, 1989), was one of several sources we consulted in regard to the unit's heritage and the Pacific campaign from 1941 to 1945. Another was the poignant article "A Long Walk through the Valley of Death" by Ronald J. Drez, which was published in the magazine *World War II Presents 1945: A Year in Review* (Primedia Enthusiast Group, 2005).

4. Postwar Experience

When talking about my years with the Great Northern Paper Company, we relied mostly on my memory. The Millinocket, Maine, Chamber of Commerce did provide us with some information pertaining to the history of that town. The routes I journeyed through the South during the period I was a newsprint salesman remain fixed in my mind.

Regarding some of the detail in this and other chapters, there undoubtedly will be readers who either say or think, "Oh come on, Bassett, you haven't committed all these things to memory!" Well, as noted earlier, of course I haven't—I don't believe anybody could. But we made great use of what is on library shelves, not only at Keeneland but throughout the Lexington area. College football, professional boxing, and major league baseball all have encyclopedias detailing the histories of those sports, and we relied on them for such things as the 42–6 score of the Notre Dame–North Carolina game in 1949.

As the years went on, John Morris and I became very close friends. We both served as directors and presidents with Thoroughbred Racing Associations Inc. John also chaired the Vanderbilt University–Grantland Rice Scholarship Committee, upon which I was a director. After John died in 1985, his heirs, upon my recommendation, established the John A. Morris Library at the Maxwell H. Gluck Equine Research Center at the University of Kentucky. The library was one of the very first electronic equine information centers in the nation.

5. State Police

Resistance on the Border: School Desegregation in Western Kentucky, 1954–1964, authored by David L. Wolford and published in *Ohio Valley History* (Summer 2004), helped us in understanding the link between the *Brown v. Board of Education* rulings (there were actually two of them, in 1954 and 1955) and the incidents in Sturgis and Clay, Kentucky, in 1956. The *Lexington Herald* provided extensive coverage of what occurred in both communities, and the paper's microfiche, which is available for use in the main branch of the Lexington Public Library, was also a source of some of the background material we used.

Among the most enjoyable experiences of this project were the interviews conducted with two men who served under me while I was with the State Police—William O'Connell Bradley and Alvie Dale Fortner. Alvie was with the force for twenty-eight years, and he remains extremely proud that he never, during all that time, unholstered his sidearm—Alvie credits his training for this.

Justice and Safety Education at Eastern Kentucky University: A Historical Perspective, edited by Richard Givan and Cynthia Miller (2002), is a publication based on the research of Dr. James McClanahan and Dr. Rhonda Smith. It details the birth of the program at EKU and its growth over the decades and is a treasure chest of information.

Sy Ramsey was the Associated Press reporter who covered my tenure as State Police director. Kyle Vance, Livingston Taylor, and Fred W. Luigart Jr. did the same for the *Louisville Courier-Journal.* Rereading the articles they wrote during that period provided a refresher course concerning such subjects as Trooper Island and the blue light law.

6. Growth of Keeneland

One of the more difficult tasks we had in constructing this chapter was determining who sat with D. Wayne Lukas in the Keeneland sales pavilion during the bidding battle for Seattle Dancer in July 1985. I had five names (including Lukas's). He had five names (including his own). But we were in agreement on only three of them. We consulted the coverage provided by the three major trade publications—the *Blood-Horse, Thoroughbred Record,* and *Daily Racing Form*—and received no further enlightenment. Keeneland has a videotape of the proceedings, but it pans past the Lukas group in an eye wink, and there are also several people standing in front of the group members, further shielding their identities. We finally solved the riddle by putting the Keeneland tape in a machine that allowed us to freeze-frame it. In doing so, we found out that my memory was faulty. But Lukas's memory was faulty as well. Thus, modern technology rescued Wayne and me from providing a false historical record.

Casey Carmichael, a master's degree candidate studying Latin and Greek languages at the University of Kentucky, has translated portions of the *Hippiater Expertus*. He says the title converts into English as "The Well-Trained Horse Doctor," which differs slightly from "The Expert Equine Practitioner," which is what we found from an unidentified source on the Internet. Six of one, half a dozen of the other—Casey is a UK boy, and we decided to go with his translation.

7. Queen Elizabeth II

Of all the chapters in the book, this is the one where I had to rely on my memory the most. We did not request an interview from the Queen, and if we had, I can give you a 100 percent guarantee she would have declined. We did obtain maps of the area around Windsor Castle and diagrams of Ascot Heath (Royal Ascot) racecourse to reinforce my recollections of the trip to the Queen's luncheon and the day at the races.

Bill Greely and I have had many conversations over the years about the Queen's visit, and we had several more during the writing of this book. I also relied heavily on Lucy's recollections in regard to both the Queen's visit to Keeneland and our visit to Windsor Castle and Ascot.

The scrapbooks that Billy Bower compiled contain many items of correspondence with the Queen's staff. Buckingham Palace sent us several photographs of the Aga Khan and me stooping down to pick up the trophy we had dropped.

8. The Blue Grass Stakes

There has yet to be a definitive history written about the Blue Grass Stakes, which is one of the reasons we developed this chapter the way we did. The Keeneland Library has copies of the charts of each edition of the race, including those conducted at the Kentucky Association track. The *Daily Racing Form* archive contains many in-depth articles about the Blue Grass, particularly from the years when Joe Hirsch journeyed in. Devoted horse racing fans may appreciate the detail we provided, while the casual reader may feel that we included too much information.

The reference to the sixty-nine editions of the Blue Grass Stakes that have been run at Keeneland to date is correct. That statistic does not include the 1943–1945 renewals of the race, which, though conducted by the Keeneland

Association, were actually run at Churchill Downs. None of those three re-newals produced a Kentucky Derby, Preakness, or Belmont Stakes winner. Keeneland's spring race meets were run at Churchill during the mid-1940s because of wartime travel restrictions—and the fall meets were not held at all.

Jim Williams, who is now in his thirty-seventh year at Keeneland, has excellent recall in regard to reporters from various publications who covered the Blue Grass over the years. The sportscaster Jim McKay, a great friend and proponent of racing, has told the story about seeing Alydar bow his head to Lucille Markey prior to the start of 1978 Blue Grass but did not mind relating it one more time. Jim passed away on June 7, 2008, and I would have so en-joyed the opportunity to present him with an inscribed copy of this book.

A number of Kentucky-based journalists have provided extensive and ex-cellent coverage of the Blue Grass and the events surrounding it over the de-cades. They include Billy Reed (a three-time Eclipse Award winner) of *Sports Illustrated,* the Louisville *Courier-Journal,* and the *Lexington Herald-Leader;* Maryjean Wall (a three-time Eclipse winner), who retired in June 2008 after covering racing for thirty-five years for the *Herald-Leader;* and Jennie Rees (a two-time Eclipse winner) of the *Courier-Journal.* We reread many of their ar-ticles, seeking nuggets of information and checking to see if my memories were in accordance with what they reported.

9. Lucy

My wife is forever a private person, but Lucy did agree to a formal interview, which occurred at Lanark Farm in January 2007. As is also the case with me, she has somewhat of a longing for the past. Lucy misses the July sale at Keene-land. "There were so many parties, so much festivity, it was a very gay time," she said. "And I don't think you have that any longer with the September sale."

The office of Geoffrey G. Russell, director of sales at Keeneland, provided us with a complete list of the yearlings Lucy has sold at the association's auc-tions. The list included prices and the names of the people who purchased the yearlings.

Jackie Hacker (formerly Jackie Chestnut) graciously contributed her memories concerning the championship golf match she and Lucy engaged in back in 1963.

10. Racing Personalities

D. Wayne Lukas and Nick Zito consented to extensive interviews, which were conducted during the summer of 2006 at the Saratoga racetrack.

Students of racing will note that Azeri was honored three times with

Eclipse Awards as Champion Handicap Mare, in the consecutive years 2002–2004. Further, she was North America's Horse of the Year in 2002. But during her first two championship seasons, Azeri was trained by Laura De Seroux. Accordingly, we list 2004 as the only year Azeri gained a championship while under Lukas's care.

The late turf writer Jim Bolus wrote several articles about Herb Stevens for *Keeneland Magazine* and other publications, and they were among the sources we used for stories about the Stevens family. The former jockey John Oldham was also a source of Herb Stevens tales.

We sent drafts of several chapters of this book to Joe Hirsch for his perusal. He specifically requested to read the one devoted to Queen Elizabeth II. Joe passed away on the morning of January 9, 2009.

11. The Breeders' Cup

From Breeders Cup Ltd., we secured race tapes that allowed us to transcribe the exact words that announcer Tom Durkin used during his calls of the events. Each year, the Breeders' Cup puts out a media guide that bulges with information—charts of prior editions of the individual races; owner, trainer, and jockey statistics; attendance figures; wagering figures. We made ample use of the 2007 guide for statistical information.

The tragic circumstances involving Go for Wand's death when she broke down in the 1990 Breeders' Cup Distaff will forever be blazed in Ron McAnally's mind. During the summer of 2007, Ron and I sat down in the cottage and had a conversation about it, which we recorded on tape. For the most part, Ron's recollections coincided with mine, and our reconstruction of the events of the day was a joint effort.

Perry Lefko's book *The Greatest Show on Turf: A History of the Breeders' Cup* (Daily Racing Form Press, 1996) provides a well-researched account of the conflict between Woodbine management and the pari-mutuel clerks that almost resulted in the event being moved to another track in 1996. Lefko, however, did not know about the telephone conversation I had with Ontario premier Michael Deane Harris while I was standing dripping wet in a New York hotel room wearing only a bathrobe.

Pam Blatz-Murff, who continues to serve as senior vice president of Breeders' Cup operations, has a superb memory concerning the participation of Ricks Natural Star in the 1996 Breeders' Cup Turf at Woodbine. Jim Gluckson, who has fulfilled the role of Breeders' Cup publicist for over two decades, was very helpful concerning the organization's dealings with Michael Letis and Michael Trager—as was Letis himself.

12. Trips as an Ambassador for Racing

Dr. Peter Timoney, former director of the Maxwell H. Gluck Equine Research Center at the University of Kentucky, explained during an interview in his UK office how important the Maktoum family's generosity was to the center's growth.

The complete texts of the speeches I prepared for the Carbine Club luncheon (which I largely didn't deliver) and the Race Horse Champion dinner (which I largely did, despite the fatal heart attack suffered by Monty Millson halfway through the speech) in 1986 are in volume two of the scrapbooks Billy Bower compiled. I also have a videotape, provided courtesy of the Victoria Racing Club, of my presenting the Melbourne Cup to Francesca de Burgh. Further, the scrapbook contains a copy of the article written by Jack Elliott, who viewed me as somewhat of a threat to Paul Hogan. Jack may have consumed several (perhaps more than several) bottles of Foster's Larger before he reached that conclusion.

For information regarding racetracks and major races in foreign countries, we primarily relied upon three sources: the *American Racing Manual* (Daily Racing Form Press, published annually—it also includes information from foreign lands); *The Directory of the Turf: The International Guide to Thoroughbred Racing and Breeding* (Tomorrow's Guide Ltd., United Kingdom, published annually); and *Thoroughbred Times Racing Almanac* (Thoroughbred Times Company, published annually).

Tom Thornbury, the associate director of sales at Keeneland, provided us with the statistics regarding the sale of horses at Keeneland auctions to buyers from Mexico.

13. The Ever-Evolving Economics of Racing

Alan Marzelli, who now serves as president and CEO of The Jockey Club, has a truly outstanding memory. We twice conducted lengthy interviews with Alan concerning the formation of Equibase.

Michael Wates and his staff were of assistance in recalling the details of the meeting with the European breeders' representatives in Newmarket in October 1989.

The Keeneland Library has a copy of the outline I used when making the "Mythical Armada" address before the Kentucky legislative committee in February 1994. It can be found in volume four of the scrapbooks that Billy Bower compiled.

14. Special People and Special Projects

Bill Cooke, the museum director at the Kentucky Horse Park; Jan Brucato, the president and director of the Lexington YMCA; and Susan Berry-Buckley and Jack Hillard, the former CEO and ongoing director of development, respectively, of the Central Kentucky Blood Center, were interviewed during the process of developing this chapter. Jan has recently changed jobs and is now a regional director for the national YMCA. And we would also like to mention that Jack, whose energy never seems to wane, is himself a cancer survivor. He is one of thousands who have benefited directly from the Blood Center.

Bill provided us with a list of those who made donations to save the Calumet trophies The list included names (except for those who wished to remain anonymous) and the amounts of money they contributed.

Margaret Glass, whose efforts figured so importantly in having Admiral and Lucille Markey at Alydar's Blue Glass in 1978 and in keeping the Calumet trophies in Kentucky, lived to the age of eighty-two. "Maggie," as her friends called her, passed away on August 2, 2003.

Phyllis Rogers, Lori Lilly, and Angel Stivers were all consulted as to their remembrances of the "mystery trip" to New York City in January 2003. With the assistance of these three ladies, we reconstructed (in chronological order) the sites and places we drove to and past that day. Angel has an archive of the trip: it includes the program from the musical *42nd Street* and the menu from the Rainbow Grill. I am quite certain she will never forget that trip. I know I won't.

15. Retirement—I Don't Have Time for That

The Keeneland Library has a copy of my itinerary during the trip to Africa in 2002. Phil Shrimpton and Cathy Davis are people I continue to see on pretty much a weekly basis.

I had a wonderful telephone conversation with Lance Liebman, who generously holds no animosity regarding that ridiculous nonrecommendation I gave him when he was applying to Yale back in 1958. You might be interested to know that Lance's cousin, Dan Liebman, is the current editor in chief of the *Blood-Horse* magazine.

The Keeneland Story: A Quarter-Century of Racing in the Finest Tradition, by J. B. Faulconer (1960), contains portions of the association's original prospectus. It also includes many interesting items of information—one being that during Keeneland's first year of operation in 1936, it experienced a net loss of $3.47.

Index

INDEX